W9-BUR-450

Multiculturalism
in the
United States

Multiculturalism
IN THE
UNITED STATES

A Comparative Guide to
Acculturation and Ethnicity

Edited by JOHN D. BUENKER
and LORMAN A. RATNER

GREENWOOD PRESS

New York • Westport, Connecticut • London

Library of Congress Cataloging-in-Publication Data

Multiculturalism in the United States : a comparative guide to
    acculturation and ethnicity / edited by John D. Buenker and Lorman
    A. Ratner.
        p.   cm.
    Includes bibliographical references and index.
    ISBN 0–313–25374–9 (alk. paper)
    1. Minorities—United States. 2. Pluralism (Social sciences)—
United States. 3. Acculturation—United States. 4. Ethnicity—
United States. 5. United States—Ethnic relations. 6. United
States—Race relations.   I. Buenker, John D.   II. Ratner, Lorman.
E184.A1M85   1992
305.8′00973—dc20   91–35116

British Library Cataloguing in Publication Data is available.

Copyright © 1992 by John D. Buenker and Lorman A. Ratner

All rights reserved. No portion of this book may be
reproduced, by any process or technique, without the
express written consent of the publisher.

Library of Congress Catalog Card Number: 91–35116
ISBN: 0–313–25374–9

First published in 1992

Greenwood Press, 88 Post Road West, Westport, CT 06881
An imprint of Greenwood Publishing Group, Inc.

Printed in the United States of America

The paper used in this book complies with the
Permanent Paper Standard issued by the National
Information Standards Organization (Z39.48–1984).

10 9 8 7 6 5 4 3 2 1

3 0000 002 812 943
LIBRARY OF MICHIGAN

E
184
.A1
M85
1992
c.2

Contents

Multiculturalism
in the
United States

Introduction

Lorman A. Ratner and John D. Buenker

The authors of the chapters in this volume have provided all manner of fact and reflection regarding the complex question of how American culture— by which we mean a widely accepted collection of values, attitudes, and beliefs—was shaped from the cultures of Europe, much of Asia, Africa, Pre-Columbian America and, in more recent times, Latin America. The contribution to American culture by people of these diverse origins, which, taken individually, reflects differences dependent on class, occupation, and religion, are duly noted. So, too, are the conflicts and tensions between the traditions of newly arrived immigrants with what came to be mainstream American culture. Finally, the contributors note the changes over time both of the cultures brought to America and of the culture that received them.

In order to enhance the value of this work as a comparative handbook or reference tool, each author has addressed a number of common topics that helped determine the pace and degree of acculturation for every ethnic group. What kind of voluntary self-help institutions served as conduits between the ethnic group and mainstream culture? What was the impact of the modernizing forces in mainstream America upon group identity and culture? What strategies, political and socioeconomic, were developed by each group to gain tangible benefits, recognition, and protection of its cultural heritage? What internal divisions arose over those who wished to become Americanized and those who wished to remain traditionalists, and how did these conflicts affect acculturation? What effect did residential and social mobility and exogamous marriage patterns have upon group cohesion? What role did formal education play in the acculturation process, and to what extent did it contribute to intergenerational conflict and estrangement? Was the group's adaptation a straight path toward acculturation, or did it ebb and flow over time and across generations? How did the group respond to the efforts of mainstream "Americanizers?" What strategies did the group develop for language maintenance and religious orthodoxy? In short, what were the specific variables that determined the course and velocity of each group's adaptation to American life?

At the same time, however, the authors were instructed that our list was meant to be suggestive, not prescriptive. They were free to organize their chapters in whatever manner seemed most appropriate, to stress the themes that each deemed more significant, and to incorporate whatever additional themes or dimensions seemed appropriate. In short, our goal was to produce chapters that addressed universal questions in a framework that permitted each scholar sufficient latitude in which to present the unique perspective gained from specializing in the history and culture of a specific ethnic group.

A glance at the table of contents might prompt the reader to question why certain cultural groups are omitted or combined in a single essay. From the outset, we recognized that any attempt or claim to be comprehensive in our coverage was foredoomed to failure and frustration and would lay us open to justifiable criticism from scholars and from ethnic groups that felt unfairly neglected. Our major goal was to provide a large enough sample of ethnic groups that we could make valid generalizations concerning patterns of acculturation and adaptation and be reasonably representative of the various waves of settlement that have, over time, populated the United States. We also wanted a sample that would provide a meaningful comparison between the experiences of European-derived ethnic groups and those from Africa, Asia, and Latin America in order to allow our readers to weigh adequately the factor of racial distinctiveness. Within those various time periods and geographical/ethnic origins, we generally tried to present the best scholarship available on the specific ethnic groups that comprised the largest numerical portions of the different waves of settlement. Thus, we decided upon a lineup that included the only indigenous ethnic group (American Indians); several that were representative of the migration waves of either the colonial period or of the great immigration wave of 1840–1890 (African-Americans, German-Americans, Irish-Americans, Scandinavian-Americans, and Chinese-Americans); and several that arrived in significant numbers mostly in the twentieth century (Italian-Americans, Jewish-Americans, Polish-Americans, and Mexican-Americans). While we seriously considered the inclusion of such ethnic groups as Japanese-Americans, Puerto Rican-Americans and other eastern European, Latin-American, or Asian peoples, our inability to match up the scholars we wanted within the time sequence involved caused us to abandon such notions. While we recognize that the differences between the experiences of Japanese- and Chinese-Americans or Mexican- and Puerto Rican-Americans, for example, are every bit as important and instructive as the similarities between them, we believe our selective sample is as representative as circumstances permitted and is large and varied enough to enable readers to make valid comparisons across time and ethnicity, to discern the major variables that condition the acculturation process and to formulate at least a tentative hypothesis regarding the essentials of that phenomenon.

These same considerations underlay our decisions about the focus and scope of the ten chapters that eventually comprised the bulk of this volume. Germans, Poles, Irish, Italians, and Chinese are examined separately, but Norwegians, Swedes, and Danes are all subsumed in the chapter on Scandinavian-Americans, because their process of acculturation was similar enough to justify doing so, at least in the opinion of the experts whom we consulted. Similarly, the emphasis in the essay on Jewish-Americans is on the experiences of eastern European immigrants and their descendants, but that of the larger resident Sephardic and German Jews are not neglected. American Indians and African-Americans are both included, even though their experiences deviate so greatly from the varieties of the immigrant experience represented in the other essays as to be considered differences of kind rather than degree. However, our primary interest is in the process of interaction between minority cultures and mainstream America, and the experiences of both American Indians and African-Americans shed much valuable light on that phenomenon. While the uniqueness of the experience in America of each of the ten cultural groups considered is readily apparent and while diversity rather than unity characterizes the totality of what follows, we firmly believe that there are enough common elements in the overall process to allow the reader to draw meaningful generalizations regarding cultural interaction leading to mutual cultural change. Our purpose in this introduction is to observe the commonalities of the cultural process and to offer some tentative generalizations.

Since the eighteenth century, observers of the American scene have been convinced that the American was "a new man." But just how people of diverse cultures, from many lands, occupations, environments and religions could be melded together into one culture, one nationality, has been in dispute. What does seem evident from the collective efforts of the authors of these chapters is that the use of such metaphors as a melting pot or a coat of many colors clouds more than it clarifies our understanding of what has happened. Having noted the complexity of the process by which people of widely differing cultures interact with one another and with a host culture, some generalizations may be drawn from the experiences of the ten ethnic groups considered. Our sample includes three immigrant groups from northern and western Europe in the nineteenth century, three from southern and eastern Europe in the early twentieth century, and four "racial minorities" of varying length of residence in the United States.

First, it is clear that, at least for the first generation of most immigrant groups, it is inaccurate to assume that the culture they brought with them was defined by their nationality. Poles, Norwegians, Italians, and Germans defined themselves by characteristics drawn from region, class, religion, and locale rather than nationality. In the same way, but not in the same time span, those diverse cultures among the various tribes of native Americans came to accept a common label, Indian. Only as time and generations in America passed did a hyphenated nationality label come to be accepted. Hence, it is probable that the phenomenon that the historian Marcus Hansen described as first-generation immigrants holding to an old identity, second-generation immigrants rejecting their origins and accepting an American one, and third-generation immigrants seeking to rediscover their roots is really a process in which the first generation held to a culture defined by factors other than nationality, the second generation identified with the culture of the host country, and the third generation developed a new "hyphenated" identity comprised of elements of both the old country and the new.

Second, to the degree that ethnic identification has persisted, and in some cases become stronger decades after the end of any significant immigration of a particular ethnic group, we might theorize that the phenomenon is largely the result of certain forces at work in American society. Given a society so open and fluid and a people so geographically mobile, Americans seek to identify themselves by membership in a variety of organizations and groups. Hence, we might suppose that the third generation's search for ethnic identity occurs for the same reason that most Americans identify with a church, a political party, a civic club, or other mediating institution. If that is true, then the search for ethnic identity is primarily a manifestation of the universal desire for social and personal location in modern mass society.

Third, the situation with regard to "racial groups," other than African-Americans, is similar to that of immigrant-derived peoples. Local, regional, and even national differences in origin have given way, and new identities such as "Asian-Americans" or "Hispanics" have appeared. Such identifications have evolved over time and have served social, political, and cultural functions for the groups involved.

Fourth, this process of identification by racial and ethnic groups, both with the mainstream culture and some subset of it, takes place at different rates of speed depending on the degree to which those already in the host society find newcomers acceptable and to which their traditions can be merged with that of the host culture without obliterating its key features. So it seems that Jews held many cultural values, attitudes, and beliefs that could be connected with those of the host society. Many, though not all, Jews were willing and able to compromise in order to accomplish that melding. Only antagonism, more evident at some points in American history than at other times, has prevented that process of a new Jewish-American culture from proceeding even further. In the case of "Native Americans," the process of forming a new Indian-American culture has proceeded much slower as a result both of cultures that were less compatible, and of antag-onisms, laws and practices of the host society that held Indians apart. In the case of Chinese-Americans, we see a dissimilarity of cultural values and host society antagonism preventing the development of the new hyphenated culture until after World War II. Since that time, the change in attitude of the host society has allowed for the rapid development of this new culture.

Fifth, while the process of identification has resulted in the development of new hyphenated cultures among all these ten groups, we should recognize that key factors (such as geographic and economic mobility) that break down group loyalties are the same forces that promote the search for group identification. What might appear to be nostalgia in the search for ones roots might in fact be a natural human response on the part of people who can only identify with massive mainstream culture through the prism of familiar subcultures. Ethnic festivals, interest in genealogy, and regional history, seem to go hand in hand with the loss of place, alternation in social mores, and change of religious affiliation. The influence of the national mass communications media in establishing a standardized mode of dress, taste in music, and blurring of distinctions in manner of speech all give reason to regain a form of complex cultural identity. The hyphenated American may well be the result of the process by which original identification was lost and a new identification found. In effect, at the same time that Americans become more like one another, they develop a sense of being a part of a subgroup that marks them as different from one other. The more we are alike, the more we are different.

The chapters that follow give us good material from which to attempt to understand and generalize about a highly complex and critical subject. In spite of our effort to find and outline a common pattern of cultural change over time of ethnic groups, there are many differences among each ethnic group's experience in the United States. In his chapter on Germans in the United States, James Bergquist makes clear that, as the first large group of non-English-speaking settlers, Germans were considered by their neighbors to be "aggressively resistant to adaptation to the mainstream of American society." He says that the creation of German-American institutions served both to preserve Old World ways and to prepare German newcomers to accept new ways. His description of the role of foreign language newspapers and social and political clubs as a bridge between old and new is applicable to all other ethnic groups. The great degree to which German-Americans, over generations and lacking any influx of new immigrants from the old country, lost contact with their past seems more pronounced than was the case of other ethnic groups described in this volume.

While German immigrants professed a diversity of religions, the later-arriving Poles were almost uniformly Roman Catholic. German newcomers consisted of nearly every possible social class, many of whom embraced farming as an occupation in both the Old World and the New, but Polish immigrants were primarily peasants, most of whom lacked the inclination or the capital to work the land. They also valued a more communal life than would have been possible if they farmed in the United States, according to Edward R. Kantowicz. Success for the Poles was measured by the establishment of community, the ownership of property, primarily a home, the opportunity to work hard and steadily and to avoid any reliance on the state or on any other entity beyond immediate family, church, and community.

The experiences of Italian immigrants in many ways mirrored that of Poles. The majority of southern Italians also came from a peasant background but the need to travel around Europe in search of seasonal employment caused Italians to be less tied to community, and their views on religion made them less committed to a militant form of Roman Catholicism. Like the Poles, Italians valued hard work and property ownership, eschewing education and movement into the professions. For both groups, the latter two attitudes have markedly changed since World War II, as Dominic Candeloro makes clear. Italians, like Poles, created fraternal and benevolent societies both as a bridge to Americanizing new immigrants and as a means of preserving some Old World identity.

The Irish experience in America has more in common with that of the Germans than with either the Poles or Italians, despite some important differences. Like the Germans, the Irish were geographically mobile but, since they spoke English and had no strong cultural base, they could integrate more readily into mainstream American society. While most Germans lacked any strong sense of old country nationalism, Irish-Americans did and do have such a sense. More than any other immigrant group, despite their dispersal in the United States, the Irish created organizations that held them together. Those organizations, according to Dennis Clark, "re-enforced identity and enhanced group morale." Their political organization was more highly developed than that of other ethnic groups and was an effective means of coping with the situation in America.

Even more dramatically than the Germans and the Irish. Jews who came to America left behind the Old World and adopted the new. To the degree that U.S. society was open to them, Jews took advantage of the opportunity to become part of their new society. At the same time, Jews have struggled to define and resolve any contradiction between being both a Jew and an American. Indeed, in his essay on the Jews, Edward Shapiro argues that "no other ethnic group has been as concerned with defining their relationship to America." For many American Jews, the hope for and ultimately the creation of a nation, Israel, served as a common bond. Paradoxically, Zionism was reconciled with a sense of integration into American life by regarding it as an act of humanitarianism toward people in need rather than as a form of Jewish nationalism in the United States. Over time, increasing interreligious marriage has further weakened the identity of Jews in America.

As described by John Robert Christianson, Scandinavians generally lacked any tie to an Old World nation, a common Old World religion, a single economic class or occupation, much like their German counterparts. Also as with the Germans, geographic mobility and economic mobility worked against a sense of Norwegian, Swedish, or Danish nationalism, hyphenated or otherwise. It only arose after 1900 and began to disappear after World War I.

The importance of the culture that immigrants brought with them and how that culture was influenced by their place in the United States is perhaps most clear in the case of the Chinese. For nearly a century, Bernard Wong demonstrates, the Chinese who arrived in America came as laborers intending to acquire wealth and return to their home country. They felt strong ties to their homeland, its culture, and the families they left behind. Faced with virulent discrimination and hostile legislation, they were forced into forming pocket communities that were culturally, if not geographically, isolated from the rest of America. Only since World War II, and most dramatically since the mid–1960s, have Chinese-Americans been allowed to enter all occupations, to intermarry legally and, in general, to build a family unit in America. With the marked increase of Chinese born in America and the pulling down of formal barriers to their integration into American society, the Chinese experience has begun to resemble that of other immigrant groups of generations earlier.

As varied as the experiences of the ethnic groups already noted are, that of the American Indian provides still different sets of conditions and responses to American culture. As Vine DeLoria, Jr. points out in describing American Indians, "Their ethnicity is a product of historical process and political ideology rather than racial and cultural homogeneity. Indeed "Indian" is a generic term akin to "Asian" or "European" in the sense that it refers to a large grouping of diverse peoples who occupy a continental land mass rather than a nationalistic entity with the historic homogeneous roots."

The American culture might have created a mythic counterculture, the Indian culture, as a way of defining itself. In short, Indian culture as described by Americans provided them with a cultural contrast that in part, by its differences, defined the American culture. Indians were described as a cultural entity when in fact no single Indian culture existed. If they had not been set up as a separate nation and a distinct racial group, Indians, as DeLoria notes, might have been assimilated a century ago. As with the Chinese since World War II, changes both in law and attitude, as well as economic condition and geographic mobility, have finally given impetus to such assimilation. Whether Indian culture in the form that DeLoria describes as "traditionalism" will take hold and preserve some of the essentials remains to be seen. In that sense, the Indian experience in the United States might come to resemble that of the Jews who seek to be both Americans and Jews.

The degree of ambiguity that characterized the relationship between these various groups and mainstream culture is apparent most dramatically in the historical interaction between Americans and Mexicans. Conflict between often hostile national neighbors, land hunger, and religious differences served to keep apart people who, in many other respects, shared a common history. Mexican-Americans, as Louise Ano Nuevo Kerr describes them, were at times a labor force, a tool in the economic development of lands taken from Mexico. At other times, they were a barrier to American economic development and geographic expansion. The Mexican-American experience provides still another set of circumstances to puzzle those who seek to understand and to generalize about American's ethnic makeup.

In many ways, the acculturation process of African Americans is the most complex of all the groups considered in this collection. Numerically, they constitute the largest single group, while the time span of their interaction with Euro-America is far larger than any other, save for the American Indians. No other single group of ethnic Americans has pursued acculturation and assimilation with more determination over such a long period of time, only to experience recurring rejection and frustration. Cynthia Greggs Fleming, quoting Bernard Makhosezwe Magubane, contends that an African-American is fundamentally "an American who is not accepted as an American, hence a kind of negative American." One hundred years of striving for acculturation and assimilation by the late 1960s left many African-American leaders wondering if conformity to Anglo-American values and cultural norms was not too high a price to pay for the integration they had so steadfastly and vainly pursued. With W.E.B. Du Bois, modern African-Americans sought a way to be both American and Negro without having to "bleach his Negro soul in a flood of white Americanism." Fleming shows that this creative tension between African roots and American experience, similar and yet different from that felt by Euro-Americans, has persisted throughout African-American history from early colonial times to the present day. Unlike most Euro-American groups, however, African-Americans have been plagued with an unsettling ambivalence about their ancestral continent that has compounded the ambivalent attitude that America has consistently displayed toward all ethnic minorities. Uncertain both about their place in American society and their relationship to a rapidly changing Africa, African-Americans in the 1980s still remained uneasily conscious of their "twoness," still "marginal, negative Americans."

It is our hope that the reader of this book will gain some insight into just how diverse, and how much alike, were the experiences of a number of ethnic groups who came to America. The process of interaction between and among these cultures was complex and always important in the shaping of what today is that welter of commonly held values, attitudes, and beliefs that is American culture.

1

African-Americans

Cynthia Greggs Fleming

The Negro American is the only American in America who says: "I want to be an American." More or less all other Americans are born Americans and take their Americanism for granted. Hence the American Negro's effort to be an American is a self-conscious thing. America is something outside him and he wishes to become part of that America. But, since color easily marks him off from being an ordinary American, and since he lives amidst social conditions pregnant with racism, he becomes an American who is not accepted as an American, hence a kind of negative American.[1]

A generation has passed since the Civil Rights Movement of the 1960s. In recent years it has become increasingly fashionable to hold reunions, forums, and all manner of meetings that attempt to assess the movement's importance. At the same time, a large number of scholarly studies have been published that examine the movement's history and the issues that it raised. A major focus of most who seek to evaluate the Civil Rights Movement is the question of whether, in fact, it actually changed anything for Americans of African descent. Have they stopped being negative Americans?

Most agree that at least some changes have occurred, for, previous to the activism of the 1960s, African-Americans all over the country suffered from the effects of segregation. In the North it was de facto, while in the South it was de jure. Because of the blatant and public nature of southern segregation, much of the early movement activity and national outrage was directed against racist conditions facing southern blacks. Yet, while northern racism was much quieter, it was every bit as effective in relegating black citizens to society's fringes. Thus, throughout the country blacks were faced with segregated and often substandard housing, medical care, occupational and educational opportunities.

From the late nineteenth century, after blacks were freed by the Civil War, and on through the twentieth century African-Americans have fought against attempts to segregate them in all areas of American life. Sometimes these fights have been waged by individuals, and sometimes they have been collective struggles. During the twentieth century one group that expended an enormous amount of energy in the fight against legal segregation was the National Association for the Advancement of Colored People (NAACP). The strategy of this interracial organization founded in 1909 was to use the court system to put segregation on trial. Indeed, the vast majority of the civil rights cases tried in the first part of the twentieth century were conducted with the support and sometimes the direct participation of the NAACP and its legal staff.

A number of the most notable cases involved the issue of segregated education. For example, in 1947, with NAACP support, Heman Sweatt, a black Texas resident, sued the University of Texas Law School for refusing him admission because of his race. The case of *Sweatt v. Painter* went all the way to the Supreme Court. The justices ordered that either Sweatt should be admitted to the law school, or that the state should provide equal facilities for black residents. Such a strategy did not challenge the constitutionality of segregation. Rather, segregation was still considered legal as long as equal facilities were provided for blacks. In an effort to keep Sweatt out of the University of Texas Law School, the state established a law school just for blacks.[2]

This tactic did not work, however, since the Supreme Court later found that this law school was not equal to the University of Texas. The Court's decision, written by Chief Justice Vinson, carefully addressed this issue:

What is more important [than the disparity in physical facilities], the University of Texas Law School possesses to a far greater degree those qualities which are incapable of objective measurement but which make for greatness in a law school. Such qualities, to name but a few, include reputation of the faculty, experience of the administration, position and influence of the alumni, standing in the community, traditions and prestige.[3]

Sweatt was admitted to the university's law school. The Texas reaction in this case clearly illustrates the lengths to which the white South was willing to go to preserve its segregated system. Yet, this reaction would prove to be mild in comparison to the firestorm created by the 1954 case of *Brown v. the Board of Education of Topeka*. In this case the NAACP legal staff challenged the constitutionality of segregation: They challenged it and won. The Supreme Court ruled that separate could never be equal, and so segregation was finally legally dead.

Even as certain judicial decisions began to support black rights, world events also began to affect black aspirations. From the late 1940s through the 1950s, developments like the advent of the cold war, the emergence of many new Third World nations, and the American ascendancy to a position of global leadership worked in concert to heighten United States sensitivity to criticism from abroad. Government officials soon realized that the United States was especially vulnerable to criticism in the area of race relations. This realization prompted increasing concern among many about racial justice. Such postwar developments helped fuel a cautious, but persistent black optimism that would lay the foundation for the activism of the 1950s and 1960s.

While black hope was nourished by government concern, white resistance was encouraged by government ambivalence. Despite the existence of a number of Supreme Court decisions favoring black rights, little changed because the federal government routinely demonstrated a reluctance to enforce these decisions. Federal action on the *Smith v. Allright* case provides a graphic illustration of government reluctance. This case, decided in 1944, outlawed the white primary, a device that had been used to reinforce black disfranchisement. The white primary had designated the Democratic primary in the South as a private club. Thus, even registered black voters were barred from voting in the Democratic primary. In the solidly Democratic South of this era, selection as a Democratic candidate was tantamount to election to office. After *Smith v. Allright* black voters who had been denied the right to participate in Democratic primaries expected the federal government to aid their attempts to extend the franchise. They were disappointed. Rather, the federal officials refused to become involved: They left this responsibility to the states.[4]

Thus, the Supreme Court ruled in favor of black rights. The legislative branch passed laws in support of black rights. The executive branch created commissions and issued executive orders supporting black rights. Yet, only half-hearted attempts were made toward enforcement and implementation. These realities, juxtaposed against each other, sent mixed signals to the white South. Many staunch supporters of segregation felt the beginnings of an assault on their cherished way of life. At the same time, they were comforted by federal reluctance to provide too much support for black rights.

In this unsettled atmosphere southern white violence against blacks continued. But by this time it began to receive increased publicity. One of the most dramatic incidents occurred just one year after the landmark *Brown* decision. In the summer of 1955 Emmett Till, a black youth from Chicago visiting relatives in Mississippi, was brutally beaten and murdered. Till was beaten so badly that only the right side of his head was intact, one eye dangled from its socket, and his tongue was swollen to eight times its normal size.[5] Two white defendants were tried for Till's murder, but it took an all-white jury just one hour and seven minutes to acquit them. One juror said, "If we hadn't stopped to drink pop . . . it wouldn't have taken that long."[6]

Against this backdrop of white violence and government ambivalence, black resistance to segregation continued to strengthen. It is important to recognize that all those cases leading up to and including the *Brown* decision came to the Supreme Court because of black instigation and NAACP legal support. Yet, black resistance to segregation was expressed in many other ways, too. Countless African-Americans became fed up with sitting in the back of buses, drinking out of dingy little "colored" water fountains, and using dirty "colored" restrooms. And so, many simply refused. In 1955 a whole movement coalesced around Mrs. Rosa Parks, a black woman who refused to give up her seat to a white man on a Montgomery, Alabama, bus. After a boycott that lasted over a year, Montgomery's buses were desegregated, and one of their local black leaders, Dr. Martin Luther King, Jr., had become famous.

On February 1, 1960, four black college students at North Carolina Agricultural and Technical College in Greensboro sat-in at a downtown lunch counter. This action launched an intense period of nonviolent direct action by black college students throughout the South against segregated facilities. By the spring of that year student demonstration leaders had met and established the Student Nonviolent Coordinating Committee (SNCC). With nothing but their belief in themselves and their courage to protect them, these students challenged segregation head on. One former SNCC member, Zohara Simmons, vividly recalled the difficulties inherent in such a challenge:

Once you actually go and have white folk come out of a restaurant and spit on you and call you nigger, and [tell you to] go back to Africa you coons, baboons, you know, the kinds of things. Then of course you're probably going to have one of two reactions. Either you're going to be so afraid that you say "Oh, I can't expose myself to that." Or you're going to be so mad that, you know it's like, "I'll be back come hell or high water."[7]

Students were not the only ones demonstrating. Many people from various backgrounds became involved in this assault on segregation. As activists picketed, boycotted, sat-in, and participated in freedom rides, the legal walls of segregation began to tumble. Oddly enough, however, many African-Americans who were veterans of the civil rights battles that changed the South and the country still did not feel like full-fledged Americans. At the beginning, integration had been their goal. Soon, many began to ask themselves: Integration on whose terms, and at what cost? The answers they found were more than a little disturbing. By 1964 and 1965, many began to recognize that the integration they had so desperately desired demanded a very high price: conformity to Anglo-American values and cultural norms.

Their realization prompted many to echo the words of W.E.B. Du Bois in his 1903 classic *The Souls of Black Folk*:

One never feels his twoness—an American, a Negro; two souls, two thoughts, two unreconciled strivings; two warring ideals in one dark body, whose dogged strength alone keeps it from being torn asunder.

The history of the American Negro is the history of this strife—this longing to attain self-conscious manhood, to merge his double self into a better and truer self. In this merging he wishes neither of the older selves to be lost. He would not Africanize America, for America has too much to teach the world and Africa. He would not bleach his Negro soul in a flood of white Americanism, for he knows that Negro blood has a message for the world. He simply wishes to make it possible for a man to be both a Negro and an American.[8]

At this point increasing numbers of activists who had been jailed, beaten and brutalized in the name of civil rights began to question their identity as Americans. Many began a serious exploration of their connection with the African continent. They began to understand that black was, after all, more than just a color. This was not the first time that Americans of African descent in this country had felt the need to understand their connection to the land of their ancestors.

In fact, that interest in Africa surfaced as early as the colonial period. Exploration of that connection, however, has always been difficult and quite emotional. Much of the difficulty has been based on the negative views of Africa and Africans that have been popularized in this country since its infancy. Indeed, even before the English established their first permanent settlement in the New World, they had a negative view of the concept of blackness. Before the sixteenth century the Oxford English Dictionary's definition of black included, "Deeply stained with dirt; soiled, dirty, foul. . . . Having dark or deadly purposes malignant; pertaining to or involving death, deadly; baneful, disastrous, sinister. . . . Foul, iniquitous, atrocious, horrible, wicked."[9]

Furthermore, the British regularly juxtaposed the "negative" color black against the "positive" color white. "White and black connoted purity and filthiness, virginity and sin, virtue and baseness, beauty and ugliness, beneficence and evil, God and the devil."[10] When the English saw their first African people, they automatically projected their feelings about the color black onto these dark-skinned people.

English settlers carried their negative views of Africans and their descendants with them when they colonized America. These views were later embellished and popularized by succeeding generations of white Americans. Many whites ascribed such characteristics as laziness, stupidity, immorality, and sexual excess to Africans and African-Americans. One nineteenth-century Baltimore physician clearly echoed these sentiments:

It is this sexual question that is the barrier which keeps the philanthropist and moralist from realizing that the phylogenies of the Caucasian and African races are divergent, almost antithetical, and that it is gross folly to attempt to educate both on the same basis. When education will reduce the large size of the negro's penis as well as bring about the sensitiveness of the terminal fibers which exist in the African's birthright to sexual madness and excess—from the Caucasian's viewpoint.[11]

Predictably enough, apologists for the institution of slavery eagerly embraced these negative notions. However, even white liberals who were sympathetic to the plight of blacks subscribed to certain stereotypical notions of black character. For example, a number of white abolitionists, including Harriet Beecher Stowe, Hollis Read, Theodore Parker, and Lydia Maria Child, believed that blacks were "predisposed toward 'feminine' languidity and softness."[12]

Given the widespread and enduring nature of such negative stereotypes, it is hardly surprising that African-Americans would be affected by them. The effects were quite varied and sometimes unpredictable. Some became ashamed of Africa, its inhabitants, and anything that connected them to such a "barbaric" background. Others refused to accept such negative images of themselves and the continent of their ancestors. Because those images were so pervasive, however, even those African descendants who championed the race's cause were unable to ignore these stereotypes completely. Consider the reasoning of Edward Wilmot Blyden, one of the foremost black intellectuals of the late nineteenth century. Blyden, who was a pan-Africanist, did not discard nineteenth century racial stereotypes. Rather, he rearranged them:

The Northern races will take the raw material from Africa and bring them back in such forms as will contribute to the comfort and even elegance of life in that country; while the African in the simplicity and purity of rural enterprises will be able to cultivate those spiritual elements in humanity which are suppressed, silent and inactive under the pressure and exigencies of material progress.[13]

Blyden's message in this passage is quite clear. Africans are different after all. There are admirable things about them, but they are different. Blyden, who was born in St. Thomas, Virgin Islands, struggled with the issue of African identity and his own relationship to it throughout his life. While he admired many things about African culture, he still measured that culture with a Western yardstick. He was a descendant of Africa, but a Westernized descendant of Africa, after all. Thus, despite his admiration for African culture, Blyden's Western viewpoint prompted him to write:

To those who have lived any time in West Africa, three things are indisputably clear; first, that it was absolutely necessary that large numbers of the people should be taken into exile for discipline and training under a more advanced race; second, that they should be kept separate from the dominant race; third, that chosen spirits from among the exiles should in course of time return and settle among their brethren in the fatherland to guide them into the path of civilization.[14]

Edward Blyden's reviews clearly indicate the complexity of the dilemma he faced. Although his ancestry was African, his views were Western. Blyden was not the first, nor would he be the last, African descendant in the New World to face this uncertainty. As clearly as the late eighteenth century, Americans of African descent began to make attempts to explore their relationship and obligation to the continent of their ancestors. One of the by-products of this exploration of identity was the establishment of a number of separate black institutions that incorporated the label of Africa in their titles. At this time, though, African-Americans were not the only ones groping toward a new identity. The drama of their search must be examined in the context of broader American attempts to define the national character. In the aftermath of the Revolution, black and white Americans sought to understand just what it meant to be an American. While both shared a number of common experiences, the definitions of their Americanness were quite different.

Descendants of Africans had participated in important early American milestones, but none more important than the Revolutionary War. Slaves and free blacks fought in the Revolutionary War in substantial numbers. On the eve of the war slavery existed in all thirteen colonies. Yet, by the time the war ended most northern states had made provisions for the gradual emancipation of their slaves. In the South, legislation designed to eliminate slavery was considered, but it was defeated and slavery continued. In such an atmosphere the status of African-Americans remained uncertain. Some were slaves, and some were free. Yet, even those who were free were not sure what their status as free people meant. Rather, the question of what citizenship rights they could exercise was determined by the policies of the state where they resided.

In the midst of this extreme and unsettling uncertainty, many African-Americans tentatively explored their relationship with the land of their ancestors. The African Institution of Boston, the Free African Society of Philadelphia, the African Methodist Episcopal Church, and the African Lodge are just a few of the separate institutions organized by blacks in the late eighteenth and early nineteenth centuries.[15] The tendency to include the word African in the title of these organizations is indicative of an identification with their African ancestry, and a sympathy for the African plight that these early blacks felt. That sympathy was tempered by a large amount of ambivalence, however.

The words of Prince Hall, founder of the African Lodge, clearly illustrate his sympathetic feelings for his enslaved African brethren: "Let us see our friends and brethren; and first let us see them dragged from their native country, by the iron hand of tyranny and oppression, from their dear friends and connections, with weeping eyes and aching hearts, to a strange land, and among a strange people, whose tender mercies are cruel—and there to bear the iron yoke of slavery and cruelty."[16] Just a few years after Prince Hall's address, officers of the African Institution of Boston wrote to Paul Cuffe, a free African-American who transported a number of blacks to Africa at his own expense: "I received yours of the 10th of last month in due season & think we ought most cheerfully to sacrifice ease & many other privileges & comforts, for the purpose of diffusing light & civilization & knowledge in Africa."[17]

These men were not the only contemporaries of Cuffe who felt that Africa needed to be uplifted. Peter Williams, a black Episcopal priest, echoed the sentiments of African Institution officials when he described Cuffe's efforts in these terms: "He [Cuffe] could not think of enjoying repose while he reflected that he might, in any degree, administer to the relief of the multitudes of his brethren, who were groaning under the yoke of bondage, or groping in the dark and horrible night of heathenish superstition and ignorance."[18]

Paul Cuffe was born in 1759, and built his fortune on his seagoing ventures. By 1806 his personal holdings included a number of oceangoing vessels, houses, and landholdings. Because of his prosperity, Cuffe was required to pay Massachusetts property taxes. Since he was not allowed to vote in his home state, however, he refused to pay taxes. This eventually led to a change in Massachusetts law allowing free blacks who met the property qualification to vote. Cuffe later converted to the Quaker religion. It was at this point that he became interested in using part of his fortune to help improve conditions among his African-American brethren. His plan for improvement was built on his conviction that emigration to Africa would improve the lot of African-Americans even as it brought the blessings of civilization and Christianity to the land of his ancestors. Accordingly, in 1815, Cuffe transported thirty-eight blacks to Africa at his own expense. His assessment of Africa as a place that needed to be civilized was entirely consistent with the views of his nineteenth-century contemporaries in the United States, both black and white.[19]

African-Americans living in these years—from the end of the Revolution to about 1820—clearly felt sympathy for the land of their ancestors and the fate of its inhabitants. At the same time, however, they filtered their views of Africa through the prism of their adopted Western perceptions. This prism distorted their view. Their unwitting acceptance of the cultural and religious arrogance of their white contemporaries prompted them to measure African culture with a Western yardstick. By such a measurement, these African-Americans judged the culture of their ancestors to be barbaric, primitive and in need of civilizing influences. Thus, at a time when blacks were not fully accepted as equals by Americans, blacks in America were not fully accepting of the integrity and equality of African culture. This reality meant that, in many ways, they were people without a country.

Later in the nineteenth century as sectional lines hardened, slavery was debated, and the fate of free blacks was questioned, African-Americans began to reassess their views of Africa and African culture. This reassessment took place in the midst of crucial developments that affected black thinking. One of those developments was the establishment of the American Colonization Society. The Society, which was founded in December 1816, was particularly interested in colonizing free blacks.[20] This group was considered quite troublesome by contemporary white Americans because their status was so unclear. One white North Carolinian succinctly expressed white concern: "It is impossible for us to be happy, if, after manumission they are to remain among us."[21]

Acting on such concerns, a number of prominent white Americans, including Judge Bushrod Washington, who was George Washington's nephew, Henry Clay, and John Randolph, organized the American Colonization Society (ACS). One of the society's major goals was the establishment of a West African colony for the resettlement of free blacks from the United States.[22] The ACS and its aims proved to be enormously popular among large numbers of white Americans. In fact, enthusiastic agreement with the society's aims prompted individuals, and even state legislatures, to donate money to the society's coffers.[23] Increasing numbers of whites, desperate for a solution to their "Negro problem," began to see colonization as that answer. The editor of the *Virginia Argus* expressed the enthusiasm that many felt for the colonization strategy:

If 12,520 Negroes of the right age and sex were sent to Africa each year, Virginia would be clear of Negroes in twenty years at an annual cost of only £103,620 which might be obtained by a tax on slave ownership; exportation of 30,000 annually would in twenty years empty the entire nation of Negroes whose places could be filled by White Europeans.[24]

This grand plan had no chance of success, though, if the society could not convince free blacks that they should emigrate. And the arguments that white colonization advocates proposed were so offensive to many free blacks that few were willing to work with the ACS. An example of one argument was published in an 1825 edition of the *African Repository*, the organ of the American Colonization Society. The *Repository* insisted that free blacks should emigrate because their situation in American society was so unfavorable: "Introduced among us by violence, notoriously ignorant, degraded and miserable, mentally diseased, brokenspirited, acted upon by no motive to honourable exertions, scarcely reached in their debasement by the heavenly light.[25] Thus, to improve this condition they should emigrate to Africa, reasoned proponents of colonization.

While many free blacks were incensed and insulted by such a characterization, there were still some who wanted to emigrate to Africa badly enough to work with the ACS. For example, one group of Cincinnati, Ohio, blacks wrote to the *African Repository* expressing their favorable view of colonization: "Resolved, that we believe that Liberia offers to the oppressed children of Africa a home where they may be free: and that it is the only place where we can establish a nationality, and be acknowledged as men by the nations of the earth."[26]

Whether they were willing to work with the ACS or not, an increasingly vocal group of free blacks in antebellum America began to support the notion of emigration to Africa. This rising tide of support came at a time when the status of free blacks in America was deteriorating steadily and precipitously. By the 1830s and 1840s, black political rights that had existed were being curtailed, and black freedom of movement was being threatened. Even though free blacks were supposed to be Americans, a number of northern and border states passed legislation that made it exceedingly difficult for them to move into a new state and establish residence.[27] This trend toward restriction of black rights culminated in the *Dred Scott* decision of 1857. In that case, the Supreme Court decided that in the century previous to the adoption of the U.S. Constitution, blacks had "been regarded as beings of an inferior order, and altogether unfit to associate with the white race either in social or political relations; and so far inferior, that they had no rights which the white man was bound to respect."[28]

This decision dealt a crushing blow to the hopes of free blacks for inclusion into American society. Against this backdrop, increasing numbers of African-Americans continued to reevaluate Africa and their relationship to it. In fact, by this time many blacks began to extol the virtues of their ancestral homeland. For example, Henry Highland Garnet, a black Presbyterian minister, insisted that Africans had been famous in the ancient world because of their many accomplishments. These accomplishments generated "a frame, which arose from every virtue, and talent, that render mortals pre-eminently great. From the conquests of love and beauty, from the prowess of their arms, and their architecture, poetry, mathematics, generosity, and piety."[29] Furthermore, this generation of antebellum African-Americans also began to see a direct and powerful link between their fate and that of other descendants of Africa: "The elevation of the colored man can only be completed by the elevation of the pure descendants of Africa."[30]

Although this generation of African-Americans began to support and popularize positive views of their ancestral homeland, however, they were still haunted by the negative African images that had plagued the views of their predecessors. The words of Alexander Crummell, a black Episcopal priest, clearly illustrated the persistence of continued negative views of Africa among African-Americans. Speaking in 1852, Crummell characterized Africa as a continent badly in need of uplift: "For ages hath she lain beneath the incubus of the 'demon of her idolatry.' For ages hath she suffered the ravages of vice, corruption, iniquity, and guilt. For ages hath she been 'stricken and smitten' by the deadly thrusts of murder and hate, revenge and slaughter."[31] Thus, on the eve of the Civil War Americans of African descent were still ambivalent about their identification with America and their views of Africa.

Just as things appeared darkest, the Civil War erupted, slavery ended, and the American definition of black citizenship rights changed—at least legally. Such dramatic developments nourished black hopes, at least for a while, that things might finally be different. Perhaps they would be treated as full-fledged American citizens. The death of Reconstruction a few years after the war, however, made it quite clear that white Americans were no more willing to accept African-Americans as fellow citizens after the war than they had been before. In this atmosphere blacks continued to evaluate their relationship to Africa and to America. Their evaluation led many to believe that they were, in fact, more African than American.

At this point the American Colonization Society, which had been virtually dormant during the Civil War, was besieged by letters from enthusiastic blacks seeking aid to emigrate. Moreover, a large number of African-Americans who were unwilling to wait for ACS support established their own joint stock companies to transport emigrants to Africa. A letter from the president of the Liberian Joint Stock Steamship Company in South Carolina clearly indicates an admission of a positive connection between African-Americans and their ancestral homeland. "Dear Sir, This will inform you that the colored people of America and especially of the Southern States desire to return to their fatherland."[32] Not only were these people interested in emigrating to improve their situation, but they also wanted to "aid in building up a nationality of Africans."[33]

Postbellum black emigration advocate Henry M. Turner even insisted that in addition to embracing Africa, African-Americans should reject American society and culture. While few were willing to go this far, most African-Americans through the end of the nineteenth century continued to wrestle with their feelings about Africa and America. As they deliberated, many tempered their praise for the fatherland with criticism engendered by their Western viewpoints. Blyden's previously reported negative judgment of African culture is illustrative of this reality.

In fact, those negative views of Africa harbored by American blacks were further reinforced by events of the late nineteenth century. At the 1884 Berlin Conference, the Europeans divided up, conquered, and colonized Africa. At the same time on the other side of the world, America annexed Hawaii, dispatched troops to the Philippines, and fully subscribed to the notion of the White Man's Burden. Widespread Western imperialism against the world's darker peoples only served to strengthen the old stereotypes based on a deeply rooted belief in black inferiority. Thus, blacks exploring

their relationship to Africa still had to contend with those familiar stereotypes that had colored the perceptions of their ancestors.

Despite the colonial abuse suffered by their fatherland, large numbers of
African-Americans in the early twentieth century began to express an une-
quivocal and enthusiastic desire to identify with their African ancestry. Into
the midst of this enthusiasm stepped Marcus Josiah Garvey. Garvey, a native
of Jamaica, was an admirer of Booker T. Washington and a student of
conditions in America. As he became increasingly familiar with the American
scene, Garvey was prompted to ask:

"Where is the black man's Government?" "Where is his king and his kingdom?"
"Where is his President, his country and his ambassador, his army, his navy, his
men of big affairs?" I could not find them, and then I declared, "I will help to make
them."[34]

Acting on his concerns, Garvey founded the Universal Negro Improvement Association. The UNIA attracted a large following among people of
African descent in various parts of the world. Yet, the UNIA's stronghold
proved to be in Harlem. Here Garvey's message of race purity, race pride,
and Africa for the Africans appealed to large numbers of African-Americans.
During the movement's heyday in the middle of the 1920s, Garvey had
more than a million followers. In addition to his emphasis on the glorious
African past, however, Garvey also preached a message of African uplift
that implied his belief in at least a certain amount of African backwardness.
Garvey's advice to his followers clearly illustrates this belief:

It strikes me that with all the civilization this Western Hemisphere affords, Negroes
ought to take better advantage of the cause of higher education. We could make of
ourselves better mechanics and scientists, and in cases where we can help our brothers
in Africa by making use of the knowledge we possess, it would be but our duty. If
Africa is to be redeemed the Western Negro will have to make a valuable contribution
along technical and scientific lines.[35]

Thus, Garvey saw an important link between the destinies of Africans and
African-Americans. Yet, he still saw Westernized blacks as leaders, and
Africans on the continent as followers.

Those who joined the UNIA were drawn by the sense of importance and
confidence it gave them. Finally, here was a movement that told them their
ancestral homeland was glorious, and that they had a great destiny to fulfill.
Garvey was able to sustain this sense of excitement and importance by
involving his followers in UNIA activities. These varied activities ranged
from participation in the Black Cross Nurses to involvement in the Royal
African Motor Corps, or the African Orthodox Church. Then there were
the parades—grand parades that wound through Harlem and gave UNIA

members the chance to wear the splendid uniforms that indicated their position in the organization.[36]

Yet, even as many African-Americans in the early part of the twentieth century gloried in their African heritage, the pernicious stereotypes about the continent and its inhabitants continued to endure. With the beginning of the motion picture industry in the twentieth century, degrading stereotypes of Africa became even more widespread. Africa became a popular backdrop for Hollywood tales of mystery and romance. In the vast majority of these early films, Africa was portrayed as an exotic place filled with unusual wildlife, colorful plant life, and ignorant savages. Invariably the white characters were the leaders, and black characters were always the followers.

Even as Hollywood popularized these negative images, some Africans who had been affected by colonization began to have ambivalent feelings about the worth of their culture when juxtaposed against Western culture. Such feelings prompted one early twentieth-century African nationalist to write:

We know that even if British rule were to be voluntarily withdrawn from West Africa, we cannot at present rule ourselves. We know further, that every other race which found itself in the predicament in which we are to-day, has had to be under the tutelage of another nation more advanced in the Science of Government than they until such time as they were sufficiently advanced to manage their own affairs, and then the idea of their continued domination by an alien power had to be decided by an overruling Providence. Ancient History is full of instances of this nature, and we have sufficient faith in God to know that we are not going to be an exception to the general rule.[37]

Thus, as twentieth-century African-Americans attempted to understand their Americanness and their Africanness, they were assaulted by conflicting views of Africa, a changing balance of power in the world, and related changes on the domestic scene. Barely a generation after the Garvey movement reached its height and large numbers of African-Americans identified their African heritage as most important, the Civil Rights Movement began. The hope engendered by the movement convinced many that they truly could be accepted as Americans after all. Yet, the more involved in the movement some became, the more alienated they began to feel from American culture. Once again, in the midst of their alienation many African-Americans looked to Africa. As they embraced Africa, many 1960s activists discovered, much to their dismay, that they could not totally identify with Africa, either.

The case of Matthew Jones, Jr., a member of the Student Nonviolent Coordinating Committee, clearly illustrates the uncertainty and difficulty that faced him and his contemporaries as they tried to defend their identity in a changing America. During the summer of 1964 SNCC unsuccessfully challenged the right of white Mississippians to exclude black voters from the delegate selection process of the National Democratic Convention in Atlantic City. SNCC members were convinced that they were morally, legally, and politically right. In the face of this conviction their unsuccessful challenge left many in the organization demoralized, disillusioned, and doubtful that their identity and destiny were in fact tied to America.

At this critical point a delegation of SNCC members were invited to West Africa. The group left the country in August of 1964, and they spent a great deal of their time in the West African nation of Guinea. Matthew Jones, Jr., who was a member of that delegation, vividly recalled how that trip affected his view of his identity: "I'll tell you what that trip did.... When we first got to Conakry [Guinea]...it was exciting for us. We looked at Sekou Toure [Guinea's leader] almost like a father. We decided we wanted to dress up, get our little dashikis, and get our hair cornrowed so we could talk to him."[38] (He says the whole delegation, to one degree or another, did this.) "He [Sekou Toure] looked at us and he said, uh, he told us that was African culture. That what we had to do was go back to the United States and organize in the black community...in other words, he did not give our cultural escapade, or whatever you want to call it, any impetus. He saw us as being Western and going over taking care of business in the United States for the benefit of all."[39]

The reaction of SNCC volunteers to Sekou Toure? "We felt a little naive because we had done it [embraced African culture in such an overt fashion]. So that was a little bit, uh, confusing for us.... That's when I found out how American I was and that's when I found that I was at that time much closer to Bill Hanson, who was a white fella from Arkansas...and myself, I was much closer to him than anybody, any of the Africans."[40]

Certain aspects of African culture perplexed Jones. "We were faced with a lot of things...that didn't quite fit what I thought were things to do. So I saw then how, number one, how Western I was."[41] Julian Bond, another SNCC staff member who went on that African trip, recalled how amazed he was when he got to Africa and saw black people doing so many things that they were not allowed to do in the United States, such as flying commercial jets. Even though this realty fascinated him, Bond's years of negative conditioning still made him remark half jokingly and half seriously, "I hope this guy knows what he's going."[42]

Yes, there was uncertainty about Africa in the 1960s. There was also excitement. Many spoke frequently about discovering their roots; learning about their ancestral homeland; glorifying their blackness. One commentator on that era asserted:

Finally and equally if not more importantly, within the past decade of the sixties there has been a significant increase in black pride and self-esteem and concomitant decrease in self-hatred among Afro-Americans. This is especially noticeable in standards of physical beauty, particularly insofar as hair styles, and dress are concerned. One rarely encounters black men with processed hair, and black women increasingly are rejecting hair straighteners.[43]

That noisy and enthusiastic expression of pride in things African and African-American soon began to show signs of diminishing by the early 1970s. Historian Alphonso Pinkney dated this waning interest from 1972. He insisted, however that it was only temporary.[44] (He was writing in 1975.) Since the publication of Pinkney's book, chemical hair straighteners have once again become popular, there is a healthy demand for bleaching creams, and excitement about Africa has been replaced by ambivalence . . . yet again.

It seems that in some ways Americans of African descent have come full circle. The laws have changed, but the ambiguity remains. After having come through a Civil War that freed them and a Civil Rights Movement that abolished legal segregation, African-Americans are still wrestling with the same basic issues that plague their ancestors. Their relationship to this country has never been clear. In the antebellum period the question was property or people. In the post–Civil War years the question became citizenship or not. This country has always had trouble defining who African-Americans are. This has contributed to their confusion in defining themselves. Such uncertainty shapes not only their attempts to identify with America, the land that enslaved them, but also with Africa—their ancestral homeland.

So, Du Bois's observation remains every bit as timely now as it was in 1903 when he first articulated it. African-Americans still feel their twoness: They remain marginal, negative Americans. They have strong emotional and cultural ties to both Africa and America. Sometimes they identify with one or the other. Sometimes they identify with both, sometimes they feel alienated from both. Du Bois's question remains unanswered: Will it ever be possible to be both black and American?

NOTES

1. Bernard Makhosezwe Magubane, *The Ties That Bind, African-American Consciousness of Africa* (Trenton, N.J., 1987), 3.

2. John Hope Franklin, *From Slavery to Freedom: A History of Negro Americans* (New York, 1980), 408.

3. Sweatt v. Painter, 339 U.S. 629 (1950), 634. Quoted in Donald G. Nieman, *Promises to Keep, African-Americans and the Constitutional Order, 1776 to the Present* (New York, 1991), 147.

4. Steven F. Lawson, *Running for Freedom, Civil Rights and Black Politics in America Since 1941* (New York, 1991), 19.

5. Steven J. Whitfield, *A Death in the Delta, The Story of Emmett Till* (New York, 1988), 22.

6. Ibid., 42.

7. Zohara Simmons interview, Philadelphia, Penn., December 17, 1988.

8. W.E.B. Du Bois, *The Souls of Black Folk* (New York, 1969), 45.

9. Winthrop D. Jordan, *White Over Black, American Attitudes Toward the Negro 1550–1812* (Baltimore, 1968), 7.

10. Ibid.

11. William Lee Howard, "The Negro as a Distinct Ethnic Factor in Civilization," *Medicine* (Detroit, Mich.), 9 (January 1903): 423. Quoted in John S. Haller, Jr., *Outcasts From Evolution, Scientific Attitudes of Racial Inferiority, 1859–1900* (New York, 1971), 55.

12. Wilson Jeremiah Moses, *The Golden Age of Black Nationalism, 1850–1925* (New York, 1978), 47.

13. Edward W. Blyden, *Christianity, Islam and the Negro Race* (London, 1888), 126, quoted in Hollis R. Lynch, *Edward Wilmot Blyden, Pan-Negro Patriot 1832–1912* (London, 1967), 62.

14. *Liberia Bulletin*, no. 16 (February 1900): 93. Quoted in Lynch, *Edward Wilmot Blyden*, 80.

15. Benjamin Brawley, *Early Negro American Writers* (New York, 1970), 97; also John H. Bracey, Jr., August Meier, and Elliott Rudwick, ed., *Black Nationalism in America* (New York, 1970), 22, 29, 4.

16. Brawley, *Early Negro American Writers*, 97.

17. Prince Sanders, Thomas Jarvis, and Perry Locks to Paul Cuffe, August 3, 1812, Paul Cuffe Papers, New Bedford, Massachusetts Public Library. Quoted in Bracey, et al., *Black Nationalism*, 22.

18. Brawley, *Early Negro American Writers*, 107.

19. Franklin, *From Slavery to Freedom*, 109.

20. Leon Litwack, *North of Slavery, The Negro in the Free States 1790–1860* (Chicago, 1961), 20.

21. Franklin, *From Slavery to Freedom*, 176.

22. Ibid., 177.

23. Litwack, *North of Slavery*, 253.

24. Jordan, *White Over Black*, 567.

25. Litwack, *North of Slavery*, 21.

26. "Movement Among the Colored People of Cincinnati," *African Repository* (Washington, D.C.) 26 (July 1850): 219. Quoted in Bracey et al., *Black Nationalism*, 86.

27. Litwack, *North of Slavery*, 66.

28. Ibid., 60.

29. Henry Highland Garnet, *The Past and the Present Condition, and the Destiny of the Colored Race: A Discourse Delivered at the 50th Anniversary of the Female Benevolent Society of Troy, N.Y., February 14, 1848* (Troy, N.Y., 1848), 12, quoted in Bracey et al., *Black Nationalism*, 120.

30. Martin R. Delany, *The Condition, Elevation, Emigration, and Destiny of the Colored People of the United States* (New York, 1969), 87.

31. Brawley, *Early Negro American Writers*, 303–4.

32. *African Repository* 53 (April 1877): 75; and 56 (July 1880): 73–74. Quoted in Bracey et al., *Black Nationalism*, 170.

33. Ibid., 170.

34. Marcus Garvey, *The Philosophy and Opinions of Marcus Garvey* (New York, 1969), 126, quoted in Moses, *The Golden Age of Black Nationalism*, 263.

35. Garvey, *Philosophy and Opinions*, 59, quoted in Moses, *The Golden Age of Black Nationalism*, 266.

36. Benjamin Quarles, *The Negro in the Making of America* (New York, 1969), 196.

37. *Gold Coast Leader*, May 13, 1916, p. 5. Quoted in Moses, *The Golden Age of Black Nationalism*, 235.

38. Matthew Jones, Jr., interview, Knoxville, Tenn., April 24, 1989.

39. Ibid.

40. Ibid.

41. Ibid.

42. Julian Bond interview, Washington, D.C., December 16, 1988.

43. Alphonso Pinkney, *Red, Black and Green, Black Nationalism in the United States* (New York, 1976), 218.

44. Ibid., 223.

BIBLIOGRAPHICAL ESSAY

Although the literature dealing with African-Americans is voluminous, much of it focuses on their subordinate position vis à vis mainstream "white" society and culture and their efforts to integrate themselves into that milieu. Works that focus directly on the evolution of African-American society and culture per se are relatively rare and generally recent, although *The Souls of Black Folk* (New York, 1969) by W.E.B. Du Bois, originally published in 1903, remains a classic, especially for its perception of African-Americans as marginal and negative. A useful introduction to the concept of "dual consciousness" is Thomas C. Holt, "Afro-Americans," in Stephan Thernstrom et al., eds., *Harvard Encyclopedia of America Ethnic Groups* (Cambridge, Mass., 1980), 5–23. An appreciation of the breadth of the literature on the general topic can be gained from four bibliographies: Elizabeth W. Miller, ed., *The Negro in America: A Bibliography* (Cambridge, Mass., 1970); James M. McPherson et al., *Blacks in America: Bibliographical Essays* (New York, 1971); John Szwed and Roger D. Abrahams, eds., *An Annotated Bibliography: Afro-American Folklore and Culture* (Philadelphia, 1978); and Robert L. Clarke, *Afro-American History: Sources for Research* (Washington, D.C., 1981). The basic facts of African-American history can be garnered from four other reference works: John P. Davis, ed., *The American Negro Reference Book* (Englewood Cliffs, N.J., 1966); Irving J. Sloan, *The Blacks in America, 1492–1976: A Chronology and Fact Book* (Dobbs Ferry, N.Y., 1977); W. A. Low and Virgil A. Clift, *Encyclopedia of Black America* (New York, 1981); and Harry A. Ploski and James Williams, eds., *The Negro Almanac: A Reference Work on the African American* (Detroit, Mich., 1989).

The evolution of African-American identity and culture is dealt with in varying degrees in a number of single-volume histories. Benjamin J. Quarles, *The Negro in the Making of America* (New York, 1969), emphasizes the integral role played by African-Americans in the development of the United States. So does Peter M. Bergman and Mort N. Bergman, comps., *The Chronological History of the Negro in America* (New York, 1969). John Hope Franklin, *From Slavery to Freedom: A History of Negro Americans* (New York, 1974), traces the history of African-Americans from their ancient Old World roots to 1970 and reflects the optimism over progress toward full equality prevalent in the 1960s. August Meier and Elliott Rudwick, *From Plantation to Ghetto: An Interpretive History of American Negroes* (New York, 1974), encompasses the path from West Africa to the 1963 March on Washington highlighted by Dr. Martin Luther King, Jr.'s "I have a dream" speech. Much more somberly, Alphonso Pinkney, *Black Americans* (Englewood Cliffs, N.J., 1988), views the Afro-American community as an "internal colony."

A number of works concentrate primarily on the views of African-Americans held by white Americans. Gunnar Myrdal, *The American Dilemma: The Negro Problem and Modern Democracy* (New York, 1975) is the classic statement, by a non-American, of the fundamental disparity between racism and the American Dream. Stanford M. Lyman, *The Black American in Sociological Thought* (New York, 1972), places Myrdal's observation in a wider scholarly context. Winthrop D. Jordan, *White Over Black: American Attitudes toward the Negro, 1550–1812* (Baltimore, 1968), traces the evolution of American racism from Elizabethan-age contacts with Africa through the end of the slave trade. George M. Frederickson, *The Black Image in the White Mind: The Debate on Afro-American Character and Destiny* (New York, 1971), examines the continuity and transformation of white attitudes from the colonization movement through the nadir of segregation. John F. Haller, Jr., *Outcasts From Evolution: Scientific Attitudes of Racial Inferiority, 1859–1900*, analyzes the deeply flawed efforts of biologists and geneticists to come to grips with their own biases. See also Rayford W. Logan and Irving S. Cohen, *The American Negro: Old World Background and New World Experience* (Boston, 1967); Lenore Bennett, Jr., *Before the Mayflower: A History of Black America* (Chicago, 1969); and Margaret Just Butcher, *The Negro in American Culture* (New York, 1971).

Perhaps surprisingly, the subject of African survivals in African-American culture has only begun to receive serious scholarly attention within the past few decades. An early exception, in addition to Du Bois, was Melville J. Hersvokits, *The Myth of the Negro Past* (Boston, 1941), which traces the survival of thousands of "Africanisms" that form an integral part of African-American culture. A good general introduction to African culture and character is Basil Davidson, *The African Genius: An Introduction to African Cultural and Social History* (Boston, 1969). More intensive and thought-provoking is John S. Mbiti, *African Religions and Philosophy* (New York, 1969). Philip Curtin, *The Atlantic Slave Trade: A Census* (Madison, Wis., 1969), demonstrates that statistics tell only slightly the terrible human cost of the commerce in human life, while Herbert S. Klein, *The Middle Passage: Comparative Studies in the Atlantic Slave Trade* (Princeton, N.J., 1978), examines the argument that the slave trade provided much of the capital for the Industrial Revolution. The theme of continuity versus discontinuity receives considerable stress in the essays contained in Daniel Crowley, ed., *African Folklore in the New World* (Austin, Tex., 1977). Bernard Makhosezwe Magubane, *The Ties That Bind: African-American Consciousness of Africa* (Trenton, N.J., 1987), explores "the phenomenon of ambivalence" through a series of essays on Back-to-Africa movements, pan-Africanism, the Italian invasion of Ethiopia, post–World War II African independence, and South Africa. In *Positively Black* (Englewood Cliffs, N.J., 1970), Roger D. Abrahams argues that a full appreciation of the meaning and style of African folklore will convince any reasonable person that African-Americans are not "culturally deprived."

The early history of blacks in the United States is told in macroscopic fashion in Donald R. Wright, *African-Americans in the Colonial Era: From African Origins Through the American Revolution* (Arlington Heights, Ill., 1990), and in microscopic fashion in Peter H. Wood, *Black Majority: Negroes in Colonial South Carolina from 1670 through the Stono Rebellion* (New York, 1974). The latter is especially useful for its insights into the impact of American slavery on African culture. Several relatively recent works have stressed the positive adaptations to slavery made by African-Americans. Chief among these are John W. Blassingame, *The Slave Community* (New York, 1972); Eugene Genovese, *Roll, Jordan, Roll: The World the Slaves Made* (New York, 1974); Herbert G. Gutman, *The Black Family in Slavery and Freedom, 1750–1925* (New York, 1976); and Lawrence Levine, *Black Culture and Black Consciousness* (New York, 1977). The perspective of those African-Americans who avoided or transcended the slave experience is carefully delineated in Leon F. Litwack, *North of Slavery: The Negro in the Free States, 1790–1860* (Chicago, 1961), and Ira Berlin, *Slaves Without Masters: The Free Negro in the Antebellum South* (New York, 1974).

The trauma of the post-emancipation era on those African-Americans who remained in the South can be apprehended from a variety of studies. Roger Ransom and Richard Sutch, *One Kind of Freedom* (Cambridge, Mass., 1977), investigate the evolution and consequences of the "new slavery" of sharecropping and the crop lien system. The imposition of legal segregation on Southern blacks in the late nineteenth century has been interpreted differently by various scholars. C. Vann Woodward, *The Strange Career of Jim Crow* (New York, 1974), argues that legal segregation was not a reaction against Reconstruction or a natural phenomenon, but rather the outcome of a conflict between Southern white conservatives and radicals. Joel Williamson, *The Origins of Segregation* (Boston, 1968), provides the viewpoints of a dozen observers organized around the general topics of genesis, historical and psychological roots, urban patterns of segregation, and on the relationship between ethnocentrism and race prejudice. The corresponding disfranchisement of African-American voters in the South has been carefully dissected by J. Morgan Kousser, *The Shaping of Southern Politics: Suffrage Restrictions and the Establishment of the One Party South, 1880–1910* (New Haven, Conn., 1974). The toll taken on Southern African Americans by the twin horrors of segregation and disfranchisement are personalized in Theodore Rosengarten, *All God's Dangers: The Life of Nate Shaw* (New York, 1974). The persistent, but generally frustrating, efforts to achieve acculturation and assimilation through formal education are chronicled in Henry A. Bullock, *A History of Negro Education in the South from 1619 to the Present* (Cambridge, Mass., 1967), and in Vincent P. Franklin and James D. Anderson, eds., *New Perspectives on Black Educational History* (Boston, 1978).

The impact of the Great Migration upon African-American identity and culture has been examined by a number of scholars. Hollis R. Lynch, *Black Urban America Since Reconstruction* (Belmont, Calif., 1981), is a pioneer effort to develop a synthesis on the entire experience. Reynolds Farley, *Growth of the Black Population: A Study of Demographic Trends* (Chicago, 1970), also deals with a variety of social and cultural topics involving urban African-Americans. The bittersweet evolution of the country's largest African-American community is analyzed in Gilbert Osofsky,

Harlem: The Making of a Ghetto (New York, 1966), while Nathan Huggins, *Harlem Renaissance* (New York, 1973) explores the tremendous explosion of African-American creative energy that characterized that black metropolis in the 1920s. Sociologist Kenneth B. Clark lays bare the enervating pathology, psychology, and power structure of the modern black slum in *Dark Ghetto: Dilemmas of Social Power* (New York, 1965).

Several other studies focus on the evolution of an African-American community in some of the country's largest cities. Allan H. Spear, *Black Chicago: The Making of a Negro Ghetto, 1890–1920* (Chicago, 1967), stresses the crucial role played by the Great Migration of 1915–1920 and the building of white resentment culminating in the race riots of the "Red Summer" of 1919. Kenneth L. Kusmer, *A Ghetto Takes Shape: Black Cleveland, 1870–1930* (Urbana, Ill., 1976) also assigns major importance to the Great Migration but sees more grounds for optimism by 1930 with the emergence of the "new Negro." Joe William Trotter, Jr., *Black Milwaukee: The Making of an Industrial Proletariat, 1915–1945* (Urbana and Chicago, 1985), explores the "proletarianization" of the Cream City's African-American population in an age of heavy industrialization. For views of the African-American urban experience over time, readers should consult Theodore Kornweibal, Jr., ed., *In Search of the Promised Land: Essays in Black Urban History* (Port Washington, N.Y., 1981), and Hollis R. Lynch, *The Black Urban Condition: A Documentary History, 1866–1971* (New York, 1973). Finally, Charles Kiel explores the significant role played in the city life of African Americans by blues musicians and preachers in *Urban Blues* (Chicago, 1966).

As with most ethnic groups, politics provided Northern African-Americans with one of the earliest and most accessible avenues of acculturation and assimilation. One of the first scholars to appreciate and elucidate the importance of that connection was Harold F. Gosnell, *Negro Politicians: The Rise of Negro Politics in Chicago* (Chicago, 1937). James Q. Wilson, *Negro Politics: The Search for Leadership* (New York, 1960), also focuses on Chicago and on the organization of Negro political and civic life and on the character of Negro public life. The relationship between political adaptation and the struggle for equal rights is deftly explored in Steven F. Lawson, *Running for Freedom: Civil Rights and Black Politics in America Since 1941* (New York, 1991). The importance of legal action to that same process is carefully outlined in Donald G. Nieman, *Promises To Keep: African-Americans and the Constitutional Order, 1776 to the Present* (New York, 1991). A more microcosmic look at the same phenomenon is found in Richard Kluger, *Simple Justice: The History of* Brown v. Board of Education (New York, 1975). The brief springtime of political emergence in the Old South is thoughtfully analyzed by Thomas C. Holt, *Black Over White: Negro Political Leadership in South Carolina During Reconstruction* (Urbana, Ill., 1977). Its reemergence nearly a century later is the subject of political scientist Everett Carll Ladd's *Negro Political Leadership in the South* (Ithaca, N.Y., 1966).

Efforts to generate a genuine African-American nationalism that would blend both sides of their "dual consciousness" antedated the Civil War, as Wilson Jeremiah Moses, *The Golden Age of Black Nationalism, 1850–1925* (New York, 1978), painstakingly demonstrates. His analysis focuses on nineteenth-century leadership and programs, as well as on black nationalism in literature. John H. Bracey, Jr., August Meier, and Elliott Rudwick, eds., *Black Nationalism in America* (New York,

1970), concentrate on the institutions that promoted nationalism and on the divergent economic, political, social and cultural themes that comprised it down to 1968. *Red, Black, and Green: Black Nationalism in the United States* (New York, 1976), by Alphonso Pinckney, locates the roots of the phenomenon in a drive for African-American solidarity, pride in cultural heritage, and a desire for political autonomy. The range of opinion on the prevailing outcome of over three centuries of African-American adaptation is displayed in Norman F. Whitten, Jr., and John F. Szwed, eds., *Afro-American Anthropology: Contemporary Perspectives* (New York, 1970), whose twenty-two essays are organized around cultural patterning, socioeconomic adaptation, and the ghetto ethnography of "black culture." Lorraine A. Williams, ed., *Africa and the Afro-American Experience* (Washington, D.C., 1981) is a series of eight essays on the ongoing connection between the people of the two continents. No study of African American nationalism should ignore *Marcus Garvey and the Vision of Africa* (New York, 1974), edited by John Henrick Clarke and Amy Jaques Garvey. See also Hollis R. Lynch, *Edward Wilmot Blyden, Pan-Negro Patriot, 1832–1912* (London, 1967).

2

American Indians

Vine Deloria, Jr.

Among American domestic ethnic groups, the original inhabitants, the Indians, constitute a special case. Their ethnicity is a product of historical process and political ideology rather than racial and cultural homogeneity. Indeed, "Indian" is a generic term akin to Asian or European in the sense that it refers to a large grouping of diverse peoples who occupy a continental landmass rather than a nationalistic entity with historic homogeneous roots. Western scientists have tried to make American Indians a racial unity by insisting that the Western Hemisphere was populated by migrants from Asia who traversed the Bering Straits land bridge, a mythical corridor created by the manipulation of water levels during certain of the ice ages. This origin theory is universally rejected by Indian tribes, who each have a particular tradition of their origin, migration, or creation.

The origin/creation emphasis of Indian tribes is important in that tribal ethics, social values, and philosophical perspectives are all grounded in the cosmic beginnings of the people and thereafter shape all of their subsequent actions. Thus, many tribes see creation as a unified activity that bestows upon all life forms a basic personality and knowledge structure. Humans are different in kind than other creatures but not set apart for special purposes. Therefore, religious duties include responsibilities to birds and animals as well as other individuals and societies. Lands that a tribe occupies are often set aside for them in the sacred plan for the present world. Tribes might have been created on these lands or commanded to migrate to them. When lands and peoples are both chosen and matched together in a cosmic plan, the attachment to the land by the people becomes something extraordinary and involves a sense of identity and corresponding feeling of responsibility for the land that transcends anything that people outside the tribe can comprehend or experience.

That tribes have been able to maintain themselves as distinct national groups can be attributed to their steadfast adherence to their mission as a distinct people as revealed to them in creation or upon one of their migrations. In the sense of tribes having a divine function within a specific world period, Indians do not see themselves as an ethnic group within a larger society but as a small but faithful remnant of a people called to a larger vocation. Prophecies suggest that the tribe is destined to vanish or at least dissipate prior to the ending of each world cycle. Presumably, the human race is reconstituted on these occasions and survivors come together to form new tribal groups and receive new commands on how to live in the new world.

Tribes are therefore always guided by internal prophetic instructions rather than external political and economic events, and the success or failure of the tribe to deal with unexpected problems can be traced to this excessive concern with fulfilling the cosmic responsibilities placed upon them. In terms of our discussion, however, and our comparison of Indians to other American ethnic groups, the important focus must be on the political/historical factors that have created American Indians as a distinct ethnic group within the American social fabric.

Initial European penetration of the interior of the continent brought contact with powerful Indian confederacies such as the Six Nations, the Creeks or Muskogees, the Miamis, and the Natchez. These Indian groups had both sufficient population to control large areas of the eastern United States and the military prowess to make colonization hazardous if not impossible without their good will and assistance. For at least half of the five hundred years after the landing of Columbus, Europeans needed a military alliance with these groups in order to protect their claims to colonial land areas against other Europeans intent on developing competing colonies. Consequently, in North America, the practice grew up of recognizing the national status of these groups by negotiating informal treaty relationships with them. For a significant period of time Indian confederacies held the balance of power between the European colonial powers who wished to dominate the continent, and the political status and military potential of Indian tribes was a well-established fact by the beginning of the American Revolution.

The Americans assiduously cultivated the neutrality of the Indians during their war for independence and during the struggle for the adoption of the Constitution. Indians constituted one of the major items on the American political agenda. Failing to anticipate how quickly they would settle and control the interior of the continent, the founding fathers saw the commerce and treaty-making clauses as capable of describing and handling their relationships with American Indians in the future and the constitutional question that involved Indians was posed in a federal-state relationships framework. Which level of government would be authorized to deal with the Indian tribes and which could do so most effectively became the political context in which Indians appeared in the constitutional setting.

The United States, fearful that its own claim to national political independence would be challenged by the established nations of Europe, went to extravagant lengths to demonstrate its own political independence by making Indian treaties formal documents of state that were submitted by the president and ratified by the Senate in the same manner that treaties with European nations were accepted as law. Within this formality, the United States then made the claim that it had stepped into the shoes of the European colonial nations regarding the Doctrine of Discovery. The Doctrine of Discovery was a pillar of emerging international law that stated that a Christian monarch could claim the legal title to lands that his subjects discovered if these lands were unoccupied or if they were occupied by non-Christian peoples. The natives, under this doctrine, had to content themselves with the equitable title to their lands, which meant, in practical terms, that only the monarch who held legal title could validly purchase their property estate. In return, the monarch accepted the responsibility to bring the natives to a full understanding of Christianity and to protect them from the intrusions of other European monarchs.

The United States emphasized the latter, and could not give the former its proper due because of its constitutional prohibition against combining the policies of church and state. This protection matured into a doctrine of American federal law whereby a particular kind of "trust" existed between the national government and the Indian tribes. This trust is nebulous in the sense that its reach and the circumstances under which it must or can be applied have never been clearly articulated by the courts or the Congress of the United States. Therefore, Indians have a separate and distinct legal/political status within the American system that generally operates as an exclusionary clause. Indians are not presumed to be included in constitutional and domestic law unless specifically mentioned. Consequently, a separate body of law has grown up dealing with the particularity of tribal and individual Indian rights. This law does not form a consistent and logical whole and is more akin to a body of equitable maxims than a regular subdivision of law such as contracts, torts, or criminal law. But it is the body of rules and regulations that distinguishes Indians from other ethnic groups. A law dealing specifically with the Irish, Polish, or Jewish people would be unconstitutional on its face. The same law, applied to American Indians, would be described by the courts as political because of the Indian treaty and trust relationship.

The United States made nearly one thousand treaties with the Indian tribes, but only about half of the treaties negotiated were ever formally ratified. Ratification often depended simply upon the manner and speed with which the treaty text was submitted to Washington for presentation for ratification. Therefore, the record is spotty at best and can be described as so haphazard as to preclude and defy efforts to formulate the principles upon which treaties were actually ratified. Some treaties represent serious and prolonged negotiations over issues critical to tribal survival or American military and property interests; others represent simply a casual meeting between Indian representatives and local field officers of the United States. The ultimate result of this confusion is that Indian tribes are presumed to possess a plentitude of aboriginal sovereign political powers unless treaties or subsequent acts of Congress specifically divest them of these rights.

Both the treaties and the trust responsibility have moral and ethical dimensions in the sense that they represent a pledge of national honor. They speak to the spirit of the law rather than its letter. In this century the combination of treaty and trust rights and responsibilities has grown together to produce a general acceptance of the legal/moral claim by Indians upon the federal government and the wholly inconsistent notion that Indian tribes are nevertheless quasi-independent political entities with a power of self-government and inherent sovereign powers in commerce and property usage. Federal law operates, consequently, on the basis of political and economic expediency and the application of federal law depends almost wholly upon the perception of Indians that each administration represents. American Indians, therefore, are wholly at the mercy of forces and personalities beyond their control, and this fact alone distinguishes them from all other American minority groups. No constitutional protections exist for American Indians insofar as they wish to emphasize their ethnic identity. By the same token, federal law recognizes in American Indians certain rights and privileges that it cannot recognize in other minority groups.

This extensive preamble to the discussion of Indian ethnicity is necessary because the history and political status of Indians has created a peculiar condition for Indians in the modern world that relates directly to their own conceptions of ethnic identity and their efforts to preserve it. Since the treaty/trust restrictions have been applied to groups in an indiscriminate manner, it is fair to point out that many Indian communities are Indian in the sense of possessing political rights but are indistinguishable from other Americans culturally, linguistically, or even religiously. The legal/political nature of Indian ethnicity is thus apparent. Some Indian groups would have completely assimilated into the American social fabric a century ago were it not for the special status of dependent nationhood that the law bestows upon them.

A further peculiarity results from the application of federal law to Indian communities. If Congress grants formal recognition of a community's Indian identity and allows it to organize under one of the laws recognizing self-government, that community is then vested with all the aboriginal sovereign powers that other tribes are presumed to possess. Congress cannot arbitrarily choose any American community and "make" them Indians, and the criteria for bestowing this tenuous status on a community is rarely defined with any precision. Here apparent ethnicity seems to create legal rights, and political privileges are properly presented to legislative authority. So culture, at least cultural traits that seem to suggest stereotypical commonality with existing Indian groups, becomes an important asset in itself. In this instance we see the ultimate power of the historical experiences of both Indians and non-Indians.

Having established the political/historical context in which Indians always appear, we are now ready to compare American Indians with other domestic American ethnic groups. Two areas immediately appear to be of critical importance in understanding the place of Indians in American society: intermarriage and education. But even these topics are fraught with historical baggage. They appear in history about the same time and have about the same influence today. Since intermarriage seems to be more influential in political consequences, we will discuss that topic first, recognizing that education could equally well deserve our initial attention and discussion.

Intermarriage can be discussed geographically as well as historically because of the nature of European colonization. Foremost in this respect has to be the intermarriage between Indians and the Spanish in the American Southwest. A large American ethnic group derives from the Indian-settler marriages in this region. In this respect it is important to note that there were never many Spaniards in the Southwest at any point in American history. The class definitions that emerged after the conquest of Mexico by Hernando Cortez were brought northward by mixed bloods who settled Texas, California, and southern Arizona and New Mexico. Over the generations the degree of Spanish blood must have become almost infinitesimal, so that most Mexican-Americans today are probably genetically full-blooded Indians, and there is probably a greater degree of Indian blood present in a Chicano barrio than there is in many Indian tribes.

In the Spanish/Mexican communities in the United States today we have evidence of the strength of Spanish culture and language, testimony of the power of Spanish feudal class distinctions. The Indian contribution to Mexican culture must have occurred on an individual basis as each man or woman left his or her tribe and became a part of the dominant society, adopting whatever behavior patterns were necessary to gain acceptance in Mexican society. We still have the Southwestern foods illustrating an Indian heritage, but where are the religious, kinship, and other cultural traits of the Indians that in other parts of the continent proved so resistant to change? Contemporary observers point out the adaptations of the Catholic ceremonies to local Indian beliefs, but they fail to recognize that these adaptations are minor elements in contemporary Mexican Catholicism. In general, Spanish/Mexican culture simply swallowed Indian culture and produced a strong and resilient Mexican ethnic group.

In areas of former French settlement or domination we also find a large population of mixed-blood peoples. The French colonial practice was to intermarry with the Indians and exchange children so that the two groups would more quickly come to understand each other. So fundamental was the French/Indian intermarriage practice that in some tribes today French ancestry is almost the equivalent of Indian ancestry, and only those people who have traceable English ancestry are regarded as whites. With the exception of the Iroquois, who have formally hated the French since Champlain sided with the Hurons against them, the Ottawa, Potawatomi, Chippewa, and Sioux all have had extensive intermarriage with Frenchmen or with mixed bloods who themselves had a French ancestor.

The importance of French intermarriage cannot be underestimated when viewed from a historical perspective. The Metis in Canada largely originate from these marriages and form a particular class of people in Canadian society. The fur trade would have been impossible in the West without the French/Indian connection, and most of the knowledge of the Western regions that English America had in the nineteenth century was derived from the mixed-blood Frenchmen. This group of mixed bloods also played a dominant role in the political affairs of the tribes from the first contact with the United States. French/Indian interpreters were present as brokers of the treaties at almost every treaty north of the Mason-Dixon line, and when treaty-making ended they emerged as the dominant group in the profitable vocations of traders, Bureau of Indian Affairs workers, and ranchers in the Great Plains. By the time the Miami Confederacy had to deal with the United States, its leading political families were primarily of French ancestry. The same can be said to a lesser degree of the Chippewa. Only since the Second World War have the French/Sioux achieved the same position in that tribe.

French intermarriage can be understood as the opposite of Spanish intermarriage. Frenchmen tended to move into the tribe, and only when there was a need for the tribe to deal with English Americans did these mixed bloods emerge as a class. Consequently, the French cultural influence on the Indian tribes was minimal, but its political and economic impact was maximized. With the single exception of French Catholicism, there is little discernible trace of French cultural characteristics in those tribes that intermarried with this nation of Europeans.

English intermarriage is difficult to trace because the people who tended to intermarry did not always regard themselves as Englishmen, although within the larger span of European ethnicity we see them as English. Probably the first large-scale intermarriage was between fugitive Scotch and Irish indentured servants and Indians in the South. The Indian frontier was not as threatening to Scotch and Irish men as historians would lead us to believe. As soon as they saw the opportunity available to free men in the New World, indentured servants fled to the Appalachians or the Deep South, usually picking up an Indian wife in the process and settling in remote places where they could not be discovered and brought back to serve out their terms. By the time the major Indian tribes in the South confronted the English settlers in frontier wars, a good many of of their political leaders were mixed bloods. The war of 1814 between the Creeks and Andrew Jackson, for example, saw the Creeks led by Red Eagle, otherwise known as William Weatherford, a man who was only one-eighth Creek.

Scotch-Irish intermarriage with the Creeks, Cherokees and Choctaws produced a separate class of people who could only be said to be "proto-Southern" in the sense that their behavior forecast the manner in which the Southern society developed. By the time of Indian Removal in the 1830s the leading families of the tribes and the Southern states were often cousins and could at least trace themselves back to a common ancestor not far removed from their own generation. Intermarriage in the South produced what can only be described as two classes of Indians—respectable and real Indians, the respectable people being but a trace Indian and the trace being sufficient to grant them authenticity and status in white society. Today we find thousands of whites who trace their ancestry back to either Pocahontas or a Cherokee "princess" who would not be caught dead with a full-blooded Cherokee.

It was the propensity of mixed-blood members of the Southern tribes to play whites and Indians against each other for their own gain that led to the belief that Indians could probably be civilized. Thus, the five major Indian groups from the South have always been called the Five Civilized Tribes. Very early they were insisting upon educational benefits in their treaty provisions and a Choctaw Academy was even established for mixed-blood sons and daughters of this elite group of people. With some rare exceptions, the political affairs of the Five Civilized Tribes have always been dominated by mixed bloods, and this condition is still prevalent in modern times. One man, W. W. Keeler, was chairman of the board of Phillips Petroleum and chief of the Cherokees at the same time, and a good many of the Oklahoma politicians have had some trace of Indian ancestry. Charles Curtis, vice-president of the United States with Herbert Hoover, was part Kaw Indian from Oklahoma.

Marriage between tribes took on important dimensions after the Indians were settled on the reservations and their children were sent to government boarding schools far away from their home reservations. In pre-reservation days it was not uncommon to have people of mixed tribal ancestry in every tribe because Indians had a propensity to adopt captives taken in war to replace family relatives lost in the conflict. Some famous chiefs were adopted members of the tribes they led in the closing days of the last century. Washakie of the Shoshones and Spokan Garry of the Coeur d'Alenes are prominent examples of this phenomenon. But government boarding schools distorted the process of tribal intermarriage completely out of proportion.

Today when the decennial census is taken, statisticians have a terrible time establishing the proper categories for tribal population. Probably three-quarters of the Indians in the country have a dual ancestry, quite often involving two or more Indian tribes, with some individuals on the west coast often representing eight or more different tribal groups. This situation is the direct result of government educational programs that have emphasized removing Indian children from their homes to be educated in off-reservation boarding schools. The pattern is predictable. The off-reservation schools were begun in the late 1880s. The first generation of students returned home and achieved some degree of prominence in tribal affairs. Some Indians earned professional degrees in law or medicine as a result of their government education and represented the beginnings of a middle class in some tribes. When their children were of an age to attend school, many of the first generation looked back with some degree of pride on their achievements and insisted that their children attend the same boarding schools. The second generation, therefore, viewed off-reservation education as a means of moving beyond the confines of the tribal community and, with the attitude that they could deal with white society as equals, this generation also broke many of the old clan and kinship restrictions and married people from other tribes who they had met in boarding schools.

The children of the second generation came of age in or after the Second World War, and these people both tended to marry outside the tribe and to relocate themselves to urban areas in the Bureau of Indian Affairs relocation vocational program. They were also inclined to marry other Indians who had attended school with them and shared the same attitude toward the larger society. Their children have tended to marry non-Indians with whom they have grown up in urban and suburban areas far from the reservations. If one were to take the possibilities of permutations and combinations from this typical scenario, it is not difficult to see that an individual could have direct ancestral ties with at least a dozen tribes.

The result of tribal intermarriage is that the sharpness of individual tribal heritages has been fused together so that a national sense of pan-Indianism has recently emerged. Individuals in a fundamental way have been forced to confront this situation when tribal lines are crossed because of the difference in customs and family responsibilities. For example, a Plains Indian marrying into an eastern or southeastern tribal family could move from the Plains extended family context to the larger clan responsibilities of his in-laws. He or she could not completely fulfill the duties that are now required by the clan and still maintain the original kinship duties. So a mixing occurs in which the two traditions are still represented but in the form of personal compromise and choice that changes the shape of individual behavior in all social situations. What might be acceptable social behavior in a naming ceremony in one context, for example, is not proper behavior in the other tribal situation. But the individual, in trying to perform some relevant social role in this dilemma, in effect creates a pan-Indian behavior pattern that subsequently becomes the manner in which people act.

The fusing of tribal particularities after the Second World War produced a general sense of "Indianness" in which similarities between kinds of tribal behaviors gradually merged into a new kind of social value that was acceptable in both tribal traditions. Such ceremonies as the sweat lodge soon transcended individual tribal customs to become one of the things that Indians did—regardless of tribal backgrounds. By the 1970s it was possible to find wholly new kinds of behavior generally accepted as "Indian" when in fact they represented changes that had occurred within the previous generation. Many tribes, for example, had special ceremonies in which friends were made. The acceptance of this friendship required a loyalty and commitment equal to or greater than the duties and support owed a sibling. In a pan-Indian setting, however, making friends became simply an act of identifying fellow Indians within a non-Indian social context as, for example, attending an urban Indian center and becoming well acquainted with other Indians who lived in the same neighborhood. The outgoing sense of hospitality and helpfulness characteristic of Indians was still experienced, but friendship itself had lost its sacred sanction and support.

On the national level this growing together of many tribal traditions provided the foundation for activist protests by such organizations as the American Indian Movement, which discovered that it could appeal to a wide audience on the basis of Indian racial identity alone by advocating unity on behalf of a larger political cause. Unless a specific goal was established by the activists, such as restoring lands for a particular tribe or ensuring fishing rights for tribes in a specific region, issues were generally framed in terms of demanding concessions from the federal government that presumably would improve the lot of all tribes. Pan-Indianism did not, therefore, seek to encourage Indians or tribes to do things for themselves. Rather, it accepted the definition of Indians as an American minority group and sought to make the group an identifiable political constituency with recognizable influence, a group to whom successful white politicians owed favors. Thus, today we often talk about the Indian vote as if it is a monolithic thing that can be courted by the pronouncement of certain emotional slogans representing political sympathy and understanding. We hardly ever speak of tribal voting to achieve specific tribal goals.

Having a multitribal genetic background is not a hindrance to most individual Indians. If a person is enrolled in one tribe, it is usually that of his or her father, and enrollment in a tribe usually means forfeiture of rights in or claims to rights as a member of another tribe. Today some tribal governments have solved this problem of multitribal background by counting the total degree of Indian blood as if it were coming wholly from the parent who makes the children eligible for tribal membership. This technique clarifies the political status of the individual and also helps to solve another problem. Since federal services are usually restricted to people of one-quarter degree of Indian blood, quite often individuals can be enrolled members of a tribe but not always eligible for some kinds of federal services. Or individuals can have sufficient Indian blood but not be enrolled in any tribe because of tribal requirements. Thus, children of a full-blood mother and a white father might not be regarded as Indians by a tribal enrollment committee. So individuals must pay special attention to their genetic ancestry so that they can continue to receive federal services.

If intermarriage with non-Indians and other tribes has been important in forming the present posture of the American Indian community, education has been nearly as important. Under the Doctrine of Discovery it was the responsibility of the European monarch to teach the Christian religion and bring civilization to the natives under his sovereign control. In North America this task was voluntarily undertaken by private citizens initially, and only in recent times has the task of civilizing the Indians been assumed by the federal government. Most of the early colleges in the New England area started as mission schools to help teach the local Indians about Western civilization. Harvard, Princeton, Dartmouth, and William and Mary are among the more prominent institutions whose initial capital was given so that Indians could be instructed in the Gospel.

Among the lasting benefits of this early concern was the translation of the Scriptures, and later other works, into the languages of some of the tribal tongues. Many tribes are still writing materials in their own languages. At first the effort was directed toward making the Indians familiar with biblical themes so that they could much more easily understand English when it was taught them. The popular bilingual programs of the War on Poverty during the 1960s also had this goal when encouraging the use of the tribal language. In both instances, however, the effect was to interest the people in using their own language, demonstrating that education should be conceived in terms of the tribal goals and not necessarily in measures pleasing to outsiders.

Education was at first a function of the missionaries, and some tribes insisted that missionary groups be given lands so that they could establish schools for the children of the tribe. Later, as federal services became a greater part of the treaty promises, the federal government embarked on an ambitious educational program for Indians that featured the creation of day schools on the reservations. But these schools generally had a difficult time when budget considerations were made; they did not seem to be producing educated Indians with sufficient speed for Congress. So the program of taking children and placing them in boarding schools was adopted. By the First World War there were nearly sixty of these schools in the United States and the idea of placing them at great distances from the reservation had changed so that the emphasis was simply on providing an education to every child on the reservation.

Vocational education long dominated federal ideas of the kind of education that Indians should receive, and even until the mid–1960s Congress believed devoutly that Indians could not master academic subjects but greatly preferred to learn skills where they could use their hands. Indians, on the other hand, always sought to learn whatever skills would best enable them to earn a living on or near their reservations, and therefore they liked vocational education. Since the reservations are all located in remote areas in the West where there are few white collar or professional jobs, there was no great demand for academic education among Indians until they became aware of the larger society in the 1960s. Since then, Indians have sought academic and professional training in record numbers.

The educational hopes of Indians always represented conflicting goals and a confused image of the substance of white society. Education was seen as a means of getting equality in material goods so that the people could live a better, more prosperous life, and as a means of protecting the tribe from the intrusions made by the whites. Indians thus sought technical knowledge without realizing that by changing their cultural values to accept this technology they were reducing the distance between themselves and the whites to such a degree that there would be little Indian substance left to protect. Thus, the Cherokees reduced their customs to written laws and Constitution, invented an alphabet and written language, made every possible overture to the southern whites, and thereby earned white resentment to such a degree that it became impossible for the federal government to protect their lands and resources and they were removed from Georgia to Oklahoma in 1838.

Indian societies were tightly organized around the sacred teaching and rituals that, it was believed, had been handed down through the centuries to ensure the continued existence of the tribe and allow for its participation in cosmic realities. Education made these cosmic realities seem remote and eventually superstitious, so that the propensity of most educated Indians was to reject the good things in their tradition and accept the worst thing in the white culture. The heroic figure of Indian history, seen from the perspective of both whites and Indians, are those Indians who held fast to their traditional ways. Educated Indians were perceived as a people set apart by their experience by both whites and other Indians. Whites resented educated Indians and believed they were not "real," while Indians saw education as an experience of alienation that made white people out of tribal members.

Educated Indians have always stood midway between Indian and white society, and as a consequence have generally become brokers of power and interpreters of culture between the two groups. As more Indians have become educated since the Second World War, this group has grown considerably, so it is fair to say that about half of each tribe consists of educated people who did not quite fit in with the central core of tribal society. One need only glance at the tribal scholarship awards or the Bureau of Indian Affairs lists of scholarship recipients to see that the people getting educated are generally not reservation residents but are Indians from families who have previously moved off the reservation or away from the community, retaining their tribal enrollment, but for all practical purposes living and learning as whites in American society.

One of the most detrimental effects of education on Indians has been the abandonment of the old ways and particularly of the old knowledge about the world. Indian health has greatly deteriorated with the loss of traditional medicines and cures. Some Indians blame the change of diet for their bad health conditions, but there is some evidence that the loss of knowledge about plants and their medicinal use has contributed even more to the inability of either the Indians or the Public Health Service to improve Indian mortality rates. This condition has become apparent in some tribes because with the resurgence of interest in traditional ways, people are once again beginning to use traditional medicines and are discovering that they can cure a multitude of illnesses with them. In the tribal context, because of the belief in the basic relatedness of the natural world, the deterioration of health indicates a bad spiritual posture and an abandonment of guiding spiritual principles. Education, many Indians believe, caused the people to lose faith in the things that they knew and followed.

The remedy for this condition is not, as some people would have it, a rejection of Western medicine, but the elevation of the medicine man or healer to his proper place in tribal society. Since many Indians fall within the educated class of tribal society, a strange phenomenon has emerged in which people who otherwise accept Western science are coming to depend upon traditional medicines and religion to maintain themselves. If this trend continues, the result will be people who are indistinguishable from other Americans, who are reasonably well-educated, but who adhere to a modernized version of the old tribal religion.

Education can also be used as a measuring stick to evaluate the spectrum of beliefs and practices within tribal societies. If we were to chart the relative educational achievements of all the members of a tribal group with the education appraised at its true worth, we might find ourselves with a steep parabolic curve in which we find a few members well-educated and a few members hardly educated at all, or stubbornly refusing any contact with the modern world. We would find varying degrees of education in the majority of tribal members, with a high school diploma and some vocational training as typical of the people at the top of the curve.

This curve can equally well represent the degree of assimilation and traditionalism to be found within the tribe. There are always a few people who vehemently deny their Indian ancestry and seek to disappear within

American society, refusing to admit that they have any Indian blood at all. And there is always a small, hard core of traditional people who act as if five hundred years of contact with whites has never happened. The majority of Indians in most tribes, however, emphasize their Indian heritage according to the manner in which they see themselves functioning in their home environment. Consequently, there is an ebb and flow within the tribes that governs the manner in which people aggressively demonstrate Indian traits and characteristics. In this respect Indians are probably not much different than members of other American ethnic groups in showing pride in their heritage.

The activism of the 1970s made it imperative for many people to emphasize their Indian heritage. Some people with a minimal claim to Indian tradition enthusiastically threw themselves into the activist movement. Unfortunately, a good many non-Indians came to believe they were also Indians, so the number of people who claimed to be Indians increased dramatically. Many of the reservation people who traditionally had shunned white society and were hesitant to show Indian characteristics took heart at the outpouring of interest in Indians and began sharing their knowledge and beliefs with less traditional people. The result was that the national Indian community as a whole took on a more militant posture regarding what it meant to be an Indian and interest in tribal culture and religion escalated accordingly. Today a near majority of each tribe seems to regard themselves as traditional people or as people who revere tribal traditions.

One symptom of this change has been the increasing emphasis on learning the tribal language. Until the early 1960s it was presumed that most tribal languages were dying out, and indeed there was good evidence that English had made great inroads even in the most conservative tribes. With the authorization of bilingual programs that sought to teach English, or at least lay the groundwork for teaching English by emphasizing the native language, many of the tribes used bilingual education to begin teaching their children the tribal tongue. But this kind of learning followed the traditional classroom methods of teaching so that Indian children often had to learn their own language as if it were Latin or Greek. In the long run native languages will probably disappear because of the inordinate influence of television on younger children. In the midst of the Navajo reservation in Arizona at Chin Lee there are three videotape rental stores, an indication of the widespread degree to which the Navajos already speak and understand English. Some tribes now have to conduct their tribal business meetings in English in order to include the TV generation of Indians, and it might not be long before only a few very traditional tribes such as the Iroquois can speak their own language with any degree of assurance and confidence.

The political strategies of American Indians differ quite substantially from those of most other ethnic groups. Until the Second World War, each tribe more or less handled its own business and dealt with important national legislation according to the way in which it felt the law would affect it. Even though there were a number of voluntary organizations dedicated to assisting Indians with their problems, Indians did not have the capability to speak with a united voice on legislation that would affect every tribe. At the very end of the war some of the Bureau of Indian Affairs employees, at the urging of Commissioner John Collier, came together to form the National Congress of American Indians (NCAI). Over the years the NCAI has come to represent the mainstream opinions of tribal councils and informed, interested Indians.

In the early 1970s a new group, partly competitive with the NCAI, the National Tribal Chairmen's Association (NTCA), was formed. It was originally designed to be the Indian counterpart to the various state and city national organizations that work for improved conditions and benefits for state agencies and city councils. The NTCA, however, adopted a stance almost indistinguishable from that of the Bureau of Indian Affairs and usually supported the Bureau in its policies and programs. Since its major funding source was the Bureau, it is not surprising that NTCA followed the government's party line so closely. Today the NTCA represents the old-line chairmen who have dominated the politics of their tribe for most of their adult life. They are, surprisingly, more aggressive at this point in policy matters than either the NCAI or some of the activist groups that had confrontation with the government as their major agenda.

The 1970s were the years of the Indian activists, beginning with the occupation of the federal prison on Alcatraz in late 1969. Even those of us who have been involved with Indian activism from its inception have a difficult time writing its chronology or providing an accurate view of the many organizations that have emerged in this area. The most persistent groups have been the American Indian Movement (AIM), which was the leading group in the occupation of Wounded Knee in 1973, and the Survival of American Indians, which began the fishing rights protests in the mid–1960s. The Indian activists were indeed activists and membership in each group at times seemed wholly dependent on which button an Indian was wearing. With the conclusion of the Wounded Knee trials in 1976, emphasis began to be placed on seeking an international forum where Indians could align themselves with aboriginal peoples from around the globe. This tendency has grown over the past decade so that the activist groups are now more interested in hemispheric problems such as the Indians in Nicaragua than in reservation conditions.

The primary political strategy among Indians can be divided into two different techniques that are easily divided into two distinct historical periods. From the end of the Second World War until 1970 the tactic was to pose as America's favorite minority and play off the favorable image of Indians against the stereotypes that whites held of blacks and Chicanos. Whenever a civil rights protest would stir up some controversy, Indians would say they had greater needs but did not feel they should take to the streets and lose their dignity over an issue that could be resolved by a simple demonstration of good will on each side. This tactic did produce results because Indian tribes were made eligible agencies under many of the national poverty program authorizations. Thus, tribes could sponsor programs for areas under their control and benefit from the large managerial overhead fees that such agencies received. By the mid–1970s tribes were eligible for a bewildering number of programs, so many that they had to start being selective in bringing programs to the reservations. The problem with this strategy was that it did not address the problems that arose because of the peculiar nature of the Indian relationship with the federal government.

The activist strategy was to call the government directly to account for its past misdeeds and omissions. Treaty rights rather than eligibility and need became the criteria for protest and the idea was to play directly on whatever reservoir of cumulative guilt lay hidden in the public psyche. That this tactic was partly successful is evident in the fact that when the Indians occupied the Bureau of Indian Affairs in Washington, doing more damage to the federal buildings than had the British when they sacked Washington during the War of 1812, the public was largely behind them. But collective historic guilt is difficult to transform into contemporary political support, and when the public came to understand that some Indian claims, although just and valid, might upset land titles in the eastern states or curtail hunting and fishing in the western states, support for Indians vanished, leaving behind a few militant anti-Indian groups that sought abrogation of all treaties.

Increasing the Indian vote in state and national elections has been a continuing goal ever since the Second World War, and a good deal of work has gone into increasing the number of Indian votes in critical states and congressional districts. However, Indians are such a small percentage of any important state or congressional district that it has been difficult to make the Indian vote count. Additionally, Indians seem to be too honest to make maximum use of their voting advantages. Since reservations are located in the most remote areas of each state, it would not be difficult for a number of the large tribes to simply wait out the election night and then return the number of votes needed to determine the outcome of close elections. Admittedly this vote withholding is not in the best tradition of democracy but it is a common practice in most of the states of the union among the two major parties and has proven important in determining the composition of many a congress. That Indians do not presently have the same skills and attitude toward the electoral process as non-Indians indicates that they have a considerable period of maturing ahead of them.

Indians, at least since the Depression, have tended to vote Democratic, and by the end of the 1960s most tribes were clearly of Democratic composition. Prior to the New Deal shift it was possible to determine the probable vote of reservation residents by the political allegiance of their agent, who seemed to have great influence over how the tribe understood the political world. This factor might also account for the political isolation of reservation people until the 1970s and their refusal to align themselves with other minorities seeking change. Following the Second World War it was almost a standard doctrine among Indians and Bureau of Indian Affairs personnel that Indians and blacks had nothing in common. The elected officers of the NCAI cringed when people suggested that Indians cooperate with blacks on certain issues of mutual concern. Folklore dictated that Indians form coalitions with Asians, another "silent" minority, and until tribal leaders had to deal with black program officers in the poverty program agencies, there was great suspicion that blacks wanted to integrate Indians into the American social mainstream and abolish the reservations.

The Poor People's March in 1968 had a number of Indian participants and probably broke the informal political color line that had existed during most of this century. With the increasing number of tribal council members in the NCAI in the late 1960s the organization was forced to deal with isolated tribes in the eastern and New England states who had worked well with the NAACP, so that by the mid–1970s it was commonplace to have Indian leaders suggesting some kind of alliance with other minorities. When Jesse Jackson began his campaign in 1984 and talked about his "Rainbow Coalition," he was surprisingly well received in Indian country.

Until 1960 it would not have been proper to have discussed American Indians in the context of American minorities because few Indians saw themselves as a minority within American society. The attitude was that Indians had a special place near but certainly not in American society and the task of tribal leaders was to determine whether protections could be established to keep the outside at arm's length. Tribal eligibility for social welfare programs broke this sense of determined isolation once and for all. With a great increase in college scholarships, thousands of young Indians headed for college and saw the world pretty much as non-Indians of the same age saw it. As Indians became more familiar with the world outside the reservation, there is no question that they began to see themselves as another minority group within American society. The activism of the 1970s only confirmed this viewpoint and made it a regular part of the Indian perspective, even of the reservation people. Indians began to see that they were connected with much larger forces in the world, and the favorable publicity that Indians have generally received because of their historical image as the Noble Savage encouraged some Indian spokesmen to insist on Indian inclusion with the various civil rights, ecological, and political co-alitions that were forming and fermenting in the larger society.

One gauge of the seriousness and permanence of this movement is the evident loosening of ties within the extended Indian family. Tribal, family, and clan membership once dominated all other Indian considerations, and it was possible for an informed member of one tribe to know or identify almost every other member of every other tribe. This extensive kind of knowledge seems remote if not impossible, but the basis for it was simple. Through their boarding school experiences many Indians knew members of other tribes and, correspondingly, their families. Elders kept track of the family and passed the information along to the younger generation so that one needed only to know tribe and last name in order to place an individual and locate his home community. This basic identity has now significantly eroded if it has not vanished in many tribes.

With family no longer acting as the dominant force in restraining behavior, there is little sense of tribal identity other than enrollment number in many Indian communities. Enrolled members of the same tribe might meet at conferences or pow-wows and discover they have no knowledge of each other's families whatsoever. They might not even have mutual friends or acquaintances. This condition is unprecedented in Indian country. On the other hand, they might discover that they share hundreds of friends in other tribes who are in the same or related professions or in the same age group. The connections in Indian Affairs have become, sad to say, networks rather than family relationships, and in this sense Indians have become an American ethnic group rather than a small collection of distinct tribal nationalities.

At the same time the old relationships are breaking down, some form of modern traditionalism is surging in many Indian communities. Modern traditionalism seems a contradiction in terms, but it is the best description of how Indians are forging a modern identity as a group. Foremost in modern Indian interest is religion, and this interest was generated initially by the participation of some well-known medicine men in some of the marches on Washington held during the mid–1970s. Additionally, beginning around 1969 and continuing for most of the 1970s, a group of traditional leaders met annually in Canada under the broad rubric of the Ecumenical Council. People from many tribes attended these sessions, which were a mixture of old teachings and demonstrated concern for the loss of language and tradition among the young people.

The Ecumenical Council succeeded in reaching people of all ages far beyond their most optimistic expectations. An impressive number of young people abandoned their careers in Indian organizational work and returned to their reservations determined to learn the tribal ways and become carriers of the traditions. Since the conditions under which the old ways were practiced no longer exist, the most satisfactory solution for these young people was to derive principles of action and understanding from the traditions and apply them to modern circumstances in which they found themselves. The movement must therefore be denominated as modern traditionalism because it seeks to transform old ways of behaving into standards of action with definable limits set by the conception of Indian identity itself.

Indians therefore find themselves at a unique point in their history. The present generation of tribal leaders can best be described in Robert Bellah's new terminology as a managerial elite, but coming right behind them, and increasingly offering a more Indian alternative, are the new traditionals who are already having quite an impact. A recent example may clarify this development. Since the authorization of self-government in 1934 it has become almost a duty of tribal councilmen to reward themselves by establishing a lucrative fee schedule for work on tribal business. Indeed, in some tribes per diem and fees constituted one of the few ways to earn a cash income for people on the reservation. Although the rank and file tribal members often complained bitterly about this practice, until recently it was unthinkable that anyone would oppose paying tribal councilmen for their attendance of meetings and other tribal business. But some tribes have now voluntarily reduced the fee schedule for tribal elected officials, leading people to assume that while there is a strong managerial inclination in tribal government, there is also a strong undercurrent of traditional belief still present that argues for the old idea of contributing to the welfare of the community as a matter of personal responsibility.

Two main attitudes can be discerned in today's Indian world. Indians who used to be called progressive, and who are primarily represented by educated younger people, still believe that with the prodigious effort tribal economies can be raised to the level of their white neighbors around them. These people work hard in tribal development programs, support educational opportunities for the coming generation, and seek to participation in state and county activities. By and large, although few Indians would admit it, the foundation of this attitude is the belief that Indians have become an American ethnic group and must accommodate themselves to the American way of doing business. The problem with this approach to tribal affairs is the inability to understand the immense amount of resources and credit that must be accumulated in order to be successful in the American economic game. Indian tribes simply do not have access to this kind of money regardless of the glitter and gleam that is present in some of the present economic opportunities. At best American Indians can only become one of the poorer and least favored ethnic groups by following this path.

The other posture present in the Indian world is the return to traditionalism in some form. Here the spectrum is wide and we find representatives of almost every nuance of tradition present. Some people want to return to the old ways in every aspect of life, and in Canada there have been experiments in living in the forests again. When this extreme behavior is found in American Indian communities it usually manifests itself in a resurgence of traditional medicines, subsistence hunting and farming practices, and revitalization of old religious ceremonies. In general traditionalism is more influential in religious circles and social organizations than in tribal governments and economic development practices. It has not yet, to any significant degree, assisted in rebuilding families and communities, and seems to be restricted to self-improvement and alcoholism activities. Traditionalism seems to be more important to many Indians because it provides a recognizable identity for both individuals and communities without coming to grips with the difficult facts of economic and political life. In this sense it resembles Christian fundamentalism in the larger society. But many Indians see traditionalism as the first step in a reconstitution of the tribal community and so it offers hope for the preservation of the people without the adoption of distasteful cultural values that connection with the industrial machine inevitably brings.

The ultimate fate of American Indians will probably be the same as that of other rural Americans with some few variations. In choosing to remain in isolated rural areas, Indians must also learn to forego the frills and gimmicks of modern American urban life. Thus, a definite choice in foods, medicines, entertainment, occupations, and participation in the larger society must be made. The fact of this necessary choice has not been clearly articulated by or for Indians, and consequently, traditionalism looks much more attractive than does eventual assimilation as an ethnic group. A stabilizing of rural America would do much to demonstrate to the tribes that a partial accommodation to industrial society can be made without losing the sense of community. Stabilizing in the Indian sense can only mean initially a consolidation and expansion of the reservation land base and proper use of its resources. We are not yet far enough along in either industrial development or in land consolidation to be able to tell which direction the people will take.

BIBLIOGRAPHICAL ESSAY

Narrowing the voluminous literature on American Indians to those works that deal directly or primarily with their interaction with Euro-American society and culture is a herculean task, especially because both Native Americans and mainstream Americans have been extremely ambivalent and fluctuating about the relative merits of separation and acculturation/assimilation. In more recent years, the leading advocates of the various Native American movements have frequently disagreed over the importance of maintaining the rich historical diversity of tribal and national identities versus the necessity of constructing a generic American Indian identity that might conceivably consolidate and maximize economic and political power. The article "Indians," written by Edward H. Spicer for the *Harvard Encyclopedia of American Ethnic Groups* (Cambridge, Mass., 1980), 58–114, provides a good introduction to and overview of that dilemma. Also very useful is his *A Short History of the Indians of the United States* (New York, 1969). The diversity and complexity of American Indian identity and culture is best conveyed by a collective reading of a number of relatively recent reference works. *The Dictionary of Indian Tribes of the Americas*, 3 vols. (Newport Beach, Calif., 1980), compiled and published by American Indian Publishers, provides brief descriptions and histories of all the Indian nations. Francis Paul Prucha, *Atlas of American Indian Affairs* (Lincoln, Neb., 1990), conveys a good sense of their changing geographical distribution and resultant cultural adaptation over time, as does Carl Waldman, *Atlas of the North American Indian* (New York, 1985). Frederick W. Hodge, ed., *Handbook of American Indians North of Mexico*, 2 vols. (New York, 1971), gives a brief description of the linguistic stock, confederacy and settlement patterns of all U.S. and Canadian tribes and subtribes. Barry T. Klein, ed., *Reference Encyclopedia of the American Indian*, 2 vols. (New York, 1986), provides valuable information on reservations, tribal groups, bands, councils, museums, libraries, schools, college courses, magazines and periodicals, and audio-visual aids, as well as extensive bibliographies. Wilcomb E. Washburn, ed., *Handbook of North American Indians*, 20 vols. (Washington, D.C., 1988), features volumes on geographical regions, Indians in contemporary society, environment, origins, population, history of Indian-white relations, technology and visual arts, and languages. It also includes a two-volume biographical dictionary and an extensive index volume.

Carl Waldman, *Who Was Who in Native American History: Indians and Non-Indians from Early Contact through 1900* (New York, 1990) focuses primarily on prominent individuals, whether Native American or those who interacted with them in important ways. So does Frederick J. Dockstatter, *Great North American Indians: Profiles in Life and Leadership* (New York, 1977). For a chronology of events and ready references to dates significant in American Indian history, see Henry C. Dennis, comp. and ed., *The American Indian, 1492–1976: A Chronology and Fact Book* (Dobbs Ferry, N.Y., 1977). Arnold Marquis, *A Guide to America's Indians: Ceremonials, Reservations and Museums* (Norman, Okla., 1974), supplies such information for 263 tribes, banks, and groups in the United States. J. R. Swanson, *The Indian Tribes of North America* (Washington, D.C., 1969) is generally considered to be the standard work. Ruth Underhill, *Red Man's America: A History of the Indians in the United States* (Chicago, 1971), focuses on the universality and peculiarity of cultural traits, while Ethel Nurge, ed., *The Modern Sioux: Social Systems and Reservation Culture* (Lincoln, Neb., 1970) uses the tribe as a prism through which to view other tribes. The anthology *North American Indian's Historical Perspective* (New York, 1971), edited by E. B. Leacock and N. O. Lurie, conveys a strong sense of chronological progression.

The tortured course of changing U.S. policy toward American Indians can be traced in many sources. Calvin Martin, ed., *The American Indian and the Problem of History* (New York, 1987) contains twenty expert essays on "the metaphysics of writing Indian-white history" from the Native American perspective. Jane F. Smith and Robert M. Kvasnicka, *Indian-White Relations: A Persistent Paradox* (Washington, D.C., 1976), the product of the National Archives Conference on Research in the History of Indian-White Relations, examines the ongoing ambivalence between assimilationist and separatist policies. The same general focus pervades Larry W. Burt, *Tribalism In Crisis: Federal Indian Policy, 1953–1961* (Albuquerque, N.M., 1982), which demonstrates that the paradox between termination and tribalism endures. James Axtell, *The European and the Indians: Essays in the Ethnohistory of Colonial North America* (New York, 1981) examines the early origins of that phenomenon, while Robert Berkhofer, Jr., *The White Man's Indian* (New York, 1978), explores the various stereotypes and misconceptions that have consistently informed Euro-American attitudes toward Native Americans. Roy Harvey Pearce, *The Savages of America: A Study of the Indian and the Idea of Civilization*

(Baltimore, 1953), traces the evolution of the "superior civilization" rationale for the destruction of Indian culture and identity. Frederick E. Hoxie, *A Final Promise: The Campaign to Assimilate the Indians, 1880–1920* (Lincoln, Neb., 1984) focuses on the era that produced the Dawes Act, the breakup of the reservations, and the use of religion and education as tools for "civilizing" Indians. Francis Paul Prucha's ironically titled *Americanizing the American Indian: Writings by the "Friends of the Indian," 1880–1900* (Cambridge, Mass., 1973) examines a similar phenomenon, while Basil H. Johnston, *Indian School Days* (Norman, Okla., 1990), concentrates on the concerted effort to alienate the younger generation from their native culture through enforced education.

Wilcomb E. Washburn, ed., *The American Indian and the United States: A Documentary History*, 4 vols. (New York, 1973) is a comprehensive collection of the reports of commissioners of Indian affairs, congressional debates, acts, ordinances, proclamations, treaties, and legal decisions that defined Indian-United States relations over two centuries. J. Norman Heard, ed., *Handbook of the American Frontier: Four Centuries of Indian-White Relationships*, 5 vols. (Metuchen, N.J., 1990) provides many insights into both sides of the frequent contact between Native Americans and Euro-Americans. Francis Paul Prucha, *The Indian in American Society: From the Revolutionary War to the Present* (Berkeley and Los Angeles, 1985), examines the relationship from the perspectives of paternalism, dependency, Indian rights, and self-determination. Wilcomb E. Washburn, ed., *The Indian and the White Man* (Garden City, N.Y., 1964) contains over one hundred documents organized around the topics of first contact, personal relations, justification for dispossession, the trade nexus, the missionary impulse, war, governmental relations, and literature and the arts. Vine Deloria, Jr., ed., *American Indian Policy In the Twentieth Century* (Norman, Okla., 1985) is a collection of essays by eleven scholars on various aspects of federal policy-making and enforcement regarding "the Indian problem." S. Lyman Taylor, *A History of Indian Policy* (Washington, D.C.), presents the U.S. government point of view.

Several other fairly recent works concentrate on the tensions within the American Indian community over acculturation, traditionalism, and progressivism. D'Arcy McNickle, *Native American Tribalism: Indian Survivals and Renewals* (New York, 1973), explores the modern origins and paradox of such concepts as Indian nationalism, pan-Indianism and Red Power. Murray L. Wax, *Indian-Americans: Unity and Diversity* (Englewood Cliffs, N.J., 1971), contends that the American Indian identity has emerged out of the relationship between the native people of the Americas and their European-descended invaders. Howard M. Bahr, Bruce A. Chadwick, and Robert C. Day, *Native American Today: Sociological Perspectives* (New York, 1972), view American Indians primarily from the standpoint of social class analysis. The growing movement toward self-help and cross-tribal associationalism is documented in Armand S. La Potin, ed., *Native American Voluntary Organizations* (Westport, Conn., 1987). Providing a variety of answers to the question of "Who is an Indian?" within a historical context, Hazel W. Hertzberg, *The Search for an American Indian Identity: Modern Pan Indian Movements* (Syracuse, N.Y., 1971), examines several fraternal and religious universalist Indian movements in the twentieth century. See also the chapter on "Pan-Indianism" by Robert K. Thomas in Stuart Levine and Nancy O. Lurie, eds., *The American Indian Today* (Deland, Fla., 1968).

The persisting conundrum between traditionalism and termination is explored thoroughly in Wilcomb E. Washburn, *Red Man's Land/White Man's Law: A Study of the Past and Present Status of the American Indian*, in which he concludes that "the Indian of the Future" cannot totally return to the past or completely retain the present culture. Robert Burnette, *The Tortured Americans* (Englewood Cliffs, N.J., 1971), surveys the tragic history of Euro-American treatment of American Indians and proposes a "Fair Indian Act" to Congress. The peculiar problems of the growing numbers of urban Indians and their greater receptivity to a "Pan-Indian" definition have received increasing attention. Jack O. Waddell and O. Michael Watson, eds., *The American Indian in Urban Society* (Boston, 1971) ranks as the pioneer work on the topic. The socioeconomic dimensions of urban settlement are examined in Henry F. Dobyns, Richard W. Stoffle, and Kristine Joes, "Native American Urbanism and Socio-Economic Integration in the Southwestern United States," *Ethnohistory* 22 (Spring, 1975): 155–79. The relationship of pan-Indianism to city dwelling forms the perspective of James Hirabayashi, William Willard, and Luis Kemmitzer, "Pan-Indianism in the Urban Setting," in Thomas Weaver and Douglas White, eds., *The Anthropology of Urban Environments* (Washington, D.C., 1972).

Over the last two decades, the growing militancy of American Indians has manifested itself in many publications. *Custer Died For Your Sins: An Indian Manifesto*, by Vine Deloria, Jr. (New York, 1969), and *Bury My Heart at Wounded Knee: An Indian History of the American West* by Dee Brown (New York, 1970) formed a powerful one-two punch. Close behind came Alvin M. Josephy, Jr., *Red Power: The American Indians' Fight for Freedom* (New York, 1971), an analysis of this new militancy. In the next few years, Deloria also contributed *Of Utmost Good Faith* (San Francisco, 1971), a study of the disparity of land-holding theory and of civil rights; *We Talk: You Listen* (New York, 1970), an impassioned plea for a new civic religion that promotes individualism through tribalism and federalism; and *The Indian Affair* (New York, 1974), a powerful brief for legal research and support, Indian control of Indian education, and diligent congressional oversight. Attempts by federal law enforcement agencies to suppress the new militancy, specifically involving the Federal Bureau of Investigation and the Lakota Indians during the 1970s and 1980s, is the theme of *In the Spirit of Crazy Horse* (New York, 1983) by Peter Mathiessen.

3

German-Americans

James M. Bergquist

For over three hundred years, German ethnicity has influenced American culture. For two of those three centuries, the Germans provided the most common example of a separate enclave of non-English-speaking foreigners, and at times the Germans seemed to other Americans to be aggressively resistant to adaptation to mainstream American society.

By the 1980s, however, as the three-century mark of German migration passed and modern-day migration from Germany dwindled to a comparative trickle, the vast majority of people of German derivation had long since found their way into the mainstream. The more recognizable elements of German separatism in American society had disappeared—the elaborate institutional framework, the ubiquitous German-language newspapers, the colorful business district that catered to German ethnic tastes in so many American cities. Millions of present-day Americans with obviously German surnames would be surprised to be addressed as "German-Americans." On the other hand, the story of the Germans' integration into American life also demonstrates forcefully that cultural adaptation works two ways. American culture has accepted many influences from the world of the German immigrants—their beer, their food, their love of good music, their customs of Sunday celebration, and, perhaps most of all, their arguments for acceptance of cultural diversity as a way of American life.[1]

There is no one answer to the question of how the Germans adapted to American life because there have been so many different groups who might somehow answer to the name of Germans. They came from different regional origins within Germany, still a patchwork of separate states before 1870. They came for a wide variety of reasons. They were parts of different waves of migration, each with a character created by its own epoch. They had had various identities within a very diverse Germany, where differences of class, religion and occupation had great meaning. Likewise, the America to which they adapted was not always the same; American culture in 1730 was a quite different thing from that of 1850 or that of 1900.[2]

Americans at many times perceived a solid, presumably stable and long-enduring institutional framework called German-America, which, they often concluded, sheltered an ethnic group that immersed itself in traditional cultural concerns and resisted adaptation to American society. Since Americans knew of German neighborhoods that had persisted for many decades, German newspapers nearly a century old, and German societies that continued the same festivals every year within memory, it was easy to take these phenomena as symbols of the group's determined adherence to the culture of the fatherland and its resistance to assimilation. These appearances, however, were illusory.

In any serious attempt to analyze the process of adaptation of German ethnic culture to American life, it is important to separate the German institutions from the successive waves of immigrants and their descendants that made their own use of those institutions—quite often as helpful stepping stones into the mainstream of American life. The institutions themselves might survive for a long time because the supply of newcomers (who needed them most) was frequently renewed by fresh waves of migration. While the many German-American regions of the country were still heavily populated by recent immigrations at the end of the nineteenth century, the second- and third-generation descendants of those who had used these institutions earlier in the century had, to a large extent, passed on into the institutional networks of the society at large.

Only a few of the German organizations functioned to serve descendants of Germans as genealogical or historical societies or as institutions seeking to preserve a culture for later generations. By far the greater number served more pragmatic ends of particular importance to the newly immigrated and their children. And many such institutions reflected the dual purpose common to all immigrant organizations. They preserved and recreated some aspects of the culture of the mother country; at the same time, they also assisted the immigrant in making the necessary adjustments to American life.[3] The German newspapers, for example, brought a daily or weekly visit from someone speaking the native language; yet they also told the newcomer of the way American society worked, the strange political practices that had to be dealt with, and the economic opportunities available. Most German organizations embodied in various proportions these dual functions of cultural preservation and social adaptation. The political clubs, of course, were directly aimed at mastering the intricacies of politics; the singing societies, at the other end of the spectrum, clearly offered a comforting refuge where old-country tradition held sway.

In the last decade of the nineteenth century, the flow of immigrants from

Germany decreased sharply, never to return to the level of the peak years of the 1850s or the 1880s. The effect upon the German institutional structure was fairly immediate, and the leadership in various sections of German-America began to complain of the lack of support, especially from the second and third generations. Those institutions that managed to survive until the First World War did so with increasing effort, and often with fervent appeals to German cultural pride and ethnic solidarity. Disillusioning as the experience was for the caretakers of German ethnic institutions, it also showed that people of German ethnic descent were not on the whole slower to adapt to American life than other immigrants were.[4]

The story of the cultural assimilation of German-Americans, then, is actually many separate stories that pertain to various groups that entered the country throughout American history. Understanding those stories involves a consideration of the changes in the flow of migration, and the rise and decline of various institutional structures, some of which served several waves of migration. German ethnicity as it was experienced at any one time really was connected to two traditions: the German-American one derived from previous generations in America; and the German one, continuously renewed by the most recent immigrants. Thus, this ethnicity continued to develop and change, and showed considerable diversity within it at any one time.

Colonial times gave America its first examples of German-America (a term scarcely used before 1850). Beginning with the settlements in eastern Pennsylvania in the 1680s, German communities began to appear in the interior of Pennsylvania and southwestward along the back country of Maryland, Virginia and the Carolinas. These communities had characteristics of insularity and cultural durability that would not always prevail in later German settlements. Most were in rural areas receiving the first influx of white Europeans. The Germans could occupy such places exclusively and have a free hand in determining the cultural framework. The churches dominated the communities, and there was little need for voluntary organizations (such as later German immigrants established) that were designed to shelter German culture within a society dominated by other groups. Those Pennsylvania German communities dominated by the pietistic sects could enforce cultural separatism as a part of religious doctrine. But these examples, which developed into cultural islands that in some cases endured to become tourist attractions in the twentieth century, were not typical even of the Pennsylvania Germans as a whole. The more numerous Lutheran and Reformed groups might cling to their particular dialect, itself so modified by American influences as to be nearly incomprehensible to native German-speakers. Yet they were rapidly Americanized in other ways—by being drawn into American politics, by the economic system within which they functioned, and also by the frontier process, for many descendants of the Pennsylvania Germans migrated westward and mixed with other populations in the newer communities being formed there. In Pennsylvania German regions outside the original Pennsylvania heartland, the use of the German language was fading fast by the 1820s.[5] By the mid-nineteenth century, Pennsylvania Germans, although still clearly possessing a distinct regional American culture, did not identify with the newer German immigrants and their desire to recreate German ways in America. The Pennsylvania Germans considered themselves Americans, and their ethnicity after at least a century was more an outgrowth of their American experience than of their ancestral German origin.[6] Even in the colonial period, Germans found their way into heterogeneous urban areas such as Philadelphia, Baltimore, and Lancaster, Pennsylvania. The urban Germans often found their place within the economy as skilled craftsmen, tradesmen and storekeepers, and these functions within the broader society speeded their integration into American society even more rapidly than those in rural areas.[7]

German immigration fell off in the years before the American Revolution, and remained at a low ebb until the end of the Napoleonic Wars in Europe. Thus, a period of nearly half a century separated the colonial German migration from the first sizable wave to enter the new republic. The German newcomers of the 1820s and 1830s were vastly more diversified than the colonial migrants had been. The economic opportunities they pursued, whether urban or agricultural, were largely in regions other than those where the colonial Germans had settled. Only a small element of nineteenth-century Germans settled in the Pennsylvania German region. Thus, the new German migration established its own communities and institutions in many new areas of the United States. Those who sought homes on the developing agricultural frontier found themselves in communities much less isolated and homogeneous than the German farmers of colonial days. Their farms depended on a widening network of transportation and communication that connected them with a national economy. The American environment and marketplace provided strong pressures for Germans to adapt to the agricultural practices of America. Although some old customs might prevail in their practices, the Germans adapted to American ways in the major aspects of farming, abandoning European farm-village models of settlement and adopting the crops that the marketplace demanded. After two or three generations on the land, the German-descended farmers showed few distinctions from their neighbors of other backgrounds.[8]

The nineteenth-century immigrants found their way to American cities more frequently than had their colonial predecessors. By 1850, 27 percent of the German-born were found in urban places, a proportion larger than in the American population as a whole.[9] Their urban character reflected the effects of the commercial and industrial revolutions already underway in Germany; the migrants included both artisans replaced by factory production and workers who had experience in the factories of Europe. American cities, especially the newer ones just taking root in the West, offered opportunities at different levels of the socioeconomic ladder that Germans were able to fill, and many could use their place in the American social structure as stepping stones to greater social mobility. A greater number of German workers could be categorized as artisans or skilled craftsmen than was true of the Irish, the other largest immigrant group of the time. In 1850, 63.6 percent of the German workers in Philadelphia were skilled workers; in Milwaukee, Wisconsin, 51 percent were classified as skilled; in New York, 60.7 percent. By 1860, Germans held over 58 percent of the skilled craftsmen's jobs in Milwaukee.[10] The Germans in many cities came to dominate certain trades and crafts that served the entire population, and were not limited to merely the German community. Other Americans came to depend on the Germans as tailors, shoemakers, pharmacists, furniture makers, tobacconists, bakers, and, of course, brewers. While ethnic solidarity might reinforce German dominance of certain sectors of the economy, these functions also worked to integrate them into the larger American economy and speeded their adaptation to the American business system.[11]

The nineteenth-century migration created societies in some American cities that seemed to outsiders heavily dominated by German culture—first Cincinnati, Ohio, and St. Louis, Missouri, later Milwaukee. But even while cities like these boasted some well-known German districts as centers of German ethnicity, their dynamic growth usually promoted both geographic and social mobility for the German. No one core German district could contain all the newcomers, and there was inevitably some process of moving outward into other areas of the city, as well as movement to other cities and rural areas.[12] Stability of the German population was not a feature of any of the great urban centers of German-America, and changes of status and location tended to speed the process of integration into American life.[13]

The growing, highly mobile, diverse, and sometimes turbulent German-born population of the mid-nineteenth century laid the basis of institutional German-America as it would emerge at its zenith just before the end of the century. This was an essentially new organizational structure; only in a few coastal cities did any institutions of the 1700s and those of the post–1815 era overlap. These organizations for the most part served the needs of a German ethnicity seeking to preserve some aspects of its culture while surrounded by other dominant cultures. It was an elaborate and complex organizational structure, partly because it had to cope with the complexities of American life, and partly because it had to serve many specific subgroups, often conflicting ones, within German-America.

Americans perceived a monolithic German America greatly turned in upon itself, but the reality was a German America greatly fragmented. The churches were still the central social institutions for many Germans, yet they were divided among Catholic and many Protestant sects, as well as a small but influential Jewish element. Obviously, no one faith could serve to unite Germans, and religious conflict often hindered efforts to rally them to ethnic solidarity. Also, there were increasing numbers of immigrants with no church affiliation, especially as liberal and radical refugees fled after the failure of the revolutions of 1830 and 1848. The mutual suspicions of religious and free-thinking Germans helped to multiply the separate institutions that served those elements.

Growth in the numbers of German immigrants fostered the development of societies and institutions that served specific subgroups of German America. Between 1830 and 1850 there were at least fifty-six different mutual aid societies among the German population of Philadelphia, and the number continued to grow thereafter.[14] The constituency of each of these might be defined by religious affiliation, region, origin, occupational group or ideological inclination. The same kind of subdivision might be found in the proliferating singing societies so dear to the Germans. In the relatively small German community of San Francisco, thirty of these were founded between 1851 and 1890.[15] The Turner societies, founded originally by refugees from the failed revolution of 1848 for physical culture and intellectual development, began as institutions of the liberal Germans, but other elements developed competing social and athletic organizations.[16] Lodges, literary societies, dramatic groups, shooting societies, labor unions, militia companies, bands—the list was endless, but most of these groups catered to a specific subgroup of German-Americans rather than to the whole. The burgeoning German press, which expanded from seventy newspapers in 1848 to 144 in 1860 and 546 by 1880, reflected an increasing diversity of the Germans in politics, ideology, culture and religion.[17]

Did these complex institutional structures hold Germans apart from American society by providing them with a separate cultural world? Or did they merely provide the Germans with more instruments by which to deal with American life, and thereby speed their integration into it? One can cite forces working in both directions, and obviously much depended on the various motivations of the people who used these structures. On the one hand, the elaborate institutional framework could be used to formulate some broad sense of common identity as Germans, replacing the narrower loyalties that many Germans had brought with them. Many of the leaders arriving after the 1848 revolutions did strive to develop this broader sense of German ethnicity. Such a purpose was vital to the German-language press, which had to forsake individual dialects for one common German language.[18] In the face of hostile anti-German pressures, there was an effort to define a German ethnicity with a culture that was worth preserving and that was capable of making its own contribution to American life. There was considerable debate among German leaders beginning in the 1840s as to the value of maintaining a separate culture, but the argument generally moved toward what in the twentieth century would be called a theory of pluralism: American society did not have to operate on the basis of a necessary homogeneity of culture, but could accept a diversity of cultural groups, all of which could contribute to American life.[19]

On the other hand, these ideals of cultural retention set forth by German-American leaders were not always those pursued by much of the rank and file. They might be more interested in narrower, often divisive goals within the fragmented structures of German America. The chronic disunity of German America based upon religion, provincial origin, class and ideology did not of itself hasten integration into American life, but it did weaken efforts to rally behind one cultural standard upon which to base ethnic solidarity. Many of the myriad German institutions thus pursued their own goals, which often had more to do with adaptation to American life than with cultural preservation. Mutual aid societies and building-and-loan associations helped to provide security and upward mobility within the American economic framework. Labor organizations grappled in various ways with the American industrial structure. Literary and discussion groups dealt with American social and political problems as frequently as with German philosophical ones. The German-language newspapers, dependent like all American newspapers upon political party support, pursued no other goal as consistently as that of indoctrinating immigrants in the ways of American politics and integrating them into the political system. The fact that institutions like these dealt with German immigrants in a familiar language and in groups separate from other Americans was secondary to the basic function of adaptation that most of them served.

During the period of remarkable German population growth just before the Civil War, no force drew the new immigrants into American life more strongly than the turbulent politics of the period. In the late 1820s and early 1830s, a pattern of German political loyalty had been set when the new Jacksonian party enlisted them as an element in the country's first mass-political organization. Usually that loyalty was easily maintained since the opposition party to Jackson and his successors, the Whig party, often seemed nativistic and hostile to the immigrants. Jacksonian Democratic politicians, especially in the urban North, habitually paid their respects to the German voters, but the predictability of the overwhelmingly Democratic German vote sometimes made a perfunctory ritual of their politics. All of this changed, however, in the early 1850s. In the general breakup of the old party system in those years, the German vote became more divided, and in many western states the Germans appeared to be a critical element hanging in the political balance. The new free-soil Republican party appealed to their interests, but the Germans were often torn in their party loyalties over issues like slavery, nativism, and temperance. Nevertheless, these more vital issues of the time and the constant appeals of competing politicians involved the Germans inexorably in the workings of politics at one of the most critical periods of American political development. The new element of German leaders that had entered the country after the revolutions of 1848 played a role in these political changes as well. Once they had abandoned hope of a revival of the European revolutions, they applied their liberal principles to the problems of American politics. A majority of the Forty-eighters aligned themselves with the antislavery cause and the new Republican party. The historical accidents of the time took German leaders and many of their followers beyond mere defense of the Germans to involvement in crucial matters affecting all of American society.

The 1850s were, however, also a period when Germans were called upon to defend their own way of life against social and political attack. The largest wave of immigration so far in American history helped to produce a strong nativist reaction, which culminated in the formation of a party with an openly nativist platform, the American (or "Know-Nothing") party. Germans regarded other reform movements of the time as part and parcel of the nativist assault, especially the temperance crusade and the strict enforcement of Sunday laws. Taken together, these appeared to be attacks on their traditional way of life and attempts to subordinate the ethnic culture to a more narrowly defined American culture described by Anglo-Saxon Protestant standards. The German response had to rest on something more than their traditional liking for beer, music and Sunday conviviality. They cast their defense in terms of the freedom promised by American ideals to all individuals; the "sumptuary laws" advocated by temperance reformers, said German leaders, were reflections of outmoded social systems that did not recognize individual rights. In arguing for such rights, which were essentially the rights of individuals to pursue their own cultural traditions, the German spokesmen were contributing to the new theory of a pluralistic society, where all played a role in the society but were able to retain their own cultural ways, and where republicanism was not rooted in one culture but in many. The natural conclusion of this, of course, was that new peoples could be integrated into American life even while preserving some of their own traditions and some of their separate social structures.

The Civil War was a period of considerable change in German ethnic life, as in many other areas of American life. The flow of immigration into the country was greatly reduced, and the great numbers who had arrived in the 1850s were forced to deal with the upheavals of the country's greatest crisis. For many young men, service in the army (either Union or Confederate) was an experience that drew them forcibly from ethnic concerns and immersed them in a common American cause. While there were German regiments, the great majority of the 200,000 German-born in the Union army served in the regular military units side by side with other American soldiers.[20] Many German-born soldiers returned to American environments far different from the ethnic communities they had left. And for those who stayed home, the war's sense of common purpose, the calls to a patriotic duty for the American nation, and the demands of both the agricultural and industrial economies to produce for the needs of the country served as strong integrating factors. The contribution of the Germans also tended to discredit the nativists' attacks upon them that had been frequently heard in the prewar years. Germans could point to the Civil War as proof of their deserved place in American society.

The post–Civil War period thus found many of the prewar immigrants in new places in American life that they had not imagined or anticipated. This increasing mobility of the German population was augmented by the arrival of a new influx of migrants. From 1877 to 1887 a major wave of German migration to the United States occurred; the peak year, 1881, with a quarter of a million arrivals from Germany, was the greatest year of German migration in all American history. As always, the influx of new-comers served to extend German America and to inject new life into its social and cultural institutions.

It was still possible in the 1880s for new German immigrants to start new and relatively isolated communities of their own. Many of these were in the Great Plains, where the railroads just opening up new lands encouraged immigrants to come and colonize new towns. Some such communities (including many settled by Russian Germans) were centered on immigrants of a particular religious group, with the church serving as the center of community life. The elements were present in such communities to create isolated German language islands, where the inhabitants could persist in their traditional ways for a long time.[21] But even in such relatively ideal conditions there were elements working the other way. The railroads that made these communities possible were also the necessary link to the national economy, offering markets for agricultural products and a supply line for the necessities of life. Groups with little background in politics were inevitably drawn into it, whether to exercise control over their local governments, to protect their way of life from cultural attack, or to protect the hardships that economic forces might place upon them. And there was always the question of the second and third generation, which, as in all of the rural communities of the time, might be impelled to leave in order to pursue their livelihoods in other regions more cosmopolitan.

Migrants to new rural areas, however, were a decreasing proportion of the last great wave of German immigration. These were the years of vast industrial development in America, and a majority of German newcomers found themselves in the cities, where industrial employment was more frequently their lot. The character of German migrants was changing somewhat; an increasing number came from the eastern parts of Germany, and fewer of them were from the skilled-worker class. Even Germans who possessed skills frequently found less employment for them, especially when factory mass-production had made these skills obsolete.[22] The result of all this was that the great urban concentrations of Germans had a growing working-class element, particularly among the recently immigrated, whose lives were dictated by concerns of industrial occupation, the workplace and class status. Though many might still treasure the old ethnic traditions, these could only be cultivated in a limited, "part-time" way.

In the last two decades of the nineteenth century, the phenomenon of German America was at its peak in the great urban centers of German concentration. It was particularly impressive in the number and scope of its organizations and institutions. The numbers of these—mutual aid societies, social groups, musical organizations, political clubs, labor organizations—multiplied rapidly, and generally reached a peak in the early 1890s. But this organizational complexity did not always reflect a structure that was oriented either toward German solidarity or toward slowing their integration into American life.

For one thing, the great diversity of organizations heightened the possibility of splintering of the German groups, because individuals had more opportunities to seek their own particular type of German, whether religious, ideological, regional or class. Many of these organizations thus served to hinder the unity or consensus that many German ethnic leaders thought necessary to defend the German culture as a whole. "Wherever there are four Germans, there will be five opinions," was the complaint common to many German ethnic leaders.[23]

It is also true that many of these institutions served more to educate the immigrants in the ways of the American environment than to maintain a separate German culture. Those institutions with overt purposes of preserving German culture, such as language schools and theater societies, were not usually the ones with the widest support from the rank and file of German-Americans.[24] While organizations devoted to recreation, economic security, religious devotion, occupational advancement and civic affairs might well have their roots in a separate German ethnic community, they could eventually evolve beyond that community and become part of a more general integrated society, even as individual German-Americans and their descendants moved into the broader community. This was in fact the history of many such organizations that survived into the first half of the twentieth century.

Some of the growth of institutional German America was related to the dispersal of its population, especially within the urban centers. The previously existing German centers in the older cities could not contain the growing population of German-Americans. New German neighborhoods inevitably began to develop in outlying sections of the city, and upwardly mobile Germans found their way into newer sections of the city that were not always as ethnically homogeneous as the neighborhoods they had left. Even in a city like Detroit, Michigan, which kept more than some other cities to a pattern of neighborhoods with distinct ethnic characters, the German districts in the early decades of the 1900s were loosening their tightly knit character as second- and third-generation Germans moved into other less-concentrated neighborhoods.[25]

There is no one model pattern of the dissolution and integration of the German ethnic communities in the American urban context. They differ because of many factors: the age of the city, the character of its commerce and industry, the nature of the geography, the ease or difficulty of public transportation, and the varieties of other ethnic groups in the environment, to name a few. But it is clear that the dynamics of the rapidly changing American city and the fluid and mobile nature of the German element were working in the long run against the maintenance of the homogeneous German neighborhood.[26] By shortly after the turn of the twentieth century, the average first- or second-generation German immigrant in the city was not part of a close-knit German district, but of a more cosmopolitan urban environment. While some could still live, work, and achieve success within a German environment, perhaps never having even to speak English, by far the greater number had to spend most of their lives outside the narrower German cultural enclave.[27]

The peak of German institutional life in the 1890s also reflected the demographic accidents created by the particular history of the German immigration. In the 1890s, most of the immigrants of the two great waves of the 1850s and the 1880s were still alive. This gave the German organizations, businesses and newspapers an unusual number of clients. But death began to remove the pre–Civil War immigrants at a more rapid rate by the turn of the century, and many organizations began to experience a decline in membership. The German newspapers numbered nearly 800 about 1893; by 1900 the number was down to 613, and by 1910 to 554. In Milwaukee, daily German-language newspapers circulated 92,000 copies in the mid–1880s; by 1910 they circulated about 45,000.[28] Figures like these were reinforced by the complaints of German leaders that the second generation was indifferent to the old cultural traditions. The first generation clearly was the great force that held German America together; when fewer newcomers came after 1885 and the older generation began to pass from the scene, the separate ethnic community began to yield rather rapidly to the wider society.

Some of the same demographic changes were reflected in the nature of the leadership of the Germans as a group. The dynamic element of the forty-eighters (if that term is used loosely to describe the leadership that had arisen from the migration wave of the 1850s) was, after 1890, quickly passing from the scene. A new element of leadership came out of the post–Civil War generation of immigrants. They were less frequently idealists with specific ideological goals as had been some of the pre–Civil War generation. More frequently they were influenced by a German nationalism stemming from the creation of a unified German state under Prussian rule in 1871.

The events of German unification did have their effects upon German-Americans, and the emergence of a great modern unified nation served as a point of pride for Germans who had themselves never lived in a united Germany. Even many of the old forty-eighters abandoned their traditional hostility to the Prussian monarchy and joined in the celebration of a united German state.[29] Unification also made it possible to assert a common German culture and to appeal to Germans of different origins to associate themselves with that common German culture. This concept of a common cultural heritage and a common great nation of origin became a useful instrument for ethnic leaders as they forged an aggressive defense for institutional German America when it passed its peak and began a steady decline.

In the last two decades of the nineteenth century there developed the anomaly of the emergence of a strong defensive mentality in organized German America, even as its institutional structure seemed to be at its strongest. The reasons for this anomaly came both from outside and from within German America. From American society in the 1880s and 1890s there emerged one of the country's periodic upsurges of antiforeign sentiment: while it was directed more at the newer waves of eastern and southern European immigrants, it had its implications for all groups who were not deemed fully assimilated.[30] The rising demand for adherence to Anglo-American cultural standards also seemed to be an assault on German cultural pride. This was reflected in efforts to forbid the use of German (or any language other than English) in school instruction, and in the renewed drives of temperance and prohibition reformers. German leaders who thus sounded the cry to rally around the standards of German pride and to unite in support of institutional German America were, however, also aware that the German-American social structure needed defense against deterioration from within. Only a minority of second-generation German-Americans retained the language or continued their association with German organizations. With the rapidly declining numbers of first-generation immigrants, the leadership increasingly directed a campaign toward the younger generations, in an effort to keep them within the cultural community. While some, doubtless, did maintain their ties to German America, there were not enough of them in the long run to maintain the vast institutional structure at the level at which it had existed in the early 1890s.

The efforts to revive and maintain German language and ethnic culture and to keep them as rallying points that would retain the loyalties of German-Americans involved a leadership that to a great extent, was closely tied to that institutional structure. German-language newspaper editors, leaders of German singing societies, businessmen who catered to the ethnic community, and a variety of types who might loosely be called "professional German-Americans" developed vigorous appeals to defend German ethnicity. While their defenses seemed addressed to those outside the ethnic community, in an effort to persuade other Americans of the cultural benefits that German-Americans brought to American society, their principal concern was more often those German-Americans, especially of the second generation, who seemed to be on the margin of ethnic life and drifting further away from it. The many German-Americans who had moved from the "core" ethnic neighborhoods and remained in touch with only one or two German societies or institutions were the ones who perhaps aroused most concern. It was not uncommon to find social societies, sporting clubs and churches that no longer used German in their functions; an increasing number of members did not know German. Some Turner societies, for example, started an emotional debate in the early 1890s over whether the commands for their gymnastic exercises might be given in English. Many German Protestant congregations about the same time entered stages of critical debate over what role, if any, the German language should play in their services.[31]

Language preservation was, however, one of the rallying points that German leaders found useful in awakening the sensitivities of the group and making its influence felt in politics. In the late 1880s and early 1890s various public debates arose over whether to require that compulsory education be conducted only in English. Such proposals threatened public and parochial schools in both rural and urban areas of the Midwest, where instruction in all subjects was carried on mainly in German. In 1890, efforts in Illinois and Wisconsin to forbid non-English instruction brought a major reaction against the Republicans who advocated the idea; the resulting upheaval in political alignments had repercussions far beyond those states, and even played a role in the Democrats regaining control of Congress in the 1890 elections.[32] While such attacks could be used to rally Germans to fend off hostility against them, it was another matter to persuade Germans to get their children into voluntary language classes, and increasingly the younger generation's acquaintance with the language weakened.[33]

By the turn of the century the German defenses were focused more upon the threat of the temperance movement, whose efforts for liquor prohibition laws had been growing in the preceding two decades. Ever since the earlier temperance crusades of the 1850s, the Germans had been sensitive on the point of liquor restriction. The drinking of beer had always been an important part of their traditional culture. The tavern and the beer-garden were central institutions of the ethnic community. The German traditions of sociability—gathering to eat and drink with noisy singing and dancing, and exuberant public celebration on Sundays—were just the kinds of things that clashed with old-fashioned Yankee Protestant cultural values. This liking for spirited public celebration was, in the long run, probably an influence that German-Americans brought upon American culture in general. At the turn of the century, however, German *Gemutlichkeit* (state of feeling jolly or jovial) and its free-flowing use of beer became one of the objects of native-born temperance reformers. The German response was encouraged by the brewing industry, which had developed in the previous half-century as an almost exclusively German enterprise, and which had close ties with the German ethnic community. Beer played a vital role in the meetings and festivals of countless German organizations, and both the brewers and the German organizations stood to be drastically affected by liquor regulation or prohibition laws.[34]

The principal effort to achieve some unified organization nationally for German America came to fruition in 1901, and was strongly influenced in subsequent years by controversies over prohibition. The National German-American Alliance eventually claimed to include over two million members, but most of these were scarcely aware that they were members. The actual structure was that of a federation of many German societies, and the Alliance claimed that all members of these constituent groups were its members. But the policies of the Alliance were made by the leaders of German organizational life, and much of the financing of its activities came from the brewing industry.[35] While many in German-America might endorse the struggle of the Alliance against prohibitionists, the Alliance did rather little otherwise to strengthen or enhance the cultural world of German-America. While beer was one of the few points of unity among nearly all German-Americans, concentration on that issue only served to conceal the great diversity and conflict that still divided the German ethnic group in many other ways.[36]

The dwindling of institutional German-America, and with it the increasing movement of many German-Americans into the larger social structures of American society, was well under way long before the guns of August 1914 sounded the opening of the First World War, creating further strains upon the ethnic bonds of Germans in America. The natural course for many Americans of German descent in the early years of the war, when the United States was not a participant, was simply to hope and to appeal for the country's continuing neutrality. There seemed little possibility that the United States as a country would aid Germany, and the practical ways in which individuals might lend support to Germany were very limited. For some German-American leaders and newspaper editors, however, especially those active in the National German-American Alliance, the support of German culture in America became identified with support of Germany's position in the European conflict. It did not seem unreasonable to them to defend the "German side" when the United States was officially neutral and others within American society praised the French and English war efforts while denouncing Imperial Germany as barbaric and militaristic. The statements of German-American newspaper editors and speakers who sought to defend German positions in such controversies would, of course, come back to haunt them in 1917 when the United States was drawn into the war against Germany. Nor did it help that German government agents had sought to provide propaganda and to otherwise assist these efforts to defend German views by way of the National Alliance.[37]

The inevitable reaction of American public opinion against German America in 1917 and 1918 provides one of the prime examples in American history of any assault upon a single ethnic group during a period of emotions heated by war. The details of that assault do not need retelling here. They included, among other things, censorship and the closing down of newspapers, prohibitions and restriction upon the use of the German language, violent intimidation of individuals, the hounding of institutions and businesses with "German" in their names, and the denigration of any cultural practice that suggested German origin. By the end of the war the National German-American Alliance had been dissolved under pressure from Congress, and the number of German language newspapers and social institutions had been drastically reduced.

Clearly the events of the war struck a blow at the institutional structures of the German-Americans, but one should not overstate the war's influence in forcing many Germans out of their ethnic communities and into the mainstream of American life. The ties of many German-stock people to the ethnic traditions were already tenuous; the heated emotions and the public controversy over symbols of loyalty might have simply served to cut the last few ties. Many nominal German-Americans simply stopped referring to themselves as such, dropped a membership or two in German organizations, cancelled their subscriptions to a German newspaper, and felt relieved when the German Bank changed its name to something more innocuous. To quietly become "less German" in this fashion was to follow the line of least resistance, but for many marginal German-Americans it was probably not a matter of great pain or loss. Much of the effect of World War I on the vast and differentiated body of German America was simply to accelerate a process of merging into American life that was already well-advanced.[38] Without doubt, others abandoned their German traditions and practices with difficulty, and some sought to recover them after the end of the war. The census of 1920 records a decrease of over 25 percent in the number of German-born in the United States. Such a decline hardly seems to be corroborated by migration and mortality statistics; in actuality, the numbers seem to indicate that many German-born were denying the place of their nativity to the census-takers in 1920. There was a mild revival of German institutions and German newspaper circulation in the 1920s, which would seem to reflect that World War I suppressed some German ethnicity abnormally.[39] Before long, however, the decline of German America was continuing in the same inexorable fashion that had shown itself in the years before 1914. The 1930s showed an even sharper decline in German-American life. The pressures came from several sources: the economic impact of the Great Depression on many weak and faltering institutions, the absence of any significant new immigration, and the rapid decline in the numbers of first-generation immigrants as those of the late-nineteenth century wave of immigration died off. It is hard to put a date on "the end of German America," but it is safe to say that by the time of America's entry into World War II, institutional German America was hardly a factor in the lives of the great majority of Americans who were of German background.

Despite their reputation among many other Americans for clannishness and isolation, the German-Americans throughout their history were among those groups who had a relatively easy process of adaptation to American society and its ways. Some of the reasons for this lie in the particular nature of the group itself, and some in the particular history of its migration—especially in a migration that was spread out and renewed over a period extending well beyond two centuries.

The vast majority of German-Americans came to America with firm intentions of staying and beginning a new life. Relatively few of them came as sojourners. That means that most Germans came fully expecting to have to alter their lives, and hoping to find a permanent place within a new social and economic system, whether by owning a farm, practicing a trade, or finding some other occupation within the context of American society. Some Germans as late as the 1830s may have held some hope for establishing an enclave of a "new Germany" somewhere in America, but by the time of the flood of migration of the 1840s and 1850s that dream had dwindled and was never really revived. Pragmatically, most German immigrants recognized that they and their children would have to be a part of American society and accepted the changes that were implied by that.

The social composition of the German-Americans during most of the periods of heavy migration meshed well with the makeup of American society in general and with its needs, especially during eras of American economic growth and territorial expansion. The Germans were not just a peasant people or a proletarian people, all concentrated at one particular social stratum or one particular point of entry into the American socioeconomic system. Rather, they included farmers able to buy land, farmhands waiting to obtain farms, industrial workers with previous experience in Europe, common laborers new to industry, skilled artisans, small businessmen, and a significant element of professionals, intellectuals, and persons of wealth. All of these different elements could make use of a variety of opportunities at various levels, when new agricultural regions were opened, new towns begun in the west, or when new industries arose. Because the ethnic community of German America itself, with its considerable complexity, often including economic opportunities at many occupational and economic levels, it was possible for some to make a start within German America and then to move laterally into a comparable place in the American social structure.

German America, like American society in general, had its divisions of class and status; yet it was often comparable to the American social structure in the predominance of middle-class values within it. The concerns of German-Americans with stability, the family, the work ethic, self-discipline, and a striving for success and security for themselves and their children were compatible with the values that prevailed among many in mainstream America. In the long run, these cultural similarities far outweighed the cultural conflicts with some Americans over matters of drinking, language and Sunday behavior. German-Americans' problems of adaptation were considerably moderated by these similarities of values.[40]

At almost any particular point in its long history of migration, German America might consist of people at many different stages of adaptation—those of the first generation, recently arrived and still considerably dependent upon German-American institutions; those who had been in the country for two or three decades; those of the second generation, most of them with no direct memories of Germany; and those of subsequent generations with various stages of ethnic awareness. At any one time, there was usually a wide continuum of people at various points in the transition from ethnic separatism to full integration into American life. Individuals could often make a comfortable transition at their own pace from membership in a pervasive ethnic environment through more tenuous ties to specific organizations to perhaps a few lingering gestures to German-America. Kindred spirits could be found at any point along the way. It was seldom necessary to undergo suddenly the shock of an irrevocable plunge from a warm enveloping ethnic environment to the cold outside world of American society. German-Americans usually had the luxury of being able to go home again to their previous culture; if nostalgia, guilt or a longing for former stability overtook them, they could take a step backward and revisit the ethnicity they had once known.

The impressive world of German America was so complex that it made possible an almost endless variety of structures and experiences for those within it. Except for those in small and isolated rural communities, people could chose among German societies and institutions, and seldom could any one institution demand the adherence of all who claimed to be German-Americans. Thus, individuals could create their own version of German America to suit themselves, and no one membership or institutional tie could be made the absolute standard of loyalty to the ethnic community. Those who wanted to use the structures of German America to retain the ethnic traditions and insulate themselves from the strange world of American life could do so. For those, on the other hand, who wished to use the institutions as instruments of transition in the process of adjustment to American life, the ethnic community seldom enforced strong demands that the process of adaptation be slowed.

The world of German America in its most prosperous and thriving times was a world of considerable movement and change for those within it. While some might cling to church or neighborhood or singing society as a secure link to an older culture, most realized that their children and others would loosen those ties. New generations would pass through, while the old institutional structures might remain. The frequent conflicts within the German community raged on over matters of religion, politics, class and ideology; seldom, however, were there conflicts over loyalty to the German community, for the natural passage through it was taken for granted by many. The story of the past half-century has been that of the final crumbling of most of the old institutions as the new migration that made them possible dwindles to a trickle and the descendants of earlier migrations move on into American life.

NOTES

1. James M. Bergquist, "Germans and the City," in *Germans in America: Retrospect and Prospect*, ed. Randall M. Miller (Philadelphia, 1984), 53–54.

2. Kathleen N. Conzen, "Patterns of German American History," in Miller, ed., *Germans in America*, 15–18.

3. James M. Bergquist, "German Communities in American Cities: An Interpretation of the Nineteenth-Century Experience," *Journal of American Ethnic History* 4 (1984): 16–17; Milton Gordon, *Assimilation in American Life* (New York, 1964), 105–14.

4. The principal argument for a German-America that was slow to adapt to the mainstream is John A. Hawgood, *The Tragedy of German-America: The Germans in the United States of America During the Nineteenth Century—and After* (New York, 1940).

5. Heinz Kloss, "German-American Language Maintenance Efforts," in *Language Loyalty in the United States*, ed. Joshua R. Fishman et al. (The Hague, 1966), 215–22.

6. For a stimulating discussion of Pennsylvania German ethnicity, see Don Yoder, "The Pennsylvania Germans: Three Centuries of Identity Crisis," in *America and the Germans: An Assessment of a Three-Hundred-Year History*, 2 vols., ed. Frank Trommler and Joseph McVeigh (Philadelphia, 1985), 1:41–65. The best general discussion of their development as a group is William Parsons, *The Pennsylvania Dutch: A Persistent Minority* (Boston, 1976).

7. Stephanie G. Wolf, *Urban Village: Population, Community and Family Structure in Germantown, Pennsylvania, 1683–1800* (Princeton, 1976), 127–53; Stephanie G. Wolf, "Hyphenated America: The Creation of an Eighteenth-Century German-American Culture," in *America and the Germans*, ed. Trommler and McVeigh, 1:66–84.

8. For a thorough study of one example of German agricultural adaptation, see Gerry G. Jordan, *German Seed in Texas Soil: Immigrant Farmers in Nineteenth-Century Texas* (Austin, Tex., 1966), especially 192–203. See also A. J. Petersen, "The German-Russian Settlement Pattern in Ellis County, Kansas," *Rocky Mountain Social Science Journal* 5 (1968): 52–67.

9. John G. Gazley, *American Opinion of German Unification, 1848–1871* (New York, 1926), 428; Conzen, "Patterns of German-American History," 22–23.

10. Leslie Ann Kawaguchi, "The Making of Philadelphia's German-America:

Ethnic Groups and Community Development, 1830–1883" (Ph.D. diss., University of California at Los Angeles, 1983), 155–56; Kathleen N. Conzen, *Immigrant Milwaukee, 1830–1860: Accommodation and Community in a Frontier City* (Cambridge, Mass., 1976), 65–74; Stanley Nadel, "*Kleinduetschland*: New York City's Germans, 1845–1880," Ph.D. dissertation, Columbia University, 1981, 128–31; Laurence A. Glasco, "Ethnicity and Social Structure: Irish, Germans and Native-born of Buffalo, New York, 1850–1860" (Ph.D. diss., University of Rochester, 1973), 84–96; Nora Faires, "Ethnicity in Evolution: The German Community in Pittsburgh and Allegheny City, Pennsylvania, 1845–1885" (Ph.D. diss., University of Pittsburgh, 1981), 219–20.

11. For general discussion, see Nora Faires, "Occupational Patterns of German-Americans in Nineteenth Century Cities," in *German Workers in Industrial Chicago, 1850–1910: A Comparative Perspective*, ed. Hartmut Keil and John B. Jentz (DeKalb, Ill., 1983), 37–51.

12. Audrey V. Olson, "St. Louis Germans, 1850–1920: The Nature of an Immigrant Community and its Relation to the Assimilation Process" (Ph.D. diss., University of Kansas, 1970), 248–49; Joseph M. White, "Religion and Community: Cincinnati Germans, 1814–1870" (Ph.D. diss., University of Notre Dame, 1980), 17–31; Conzen, *Immigrant Milwaukee*, 131–36; Kellner, "German Element on the Urban Frontier," 118–45. White points out (p. 29) that even in heavily German Cincinnati the Germans were not more than half the population in any single ward in the city in 1840.

13. Jay Dolan, studying a sample of German Catholics in New York City, found that 58 percent of those present in 1850 had left the city by 1869. Dolan, *The Immigrant Church: New York's Irish and German Catholics, 1815–1865* (Baltimore, 1975).

14. Kawaguchi, "The Making of Philadelphia's German-America," 257.

15. Irving Bobow, "The Singing Societies of European Immigrant Groups in San Francisco: 1851–1953," *Journal of the History of the Behavioral Sciences* 5 (1969): 16–18. See also Mary Jane Corry, "The Role of German Singing Societies in Nineteenth-Century America," in *Germans in America: Aspects of German-American Relations in the Nineteenth Century*, ed. E. Allen McCormick (New York, 1983), 155–68.

16. Augustus J. Prahl, "History of the German Gymnastic Movement of Baltimore," Society for the History of Germans in Maryland, *Twenty-Sixth Report* (Baltimore, 1945), 16–29; Guido Dobbert, "Disintegration of an Immigrant Community: The Cincinnati Germans, 1870–1920," (Ph.D. diss., University of Chicago, 1965), 16–29.

17. James M. Bergquist, "The German-American Press," in *The Ethnic Press in the United States: A Historical Analysis and Handbook*, ed. Sally M. Miller (Westport, Conn., 1987), 136–42. The figures are for newspapers only and exclude magazines and other special-interest publications.

18. Kawaguchi, "The Making of Philadelphia's German America," 248–96, 404–6.

19. This evolution of a broader concept of German ethnicity in America is described in detail in a ground-breaking essay by Kathleen N. Conzen, "German-Americans and the Invention of Ethnicity," in *America and the Germans*, ed. Trommler and McVeigh, 1:131–47.

20. William L. Barton, *Melting Pot Soldiers: The Union's Ethnic Regiments* (Ames, Iowa, 1988), 110.

21. LaVern J. Rippley, "German Assimilation: The Effect of the 1871 Victory on Americana-Germanica," in *Germany and America: Essays on Problems of International Relations and Immigration*, ed. Hans L. Trefousse (New York, 1980), 121–28.

22. Hartmut Keil, "Chicago's German Working Class in 1900," in *German Workers in Industrial Chicago*, ed. Keil and Jentz 21–29; Mack Walker, *Germany and the Emigration, 1816–1885* (Cambridge, Mass., 1964), esp. 181–94; Nadel, "*Kleinduetschland*," 45–48.

23. Guido Dobbert, "German-Americans between Old and New Fatherland, 1870–1914," *American Quarterly* 19 (1967): 665–66, quoting *Duetsche Pionier* 11 (June 1879): 140.

24. Olson, "St. Louis Germans," 133–68.

25. Olivier Zunz, *The Changing Face of Inequality: Urbanization, Industrial Development, and Immigrants in Detroit, 1880–1920* (Chicago, 1982), 348–49.

26. For some review of the complex literature on ethnic dispersion, see Kathleen N. Conzen, "Immigrants, Immigrant Neighborhoods and Ethnic Identity: Historical Issues," *Journal of American History* 66 (1979): 603–15; Zunz, *The Changing Face of Inequality*, esp. 40–60; and Alan N. Burstein, "Immigrants and Residential Mobility: The Irish and Germans in Philadelphia, 1850–1880," in *Philadelphia: Work, Space, Family and Group Experience in the Nineteenth Century* (New York, 1981), ed. Theodore Hershberg, 174–203. For other discussions of German urban population movement, see Dobbert, "Disintegration of an Immigrant Community," 37–42; Nadel, "*Kleindeutschland*," 55–75, 275–76; Gerd Korman, Industrialization, Immigrants and Americanizers: The View from Milwaukee, 1866–1921 (Madison, Wis. 1967), 41–43.

27. Zunz's study of Detroit found that 15 percent of the German-born there in 1900 did not speak English. *Changing Face of Inequality*, 186. Two-thirds of these were women, who presumably could remain more consistently within the limits of the German neighborhood.

28. James M. Bergquist, "The German-American Press," 143; Carl F. Wittke, *The German Language Press in America* (Lexington, Ky., 1957), 206–9. The decline of the German newspapers in the 1890s was also hastened by a major depression.

29. Dieter Cunz, *The Maryland Germans: A History* (Princeton, N.J., 1948), 374–77; Dobbert, "Disintegration of an Immigrant Community," 148–56; Carl Wittke, *Against the Current: The Life of Karl Heinzen (1809–80)* (Chicago, 1945), 276–81.

30. John Higham, *Strangers in the Land: Patterns of American Nativism, 1860–1925* (New York, 1963), 35–105.

31. Bergquist, "German Communities in American Cities," 22–23.

32. Robert J. Ulrich, "The Bennett Law of 1889: Education and Politics in Wisconsin" (Ph.D., University of Wisconsin, 1965); Richard Jensen, *The Winning of the Midwest: Social and Political Conflict, 1888–1890* (Chicago, 1971), 122–53; Paul J. Kleppner, *The Cross of Culture: A Social Analysis of Midwestern Politics, 1850–1900* (New York, 1970), 158–78.

33. Kloss, "German-American Language Maintenance Efforts," 233–37; Ernest J. Becker, "History of the English-German Schools of Baltimore," *Twenty-fifth*

Report, Society for the History of the Germans in Maryland (Baltimore, 1942), 13–17; Olson, "St. Louis Germans," 91–132.

34. William L. Downard, *The Cincinnati Brewing Industry: A Social and Economic History* (Athens, Ohio, 1973), 64–78.

35. La Vern J. Rippley, "Ameliorated Americanization: The Effect of World War I on German-Americans in the 1920s," in *America and the Germans*, ed. Trommler and McVeigh, 2:220–21.

36. Clifton J. Child, *The German-Americans in Politics, 1914–1917* (Madison, 1939); David W. Detjen, *The Germans in Missouri, 1900–1918: Prohibition, Neutrality, and Assimilation* (Columbia, Mo., 1985), 31–71.

37. Frederick C. Luebke, *Bonds of Loyalty: German Americans and World War I* (De Kalb, Ill., 1974).

38. Conzen, "Immigrants, Immigrant Neighborhoods and Ethnic Identity," 614.

39. Rippley, "Ameliorated Americanization," 223–29.

40. Frederick C. Luebke, "Images of German Immigrants in the United States and Brazil, 1890–1918: Some Comparisons," in *America and the Germans*, ed. Trommler and McVeigh, 1:209–12.

BIBLIOGRAPHICAL ESSAY

Kathleen Niels Conzen's essay on Germans in Stephan Thernstrom et al., ed., *Harvard Encyclopedia of American Ethnic Groups* (Cambridge, Mass., 1980), 405–25, is the most convenient starting point for an understanding of the German-American experience. Heinz Kloss, *Atlas of 19th and Early 20th Century German-American Settlement* (Marburg, 1974), provides a useful guide to understanding the complex, widespread pattern of German dispersion throughout the United States during the century of peak immigration. Henry A. Pochman and Arthur R. Schultz, eds., *Bibliography of German Culture in America to 1940* (Madison, Wis., 1953) includes an alphabetical listing of over 12,000 published items, as well as information on American depositories of source materials and on German-American research associations. The bibliography is especially worthwhile if used in conjunction with Pochman's *German Culture in America: Philosophical and Literary Influence, 1600–1900*, a two part analysis of German thought in America and of German literary influences. Michael Keresztesi and Gary R. Cocozzoli, eds., *German-American History and Life: A Guide to Information Sources* (Detroit, Mich., 1980) is the most comprehensive and up-to-date bibliography. It should be supplemented with two bibliographies edited by Don Heinrich Tolzman, *German-Americans* (Metuchen, N.J., 1975) and *German-American Literature* (Metuchen, N.J., 1977). The former features a discussion of the holdings of the major German-American archives.

The classic survey of German-American society and culture is Albert Bernhard Faust, *The German Element in the United States*, 2 vols. (New York, 1969), originally printed in 1927, which details population figures, economic activity, political attitudes, contributions in education, theater, literature, music, religion, and recreational activities. Much briefer and more popularly written is Richard O'Connor, *German-Americans: An Informal History* (Boston, 1968), which devotes much attention to the anti-German sentiment attendant upon both world wars. Robert Henry Billigmeier, *Americans From Germany: A Study in Cultural Diversity* (Belmont, Calif., 1974), stresses the tremendous diversity of the German immigration to the

United States over more than two centuries, explores the unique experience of the Pennsylvania Germans from the American Revolution to World War I, and discusses the effects of two world wars on German-American identity and diversity. *The Pennsylvania Dutch: A Persistent Minority* (Boston, 1976) takes a much more detailed look at this special community of German-Americans, as do the eight scholars who explore their religious sects, education, literature, newspapers, and military experience in Ralph Wood, ed., *The Pennsylvania Germans* (Princeton, N.J., 1942). La Vern J. Rippley, *The German-Americans* (Boston, 1976) is a brief, readable survey with an emphasis on political and social developments. Gerhard K. Friesin and Walter Schatzberg, eds., *The German Contribution to the Building of the Americas* (Hanover, N.H., 1977) stresses the debt owed by all of the Americas to German immigrants and ideas.

Studies of the German immigrant experience in a variety of specific locales abound. Kathleen Niels Conzen, *Immigrant Milwaukee, 1836–1880* (Cambridge, Mass., 1976), argues that the tremendous numbers, diversity, and "institutional completeness" that made Milwaukee "the German Athens," also prevented the development of a unified community with political clout proportionate to its size. John F. Nau, *The German People of New Orleans, 1850–1900* (Leiden, Netherlands, 1958) presents the social and economic history of German immigrants in a city dominated by Spanish and French influences and with a climate radically different from that of the Old Country. Helmut Keil and John B. Jentz, ed., *German Workers in Industrial Chicago, 1850–1910: A Comparative Perspective* (DeKalb, Ill., 1983) places working-class culture in the wider context of a burgeoning industrial city operated largely by European immigrants of various origins. Several books examine the experience of the sizable German-American population of Missouri. Walter O. Forster, *Zion on the Mississippi: The Settlement of the Saxon Germans in Missouri, 1839–1841* (St. Louis, 1953), focuses on the experience of a typical settlement of evangelical Lutherans. David W. Detjen, *The Germans in Missouri, 1900–1918: Prohibition, Neutrality, and Assimilation* (Columbia, Mo., 1985), analyzes the devastating impact of cultural conflict and war-borne hysteria over loyalty upon the integrity of the German-American community in the state. Charles Van Ravenswaay, *The Arts and Architecture of German Settlement in Missouri* (Columbia, Mo., 1977), explores the creative interaction between German forms and values and American environment and materials. Finally, Russell L. Gerlach, *Immigrants in the Ozarks* (Columbia, Mo., 1976), concentrates on the experience of German-Americans in one of the country's most beautiful, but remote, areas. Moving farther south, Terry G. Jordan, *German Seed in Texas Soil: Immigrant Farmers in Nineteenth-Century Texas* (Austin, Tex., 1966), utilizes census schedules for the second half of the nineteenth century to demonstrate how German immigrants adapted their Old World farming methods to local conditions, while continuing to farm more intensively and to invest more time than did other ethnic groups. Dieter Cunz, *The Maryland Germans* (Princeton, N.J., 1948), details the sizable immigration to that state from colonial days through World War II. Klaus Wust, *The Virginia Germans* (Charlottesville, Va., 1969), performs the same service for those who settled on the other side of the Potomac River.

As did every major immigrant group, German-Americans sought to adapt to life in the United States through the establishment of a series of mediating institutions. Chief among these were religious congregations. Emmet H. Rothan, *The German*

Catholic Immigrant in the United States, 1830–1860), Washington, D.C., 1946) focuses on their efforts to persuade the Yankee- and Irish-dominated Catholic Church to accommodate to their peculiar language and religious devotions. Colman J. Barry, *The Catholic Church and German Americans* (Milwaukee, Wis., 1953), examines the divisive effect of the demands for German national parishes, on the one hand, and for Americanization of liturgy and ritual, on the other. Philip Gleason, *The Conservative Reformers: German American Catholics and the Social Order* (Notre Dame, Ind., 1968), details the increasing involvement of German Catholics in social reform during the Progressive Era, primarily as a means of maintaining their identity in the face of acculturationist pressures. Carl E. Schneider, *The German Church on the American Frontier* (St. Louis, 1939), examines the central role played, primarily by Protestant churches, in the opening up of the western territories. Paul F. Douglas, *The Story of German Methodism* (New York, 1939), demonstrates that the communicants of that immigrant church were more easily acculturated than were their Catholic or Lutheran compatriots. Carl F. Wittke, *The German Language Press in America* (Lexington, Ky., 1957), argues that its primary function was to provide a stabilizing influence on the immigrant population and to facilitate the transition from German to German-American. The collection of essays in Glenn C. Gilbert, ed., *The German Language in America* (Austin, Tex., 1971) demonstrates the critical importance of language as a component of the acculturation process.

Although German-Americans were generally less politically active than some other ethnic groups, they did make their mark at certain times and places. Despite their small numbers, none had a greater impact than did the refugee intellectuals of the late 1840s. The classic monograph is Carl F. Wittke, *Refugees of Revolution: The German Forty-Eighters in America* (Philadelphia, 1952), which comprehensively treats their influence on every important aspect of American life and politics for the next two decades. Several scholars have contributed topical essays on many of those aspects to A. E. Zucker, ed., *The Forty-Eighters: Political Refugees of the German Revolution of 1848* (New York, 1959). Frederick C. Luebke, *Immigrants and Politics: The Germans of Nebraska, 1880–1900* (Lincoln, Neb., 1969), argues persuasively that ethnocultural issues, such as language retention, Sunday observance and prohibition of alcoholic beverages, generally took preeminence over socioeconomic considerations, except for a brief period during the Populist Era.

There can be little doubt that the great crisis for German-America, and its ultimate acculturation, took place during World War I. Clifton J. Child, *German-Americans in Politics, 1914–1917* (Madison, Wis., 1939), focuses on the crucial role of the German-American Alliance, which he interprets primarily as a coalition against prohibition and the pro-British policies of the Woodrow Wilson administration, rather than as a tool of German foreign policy. John A. Hawgood, *The Tragedy of German America* (New York, 1970), originally published in 1940, analyzes efforts to found "New Germanies" in Missouri, Texas, and Wisconsin and the failure to avoid acculturation and assimilation, especially during World War I. In a similar vein, Frederick C. Luebke, *Bonds of Loyalty: German-Americans During World War I* (DeKalb, Ill., 1974), portrays the Great War as "the traumatic climax of an ethno-cultural struggle that long had festered below the headlines." The more politically involved Germans became, the more their neighbors perceived them as dangerous and subversive. Centering his attention on Cincinnati, Guido A. Dobbert, *The Disintegration of an Immigrant Community* (New York, 1980), attributes

Deutschtum's rapid decline there to the pressures unleashed by prohibition and Americanization crusades. Although there was much less cause for concern by American loyalists during World War II, Sander A. Diamond, *The Nazi Movement in the United States, 1924–1941* (Ithaca, N.Y., 1974), argues that a significant number of post–World War I German immigrants, mostly skilled workers hard-hit by the Great Depression, were attracted to the German-American Bund, a pro-Nazi organization, by the argument that American Jews were responsible for their economic plight.

The phenomenon of chain migration and ongoing cultural exchange has shaped the adaptation of German-Americans for at least a century and a half. E. Allen McCormick, ed., *Germans in America: Aspects of German-American Relations in the Nineteenth Century* (New York, 1983) examines the impact of German culture, especially literature and music, on the United States and on the intensive, yet unsuccessful, effort to create a unified German culture in America during the decade of 1890s. Hans L. Trefousse, ed., *Germany and America: Essays on Problems of International Relations and Immigration* (New York, 1980) contends, in part, that the establishment of the German Empire in 1871 provided a great impetus for the preservation of German culture that did not subside until World War I.

Not surprisingly, the observance in the 1980s of three centuries of German immigration gave rise to a number of efforts at long-term assessment of the adaptation process. See, for example, Randall M. Miller, ed., *Germans in America: Retrospect and Prospect* (Philadelphia, 1984), and Frank Trommler and Joseph McVeigh, eds., *America and the Germans: An Assessment of a Three-Hundred-Year History*, 2 vols. (Philadelphia, 1985). Finally, Frederick C. Luebke, *Germans in the New World: Essays in the History of Immigration* (Urbana and Chicago, 1990) is a collection of ten essays by perhaps America's most distinguished scholar of German-American ethnicity. He defines German assimilation as an interactive process in which both the immigrant group and the receiving society are changed, a phenomenon that is infinitely complex and time- and space-variable, as opportunities are presented to individuals in both contexts.

4

Irish-Americans

Dennis Clark

The Irish-Americans could well be considered the ethnic group that best reveals the extraordinary extent and variations of acculturation in the United States. Their record as an identifiable ethnic minority begins so early that it is interwoven with our opening history of exploration and colonial status. As frontier wanderers and indentured servants, as military adventurers and seaport merchants, their names are noted in the parchments of American history from the outset.[1] Hence, the increase in immigration that began in the 1830s must be seen as part of a continuum that reaches from colonial times right up to the jet age. The geographical dispersion, the regional differences, the variations from decade to decade, and the manifestation of a wide spectrum of social behavior all testify to the distinctive character of this long Irish subcultural tradition in this country and add to the fascination in studying the group and its past.

In order to evaluate the adaptations of this group, therefore, it is necessary to recognize that the social configurations of one period or region may contrast notably with those of other times and areas. Interpretation must accommodate a flexibility that has been one of the main features of the Irish-American engagement with American life. The identity of the group, both self-realized and attributed, changed over the generations and took a number of different colorations. The expectations and conditions in the broader society also altered with all the swiftness inherent in the fluid vitality of American life. Even the heritage derived from Ireland changed over the course of religious repression under English rule and remarkable misfortunes of famine, social disruption and cultural change that altered the demographic and cultural basis of Irish life.[2]

In spite of these disruptions of social depredation and emigration, millions of Irish-Americans were able to assume stable cultural positions within American life. Marjorie Fallows asserts that they were culturally assimilated into a system that "can encompass differences without having to eradicate them.[3] This was part of the broader achievement extolled by Gunnar Myrdal:

To outside observers . . . the relative success will forever remain the first and greatest riddle to solve when he sees that the children and grandchildren of these unassimilated foreigners are well-adjusted Americans. . . . He will be tempted to infer the influences upon the immigrant of a great national ethos in which optimism and carelessness, generosity and callousness, were so blended as to provide him with home and endurance.[4]

The development of a consonance between the Irish and the broader American ethos has to be explained in the face of disparities of culture, clashing social interests, religion, and historical timing of the waves of immigration. The difficulty of the task is formidable. This chapter deals mostly with nineteenth-century examples, including the generation following the 1845–1846 famine, but only with the understanding that these are convenient and do not represent by any means the great span of Irish-American experience. I will focus on just one dimension of diversity within the Irish-American tradition, that of interactive networks, but the achievement of Irish-American adjustment must be explained in relation to the powerful factor of geographical distribution and regional variations within the country. Did the regional variations make a real difference in the social experience of the group as it moved toward pluralist acceptance? David Doyle has argued that by the late nineteenth century the Irish-Americans were sufficiently "mature" so that their institutions and activities exhibited a high degree of complexity.[5] This is an important insight, for scholars have usually failed to comprehend the complexity of American ethnic subcultures. It has been generally assumed that they depend on ghetto solidarity and simplicity verging on the primitive. The subcultures are seen as unequal to the technical virtuosity and social power of the host culture. Hence, the view of them has been foreshortened so that Irish or Italian or black figures are placed throughout the landscape in a sort of academic stereotyping that drastically underestimates the realities of social differentiation that have occurred in different settings. This process is part of the American disposition toward simplification that has generated egregious distortions of our history and an unworthy panorama of popularized misconceptions about minorities, cultural differences and the truth of our life as a people.

Kathleen Neils Conzen has shown that ethnic identity in America did depend "originally on some level of neighborhood concentration, but does not depend equally on neighborhood survival.[6] This is true particularly for the Irish, because they distributed themselves early across many localities.

The pluralism that permitted this distribution was strained repeatedly, but it did compound a formula of limited tolerance. The decentralization and localization of power in nineteenth-century America allowed innumerable separations to flourish within the national unity, moderating both conflict and assimilation. John Higham stresses the importance of local experience in this process, and the relationships on many levels that occurred to blend the ethnic groups internally and connect them externally to the larger society.[7] It has been difficult to apprehend this process because we have not fully explored the regional adjustments the groups made, nor have we understood their creative energies. For generations, immigrants, were considered to be ignorant and incompetent, requiring a distinctively American transformation to effect their social advancement.

American regions were early viewed as physiographic units, and only later was a cultural dimension added to their definition. Regions are best conceived in terms of an interplay between an environment and a culture or cultures.[8] Nathan Glazer has contended that regional variations in ethnic political behavior are clearly evident. Irish-American distribution is responsible for differences in family life, religion, employment and orientation toward other groups. The most impressive single feature of this pluralist adaptation of the Irish, however, is the resourcefulness of the group in sustaining its identity amid differing regional conditions. It cannot be easily conceded that a group over the entire span of American history has continuously interwoven itself with the regional dramas of national development and yet persisted in its own subcultural definition and influence. Yet, this group did it.

This interaction of local ethnic identity, regional events and national growth has been a testimony to the group morale and historical consciousness of the Irish-Americans. Although their background has been tirelessly portrayed as one of poverty and cultural deprivation, this portrayal has missed the matrix of the resilient, malleable, persevering and irreducible elements residing in even the truncated and fragmented forms of the Irish heritage transported to America. This people wore persecution as a daily garment, evaded extinction in a multitude of ways, and contrived to continue life in inauspicious conditions over a long period of time. As a result, there were reservoirs of cunning, ambition, self-esteem and intrepidity in the group's background that were rarely perceived by those who saw the Irish only as destitute flotsam cast into the America current. The enervating effect of America itself drew forth these qualities, enhanced them and gave them amplitude for expression in exciting new roles and situations. Policemen in New York, merchants in the south, railroaders on the prairies, cowboys on the range, miners in the mountains and priests on the Pacific all acted out an Irish-American fulfillment in the midst of detractions and difficulties. We can see this now in retrospect as a demonstration of a heretofore overlooked display of cultural vitality and historic toughness not usually credited to those from poor and derogated societies. As a young nation, the United States must recall that this essential vitality existing below formal elaborate institutions and this historic toughness have characterized ancient peoples that have withstood the batterings of centuries.

The regional variations and extended interactions of the Irish, therefore, required a cultural elasticity and adaptation that would make an acceptable degree of acculturation possible. In successive areas of social enterprise the group did develop notable solutions. However, this should not obscure the grim record of exploitation, pathology and social failure that looms very large, indeed, for the Irish. Granting this, it is appropriate to review some of the areas of positive social adaptation, subject to the necessary limitation with respect to both time and area of social adjustment.

What kinds of institutional arrangements did the Irish construct to adapt their rural, preindustrial, culturally circumscribed experience to the American scene? How did they grasp onto America? To ask these questions is to raise a host of issues, but a broad inquiry makes it immediately evident that, based on their own cultural affinity, the group was able to maintain affiliations across great distances and through generations of minority status. The periods of frontier penetration, canal labor dispersion and railroad construction in which they were prominent are part of the earliest history of the Americans as a people. The vast reach of America had to be matched by the imagination of immigrants if they were to be part of this far-ranging nation. They had to identify with the new American enterprise and not huddle themselves into cloistered colonies of perpetual strangers.

Family ties were probably the single most powerful influence on Irish migration. The measures taken by early frontier Irish such as George Croghan and William Hohnston to bring relatives to America are illustrative of the propensity to form migration chains based upon blood relationships. Kerby Miller, in his splendid work, *Emigrants and Exiles: Ireland and the Irish Exodus to North America*, provides historians for the first time with a full range of Irish-American correspondence among emigrants and between emigrants and those remaining in Ireland.[9] This compilation of letters makes clear their centrality of the family in the emotional and social orientation of these people. It shows, even among those Miller believes to be more individualist, how persistent family ties were.

The family ties and migratory links described by Joseph A. King in his account of the Harrigan and Fitzgerald families in labor and farming situations from Maine to Wisconsin from the 1830s to the 1930s are equally revealing. The recruitment of relatives and friends in Ireland to come to Oregon is also evidence of the potent informal relationships that underlay Irish dispersion across the United States.[10] These were the beginnings of the far-flung networks through which the Irish-Americans maintained a national cultural identity as a group and interacted with one another.

Part of this immigrant family system was the cult of thrift that was practiced by Irish wage-earners in multitudes. The records of savings and loan associations and banks in various cities reveal the assiduous fashion in which the immigrants saved. The identification books of the Western Saving Fund Society in Philadelphia show that in 1870 a predominantly female clientele of depositors was busily saving despite low wages and difficult circumstances. Single women working as cooks and children's nurses, widows, and male laborers, porters and waiters all saved. The Philadelphia Saving Fund Society's records show about one-third of the depositors were female in the 1860s, and by 1889 one-sixth of the depositors were Irish-born in this bank alone. The savings began as soon as six months after immigrants arrived, and some were still depositing regularly forty years after entering the country. The funds accumulated were, of course, frequently used for remittances to Ireland, to bring out other family members, and to provide a family nest egg against bad times—hard savings amid hard work and self-denial.[11]

Since the Irish were overwhelmingly a laboring population in the nineteenth century, they had grave social needs, whether in major cities, mining camps or rural settings. Poverty, poor nutrition, overcrowded housing, bad sanitation and job-related illnesses and accidents caused serious health problems. Tuberculosis was common. Epidemic diseases such as cholera and typhus, as in the slums in Memphis, Tennessee, and the canal camps, took a heavy toll. Hospitals were not really public community-serving institutions for much of the nineteenth century.[12] It was only when the American public health movement became widespread that conditions began to improve. This need for health care among the Irish was at length most directly served by an extensive network of Catholic hospitals and clinics, by orders of nursing nuns, and by doctors who served the Irish communities and who were themselves of Irish backgrounds. The influence of the church with its ethic of ministering to those in need and its view of medical ethics was a strong motivating force in health care for the immigrants and their children. Thus, there was projected across the country a sizable network of health care facilities that was largely staffed, operated and supported by an Irish clientele. Other groups, most notably the German Catholics, also set up such facilities, but the Irish held predominance in health services under church auspices after 1850.

Irish-American physicians were part of the medical world in the country in the early nineteenth century, but only in small numbers. Dr. James MacNavan, an exile after the Rising of 1798, was one of the founders of American obstetrical practice. Dr. James McHenry in Philadelphia treated a clientele, but found time to write numerous works. Dr. John C. Riley wrote one of our early medical textbooks, Dr. Joseph O'Dwyer of New York invented intubation, and General Robert M. O'Reilly was surgeon general of the U.S. Army. However, Catholic medical schools were slow to develop, and after Georgetown University founded one in 1851, others did not form until after 1900, when Fordham University and St. Louis University set up medical training.[13]

The earliest editions of the *American Medical Directory* list scores of Irish-American physicians in the early part of the twentieth century, and these include the first large wave of medical leaders from this ethnic group that was very active in founding hospitals through the period beginning in 1880. Older Irish Catholic centers had hospitals by the mid-nineteenth century. The Mullanphy Hospitals served St. Louis beginning in 1829. Dr. J. J. Ryan directed St. Joseph's Hospital in New Orleans, Louisiana, founded in 1858. St. Mary's in Detroit dated from 1854. St. Vincent's Hospital in New York was opened in 1849, as was St. Joseph's Hospital in Philadelphia. Cincinnati, Ohio, Louisville, Kentucky, and Chicago also had Catholic hospitals from this period.[14]

After 1880, however, economic standing of the Irish improved and an extraordinary effort was made in founding health care institutions. Credit must be given to the Sisters of Mercy for the vigorous role they took in this development. This sisterhood was established by Catherine McAuley, a wealthy Dublin heiress, whose zeal sent her fellow sisters to England and America to serve the sick and poor in the midst of the Great Famine migration of the 1840s. In Pittsburgh and Chicago these sisters set up hospitals in 1848 and 1850, but in the 1890s, in a remarkable burst of activity, they founded hospitals in Springfield, Massachusetts, Wilkes Barre, Pennsylvania, Des Moines, Iowa, in the Cripple Creek mining area in Colorado and in San Diego, California. Other hospitals followed in Columbus, Ohio, Denver, Colorado, and in Utah. Clinics and hospices for the acutely ill were also instituted. And, this was just one sisterhood. Others acted similarly, so that by 1912 there were fifteen Catholic hospitals in the Northeast, fifteen in the Midwest, eleven in the South, four in the Southwest, twelve in the far West including California, and three in Washington and Idaho. These were not exclusively Irish-American enterprises, but the clearly dominant names among the boards, benefactors, staffs and affiliated physicians were of that group.[15]

If health services were a critical need for the nineteenth-century Irish-Americans, schools were also a pressing requirement. After 1830, the consciousness of the importance of education grew among the working people in all the more advanced nations. In Ireland, paradoxically, the efforts of the British to completely colonialize the population led to a rather precocious development of schooling.[16] Still, the collapse of Gaelic culture, the poverty of the island, and the restrictions upon Catholic educational work due to government hostility and discrimination all compromised school progress. In the United States, although there was Protestant hostility toward Catholic institutions, much more progress was possible among the immigrants. After the initial periods of difficulty of settlement and the formation of stable family life, the Irish Catholics moving steadily toward greater education largely patronized the public schools. Where Irish Catholics formed a significant sector of an urban community, or where they were sufficiently concentrated in rural districts, Catholic schools were quickly established.

In the Eastern cities at the outset of the rising demand for primary schools, men like Matthew Carey in Philadelphia served on public school boards in the 1830s. As religious controversy flared, leaders such as Archbishop John Hughes of New York insistently campaigned for Catholic schools, and Irish Christian Brothers were brought to the United States to found schools in Brooklyn, New York and Baltimore in 1846. Irish Franciscan priests set up a Brooklyn school that same year. In a burst of enterprise predating their impressive health care work, the Sisters of Mercy under Mother Mary Warde set up schools by 1860 in Pittsburgh, Philadelphia, Cincinnati and in the distant cities of St. Louis and San Francisco. Father James O'Gorman and some Sisters of Mercy founded the first Catholic school in Iowa, and in other areas on the plains Catholic schools flourished, including early Indian schools with largely Irish-American teachers in Kansas in the 1840s. In Wisconsin, Mother Regina Mulqueeny expanded the schools of the Dominican Sisters in the 1870s, and Mother Mary Megehan's Sisters of Charity worked in numerous areas across the country.[17]

The Sisters of St. Joseph, headquartered near Philadelphia, were typical of the strong East Coast religious orders that sent their members ranging across the landscape to serve. Between 1847 and 1891 approximately two-thirds of the nuns of this congregation were Irish-born or from Irish-American families. Two strong Irish-born leaders of the sisterhood led it to prominence and influential service in the fields of health, social services and especially education. Eliza Kieran was one of five members of her family from County Armagh who were in religious congregations. She joined the St. Joseph's sisters in 1853 and led the congregation from 1871 to 1894. Ella Lannen from Waterford followed her in a period of even greater expansion of the sisterhood's work.[18]

Another example is that of the Sisters of St. Francis of Glen Riddle, Pennsylvania. This congregation arose at the time when the emigration of females from Ireland was at its height in the 1880s. Beginning in 1888 and through the ensuing history of the sisterhood, 488 members of this organization, more than one-fourth of the total enrollment, were Irish-born, and scores of others were from Irish-American families. Six of these Irish-born women became heads of the organization's provinces. One-half of the Irish-born nuns were engaged in education, and about one-fifth were in health services as nurses, technicians and in hospital administration. In addition to the Irish-American communities they served, they were also assigned to Hispanic, Black and Indian missions. Three women named O'Hara from one family in County Tyrone became, respectively, a teacher, a head of a Franciscan province, and a frontier missionary in Oregon. This sisterhood illustrates well the dual health and education missions especially needed in the nineteenth century. As nurses in wartime and in times of epidemics, as teachers in railroad camps, as defenders of female immigrants on the docks, and in the slums, these women performed an extraordinary humane and disciplined service.[19] More than priests and bishops, they were the daily heart of the Irish-Catholic drive for social advancement. It is little wonder that the Irish became proud to support their efforts.

From the first Plenary Council in Baltimore in 1853, the Catholic bishops strove to provide more and more schools. In Colorado and Montana in 1869 the nuns taught the children of gold miners. In Utah, they set up an academy in Salt Lake in 1875. In Wyoming they built Indian schools, and by 1880 they had schools in Idaho and Washington.[20] Their record is astonishing and is largely unknown, except for some few historical references. Their achievements in an age when women worked under formidable constraints has gone largely uncredited by American historians, feminists and even Catholic historians, who have been more interested in sentimental and pious recitations than in rendering the harsher truths of religion's social role even when that role is so admirable.

It was on this foundation of great educational endeavor that the Catholic institutions of higher learning were established. Between 1786 and 1900 Catholics created 167 colleges and universities for men and dozens of colleges for women.[21] Culturally, the coloration of this educational system was a combination of Latin Catholicism, French educational rationalism and pietism, Victorian curricula with classical and English influences, and American innovations and adaptations. Ironically, the traditional culture of Ireland was barely reflected in the schools themselves, since Ireland's traditional culture had been so severely damaged by poverty and persecution, and since the revived Catholicism of the country had been so strongly influenced in the nineteenth century by French and Latin influences. Thus, the institutions of education that were built and patronized by the Irish-Americans were in one sense broader and more cosmopolitan than would be expected from such an immigrant group, yet, in another sense, they failed to transmit adequately a distinctive cultural heritage from the homeland.[22]

Journalism was, of course, a cultural lifeline for the Irish from the days of the founding of *The Shamrock* (New York, 1815) and *The Erin* (Philadelphia, 1823). Specifically Irish newspapers were usually local, as were most of the Catholic papers, but in Philadelphia alone over a century-and-a-half there were some twenty Irish newspapers founded, most of which did not have long lives. As mail and rail service improved, however, *The Irish World* of New York and *The Boston Pilot* circulated far beyond their cities. The former was eagerly read in distant places and its correspondence and articles came from all parts of the country, and the latter was the chief voice of Catholic opinion in the nation for several decades.[23]

Editors, correspondents and publishers are key figures in a democracy, and the Irish entered the newspaper field with alacrity. It was, at first, a distinctly *déclassé* and bohemian profession, but unfair discrimination in other occupational areas did not leave a wide choice for many literate Irishmen. The ties among these Irish journalists were, naturally enough, based on common backgrounds, mutual interests, organization member-ships and cultural affinity. Thus, members of the Fenian Brotherhood aided one another, as did those in the *Clan na Gael*. Irish editors arranged articles and speaking engagements for Irish notables. Although competition and rivalry alienated some publications from others, communicating and col-laboration was inevitable among those in the newspaper field. Throughout the hundreds of Irish-American newspapers and the thousands of general circulation papers employing Irishmen in the nineteenth century, the pro-fusion of gossip, exchange and calculated advertence to Irish interests could not but form a milieu of ethnic interaction. From *The Irish Citizen* in New Jersey to *The Celtic Cross and Western Irishman* in Colorado, the network was kept live. *The Dove of Ireland* magazine might not circulate far from the Eastern states, but Irish-American publishers and editors were part of the press from Kansas and Nebraska to Montana, and from Chattanooga to Oregon.[24]

It is obvious that with such a pronounced working-class character the Irish-Americans would develop strong occupational associations. Common work experience gave rise to loyalty to the work group, so that dockworkers, bricklayers, railroad men and miners all developed a lore, a morale and a camaraderie related to their daily labor. Ideologies such as socialism were usually secondary to these more direct occupational affinities. After all, the greater part of the worker's waking life was spent in the work group. A good example of the occupational relationships that grew into a national network of Irish-American association were those of the ironworker.

German and English workers at first dominated the early iron work and ornamental iron trades that flourished with the ornate decorative construc-tions of the Victorian age. The coming of iron frameworks for building erection, and then the invention of the elevator, increased the use of iron and the men who assembled it. Bridgebuilding increased, and high-rise con-struction was pursued in one city after another. The International Associ-ation of Bridge and Structural Iron Workers was formed in 1896 with delegates from Boston, Chicago, Buffalo, New York and Cleveland. By 1900 membership had grown to 6,000. Edward John Ryan of Boston was the first international president. The executive board was almost all Irish, in-cluding P. J. Dalton, James G. Crowley and George W. Geary of Chicago, and John Brady of New York.[25]

Structural iron work was extremely hazardous. Workers in 1890 were expected to climb narrow beams six, and at times seven, days a week in all kinds of weather for $2.10 a day. Accident and mortality rates were higher than in most other trades at the time, and ten years of work life in the trade was about the maximum. Young Irishmen were drawn to the work through natural association with those already in it. If there were dangerous jobs in the 1890s, such as mining and bridgebuilding, such jobs were usually given to the Irish. The work of bridgebuilding was of its nature migratory, and young men moved from one job to another, their only immediate social bonds being to their fellow workers. As *The Bridgeman's Magazine* said in 1909, "There's not a job from Broadway to the moon they wouldn't jump at." There was an elan to the work, a daring quality that attracted vigorously young males.[26] The ironworkers were widely known as tough, hard-drinking but steady men.

By 1902 there were 10,000 members of the Bridge Structural Iron Workers, and in 1905 Frank Ryan of Chicago took over the presidency. The earliest activity of the union had been to make payments to widows of workers and weekly payments to disabled members. Disaster was never far away. In 1907, fifty members of the union died in a single bridge collapse in Quebec. There were tough strikes against the American Bridge Company and the National Erectors Association. Layoffs, employer preference for open-shop policies, and disputes over wages and hours produced a militant union under the Irish leadership.[27]

The most sensational episode involving the union followed bitter labor-management conflicts in Los Angeles. An American Federation of Labor committee reported that the steel industry heads had fought unions tooth and nail and had destroyed not only steelworker unions, but those of machinists, carpenters, bricklayers, stone masons and longshoremen. The Los Angeles area was an especially antiunion locality. On October 1, 1910, the *Los Angeles Times* building, seat of the stridently antiunion local newspaper, blew up. Some contended that unrepaired gas leaks caused the explosion in which twenty people were killed. Business spokesmen, however, cried that the unions were responsible. William J. Burns, head of a large detective agency, went to Detroit and actually kidnapped two suspected men, Ortie McManigal and James B. McNamara, who were transported to Chicago and then Los Angeles by train. McNamara was the brother of John J. McNamara, secretary-treasurer of the ironworkers. The latter was arrested in 1911 at a union meeting and accused of masterminding the Los Angeles explosion. The case become a *cause célèbre*, with the labor movement rallying behind John McNamara. In a plea bargain to save his brother from capital punishment, John J. McNamara pleaded guilty without any confession and was given a fifteen-year sentence. A further drive by employers and compliant law enforcement officials rounded up fifty ironworkers on fake charges of keeping explosives. Excavation at the time often required blasting holes with dynamite to erect steel beams. The charges were dismissed, but the pressure on the union continued. The expenses of the trials between 1911 and 1913, according to the union's head, J. E. McClory, nearly wiped out the union.[28]

Life could not be all work for the Irish-Americans by any means, so that they also contrived to provide themselves with entertainment on an extensive scale. The folk basis for informal amusement that had been a traditional cultural medium in Ireland was considerably curtailed by emigration. Old customs, patterns of gathering and *ceilidh* entertaining in rural settings were all undercut. The vigor of the old Gaelic traditions of story-telling, ballad singing and proverbial hospitality were diminished by the increasing debility of impoverished Gaelic areas in Ireland. Despite these factors, the Irish in the United States continued to maintain lively though fragmentary informal entertainment activity in homes, parishes and local communities. But they also moved into American entertainment with alacrity. In the early nineteenth century they became part of the nascent commercial theater and later the traveling minstrel troupes, then joined in the great expansion of theatrical life after the Civil War, and became part of the vaudeville circuit thereafter.[29] When motion pictures were invented, they were in a good position to become part of that industry.

The stage Irishman, replete with clownish affectations and full of buffoonery, became a fixture of American theater almost from its inception. The Irish reaction to this public mockery was ambiguous. Irishmen played the roles, Irish people laughed at the follies of such characters, and Irish playwrights endlessly scripted their antics. As early as the 1840s, however, some Irish protested the stereotyped foolery of these characters.[30] But there were also other standard characters that became traditional theatrical favorites at the footlights, and these included the handsome nationalist hero, the lovely colleen, the wise old man and the good-hearted mother.

From the 1820s there were Irish plays presented in New York and New Orleans. By the 1850s, Irish plays and players ranged from the East Coast to Chicago, and a figure called Mose was portrayed visiting Philadelphia and California, while Irish firemen became images of daring and adventure for audiences in numerous cities.[31] The plays of Dion Boucicault gave rise to melodrama about romantic nationalism that glorified the Irish nation all the way back to the fabled Brian Boru who won the Battle of Clontarf against the Vikings in A.D. 1014. Edward Harrigan, who was influenced by Boucicault, led this playwriting tradition through the second half of the nineteenth century.[32] What had been created was an entire circuit of Irish-American theater that featured favorite plays about Robert Emmett, the patriot executed in Ireland by the English in 1803, and a whole repertoire of comedy, melodrama and musical presentations. It should be recalled that this large theatrical enterprise was precocious as American ethnic theater. For the Irish, it was also a new experience, for in Ireland itself the families of most of the rural emigrants would not have ever seen a stage presentation.

Mari Kathleen Fielder, herself a representative of an Irish-American family

with a long theatrical history, has traced this ebullient stage tradition in all
its remarkable elaboration through the nineteenth and twentieth centuries.
She has documented the extraordinary extent of this activity across the
continent one decade after another. In the 1840s, the national and federal
theaters in Boston were presenting Dion Boucicault's "West End" or, "The
Irish Heiress," a play that had been given in London. It moved on to
Baltimore, Philadelphia, Buffalo, New York, Montreal and New Orleans.
Plays like "Katty O'Sheal" by James Pilgrim were presented in Norfolk,
Virginia, Wheeling, West Virginia, Cincinnati and St. Louis. In the Eastern
cities such Irish theater was steady fare, and not just in major centers like
New York and Philadelphia, for the acting companies traveled to smaller
cities like Worcester, Massachusetts, Providence, Rhode Island, and Wilkes
Barre, Pennsylvania as well. The troupes frequently were sponsored by local
churches and schools and proceeds were divided so that the institutions
used the entertainers in fundraising endeavors that became annual affairs.
Thus, in addition to the entire strictly commercial theater circuit, there was
a high professional as well as amateur circuit attached to the Catholic
institutional network.[33]

All through the western mining towns where the Irish were at work this
kind of theater was welcome. John Maguire from County Cork, by way of
Australia, for instance, built the first theater in Butte, Montana, where he
gave his own recitations of "Shamus O'Brien" and "Over the Hill to the
Poorhouse" in the 1879s to audiences of copper miners.[34] Troupes worked
in St. Louis and then toured westward. The famous Lola Montez, originally
Lily Gilbert from Limerick in Ireland, toured mining camps. San Francisco
was its own great audience, but players went to the Gold Rush boom towns
as part of a colorful period of gaudy frontier entertainments.[35]

Fielder's work also describes the independent stock companies that served
the Irish-American circuit. A good example is the Mae Desmond Players,
based in Philadelphia from 1918 to 1932. Presenting the plays of Edward
Everett Rose and others, the troupe specialized in productions that showed
Ireland in the most romantic fashion. J. Hartley Manner's "Peg O' My
Heart" was a perennial favorite, with the lovely Mae Desmond as the lead.
Plays with British characters as the foils of wily Irishmen, plays about the
Irish as patriots in American settings, and plays extolling Catholic virtues
and kindly priests were all part of this company's repertoire.[36] There were
a number of such troupes, but they faded when motion pictures beguiled
away their audiences. This distinctive Irish-American theatrical tradition, it
should be noted, preceded the popularization of the great creative achievements of the literary renaissance in the theater in Ireland at the dawn of
the twentieth century.

Even while this institutional theater was thriving the Irish folk tradition
in music and dance replenished itself on the American scene. The Irish
organizations throughout the country sponsored balls, dances, *feiseanna*

(outdoor music and dance competitions) and dancing classes in practically all communities where there were sizable Irish populations. Musicologist Mick Moloney has recorded much of the music customary at these events in renditions by traditional musicians. Some of the most noted folk musicians continued their careers into the twentieth century, including Patrick Reidy, Thomas O'Sullivan and Michael Coleman. This folk music inheritance flourished until ease of travel, motion pictures and radio provided other diversions, but it remained vital enough in cities across the United States to be revived when interest in folk music increased in the 1960s, and Moloney estimated that in the 1970s there were about 25,000 youngsters enrolled in Irish dancing classes across the country.[37] The Clancy Brothers and Tommy Makem and dozens of other musical groups using Irish-traditional music became regular features of campus concerts and folk concerts all through the United States in the decades after the 1960s. This revival could only take place as the legacy of the earlier persistent and largely informal Irish-American music and dance tradition.

There existed throughout the country an Irish-run social institution so common as to be taken for granted, and that was the Irish tavern or saloon. In major cities they were a fixture both of downtown life and neighborhood convenience. In midwestern and southern areas where alcoholic drinks were prohibited, the bootlegger worked surreptitiously, but in most of its history the saloon was all but a local necessity. Whether it was Connelly's tavern in Natchez, Mississippi, or Isadora Barry's inn in Philadelphia, the Irish tavernkeeper was already an established folk character in the eighteenth century. Minimal capital and a gregarious disposition were all that were needed to enter the trade. Over the generations the saloon business became an adjunct of the brewing and distilling business, but this changed in the early twentieth centuries. The Irish saloonkeeper had to contend with the Prohibitionists, criminals, purity crusades and all manner of social intimidation, but this business remained the resort of his compatriots through it all. In larger centers and in the most remote places these establishments were often the points of reference for Irish seeking to locate jobs, relatives and guidance. In Boston and Chicago the saloon networks remained heavily Irish even when Germans and others came into the field. In the West, although the proportion of Irish-born saloonkeepers was smaller, the American-born Irish were still active in frontier watering holes from Texas to Montana. From McSorley's Wonderful Saloon in New York City to the groggeries of San Francisco's Barbery Coast, the full glass remained part of the full life for the Irish in America.[38]

The Irish network that is probably most fully documented is that involving groups of a nationalist character. The Society of the United Irishmen had members in major port cities in the 1790s, but considering the difficulties of communication at the time, their efforts to maintain liaisons were not too successful. Daniel O'Connell's Repeal Association's sympathizers in

America organized and collected funds in Eastern cities in the 1840s. The broadening of Irish-American nationalism, however, took place with the spread of the Fenian Brotherhood in the 1860s. From its inception in New York it moved to all major American cities where it worked to gain Irish independence, by force if necessary. Its most notable early achievement was the organization of commemorations across the country for Terence Bellew McManus, a man who figured in the thwarted rebellion of 1848 in Ireland. Beginning in San Francisco where McManus died, the cortege was met by delegations repeatedly in its passage from West to East in New York. When the patriot's body arrived in Dublin, there was a huge outpouring demonstrating the suppressed nationalist sentiment in the country in a way that had not been seen for a generation.[39]

The Fenians in America were organized from coast to coast among the sizable Irish communities. Boston, New York and Philadelphia were joined by inland cities like Pittsburgh and Buffalo. Ohio, Indiana, Michigan and Illinois had branches, as did Virginia, Missouri and Louisiana. In 1865 there were 273 "circles" of the Fenians at a meeting in Cincinnati where the nationalists came together from across the country. Even in states like Iowa where there were not the large concentrations of Irish characteristic of the East coast there were Fenian circles in Dubuque, Des Moines, Sioux City and Webster City.[40]

After the failure of the Fenians to produce an armed uprising in Ireland, the nationalists turned to the *Clan na Gael*. It was founded in New York in 1867. It was organized in "camps," and soon spread to such distant places as Little Rock, Arkansas. As a secret society pledged to establish an Irish republic, it had 7,000 members by 1874. Repeatedly split by factionalism, it still maintained its ideological nationalist course. Severe splits occurred in the 1880s between the elements led from Chicago by Alexander Sullivan and those led from New York by John Devoy. Regional differences in political views and personalities were part of this tendency toward divisiveness. Nevertheless, the *Clan na Gael* survived and was strategically highly important in mobilizing support for the Irish revolutionary movement that coalesced in the period around World War I.[41]

It is worth recalling that although the militant and overtly nationalist organizations maintained an uneven pattern of propaganda and agitation, other large Irish groups complemented the formal nationalist groups by informing broad memberships and consolidating Irish-American opinion. The Ancient Order of Hibernians, for instance, was a largely moderate nationalist group with branches across the United States. The Irish Catholic Benevolent Union in the 1870s was also widely influential and had goals relating to nationalism. All kinds of church and fraternal groups filled out this elaborate nationalist bloc that by 1880 was a vigorous ideological and political force in American life.[42]

Charles Stewart Parnell's momentous drive to secure land redistribution in Ireland generated an extensive supportive effort in the United States for fundraising and political expression. A key figure in the organization of this Land League network was Michael Davitt, Mayo-born Fenian veteran, former political prisoner in English jails, and an eloquent apostle of land reform for Ireland. In 1878 Davitt toured the United States to develop support for the cause. Traveling along the East Coast he was able to address Irish-American audiences in the major cities. He then moved on to Cleveland and St. Louis, Dubuque, St. Paul and Chicago before again visiting New York and New England. In all these places sympathizers organized and collected funds in response to his message. Davitt visited his own emigrated family members in Scranton, Pennsylvania, and Philadelphia as well. In 1880 he again toured the United States, visiting many of the same cities, but this time he went on to speak to the Irish who had gone West, so that he found audiences prepared to hear him in Omaha, Nebraska, Cheyenne, Wyoming, Denver, Reno, Nevada, Virginia City, Nevada, Sacramento, California, and San Francisco.[43] The scope of this ardent nationalist visitation demonstrates the far-flung character of the Irish-nationalist network. Enthusiasts and organizers could be found and activated from one end of the country to the other, and this was a condition that persisted from the days of the Fenians into the twentieth century.

This pattern of nationwide activity in behalf of Irish nationalism continued into the twentieth century. When the Irish war of independence flared throughout the period from 1918 to 1921, Irish-American groups rallied to the rebels and conducted extensive propaganda and fundraising campaigns across the country as they strove to politically induce the United States government to aid the fledgling Irish state. The American Commission on Conditions in Ireland in 1920 and 1921 sent emissaries to that country to investigate British repression and destruction, and this commission included not only representatives from major cities throughout America and representatives from non-Irish organizations, but participants from such places as Bismarck, North Dakota, Portage, Wisconsin, and Asheville, North Carolina. The American Commission for Relief in Ireland, while centralizing its administrative functions in New York City, was similarly broad-based and inclusive, and its reports for 1921 and 1922 include twelve pages of names of leaders in the relief work from all states in the union.[44]

Various organizations continued this pattern of nationwide activity. The Ancient Order of Hibernians had representatives in many states. The American Irish Historical Society, founded in 1896, had representatives in each state until the 1960s, and its journal and studies were nationwide in scope. Even a much less numerous group like Irish Northern Aid in the 1970s was able to show representation in all the states.[45]

It is significant that major Irish-American organizations did not devolve themselves into regional groupings as an organizational practice. Factionalism did cause splits that followed regional lines, as in the cases of the

Fenian Brotherhood and the *Clan na Gael*, and some organizations shrank to a scale that permitted them to operate only in one section of the country, as was the case with the *Clan na Gael* after 1940. But, the prevailing aspiration was to have organizations that represented the group across the nation, not just in the South or in New England or in the West. Even the American Association for Recognition of the Irish Republic in its decline in the 1940s aspired to this goal and sought to draw representation from the West Coast as well as the East and Midwest to show the broadest possible outreach.[46]

Because of the far-flung dispersion of the Irish-Americans, a constant plea for unity existed, and it was ever difficult to attain. The rhetoric seeking this unity extends from the eighteenth century forward, and echoes the pleas of Theobold Wolf Tone, Thomas Davis and other Irish nationalists for whom it was a central concern. Set against these entreaties for unity was a theme of lamentation about the failure to attain it. Fenians, *Clan na Gael* spokesmen, leaders of the Sinn Fein movement, politicians, churchmen and visiting leaders from Ireland all repeatedly complained of the failure to combine Irish people into a thorough solidarity. The strains preventing unity are understandable in retrospect. As a group from a dissociated rural background with limited organizational models, the nationalist emergence and religious revival in America was a novel experience. Common organizational defects, distance and barriers to continuity made the development of their networks uncertain. In view of the group's social disabilities, the record of organizational achievement across the generations must be judged as remarkable in itself.

The organization and cooperation of Irish people across great distances in various regions of the United States was not, of course, an entirely positive feature of their ethnic life. Distance itself hampered their cooperation and communication. Where the networks were bound by a strong internal discipline, as in the case of the Irish-dominated religious sisterhoods, there was much less conflict. The benefits of this extensive liaison of the Irish-Americans, however, were manifold. Their networks permitted them to cope with the geographical mobility of the group, reaching the Irish in the most remote corners of the country. It gave them regional influence toward the satisfaction of specific needs and toward the exercise of leverage in politics. Their presence in one region enabled them to offset the tensions in another. If they were especially confined in New England or the South, the more expansive social conditions in the West tended to balance out their status in the country as a whole. The very existence of far-ranging ties and organizations was a boon to the morale of a group that faced difficult problems in American life. The alienation and isolation caused by emigration and prejudice against the Irish was countered by the affiliations fostered by organizations that reinforced identity and enhanced group morale. Finally, these national bonds conferred an image on the group of distinctive Americanism. The Irish were not just a phenomenon of the heavily immigrant cities of the East. In all parts of the nation they had organized on a characteristically voluntary American basis. They expressed De Tocqueville's insight into the American capacity to imitate, to organize, to get things done. A people without the freedom to fully develop socially in their homeland demonstrated in prodigious fashion their abilities to do so in the United States.

Although the historic creation of an overseas tradition of identity and adjustment in the new American society would be the outstanding achievement of the Irish-Americans, the political dimension of this creation would have far-reaching implications for the group within American life, for Ireland itself in its evolution as a modern state, and for the American political system as a pluralist configuration. The stereotypical view of this political development summarizes it as a succession of Irish-Catholic urban bosses, corrupt and antithetical to democratic values, failures in the interpretation of Lord James Bryce, whose censorious attitude toward American institutions reflected the Anglophilia of his own class and time. This is a badly foreshortened view of the Irish-American political interaction with American life, and does not assess the real extent of ethnic innovation in what is admittedly a realm of American life that has been full of turbulence and contradictions.

The inauspicious prospects for political stability of the early republic were underscored by the novelty of its institutions and the hazards of "big power" hostility, as well as the tempestuous character of a society that was fluid, pluralist, regionally varied and rapidly expanding. How this new society and infant government would handle its grievances was crucial. Very early in the progress of its political life the Irish became part of the expression and arrangements by which the grievances were given public attention. As pioneer populists the Irish played a vigorous role from the outset. Irish-Americans were among the earliest clarions vocally haranguing against the Alien and Sedition Acts, debtors prisons, and lack of public education and the Whiggish and bourbon magnates of the first generations after the Revolution. Some were veterans of the failed 1798 rebellion in Ireland, others were opportunists on the American scene. They were in action even before Andrew Jackson summoned forth the roar of the crowd to express the impatience of both the frontier and the city underclass. There were dozens of Irish-Americans with strong leadership profiles by Jackson's time. Eight made it to Congress as elected representatives by 1835, and by 1870 there had been eighteen Irish-Americans sent to Congress despite anti-Irish and anti-Catholic rancor. These included spectacular characters like Mike Walsh, the editor of the fiery New York protest paper, *The Subterranean*. Hence the oratorically vigorous Irish-American politician was part of the public pantheon long before the emergence of big-city boss rule after the Civil War.[47]

The urban political machine based on bloc voting and immigrant needs has become a fixture of American political history with almost as much influence as our formal governmental institutions. It is seen by some as a corrupting disease of democracy, and by others as an ingenious popular device for coping with an otherwise uncontrolled environment. The Irish-American figures who guided these urban political constructions were a widely varied cast, from street fighters who dominated polling wars to playboy bounders like New York's Jimmy Walker. The Irish-American cavalcade of these politicos is huge, ranging from the inimitably rascally James Michael Curley of Boston to San Francisco's "Blind Boss" Chris Buckley. In retrospect it is notable that this political machine sovereignty under Irish leadership often had powerful currents of reformist activity as well as a distinctive democratic medium for the key function of mobilizing public opinion and the franchise. To see it as a mere instrumentality of predation is shortsighted. It was a momentous invention, and its grass-roots character, rhetorical style and bloc-voting specificity is markedly Irish in origins and momentum.

As Irish power in the major cities has waned, however, a new political system has arisen. Localized bloc voting has yielded to special interest politics of a different kind. Mass media have superceded ward leader circuits of influence. The images of television campaigning have replaced the "pork chop" politics of local communities. In this development the Irish have continued to maintain a disproportionate role as political fixers and campaign fixtures. They have done this by appearing as representatives of the common man of democracy somewhat sanitized and made smoother by television makeup and extended schooling. The post-Kennedy image of the sartorially appropriate fellow who looks like a trustworthy high school coach has legions of fans, and throngs of ambitious Irish-American practitioners seek office based on its currency. Their Irish-American identities and allegiances are often quite fragile, but they cannot help but be related to the generations of Irish politicians whose antics and records have indelibly been stamped upon the nation's political history.

What is significant about this political contribution is that it really does not fit into the formal political history of the nation seen as constitutional elaboration or administrative record. It has not been an achievement in only one region or among one class or related to some single set of issues. It is too broad to be pigeonholded, and is probably best studied as a manifestation of a certain kind of political culture through which the politics of the country were gradually nationalized through the experience of the constituent elements of our democracy.

What are the implications of the Irish construction of these networks of family affinity, health service, schools, labor ties, journalism, theatrical camaraderie and nationalist endeavor across America? In addition to their pivotal role in urban contracting and building and in urban politics, these networks of influence represented both a second tier of adaptation over and above their local community adaptations, and also an extension of their own culture of emigrant ingenuity, a cult that had become international in the nineteenth century. Further, it is evident from the foregoing that it is difficult to set forth generalizations about this ethnic group's behavior unless a specific time, locale and social context are posited. The voluntary associations stimulated by American experiences, the educational work, the political strategies are all diffused through a broad panorama of life and events in a changing United States. The studies of Irish-American outlook and social mobility that have appeared in the last twenty years are mainly focused on the northeastern part of the country, with some fine individual studies of San Francisco and New Orleans.[48] Concentrated as they are on the middle and second half of the nineteenth century and on social mobility under industrialization, they are only partial in relation to the enormous spread of the Irish-American dispersion. It would be misleading to pretend that we as yet have a real grasp of an adequate interpretive design through which to evaluate this group's history in the United States.

By concentrating on a social history that deals with urban workers, by omitting rural and frontier dimensions, migratory trades, occupational networks like those in the theater and journalism; and by scanting the contributions of such groups as nuns, the broader picture of the Irish penetration of American life in all its flexibility and regional diversity is foreshortened. The manner in which the group has flexibly prolonged its cultural presence and social memory has been underplayed in the interest of specificity about individual locales and statistical measurement of occupational mobility. The more extensive ethnic proliferation sustained by the persistence of family names and recollections, a huge tableau of associations, and an imagery of ethnic history that is partly accurate record and partly folk mythology has thus been obscured. Through the breadth of this ethnic experience, the Irish-Americans have maintained a primary identity of secondary derivation based on specific events and memories embedded in American culture. Our interpretive instruments have barely been able to comprehend this process.

Attempts to align a theoretical explanation of what John D. Buenker calls the "American Equation" of ethnic mingling and interaction have been less than successful. Melting pot, pluralism and tryptychs of Protestant, Catholic and Jewish orbits have failed to comprehend all of the manifold incongruities of the American experience because that experience has been so diverse socially, so wide-ranging geographically and so diffuse in its adaptations that scholars have constantly yielded to the temptation to exalt the part for the whole in seeking some unifying exposition. Eric Wolf in his work, *Europe and the People Without History*, has shown how these theories fall short of describing the reality of social experience implicit in the great migrations.[49] People came in trajectories and mingled in situations so diverse that their adjustments can only be seen as a "totality of netlike connections."

Wolf finds a key to their situations in their "social labor." Others would find it in the process of adaptation itself that required the exchange and creation of cultural forms to suit a widely varied array of social, economic and environmental conditions. Buenker's distinction of "tiers" of governmental, industrial and popular social life at least provides the flexibility needed to encompass this diversity.

The Irish-Americans were able to devise networks of communication, association and leadership that permitted them to make a communal formulation of primary family and religious bonds at the local level that had political and cultural expressions over long periods of time. Underlying this formulation was a legacy of identity and a cult of ethnic consciousness that was sufficiently elastic to foster emotional and psychological affinities that projected networks in such fields as health care, education, journalism, labor, the theater and nationalist advocacy. The process by which this evolution took place was one of cultural invention, adaptation and reconstruction that shaped Irish-American traditions over an extended period of swelling and receding immigration and ethnic prominence.

In a country as large as the United States with such a broad spectrum of ethnic infusion into a panorama of differing situations subject to great tides of change, it is simply not wise to try to impose some universal theoretical constructs. It is more prudent to permit explanatory and interpretive designs to emerge from perspectives across and through local and regional conditions. The contradictions and disparities involved in trying to fit some interpretive models onto the Irish-American experience provide an extended example of the shortcomings involved. The scope of the Irish-American historical career involves ambiguities that make the case of this ethnic group especially resistant to generalization, particularly because of its familiarity with English, its previous dealings with Anglo society, and because the sheer span of Irish-American culture continues to decline in this period of immigration restriction and erosion of its institutions. Thus the reckoning of Irish adjustment to America remains what it was in the opening era of the country's development—problematical and fascinating.

NOTES

1. Dennis Clark, *Hibernia America: The Irish and Regional Cultures* (Westport, Conn. Greenwood Press, 1986), 1–34.

2. Joseph Lee, *The Modernization of Irish Society, 1848–1918* (Dublin: Gill and Macmillan, 1973), 1–20.

3. Marjorie Pallows, *The Irish-Americans: Identity and Assimilation* (Englewood Cliffs, N.J.: Prentice-Hall, 1979), 145.

4. Quoted from Gilbert Ostrander, *American Civilization in the First Machine Age* (New York: Harper and Row, 1970), 30.

5. David Doyle, *Irish-Americans: Native Rights and National Empires 1890–1901* (New York: 1976), 38–76.

6. Kathleen Neils Conzen, "Immigrants, Immigrant Neighborhoods and Ethnic Identity: Historical Issues," *Journal of American History* 66, no. 3 (December 1979): 603–15.

7. John Higham, "Integrating America: The Problem of Assimilation in the Nineteenth Century," *Journal of American Ethnic History* 1, no. 1 (Fall 1981): 7–25.

8. Frederick Luebke, *Ethnicity on the Great Plains* (Lincoln, Neb.: University of Nebraska Press, 1980), 214–18.

9. Kerby Miller, *Emigrants and Exiles: Ireland and the Irish Exodus to North America* (New York: Oxford University Press, 1985), 102–30.

10. Joseph A. King, *The Irish Lumberman-Farmer* (Lafayette, Calif.: Joseph A. King, 1982), 225–31. John F. Kilkenny, *Shamrocks and Shepherds: The Irish in Morrow County* (Portland, Ore.: Oregon Historical Society, 1981), 22–54.

11. Identification Book No. 1 (1871), Western Saving Fund Society, Philadelphia. Annual Reports of the Philadelphia Saving Fund Society, 1851, 1861, 1889. Archives of the Philadelphia Saving Fund Society, Philadelphia, Penn.

12. Maurice Voge, *The Invention of the Modern Hospital. Boston, 1870–1930* (Chicago: University of Chicago Press, 1980).

13. Howard A. Kelly and Walter L. Burrage, eds., *Dictionary of American Medical Biography* (Boston: Milford House, 1928), 288, 689, and passim. Abraham Flexner, *The Flexner Report on Medical Education in the United States and Canada* (New York: The Carnegie Foundation, 1910), cf. entries for Georgetown, Fordham and St. Louis universities.

14. *American Medical Directory—1912* (Chicago: American Medical Association, 1912), Index to Physicians. The references to hospitals are drawn from the geographical listings by states throughout the directory. For a local development history see Gail Farr Casterline, "St. Mary's and St. Joseph's: The Origins of Catholic Hospitals in Philadelphia," *Pennsylvania Magazine of History and Biography* 108, no. 3 (July 1984).

15. Ibid., passim. The Sisters of Mercy institutions are usually designated as such in the *American Medical Directory—1912*. M. Joanna Regan, *Tender Courage: A Brief Sketch of the First Sister of Mercy* (Gwynedd Valley, Penn.: Gwynedd-Mercy College, 1978), 1–12.

16. Donald Akenson, *The Irish Education Experiment* (London: Routledge and Kegan Paul, 1969), 1–90.

17. Rev. J. A. Burns, *The Growth and Development of the Catholic School System in the United States* (New York: Oxford University Press, 1979), 66–72, tells of anti-Irish bias in public schools.

18. Register of the Sisters of St. Joseph, 1847–1900, Archives of the Sisters of St. Joseph, Chestnut Hill College, Philadelphia, Penn. Sister Maria Kostka Logue, *The Sisters of St. Joseph of Philadelphia* (Westminster, Md.: The Newman Press, 1950), passim.

19. Biographical notes and analysis of Sister M. Aiele Gorman, O.S.F., June 13, 1983, The Sisters of Saint Francis of Philadelphia, Glen Riddle, Penn.

20. Burns, *The Growth and Development of the Catholic School System*, 152–65.

21. Edward J. Power, *A History of Catholic Education in the United States* (Milwaukee, Wis.: Bruce Publishing Co., 1958), 332–53.

22. See, for instance, Philip Gleason, "The Curriculum of the Old-Time Catholic College: A Student's View," *Records of the American Historical Society* 88, nos. 1–4 (March-December 1977): 101–2.

23. William V. Shannon, *The American Irish* (New York, 1966), 188–91. Carl Wittke, *The Irish in America* (Baton Rouge: Louisiana State University Press, 1956), 202–15. See also William Leonard Joyce, *Editors and Ethnicity: A History of the Irish-American Press, 1848–1883* (New York: Arno Press, 1976).

24. Eugene P. Willging and Herta Hatzfeld, *Catholic Serials of the Nineteenth Century in the United States*, 2 vols. (Washington, D.C.: Catholic University Press, 1968), 1: 16, 17, 75, 100, 105, 120, 158; 2: 185.

25. John H. Lyons, ed., *An Informal History of the Iron Workers* (Philadelphia: International Association of Bridge, Structural and Ornamental Ironworkers, 1971), 1–12.

26. Ibid., 4.

27. Ibid., 7.

28. Ibid., 13–27.

29. Wittke, *The Irish in America*, 33–63.

30. Maureen Murphy, "Irish-American Theater," in *Ethnic Theater in the United States*, ed. Maxine Schwartz Seller (Westport, Conn.: Greenwood Press, 1983), 223.

31. Ibid., 222.

32. Playbills and notices in the collection of Mari Kathleen Fielder document these productions. Letter and documentation of Mari Kathleen Fielder to Dennis Clark, January 23, 1984.

33. Mari Kathleen Fielder, "Wooing a Local Audience: The Irish-American Appeal of Philadelphia's Mae Desmond Players," *Theater History Studies* 1 (1981): 50–63. William B. Carson, *The Theater on the Frontier: The Early Years of the St. Louis Stage* (Chicago: University of Chicago Press, 1932), 45. Constance Rourke, *Troupers of the Gold Coast or the Rise of Lotta Crabtree* (New York: Harcourt Brace and Co., 1928), 121–212. Glenn Hughes, *A History of the American Theater: 1700–1950* (London: Samuel French Co., 1951), 282–97. Hans Nathan, *Dan Emmett and the Rise of Negro Minstrelsy* (Norman: University of Oklahoma Press, 1962), 1–41.

34. Workers of the Writers Program of the Works Progress Administration, *Copper Camp: Stories of the World's Greatest Mining Town: Butte, Montana* (New York: Hastings House, 1943), 72.

35. Rourke, *Troupers of the Gold Coast*, 120–24.

36. Mari Kathleen Fielder, "Green and Gold Reconsidered: The Identity and Assimilation Dilemma of the American Irish as Reflected in the Dramas of Edward Everett Rose," paper, April 1983.

37. Mick Moloney, "Irish Traditional Dance in America," *Balkan Arts Tradition* (New York: Balkan Arts Center, 1977), 5–8.

38. Perry R. Duis, *The Saloon: Public Drinking in Chicago and Boston, 1880–1920* (Urbana: University of Illinois Press, 1983), passim. Dennis Clark, *The Irish Relations: Trials of an Immigrant Tradition* (Rutherford, N.J.: Fairleigh-Dickinson

University Press, 1982), 61–75. John Mitchell, *McSorley's Wonderful Saloon* (New York: Duell, Sloan and Pearce, 1943), 1–40. Elliott West, *The Saloon on the Rocky Mountain Frontier* (Lincoln: University of Nebraska Press, 1979), 54–59.

39. Wittke, *The Irish in America*, 151–53.

40. Philip E. Myers, "The Fenians in Iowa," *Palimpsest* 62, no. 2 (March-April 1981): 56–57.

41. Michael F. Funchion, ed., *Irish-American Voluntary Organizations* (Westport, Conn.: Greenwood Press, 1984), 75–92.

42. Ibid., 50–61.

43. T. W. Moody, *Davitt and Irish Revolution, 1846–82* (Oxford, England: Clarendon Press, 1981), 211–70, 282.

44. *Report of the American Committee for Relief in Ireland* (New York: Emigrant Savings Bank, 1921), 1–12. Funchion, *Irish-American Voluntary Organizations*, 12–31.

45. Ibid., 200–206. Dennis Clark, *Irish Blood: Northern Ireland and the American Conscience* (Port Washington, N.Y.: Kennikat Press, 1976).

46. Papers of John J. Reilly, Historical Society of Pennsylvania, Philadelphia, Penn. Reilly was an activist for this group from 1919 to 1960, and his papers show the aspiration for national ties for it.

47. *The Biographical Directory of the American Congress, 1774–1971* (Washington, D.C.: Government Printing Office, 1971), passim. Lists Stephen Ormsby, John D. O'Neill, Jeremiah O'Brien, Richard McCormick, Felix McConnell, Blair McClenachan, Dennis McCarthy, Richard McCarty, George McDuffie, James McIlvaine, James McSherry, James Kelly (Washington) James Kelly (Pennsylvania), Patrick Sullivan, Thomas Walsh, William Walsh, Michael Walsh and Terence Quinn, all of whose careers began before the Civil War.

48. See, for instance, Stephan Thernstrom, *The Other Bostonians: Poverty and Progress in the American Metropolis* (Cambridge, Mass.: Harvard University Press, 1973); Clyde and Sally Griffin, *Natives and Newcomers: The Structure of Opportunity in Mid-nineteenth Century Poughkeepsie* (Cambridge, Mass.: Harvard University Press, 1977); Theodore Hershberg, *Philadelphia: Work, Space, Family and Group Experience in the 19th Century* (New York: Oxford University Press, 1981); Timothy J. Meagher, *From Paddy To Studs: Irish-American Communities in the Turn of the Century Era, 1880 to 1920* (Westport, Conn.: Greenwood Press, 1986); and for other references: Seamus P. Metress, *The Irish-American Experience: A Guide to the Literature* (Washington, D.C.: University Press of America, 1981), 17–42.

49. Eric Wolf, *Europe and the People Without History* (Berkeley: University of California Press, 1982), 11–25.

BIBLIOGRAPHICAL ESSAY

The starting point for further study of Irish adaptation to life in the United States is the essay by Patrick J. Blessing in Stephen Thernstrom et al., eds., *Harvard Encyclopedia of American Ethnic Groups* (Cambridge, Mass., 1980), 524–45. Access to the abundant literature on Irish-Americans can best be gained through Michael Funchion, "Irish-America: An Essay on the Literature," *Immigration History Newsletter* 17 (November, 1985): 1–8; Walter R. Rose, *A Bibliography of the Irish in the United States* (Afton, N.Y., 1969); Seamus P. Metress, *The Irish-American Experience: A Guide to the Literature* (Washington, D.C., 1981); and Alan R. Eagar, *A Guide to Irish Bibliographical Materials* (London, 1964).

The best account of the great Irish migration of the pre–Civil War era is Kerby Miller, *Emigrants and Exiles: Ireland and the Irish Exodus to North America* (New York, 1985), a model for the study of causation and patterns of emigration. George W. Potter, *To The Golden Door: The Story of the Irish in Ireland and America*, tells somewhat the same story in a more popular, sentimental vein with greater emphasis on the American experience. William V. Shannon, *The American Irish*, (New York, 1966), examines Irish-American activities in politics, religion, entertainment, literature, athletics, and law enforcement and concludes with an assessment of the "Irishness" of Joseph R. McCarthy and John F. Kennedy.

Focusing primarily on the Irish-Americans of Chicago's South Side, Andrew M. Greeley, *That Most Distressful Nation: The Taming of the American Irish* (Chicago, 1972), analyzes their attitudes, institutions, and behavior in comparison to other Windy City ethnic groups. Carl F. Wittke, *The Irish In America*, (Baton Rouge, La. 1956) although somewhat dated, surveys Irish-American culture, institutions, economic activities, political behavior, relations with other ethnic groups, and efforts to influence Old World developments. Focusing primarily on religion, politics, and nationalism, John B. Duff, *The Irish In the United States* (Belmont, Calif., 1971) succinctly synthesizes the findings of most important earlier studies.

Several more recent works have concentrated more directly on the adaptation process of Irish-Americans. In *How the Irish Became Americans* (New York, 1973), Joseph P. O'Grady surveys the Irish-American experience from colonial times to the 1920s, with a focus on the nineteenth century, and emphasizes the centrality of the Anglo-Irish struggle in the Old Country as the cause that bound together immigrants and their descendants and molded them into an effective political pressure group. Marjorie Fallows, *The Irish-Americans: Identity and Assimilation* (Englewood Cliffs, N.J., 1979), contends that Irish culture experienced a process of syncretism in which elements flowed both ways and were combined into new forms. The evolution of an identifiable Irish-American "type," personified by James T. Farrell's Studs Lonigan, is the central theme of Timothy J. Meagher, ed., *From Paddy to Studs: Irish-American Communities in the Turn of the Century Era, 1880 to 1920* (Westport, Conn., 1986). The various scholars investigate Irish-American communities in Lowell and Worcester, Massachusetts, Philadelphia, Chicago, St. Louis, and San Francisco; Meagher concludes that the resultant culture blended fidelity to Catholicism with American patriotism, but lost the rich folk culture of Ireland.

Acknowledging the importance of regional differences among the American Irish, several scholars have concentrated their attention on particular geographical settlements. Lawrence J. Caffrey, Ellen Skerrett, Michael F. Funchion, and Charles Fanning, *The Irish In Chicago* (Urbana and Chicago, 1987), examine "the Irish-American dimension" in the city's religion, politics and literature, and the group's seemingly inexorable evolution toward suburbanization and assimilation. No Irish habitat has received more scholarly attention than has Boston, the first major point of debarkation. Oscar Handlin, *Boston's Immigrants*, (Cambridge, Mass., 1959) is a classic study of the pathology of the early Irish ghetto and the hardships and discrimination that the group struggled to overcome. The two pioneer social mobility studies by Stephan Thernstrom, *Poverty and Progress* (New York, 1969) and *The*

Other Bostonians (Cambridge, Mass., 1973), capture the status of the Hub's Irish-Americans, in a comparative framework, after a generation or more of socioeconomic struggle. Most recently, Dennis P. Ryan, *Beyond the Ballot Box: A Social History of the Boston Irish, 1845–1917* (Amherst, Mass., 1991) provides an overview of the group's emergence into the middle class over three generations of striving and conflict. Comparing the city's Irish immigrants to their German contemporaries, Robert Ernst, *Immigrant Life in New York City, 1825–1863* (New York, 1949), examines their respective settlement patterns, economic life, institutions, and political behavior. In *The Irish in Philadelphia: Ten Generations of Urban Experience* (Philadelphia, 1974), Dennis Clark analyzes the reasons why the Philadelphia Irish generally enjoyed greater socioeconomic success, while wielding less political influence, than their counterparts in Chicago, Boston, or New York. The influence of a distinctive Southern urban environment is apparent in Earl F. Niehaus, *The Irish in New Orleans, 1800–1860* (Baton Rouge, La., 1965). Niehaus explores the conflict between the more established French Catholics and their Hibernian co-religionists, the competition between the latter and the city's black community for employment and housing, and the Irish-Americanizing influence on Catholic institutions and practices. The experience of *The San Francisco Irish, 1848–1880* (Berkeley, Calif., 1980) as examined by R. A. Burchell was one of reasonably rapid acculturation and assimilation. Demonstrating that the Irish-American experience was not all metropolitan in locale, Sr. M. Justille MacDonald, *History of the Irish in Wisconsin in the Nineteenth Century* (Washington, D.C., 1954), examines many rural settlements throughout the Badger State and discusses their role in the state's economic, social, and political life. John F. Kilkenney, *Shamrocks and Shepherds: The Irish in Morrow County* (Portland, Ore., 1981), examines the impact of a different type of rural environment on Celtic newcomers. Finally, Dennis Clark, *Hibernia America: The Irish and Regional Cultures* (Westport, Conn. 1986), demonstrates the importance of regional influences on the development of Irish-American culture.

Nor have scholars entirely neglected the internal dynamics and variety of the Irish-American community. Stephen Birmingham, *Real Lace: America's Irish Rich* (New York, 1973), dissects the fortunes, recreations, and manners of the country's "first Irish families." At the other end of the socioeconomic spectrum, Joseph A. King explores the life of *The Irish Lumberman-Farmer* (Lafayette, Calif., 1982). The impact of immigration on Irish reproduction and family patterns is the major subject of Robert E. Kennedy, Jr., *The Irish: Emigration, Marriage, and Fertility* (Berkeley, Calif., 1973). Two recent books examine the experiences of Irish-American women in impressive detail. Janet A. Nolan, *Ourselves Alone: Women's Immigration from Ireland, 1885–1920* (Lexington, Ky., 1989) concentrates on the Irish conditions that propelled the heavy outmigration of young women from the 1880s on, but also examines how those women adapted to life in the New World. Hasia R. Diner, *Erin's Daughters in America* (Baltimore, 1983), devotes much more attention to the peculiar pattern of adaptation formed at the juncture of Irish ethnicity and female gender.

Several other works deal primarily with the mediating institutions developed by Irish immigrants to facilitate the adaptation process. Edward J. Power, *A History of Catholic Education in the United States* (Milwaukee, 1958), establishes the pivotal role played by Irish-Americans in the articulation of the parochial school system. J. A. Burns, *The Growth and Development of the Catholic School System in the*

United States (New York, 1979), presents a much more sophisticated and balanced analysis of the same phenomenon. Jay Dolan, *The Immigrant Church* (Baltimore, 1977), performs the same service for the Roman Catholic Church, an institution that owes much of its peculiarly American character to Irish immigrants and their descendants. William Leonard Joyce, *Editors and Ethnicity: A History of the Irish American Press, 1848–1883*, discusses the critical position of newspaper editors in formulating Irish-American identity and culture. Michael F. Funchion, ed., *Irish-American Voluntary Organizations*, (Westport, Conn., 1984), provides an intensive look at the myriad ethnic, benevolent, and cultural institutions through which millions of Americans have discovered and expressed their "Irishness." Drawing much of his material from the Chicago experience, Edward M. Levine, *The Irish and Irish Politicians* (South Bend, Ind., 1966), explores the mutually reinforcing relationship between Hibernian politics and the American political system.

Finally, several works examine the continuing symbiotic relationship between Hibernian Americans and the Old Sod and its role in the formation of ethnic identity and nationalism. William D'Arcy, *The Fenian Movement in the United States, 1858–1886* (Washington, D.C., 1947), discusses the rise and fall of the American-based movement to launch an invasion to liberate Ireland during the U.S. Civil War and its eventual defeat by the British. Florence E. Gibson, *The Attitudes of the New York Irish Toward State and National Affairs, 1848–1892* (New York, 1951), examines their reaction to such nineteenth century issues as the Know-Nothing movement, the Tweed Ring, the Grant era, Grover Cleveland, and Tammany Hall. Thomas N. Brown, *Irish-American Nationalism, 1870–1890* (Philadelphia, 1966), analyzes the critical role of the Fenians and similar efforts to influence events in Ireland on the formation of hyphenated nationalism in the United States. Dennis Clark, *Irish Blood: Northern Ireland and the American Conscience* (Port Washington, N.Y., 1976), demonstrates that the lingering tragedy of the six northern counties continues to fuel that same nationalism to the present day. David Noel Doyle, *Irish-Americans: Native Rights and National Empires: The Structure, Drives and Attitudes of the Catholic Minority in the Decade of Expansion, 1880–1901* (New York, 1976), contends that by the turn of the century, the Irish Catholic community had matured to the point where they divided between traditionalists and Americanizers over a variety of issues involving American expansion. For an interpretive overview of two centuries of Irish-American interaction by two dozen prominent scholars, see *America and Ireland, 1776–1976: The American Identity and the Irish Connection. The Proceedings of the United States Bicentennial Conference of Cumann Merriman, Ennis, August, 1976* (Westport, Conn., 1980), edited by David Noel Doyle and Owen Dudley Edwards.

5

Scandinavian-Americans

John Robert Christianson

Scandinavian acculturation in America was not a one-way street of assimilation into a dominant Anglo-American community. It was rather, a process of fragmentation into a variety of ethnic communities, each with its own particular identity and institutions. These localized communities varied considerably, and they all changed as time passed. A broader ethnic identity finally emerged out of the very process of assimilation, so that as the Scandinavian-American communities became more "American," they came to consider themselves more "Scandinavian."

Look at any ethnic group within this nation of nations and you will find a nation in miniature, composed of numerous subgroups that differ from one another by social class, regional origins, religion, time of arrival in America, or other factors. Scandinavians in America, like other American ethnic groups, shared this diversity from the very beginning. The America into which they came was also a place of great cultural diversity.

COLONIAL SETTLEMENT

Their Viking ancestors had established colonies on Greenland around 985, and on Newfoundland before the year 1000.[1] The Greenland settlements lasted five hundred years. This was longer than any other Scandinavian settlement in the New World until the present, but not long enough to establish links with later European colonies in America. The culture of Scandinavian Greenland fossilized into patterns that were unable to survive

Copyright © 1990 by J. R. Christianson

the late medieval crisis, and the settlements vanished during the last half of the fifteenth century.[2]

Less than two hundred years later, in 1638, Finnish and Swedish colonists established New Sweden on the Delaware. They brought two distinct ways of life to America. The Swedish colonists were mainly peasant farmers, soldiers, and former estate administrators who built permanent communities along or near the Delaware. The Finnish colonists, on the other hand, were backwoodsmen with a mobile wilderness culture that was admirably preadapted to American frontier conditions.[3] The Finns got on well with the Lenape (Delaware) Indians, who were also slash-and-burn farmers and enjoyed taking sauna baths. They added maize to their high-yielding Finnish ryes, and the Indians learned splint basketry from them. A new physical environment also caused some cultural change among the Scandinavians. They did not use skis, for example, on the American frontier.

The first effective colonial settlement in a region can establish a cultural pattern that more numerous groups will pick up as they arrive. This was largely the case in the Middle Atlantic region. English Quakers, German sectarians, and Scotch-Irish Prebysterians who arrived in the late seventeenth and eighteenth centuries were met by Swedes and Finns as well as Lenape. Those who moved to the frontier put on the Finnish fur caps and buckskins, picked up Finnish woodsmens' lore, learned how to build the Finnish type of log structures using broadaxe and adze, and adopted the Finnish practice of swidden agriculture with frequent movement to new clearings. At the same time, the scattered Finnish, German, and Swedish frontier families shifted to speaking English. In this way, a syncretic Midland frontier culture emerged, English in its language, largely Scandinavian in its material culture, and adopted by settlers of diverse racial and ethnic backgrounds. By the nineteenth century, this culture was widely diffused, and the colonial Scandinavian log cabin had become a powerful symbol of American frontier values.

The Scandinavian colonists had come to America with dissimilar backgrounds, and they were fragmented even more by the process of acculturation. Along the Delaware, they still spoke Swedish in the late eighteenth century and still imported their Lutheran clergymen from Sweden, though the Scandinavians of the frontier had long since switched to English. Other Scandinavian colonists along the Hudson had learned to speak Dutch.[4] In Pennsylvania and North Carolina, Scandinavian Moravians assimilated into the predominantly German language and customs of the Moravian colonies.[5] In virtually every seaport of North America were scattered middle-class Scandinavian colonists. They were numerous enough in Philadelphia to form a Scandinavian Society in 1768, and they were among the early pillars of the Lutheran congregation in New York.[6] Generally, however, they assimilated without much trace into the local colonial society. As a colonial minority group, they had little choice.

By the second or third generation, Scandinavian-American colonists were speaking Dutch, German, English, and in a few communities, Swedish. Under these circumstances, little could remain of a shared Scandinavian ethnicity. For Scandinavian Americans, colonization had already become a process of cultural fragmentation.

SCANDINAVIA IMMIGRATION TO 1865

The one common characteristic of all Scandinavian-Americans is their origin in Scandinavia, where the five modern nations of Denmark, Finland, Iceland, Norway and Sweden were emerging during the early nineteenth century. The Scandinavian economy was still pre-industrial in 1815, but the transition to a modern society had begun. During the next half-century, the population of Scandinavia doubled, transportation networks were modernized, and crises of underproduction became increasingly rare. When they did occur, as in the famine years of 1849–50 in Norway and 1866–69 in Finland and Sweden, the result would be a surge of emigration, not demographic catastrophe.

The landowning peasantry was an important class in Scandinavia.[7] Literacy was high and rising, and the more prosperous peasants were increasingly assertive in politics. Class lines remained sharp, however, and the peasant elite rankled under the condescension of their social superiors. As the traditional order of Scandinavian society gradually collapsed, these upwardly mobile peasants helped to shape a more individualistic and dynamic world. The old customary and communal forces of social cohesion gave way to a welter of new voluntary associations. Many of them were religious. The all-encompassing Lutheran state church remained in place, but below its surface, revival movements led by literate peasants gave vigorous expression to the drive for a transformed religious and social order.

Scandinavian emigrants of this era came largely from this active, well-to-do, educated, and dissatisfied peasant elite. Numerous combinations of religious, political, and economic discontent pushed them to leave, so they were a varied and fragmented group from the beginning. Some hoped to reestablish the vanishing world of their ancestors on the American frontier, while others dreamed of diverse new and better worlds. A few examples will illustrate how some of these groups developed their own particular community institutions and identity in America.

Nineteenth-century Scandinavian mass emigration began in the summer of 1825, when a party of fifty-two Quakers and Haugean Lutherans purchased a single-masted sloop of thirty-nine tons, the *Restaurationen*, and set out from Stavanger, Norway, for America. They had an English-speaking guide, and their contacts with American Quakers helped them to sell their ship and cargo in New York harbor, and to find land in western New York state.

The "Sloopers" were coastal people who were used to contacts with foreigners. Their small numbers, open-mindedness, and liberal religious views eased assimilation into the local English-speaking community. At the same time, their letters home began the process of pull toward a specific Scandinavian settlement in America. In 1836, two more ships containing a total of 167 immigrants arrived from Stavanger.[8] These people, together with some of the Sloopers, followed the flow of Americans heading toward the prairies of northern Illinois.

Most of their neighbors in the Fox River valley of Illinois were English-speaking, but the Norwegian language remained alive because of the steady flow of new immigration. In general, however, the Fox River settlers assimilated to American ways with comparative ease. In particular, this settlement came to be characterized by a diversity of beliefs reflecting American religious pluralism and their own revivalistic background. Some of the Norwegians attended Mormon river baptisms or Methodist tent meetings, while others remained Quakers, pietistic Haugean Lutherans, or even liturgical Lutherans.

Meanwhile, the pull was spreading into different parts of Norway. Two wandering sheep traders, Ole and Ansten Nattestad, came out of the mountains to buy stock in the coastal lowlands around Stavanger. There they heard for the first time about the land called America.[9] They took the news into the high valleys of Telemark, Numedal, and Setesdal. In 1837, a clan of over fifty mountain people left Telemark for America, and others followed in 1839. Economic stress was the main push, and the rich land of the Fox River valley was their specific destination.

When they arrived in Illinois, they were overwhelmed by the richness of the land—and shocked by the religious variety. To them, Fox River was a hornet's nest of heresy. These mountain people might not have been overly pious, but they were innately conservative, suspicious of foreign ways, and therefore stubbornly loyal to the Church of Norway. Moreover, the dialect they spoke was quite different from that of the Stavanger region. These differing cultural values led to the fragmentation of the Norwegian immigrant community.

The mountain clansmen did not settle in the Fox River valley. They headed north, toward the Wisconsin frontier, where they established their own settlements at places like Muskego, Jefferson Prairie, and Koshkonong. Their Scandinavian mountaineer background preadapted them to success on the American frontier. They were the ones who introduced skis to North America, and they moved with great speed across the winter snows, outrunning deer.[10] By 1843–44, they were organizing Lutheran congregations to be the central institution in each of their communities and even calling middle-class clergymen from Norway to duplicate the rituals and social hierarchies of the Old World.[11] Their settlements were close-knit, compact, conservative and unified in religion. For a long time, they maintained their Norwegian mountaineer speech and values.

The Mormons were equally close-knit but far different in their religious beliefs. In 1839, the Latter-Day Saints under their prophet, Joseph Smith, had settled in Nauvoo, Illinois. Mormon missionaries fanned across the prairies. Some Norwegians in the Fox River settlement attended Mormon meetings and became converts. In 1844, Joseph Smith was assassinated. Two years later, when the Mormons began their long trek to Utah Territory, Scandinavians were among them. The Scandinavians became active participants in the process of ethnogenesis that created the Mormon culture of Deseret. Their extensive kinship networks, predeliction for organized community cooperation, and strong interests in education and the arts reinforced emergent Mormon values and institution. The primary identity of these Scandinavian-American Mormons was always religious, and they were ostracized by other Scandinavians from the moment of conversion. The mixed communities of Danish, Norwegian and Swedish Mormons in the Sanpete Valley lived in isolation from other Scandinavian-Americans, recruiting new members directly from Scandinavia by means of missionary activity. Their institutions became those common to the Mormon empire, and they shifted rather quickly to the use of English. Religion, rather than regional background, gave them their particular identity and institutions. At the same time, by dividing them from their fellow Scandinavian-Americans, it led to further fragmentation of the Scandinavian-American population.

The same was true of the Janssonists. In the Swedish provinces of Uppland and Hälsingland during the 1840s, popular religious ferment centered around Erik Jansson, a layman whose prophetic message was perfectionist and utopian. In 1846, fleeing prison and persecution, Erik Jansson came to America, and 1,200 to 1,500 of his disciples followed within a year. At Bishop Hill on the Illinois prairies, not far from Nauvoo and the Fox River settlement, they founded a communal utopia under the dictatorial leadership of the prophet and his successors. By 1858, the Janssonists held 14,000 acres in common, besides mills, factories, a plain house of worship, and handsome communal residences and dining halls built in the style of Swedish manor houses. The Janssonists worked in gangs, worshipped, sang, and conducted all their affairs in the Swedish language.

Erik Jansson was assassinated in 1850. Within less than twenty years, the Bishop Hill colony had destroyed itself with acrimonious lawsuits. Most of the colonists moved away, vanishing into the mainstream of Swedish America. For as long as it survived, however, it was a place with institutions and a collective identity quite unlike any other Scandinavian-American community.

By 1850, Scandinavians were arriving in Minnesota. Here the old and new Scandinavian-Americans crossed paths and discovered that they were strangers. Immigrants from Sweden arrived in the territory as early as 1850, and they organized their first Swedish Lutheran congregations in Minnesota. Gunnar Thompson was of Delaware Swedish descent.[12] He had migrated with a group of Lutherans from Columbiana County, Ohio, descendants of Delaware Swedes and Pennsylvania Germans. This community located in Rice County, close to the extensive settlements of recent Swedish and Norwegian immigrants in Goodhue County. Although they were also Lutherans, the recent immigrants discovered that they had little in common with the Americanized Ohioans, and vice versa. Different times of arrival in America had turned them into different peoples.

Nineteenth-century Finnish emigration began in the early 1860s. The first Finns came by way of northern Norway, where the population was a mixture of Norwegians, Finns, and Sami (Lapps). American recruiters in 1863–64 found both Finns and Norwegians who were willing to leave the declining copper mines at Kaafjord. Some of the Finns settled in the mining community of Hancock, Michigan, but others went into farming on the Minnesota frontier.[13]

They spoke a language completely different from the other Scandinavian tongues, and they tended to adhere to the Laestadian revival, which more orthodox Scandinavian Lutherans considered to be wildly emotional and fanatical. These differences strained relations with other Scandinavians and led them to establish their own communities and churches.[14]

On the eve of the Civil War, there were over 70,000 native-born Americans of Scandinavian ancestry. Small islands of Scandinavians were scattered across the face of North America, from upstate New York, old New Sweden, the Moravian and Appalachian Midlands and South, to the Midwest, Texas, Utah Territory, and California. Some of these settlements were two centuries old and had lost their original ethnic character. In all areas, local variations in the patterns of cultural continuity and acculturation gave each settlement a character of its own, differentiating it from its non-Scandinavian neighbors, but also from other Scandinavian-American settlements and from the Scandinavian homeland. It was a fragmented world of isolated communities, each developing in its own direction.

The greatest density of Scandinavian settlement was in the Upper Mississippi basin: northern Illinois and Iowa, southern Wisconsin and Minnesota. In urban areas like Chicago, Milwaukee, Madison, the river towns of the Upper Mississippi, and in many rural areas, small Scandinavian communities were scattered among a wide variety of other peoples and tongues. A Scandinavian-American mainstream was taking shape in this region by 1860, composed of these numerous dispersed, local communities.

Jon Gjerde described the rural communities of immigrants from Balestrand in the Norwegian district of Sogn.[15] Although the gap between land-owning farmers and landless cottagers was widening in nineteenth-century Balestrand, the expanding rural economy eased household formation. Earlier marriages, larger families, and soaring illegitimacy rates created concerns about moral decline that found expression around 1846 in a pietistic revival, but this in turn brought a division in community values. Meanwhile, farmers used the abundant cottager labor supply to shift toward more profitable market production, though the risk and costs were considerable.

Emigration from Balestrand began as a movement of prosperous farming families made insecure by the rapidity of change, and of younger sons faced with downward mobility into the cottager class. These early Balestrand immigrants settled on Spring Prairie, Wisconsin, in 1845. Their networks of family and friends were intact, and they soon established a Lutheran church as the center of community life. But not everything was the same. The land-to-labor ratio on the Wisconsin frontier was the reverse of Balestrand—labor was scarce, land abundant—so they had to change their ways of farming. The family, not cottagers, became the source of farm labor, resulting in immense flocks of children, and there was also a shift from labor-intensive animals to grain production.

In 1853, a Haugean revival on Spring Prairie brought a schism in community values between the pietistic Haugeans and those who adhered to the more traditional Norwegian Lutheran Synod. Religious ideology now became the basis of community fragmentation and reformation. In 1854, the Spring Prairie pietists sold their land and moved to Minnesota, where they founded a Haugean rural community at Arendahl. They established ties with other Midwestern communities of Haugeans from Sogn, while the Spring Prairie people had links to other Norwegian Synod communities.

Similar forces were at work throughout the Midwestern mainstream of Scandinavian America on the eve of the Civil War, linking and then differentiating local communities in an endless dialectic. Groups left older settlements to establish daughter settlements further west, but they brought along their ties of kinship and friendship, and frequently also kept up their connections with the older settlement. Circuit-riding Lutheran pastors and itinerant lay preachers shared in the leadership of five, six, or more communities. Larger networks of pastors and congregations met in annual Lutheran synods, from the low-church Augustana and Eielsen's synods to the liturgical Norwegian Synod. Newspapers in the Dano-Norwegian and Swedish literary languages began to link the scattered Scandinavian-American settlements in the 1850s. Many of the Scandinavian immigrants of this era were political activists who quickly became involved in American local and county politics, building on the base of their fellow countrymen.

Around 1860, midwestern Scandinavians also made their first ventures into American higher education. In Chicago and Decorah, Iowa, they established bilingual Lutheran colleges in an attempt to train their own community leaders. Though small, these institutions strove to maintain the academic rigor of the Old World. At Luther College in Decorah, for example, the curriculum went far beyond bilingualism: For over fifty years, Latin,

Greek, Hebrew, and the three "American" languages, Norwegian, English, and German, were all required for graduation.[16] The goals of such an education were clearly cosmopolitan and pluralistic, not local and particular.

Within the Scandinavian-American mainstream in the Midwest, there was still no clear sense of ethnic identity on the eve of the Civil War. Elite groups like pastors and journalists had a cosmopolitan education and promoted a common "Scandinavian" identity that reflected the pan-Scandinavian movement of mid-nineteenth century Scandinavia. This coincided in a rough way with the perception of other Americans, who could not really see the difference between a Dane, a Norwegian, and a Swede. The average Scandinavian-Americans of this era simply accepted their ethnic identity as a fact of life. They did not usually think of themselves in national terms as Norwegians or Swedes, but in terms of their dialect, social class, religion, or regional subculture. Their communities were organized the same way, not on national lines. They were Langelanders, Telemarkings, Janssonists, or Mormons, not Danes, Swedes, or Scandinavians. They also perceived their Anglo-American neighbors as a distinct people, called "Americans" or "Yankees." To the Scandinavians, "Americanization" did not mean assimilation to the culture or structured communities of the Yankees. It simply meant learning enough about American institutions and the English language to participate in public life. In that sense, they were strongly in favor of it, and it did not disrupt their own sense of community.[17]

THE CIVIL WAR

The Civil War brought a slump in Scandinavian immigration. At the same time, the Dakota War in Minnesota stopped the westward movement of the frontier. During the war, substantial numbers in the Scandinavian regiment, the Fifteenth Wisconsin, saw heavy action under Colonel Hans Christian Heg of Muskego.

The war added two new dimensions to the meaning of Americanization: participation in a common American cause, and creation of Scandinavian-American heroes. Ethnicity and patriotism remained quite compatible in this era. Scandinavian-Americans could be loyal Americans while living in ethnic communities with a language, customs, social networks, and institutions of their own. In fact, the very battle cry of the Fifteenth Wisconsin Regiment was in Norwegian: *For Gud oo vort Land* ("For God and Our Country").

SCANDINAVIA FROM 1865 TO 1890

The population of Scandinavia doubled in the years 1815–65. These masses of young people were absorbed into a rural economy through the explosive growth of the cottager class. By 1870, cottagers made up roughly

40 percent of the total population of Norway. They squatted on land belonging to a farm or estate, paid their rent by working for their landlord without wages, and subsisted as farm laborers, lumberjacks, fishermen, rural craftsmen, and small-scale tenant farmers. Their conditions were miserable. To the peasant farmers, however, they were a source of cheap labor that allowed modernization and increased market production.[18]

Then came the flood of cheap foreign grain of the late 1860s, brought to Scandinavia by new global transportation networks. Small coastal towns with sailing fleets were devastated, and Scandinavia was the most strongly maritime region in Europe. Agricultural traditions were undercut and destroyed by foreign competition. Regional underproduction compounded the crisis of global overproduction. Crop failures in the years 1866, 1867, and 1868 drove Finnish and Swedish peasant families to emigrate in great numbers. The first parties of Icelanders came to America around the same time. Scandinavian mass emigration was under way.

There was a growing political consciousness. Virtually all younger Scandinavians were literate, and they were the ones who emigrated. Women, cottagers, and then workers struggled to enter the political arena. Parts of Scandinavia under foreign rule—Finland, Iceland, Norway, and North Schleswig after 1864—developed assertive, extremely resilient national identities as a form of resistance, and emigrants from these regions carried it abroad.[19]

The early 1880s, when Scandinavian emigration peaked, was a time of rapid urban growth and early industrialization. All segments of the Scandinavian population were disrupted and dissatisfied. The emigration included cottagers, sailors, marginal farmers, and the politically oppressed, but also a "brain drain" of skilled craftsmen, machinists, engineers, clergymen, physicians, shipowners, and others who could not find opportunities in the constricted, developing economies of Scandinavia.

Many migrated by stages, moving first to an urban area and then overseas. Women could often find jobs in the Scandinavian cities, and the more highly urbanized areas like Denmark consequently sent out a preponderance of male emigrants. Cottager families frequently sent one member overseas to earn passage money for the others. One-third of the emigrants departing from Gothenburg in the early 1880s traveled on prepaid tickets sent from America. Young single men and women made up a larger percentage of Scandinavian immigrants, and remigration, permanent or temporary, became much more common.

By 1890, over 10 percent of all foreign-born in America were Scandinavians. They numbered nearly a million, not counting their American-born descendants.

These boom years of Scandinavian immigration came to an abrupt end with the panic of 1893 and the hard times that followed. By 1903, however, the flow of Scandinavian immigration was renewed. It reached high levels again in the first decade of the twentieth century. Scandinavians were a part of the "new immigration" of that era, as they had been of the older trans-Atlantic movements.

SCANDINAVIANS IN AMERICA, 1865–1914

Such a varied group as the Scandinavian immigrants of the 1870s and 1880s could hardly be expected to have similar goals or similar patterns of acculturation. Engineers and other professionals pursued their careers in the cities, industrial, and mining areas of America. Some of them assimilated rapidly into the American middle classes, but there were so many of them in cities like New York, Chicago, and Minneapolis that they maintained their middle-class Scandinavian social patterns and even established Scandinavian-American professional organizations.

Many social layers of Scandinavians came to American cities. Sometimes whole communities were reestablished in the New World. Sailors, skippers, shipwrights, ships' chandlers, and shipowners from the devastated Scandinavian coastal towns established durable, well-integrated waterfront colonies in Brooklyn, San Francisco, Milwaukee, Manitowoc, and other American port cities.[20] Skilled Scandinavian machinists and other craftsmen clustered in Boston, New York, Philadelphia, Chicago, Omaha, and many smaller industrial cities including Hartford (Connecticut), Jamestown (New York), Moline (Illinois), Racine (Wisconsin), and Rockford (Illinois). Immigrant clergymen, journalists, physicians, pharmacists, merchants, and politicians pursued careers in urban Scandinavian communities among former cottagers, farmers and town people now working as journalists, carpenters, masons and common laborers. In every city, there were many diverse Scandinavian communities, not one, by the end of the 1880s. The pan-Scandinavian communities of an earlier era became segregated along regional and social lines. For the masses, the process of Americanization was becoming a process of urbanization.[21]

These new immigrants came from a Scandinavia far different from earlier times, and their America was different from that of the rural pioneers, who still lived their lives not far from the burgeoning cities. The community institutions of the urban settlements were saloons, clubs, theaters, mutual aid associations, choral societies, marching societies, trade or professional organizations, orphanages, and deaconess hospitals. All of these, and even the pattern of urban church life, differentiated these new communities from the older rural settlements, augmenting the fragmention of Scandinavian-American life.

Assimilation into non-English communities was another process that fragmented the Scandinavians in America. Some assimilated into the large German Protestant communities that were scattered throughout urban and rural America. Lutheran culture, despite its many variations, gave Germans and

Scandinavians so much in common that it was sometimes easier for Scandinavians to assimilate into German-American than into Anglo-American life.[22] There was also a great deal of assimilation between different Scandinavian communities in America. Danes arrived later than Norwegians and assimilated in large numbers into the well-established Norwegian-American communities. By the 1890s, perhaps 10 percent of all Norwegian-Americans were actually of Danish origin. As these Danes, who were generally more urbane and liberal, began to play their role in shaping some Norwegian-American communities, those communities were differentiated from others that lacked a Danish minority.[23]

Intermarriage was one factor that facilitated interethnic assimilation. There was a predominance of unmarried males among Danish and Finnish immigrants and among all Scandinavian immigrants on the West Coast. This led to higher rates of exogamy, especially with other Scandinavians and with Germans. It also helps to explain why Danes—aside from the nationally conscious North Schleswigers and Grundtvigian Lutherans—assimilated more rapidly than other Scandinavians, though not always into the Anglo-American community. In general, Scandinavians in America were slow to marry outside their ethnic group and social class. When they did so, they inevitably moved to the margins of their ethnic community.

Rural areas still exerted a powerful attraction to Scandinavian immigrants of the 1870s and 1880s. Danes, Finns, and Icelanders established rural settlements of their own. Norwegians and Swedes immigrated to well-established ethnic settlements in Illinois, Wisconsin, eastern Iowa, and Minnesota.

The newcomers worked as farm laborers, seasonal lumberjacks, railroad laborers and tenant farmers. There were so many of them that the process of assimilation slowed down and backed up. Scandinavian-American communities of the Midwest became more Scandinavian in the 1880s than they had been in the 1860s. At the same time, newcomers could learn the language and lore of America in the older ethnic settlements. It was a strange, unsettling experience, even among relatives and others from the same home area. The two patterns of change among the immigrants—rapid acculturation and its opposite, fossilization—both had the effect of differentiating the immigrant communities from the Old World. One Danish immigrant who arrived alone in central Iowa around Christmas of 1888 recalled,

I was transplanted into an entirely new world where even the landscape was different. The people spoke a language I could not understand, and even when they spoke Danish, the trend of conversation was along lines of which I had no knowledge. The houses, the stores, and even the streets were different and unfamiliar. The food we ate was entirely different; while much better food was served than I was used to, yet it was unfamiliar. The table manners and the actions of people were all strange.[24]

Different times of arrival in America had transformed culture so that these immigrants from the same Old World class and community found themselves to be strangers sitting at a common table.

After one to five years in the older settlements, the rural newcomers either went to the city to seek a job, or they loaded their possessions into prairie schooners or railroad boxcars and set off for the frontier. Each new settlement still had a core of people from a single Scandinavian family, village, or region, both newcomers and younger people who had grown up in America, but the pioneers of the 1870s and 1880s were not like those of earlier decades. Many of them were former cottagers or poor, marginal farmers, and many had lived for a time in the urban slums. On the plains of Kansas, Nebraska, and the Dakotas they met a harsh environment suited to wheat ranching but not traditional Scandinavian mixed farming. Railroads provided access to seemingly insatiable global markets, but at the price of a fluctuating market and economic dependence. The physical environment, economic situation, and social origins of the plains farmers all differentiated them from the older Scandinavian settlements.

They also seemed to be more progressive in their politics. Back in the 1930s, when the general tendency was to equate immigrants with bomb-throwing radicals, the Scandinavian-American historian Marcus Lee Hansen had asserted that immigrants in general were actually a conservative force in American politics.[25] Jon Wefald challenged this view in 1971. He compared Norwegian-American voting records and the editorial position of Norwegian and English-language newspapers in the same localities, and he concluded that Norwegian-Americans of the late nineteenth century were "unrelentingly progressive, frequently radical," and consistently left of center in American politics.[26] David Brye's study of Scandinavian voting behavior in Wisconsin from 1900–50 generally supported Wefald's thesis. Brye demonstrated that the Progressive movement drew its strength from rising ethnic groups including Norwegians and other Scandinavians, not from declining Yankees, as Richard Hofstadter had believed. Brye came to the conclusion that Joseph McCarthy would not have been elected to the U.S. Senate in 1946 if everyone in Wisconsin had voted like the Scandinavian communities.[27] Carl H. Chrislock's study of Norwegian voters in Minnesota, on the other hand, led him to challenge the Wefald thesis. He found the Populist movement of the 1890s and the later Nonpartisan League and Farmer-Labor movements to be stronger on the plains of the Red River valley than in the traditional Norwegian-American areas of southeastern Minnesota. He saw this as a difference shaped by regional factors rather than by different Norwegian backgrounds, and he doubted that Norwegian-American voters in general were left of the center.[28] Sten Carlsson found that Norwegians were exceptionally active in American politics, and that Scandinavians in the upper Midwest region wielded political influence far beyond their numbers.[29]

In addition to politicians, there were many Scandinavian voices among the spokesmen for reform at the turn of the century. The Industrial Workers of the World songwriter and martyr, Joe Hill, was a Swedish immigrant. The New York journalist Jacob A. Riis, and his Chicago friend, the urban planner, Jens Jensen, were both natives of Denmark. Thorstein B. Veblen, the iconoclastic economist, was born in Wisconsin of Norwegian immigrant parents. All of them drew on their Scandinavian backgrounds in looking for solutions to broad American problems. They expressed an emerging Scandinavian-American stance on public issues and social policy that was fragmented but decidedly at odds with the Anglo-American mainstream.

Despite the unifying institutions of politics, the press, the church, and personal ties between local communities, the fragmentation of Scandinavian America continued in the later years of the nineteenth century and beyond. Some of the rural immigrants of this era arrived with capital and skills. North Schleswig Danes, for example, fled for political, not economic reasons, and they came from one of the most modern agricultural areas in Scandinavia. One of them brought the first cream separator to America. Scandinavian immigrants of this type headed for the older settlements or for California and took the lead in establishing modern dairies, greenhouses, egg and poultry farms, fruit and vegetable operations, and various kinds of rural cooperatives. The misery and hardship of the plains was seldom their lot. At the same time, Mormon immigrants continued to head for Utah, and some Scandinavians went to the mining frontiers of the West and Alaska. Fishermen from western and northern Norway discovered the waters of Tacoma Bay and Alaska late in the century. People from these fishing regions of Norway had not emigrated previously, but now they flocked to the Pacific Northwest, where they formed communities apart from the Norwegian farmers and lumberjacks coming out from the Midwest. As ever new and more varied Scandinavian-American communities came into existence, the process of fragmentation continued.

By the end of the nineteenth century, the total Scandinavian community in America was larger, more diverse and fragmented than ever before. The older communities of the Midwest had developed persistent local cultures combining American informality and technology with archaic Scandinavian customs, dialects and mentalities. Newer communities reflected a more urbane, highly educated and secularized Scandinavia. Scandinavian cooperative, socialist and radical ideas flourished on the northern plains, in Chicago, and in the mines and mills of the North and West. Utopian and planned communities multiplied around the turn of the century. Finnish socialists started a utopia on an island in the Northwest. The Swedish Mission Covenant established successful, carefully planned suburban communities near Chicago and in California. The liberal, nationalistic Danish Lutheran Grundtvigians laid out farming communities, complete with churches and folk schools, in Minnesota, Texas and California. Once established, these highly integrated communities were resistant to assimilation.

So were the larger settlements with a wide range of social, religious, educational, political, and economic institutions. These large settlements were in urban, small town, and rural areas.

An example of the density of Scandinavian-American institutions in this era can be found in the Norwegian settlements of northeastern Iowa and southern Minnesota. These settlements were established on the frontier around 1850 and comprised from one-third to one-half of the total population in six contiguous counties by 1900. There were over eighty Norwegian Lutheran churches in these six counties, in addition to a scattering of Norwegian Methodist congregations. Services were mainly in Norwegian. Norwegian-language church schools supplemented the common school education. In one town, Decorah, Iowa, there was a Norwegian Lutheran elementary school, academy, and college, offering bilingual education in English and Norwegian from first grade through four years of college. Most of the county seat towns and many of other towns of the region had Norwegian-speaking merchants, craftsmen, bankers, physicians and other professionals, and Norwegian specialty shops such as bookstores, groceries and apothecaries. Norwegian-language newspapers were published in Decorah and in nearby LaCrosse, Wisconsin. Decorah was the seat of Winneshiek County, and all of the county officials were of Norwegian descent, as were the county's representatives in the state legislature and the Congress of the United States. The situation was similar in a couple of the other countries. In addition, there were innumerable Norwegian-language social circles, women's organizations, choral societies, mutual insurance companies, and other voluntary organizations in the region. In Decorah, there was a large Norwegian-language library, two publishing houses specializing in Norwegian publications, and a nascent Norwegian-American museum. Besides a newspaper and half a dozen journals in Norwegian, calendars, songbooks, poetry, stories, novels and nonfiction in Norwegian were published in Decorah. In short, although the common schools were conducted in English and there were many other ethnic and linguistic groups living in the region, it was entirely possible for whole communities in this region to conduct virtually all the affairs of rural and small-town life in the Norwegian language. This was cradle-to-grave ethnicity.

The same was found in many parts of Scandinavian America around the year 1900—the Danish and Swedish settlements of western Iowa and Nebraska, the Finnish mining towns of northern Minnesota and Michigan, the Swedish side of Jamestown or Rockford, "Kringle Town" in Racine, Bay Ridge in Brooklyn, Humboldt Park in Chicago, Seven Corners in Minneapolis, Ballard in Seattle, Solvang in southern California, Sanpete County in Utah, and many other scattered places. Every place was different. Some of these communities were two or three generations old, and their ethnic life seemed to grow stronger and more firmly rooted in their own local patterns with each passing year. There was no reason to think that it would not last forever. By 1910, there were over three million first- and second-generation Scandinavians in America.

National networks of contact between these communities were also growing stronger. For the first time, a sense of national Scandinavian-American identity began to superimpose itself upon the diversity of local identities. A few Scandinavian-language newspapers achieved national circulation. Rail transportation facilitated national gatherings of Scandinavian-Americans. Church conventions, choral festivals and Scandinavian-American patriotic events turned into mass meetings. Ski-jumping meets and other athletic events, conventions of ethnic professional and social organizations drew together Scandinavian-American national pride. The dramatic separation of Norway from Sweden in 1905 reverberated through the Swedish and Norwegian communities of America. A patriotic national consciousness began to overpower the particular social, regional, and religious identities of earlier years. More and more, the Scandinavians in American began to identify with broader national ethnic communities and think of themselves as Danish-Americans, Finnish-Americans, Norwegian-Americans, or Swedish-Americans.

On May 17, 1914, Norwegian-Americans celebrated the centennial of the Norwegian constitution with parades, picnics, music and mass meetings in many cities. Hundreds made steamship pilgrimages to Norway that spring and summer. Many were still in Europe when the First World War broke out in August.

SCANDINAVIAN-AMERICANS AND WORLD WAR I

The outbreak of World War I led to intense attacks on unassimilated immigrants in the United States. President Woodrow Wilson and former President Theodore Roosevelt were among those who criticized "hyphenism." At the same time, immigrants came to be associated with political radicalism. Scandinavians were among those who came under attack. Swedish-Americans and Lutheran clergy were called disloyal.[30] Finnish-Americans were branded as "non-Nordic" radicals and maligned for their role in the bitter Michigan copper strike of 1913–14.

During the height of the war in 1917–18, attacks on hyphenism approached collective hysteria. One Minnesota judge, John F. McGee, called for "firing squads" for German and Swedish Americans. Minnesota established a state Commission of Public Safety to ferret out disloyalty, with Judge McGee as a member. Similar campaigns took place in other states. Foreign language newspapers were censored, and the editors of a Finnish-language socialist paper in Oregon were arrested. Under this extremist pressure, Scandinavian-Americans did all they could to give public evidence of their patriotism. In 1918, without the support of legislation, Governor William L. Harding of Iowa issued a proclamation banning the public use of all languages other than English. This went too far. Strong protests arose from many ethnic communities in Iowa, not least from the North Schleswig Danes who had fled similar persecution under Prussian rule.

Before things got better, however, they got worse. On the heels of the most virulent attacks on hyphenism came the "red scare," touched off by the outbreak of the Bolshevik Revolution in Russia. In Scandinavia, a socialist revolution was barely aborted in Norway, and civil war raged in Finland.[31] When the Finnish Reds were defeated, they fled, some to Russia and some to America. Their squabbles on the far left caused further ethnic fragmentation but had little effect on the Scandinavian-American mainstream, which was loyally and doggedly struggling to survive the nativist and right-wing attacks.

A Scandinavian ethnic preponderance in many small towns and rural areas of the Midwest was able to cushion the worst effects of nativist attacks, but in a general sense those attacks proved fatal. The cultural self-confidence and ethnic institutions of Scandinavian America never really recovered. Many Scandinavian-Americans bear the psychological scars of that era to the present day. The dream of a permanent Scandinavian-American sub-culture was shattered.

THE LAST HURRAH

Scandinavian America survived. There was a postwar backlash against nativist extremism. "We demand recognition as a part of the nation," wrote a Minnesotan of Scandinavian descent, "and we will not tolerate being viewed as a flock of strange foreigners because we speak a language besides English."[32] The Scandinavian-American press reached its highest circulation in the 1920s. Family and institutional use of Scandinavian languages picked up, and the flow of immigration was renewed at moderately high levels through the 1920s. Swedes, Finns, and Norwegians continued to maintain high levels of endogamous marriage.

Scandinavian-American literature reached a high point with writers like Waldemar Ager, Enok Mortensen, and O. E. Rölvaag, whose *Giants in the Earth* (1927) became an American best-seller. Immense ethnic festivals like the Norse-American Centennial of 1925 in Minneapolis and the New Sweden Tercentenary of 1938 in Philadelphia attracted the national attention associated with presidential attendance and commemorative postage stamps. All of the small, varied, and scattered Scandinavian outposts of America seemed to be uniting into great national ethnic communities. In Minneapolis in 1925, President Calvin Coolidge even supported the effort to recognize Leif Erikson as the discoverer of America.

An inexorable change in language patterns was part of the shift toward a broader Scandinavian-American ethnic identity. The use of Scandinavian languages in schools and churches declined steadily during the 1920s and 1930s, despite the resistance of nationally conscious groups like Finnish Lutherans, Danish Grundtvigians, and the Swedish Mission Convenant. Many leading Scandinavian-Americans now preferred to express themselves in English. Scandinavian-American organizations were coming into existence on the basis of English. Old loyalties had been reinforced by the innumerable cultural associations of a common language or dialect. The shift to English laid those loyalties to rest forever and allowed a new, broader Scandinavian-American identity to emerge.[33] It also allowed Scandinavian-Americans to make an impact upon the American mainstream. Until the shift to English occurred, a unified Scandinavian-American ethnicity had been unthinkable. Now it seemed inevitable.

Against the background of these paradoxical developments, Marcus Lee Hansen asserted his famous "law" that what the second generation wants to forget, the third generation remembers.[34] In retrospect, it is clear that the changes of the 1920s were shaped more by the developments of the era than by the passage of generations. The shift to English was due to nativist pressures, the decline of immigration, and the almost exclusive use of English in public education, rather than to a cultural generation gap. Some Scandinavian-American families had already exceeded the two-generation limit by maintaining their language and ethnicity for sixty or seventy years, only to switch to English in the face of the great, new obstacles to ethnicity that arose around the time of World War I.

Scandinavian-Americans assimilated linguistically but they remained apart socially.[35] Most of their churches retained an ethnic character. Individuals and communities remained conscious of their ethnic origins. Many Scandinavian-Americans still preferred to socialize and marry within their own ethnic group. Certain habits of daily life still differentiated Scandinavian-Americans from other Americans. There were innumerable variations. An elaborate, solemn formality in personal relationships was so natural to many Scandinavian-Americans that they did not realize it was an ethnic trait. Many Scandinavian-Americans were unaware that the celebration of Christmas Eve was not a universal American practice, or that some ethnic groups preferred to entertain guests "out" instead of at home, or that some well-mannered Americans left the dinner table without thanking the hostess. Scandinavian-Americans, in other words, took their ethnic values for granted without realizing that they were ethnic. This "hidden ethnicity" was expressed in habits of Scandinavian-American daily life and persisted long after the shift from the bilingualism to English monolingualism.

By 1930, Scandinavian immigration was a thing of the past, which meant that the Scandinavian-American communities were on their own. Through the hard times of the 1930s and the World War II era, into the 1950s and beyond, the Scandinavian-American ethnic communities persisted without much self-confidence or hope for the future. The war brought organized relief efforts and renewed feelings of solidarity with the Scandinavian countries, but the effect was temporary. In general, Scandinavian-Americans of these years assumed that their ethnicity was the remnant of a fading past. Around 1960, Scandinavian-American churches and cooperatives finally abandoned their ethnicity and merged with non-Scandinavian organizations.

THE NEW ETHNICITY

The defeatist attitude changed with the "new ethnicity" of the 1970s. For many Scandinavian-Americans, the catalyst was ScanPresence in Minneapolis in the spring of 1973. This conference on the Scandinavian Presence in North America brought together a wide range of leaders from government, industry, cooperatives, the church, and the academic community, representing all five Scandinavian countries and innumerable Scandinavian-American communities. The result was that ethnic pessimism soon gave way to optimism.[36]

Undergraduate majors in Scandinavian studies and junior-year-abroad programs in Scandinavia proliferated during the 1970s and 1980s. Many of these were at private liberal arts colleges founded by Scandinavian-Americans. Undergraduate and graduate programs were offered at major universities. Students in these programs looked to careers in international affairs. Their task would be to maintain ties between two global regions, Scandinavia and North America, which were no longer connected by substantial bilingual Scandinavian-American communities.

Scandinavia and Scandinavian America achieved higher visibility in American cultural life during the 1970s and 1980s. Poets like Robert Bly, Joseph Langland, and Gracia Grindal reflected sensitively on their Scandinavian-American roots. Scandinavian films, the Danish Royal Ballet, and Swedish and Finnish opera were admired by American audiences. Two Swedish films, *The Emigrants* and *The New Land* made Scandinavian-American immigration a theme of mass popular culture. The American humorist, Garrison Keillor, drew on small town Scandinavian-American ethnicity in his tales of Lake Wobegon. In 1982–83, a joint governmental cultural project, "Scandinavia Today," brought modern Scandinavian royalty, art, music, theatrical events, and luxury products to selected American cities.[37] Under the impact of all this, the mainstream cultural identity of states like Minnesota and Washington began to take on a decidedly Scandinavian color. For the first time, a significant number of people began to think of "Scandinavian-American" as their primary ethnic identity.

Institutions like Vesterheim, the Norwegian-American Museum, in Decorah, Iowa (the largest ethnic museum in America), the American-Swedish Historical Museum in Philadelphia, the American Swedish Institute in Minneapolis, the Bishop Hill restoration in Illinois, the Danish Windmill and Danish Immigrant Museum in Elk Horn, Iowa, and the Nordic Heritage

Museum in Seattle, as well as the House of Emigrants in Växjö, Sweden, came into existence or took new vitality in this era.

The "new ethnicity" was obviously far different from the old. Most Americans of Scandinavian descent were not really affected because they no longer had a strong ethnic identity. Some twelve million Americans claimed Scandinavian ancestry in the United States census of 1980. But social and geographical mobility had dispersed most of the urban Scandinavian-American communities, and postwar immigrants in Los Angeles, Chicago, New York, and other cities had little in common with the assimilated Scandinavian Americans. In the dense rural and small town settlements, there had been less geographical mobility and less structural assimilation because of the comparative lack of non-Scandinavian structures. Even in these places, however, most Scandinavian-American ethnicity was now a combination of "hidden ethnicity," ethnic hobby activities, and attendance at ethnic festivals. Visitors from the Scandinavian countries found it all rather strange and not really very Scandinavian.

By the 1980s, conscious Scandinavian-American ethnicity was moving simultaneously along two tracks. One was the track of professional scholarship, diplomacy, and international trade. A few young people entered this track by immersing themselves in academic studies of Scandinavia and spending a year or more in Scandinavia. The other track was that of ethnicity as a leisure-time activity. Scandinavian-American organizations had short courses in genealogy, cooking, music, folk dancing, arts and crafts such as folk painting, woodcarving, embroidery and weaving. They also sponsored group flights that brought Scandinavian-Americans into direct contact with modern Scandinavia.

Both tracks of the new ethnicity were voluntary, which meant that the participants were not necessarily of Scandinavian descent. Many were not. In Minneapolis during the 1970s, for example, a native of Pakistan taught Scandinavian languages, a native of Puerto Rico led a Danish folk dancing group with at least one Chinese-American dancer, and the leading exponent of Scandinavian-American folk music was of East European Jewish background.

The story of Scandinavian-American fragmentation and acculturation is long and complex. Medieval Scandinavians established the first European communities in the New World. Colonial Scandinavians helped to shape the culture of the American frontier. Nineteenth-century Scandinavian immigrants established innumerable widely scattered communities with highly diverse ethnic institutions based on their particular religion, social origins, regional dialect and culture, and reflecting their Scandinavian origins as well as their experiences in the New World. Gradually some of these diverse communities became linked into wider ethnic networks. During the first half of the twentieth century, immigration from Scandinavia virtually ceased and the Scandinavians in America assimilated to the English language. At the same time, they developed a broad, nationalistic sense of ethnic identity. English-speaking Scandinavian-American communities persisted in a half-hidden state until the ethnic revival of the 1970s. By that time, ethnicity was voluntary, and Scandinavian-American ethnic boundaries were no longer community-based or impenetrable. This allowed non-Scandinavians to play leading roles in the "new ethnicity" that restored the optimism and vitality of Scandinavian ethnic life in America.

NOTES

1. Knus J. Krogh, *Viking Greenland* (Copenhagen: National Museum, 1967). Anne Stine Ingstad and Helga Ingstad, *The Norse Discovery of America*, 2 vols. (Oslo: Norwegian University Press, 1985).

2. Gwyn Jones, *A History of the Vikings*, revised edition (New York: Oxford University, 1984), 306–11.

3. Matti E. Kaups, "Finnish Practices in Early Pioneer America: A Short Report," paper delivered October 24, 1985, to *SIMCON III: Scandinavian Immigration Conference*, Luther College, Decorah, Iowa.

4. Torstein Jahr, "Nordmaend i Nieuw-Nederland," *Symra* 5 (1909): 65–79. Torstein Jahr, "Nordmenn i Ny Nederland," *Symra* 9 (1913): 9–34. P. S. Vig, "Danske blandt hollaenderne i Ny Amsterdam (New York) i det 17. og 18. år-hundrede," *Danske i Amerika*, 1:1 (Minneapolis: C. Rasmussen, 1908), 39–45.

5. P. S. Vig, "Danske i brödrekirken i Nordamerika fra 1742," *Danske i Amerika*, 1:1, 46–88.

6. On the 1768 society, see Johannes B. Wist, ed., *Norsk-Amerikanernes festskrift 1914* (Decorah, Iowa: Symra, 1914), 268.

7. Oyvind Osterud, *Agrarian Structure and Peasant Politics in Scandinavia: A Comparative Study of Rural Response to Economic Change* (Oslo: Universitetsforlaget 1978). Sune Akerman, "Theories and Methods of Migration Research," in *From Sweden to America: A History of the Migration*, eds. Harald Runblom and Hans Norman (Minneapolis: University of Minnesota, 1976), 25–32, posits a process of emigration moving through introductory, growth, saturation, and regression phases; the growth phase in Scandinavia was roughly 1836–65.

8. Henry J. Cadbury, "Four Immigrant Shiploads of 1836 and 1837," *Norwegian-American Studies* 2 (1927): 20–52.

9. C. A. Clausen, ed., *A Chronicler of Immigrant Life: Svein Nilsson's Articles in Billed-Magazin, 1868–1870* (Northfield: NAHA, 1938), 42. See also Andres A. Svalestuen, "Emigration from the Community of Tinn, 1837–1907: Demographic, Economic, and Social Background," *Norwegian-American Studies* 29 (1983): 43–88.

10. Clausen, *A Chronicler*, 72. Olaus Fredrik Duus, *Frontier Parsonage: The Letters of Olaus Fredrik Duus, Norwegian Pastor in Wisconsin, 1855–1858*, ed. Theodore C. Blegen, trans. Verdandi Study Club (Northfield: NAHA, 1947), 50. On Norwegian-American skiing, see also John Weinstock, "Sondre Norheim: Folk Hero to Immigrant," *Norwegian-American Studies* 29 (1983): 339–58, and Kenneth O. Bjork, *West of the Great Divide* (Northfield: NAHA, 1958), 274–99.

11. On the "people of condition," a middle-class Scandinavian elite transplanted

to Scandinavian-America see J. R. Christianson, "Literary Traditions of Norwegian-American Women," in *Makers of an American Immigrant Legacy*, ed. Odd S. Lovoll (Northfield: NAHA, 1980), 92–110.

12. Dorris A. Flesner, "The Beginning of English Lutheranism in the Upper Midwest," *The Lutheran Historical Conference Essays and Reports, 1984* 11 (St. Louis, 1986): 43–69.

13. Arnold R. Alanen, "The Norwegian Connection: The Background in Arctic Norway for Early Finnish Emigration to the American Midwest," *Finnish Americana* 6 (1983–84): 23–33. Samuli Onnela, "Emigrationen från Finland till Amerika över Nordnorge 1867–1892," *Beretning: Foredrao oo forhandlinger ved det nordiske historikermöde i köbenhavn 1971 9–12 august* (Copenhagen: Fr. Bagge, 1971), 165–77.

14. N. P. Xavier to H. A. Preus, July 31, 1876: March 15, 1879, in Luther College Archives, Decorah, Iowa.

15. Jon Gjerde, *From Peasants to Farmers: The Migration from Balestrand, Norway, to the Upper Middle West* (Cambridge, England: Cambridge University, 1985).

16. Laur. Larsen, "Undervisnings-plan," *Katalog for det norske Luther-College i Decorah, Iowa, 1861–1872* (Decorah, Iowa: B. Anundsen, 1871), 17–28. Leigh D. Jordahl and Harris E. Kaasa, *Stability and Change: Luther College in Its Second Century* (Decorah, Iowa: Luther College Press, 1986), 9–10.

17. Peter A. Munch, "In Search of Identity: Ethnic Awareness and Ethnic Attitudes Among Scandinavian Immigrants 1840–1860," in *Scandinavians in America: Literary Life*, ed. J. R. Christianson (Decorah, Iowa: Symra, 1985), 1–24.

18. Einar Hovdhaugen, *Husmannstida* (Oslo: Det norske samlaget, 1976). S. Skappel, *Om husmandsvaesenet i Norge, dets oprindelse oo utvikling*, "Videnskapsselskapets skrifter, II. Hist.-filos. klasse 1922, no. 4" (Oslo: Jacob Dybwad, 1922).

19. On North Schleswig, where Gottlieb Japsen linked the rise of national feeling with the emergence of a bourgeois society, see Gerda Bonderup et al., "National udvikling og borgerliggörelse: Hovedlinier i Gottlieb Japsens forfatterskab," *Historie (Jyske Samlinger)*, new series, 13 (1949): 80–107.

20. On the Norwegian maritime community in Brooklyn, see Christen T. Jonassen, "Macro and Micro Ecological Factors in the Founding and Evolution of an Urban Norwegian Immigrant Community," in *Scandinavians and Other Immigrants in Urban America*, ed. Odd S. Lovoll (Northfield: St. Olaf College, 1985), 75–89.

21. Odd S. Lovoll, "*Washington Posten*: A Window on a Norwegian American Urban Community," *Norwegian-American Studies* 31 (1986): 177–79.

22. John L. Davis, *The Danish Texans* (San Antonio: Institute of Texan Cultures, 1979), 40–42. Kristian Hvidt, *Flight to America: The Social Background of 300,000 Danish Emigrants* (New York: Academic Press, 1975), 168–69.

23. J. R. Christianson, "Danish Assimilation Into the Norwegian-American Community," paper delivered August 29, 1984, to the *Conference on Scandinavian Immigration, Settlement, and Acculturation*, University of Wisconsin, Madison.

24. "Autobiography of C. P. Peterson, D.D.S" (1938), manuscript in possession of the author.

25. Marcus Lee Hansen, "Immigration and Democracy," in *The Immigrant in American History*, ed. Arthur M. Schlesinger (New York: Harper Torchbook, 1964), 77–96.

26. John Wefal, *A Voice of Protest: Norwegians in American Politics, 1890–1917* (Northfield: NAHA, 1971).

27. David L. Brye, "Wisconsin Scandinavians and Progressivism, 1900–1950," *Norwegian-Americans Studies* 27 (1977): 163–93.

28. Carl H. Chrislock, "The Norwegian-American Impact on Minnesota Politics: How Far 'Left-of-Center'?" in *The Norwegian Influence on the Upper Midwest*, ed. Harald S. Naess (Duluth: University of Minnesota, 1976), 106–16.

29. Sten Carlsson, "Scandinavian Politicians in Minnesota Around the Turn of the Century: A Study of the Role of the Ethnic Factor in an Immigrant State," *Americana Norvegica* 3 (Oslo 1971): 237–71.

30. For the case of a Swedish Lutheran clergyman hounded out of Minnesota, see Nels T. A. Larson, "Life in Saskatchewan, 1918–1925: A Story of a Pioneering Missionary Family," *Swedish-American Historical Quarterly* 36, no. 1 (1985): 39–55.

31. T. K. Derry, *A History of Modern Norway 1814–1972* (Oxford: Clarendon Press, 1973), 298, 310–17. The Finnish-American left is discussed in Reino Kero, "The Background of Finnish-American Working Class Writers," in *Scandinavians in America: Literary Life*, 176–87, and A. William Hoglund, "Finnish-American Humor and Satire: A Cultural Self-Portrait, 1890–1930s," ibid., 160–75.

32. Quoted in Odd S. Lovoll, *The Promise of America: A History of The Norwegian-American People* (Minneapolis: University of Minnesota, 1984), 195.

33. Einar Haugan, "Svensker og nordmenn i Amerika: en studie i nordisk etnisitet," *Saoa och sed: Klungl. Gustav Adolfs akademiens årsbok* (1976): 38–55.

34. M. L. Hansen, *The Problem of the Third Generation Immigrant* (Rock Island, Ill.: Augustana Historical Society, 1938).

35. Peter A. Munch, "Segregation and Assimilation of Norwegian Settlers in Wisconsin," *Norwegian-American Studies* 18 (1954): 102–40; and Rigmor Frimannslund, "Blant norskamerikanere i Wisconsin," *By og bygd* 14 (196): 1–34.

36. Erik Friis, ed., *The Scandinavian Presence in North America* (New York: Harper's Magazine Press, 1976). See also J. R. Christianson, "Cooperation in Scandinavian-American Studies," *Swedish-American Historical Quarterly* (October 1984): 380–84.

37. "Twin Cities' Scandinavia Today Issue," *TC: Twin Cities* 5, no. 8 (1982–83).

BIBLIOGRAPHICAL ESSAY

General surveys of Scandinavians in America do not exist, but a survey of each Scandinavian national group (Danes, Finns, Icelanders, Norwegians, and Swedes) is in Stephan Thernstrom, ed., *Harvard Encyclopedia of American Ethnic Groups* (Cambridge, Mass.: Harvard, 1980). See also the articles on the same groups in J. D. Holmquist, ed., *They Chose Minnesota: A Survey of the State's Ethnic Groups* (St. Paul, Minn.: Minnesota State Historical Society, 1981).

Comparative studies include Bo Kronborg, Thomas Nilsson, and Andres A. Svalestuen, eds., *Nordic Population Mobility: Comparative Studies of Selected Parishes in the Nordic Countries 1850–1900 (Oslo: Universitetsforlaget, 1977); Ingrid Semmingsen and Per Seyersted, eds., Scando-Americana: Papers on Scandinavian Emigration to the United States* (Oslo: American Institute University of Oslo, 1980);

and J. R. Christianson, ed., *Scandinavians in America: Literary Life* (Decorah, Iowa: Symra, 1985).

For the Scandinavian background, see Florence Edith Janson, *The Background of Swedish Immigration 1840–1930* (Chicago: University of Chicago, 1931); and Michael Drake, *Population and Society in Norway 1735–1865* (Cambridge, England: Cambridge University, 1969); as well as the community studies by Gjerde and Ostergren cited below.

Scandinavian emigration is discussed in Kristian Hvidt, *Flight to America: The Social Background of 300,000 Danish Emigrants* (New York: Academic Press, 1975); Reino Kero, *Migration from Finland to North America* (Turku: Turun Yliopisto, 1974); Harald Runblom and Hans Norman, eds., *From Sweden to America: A History of the Migration* (Minneapolis: University of Minnesota, 1976); and in eight articles on the regional background to Norwegian emigration in *Norewgian-American Studies* 19 (1983).

Colonial Scandinavians in America is the subject of Amandus Johnson, *The Swedish Settlements on the Delaware, 1638–1664*, 2 volumes (Philadelphia: University of Pennsylvania, 1911), and John O. Evjen, *Scandinavian Immigrants in New York, 1630–1674* (Minneapolis: K. C. Holter, 1916). On New Sweden as the heart of Midland American frontier culture, see Terry G. Jordan, *American Log Buildings: An Old World Heritage* (Chapel Hill: University of North Carolina, 1985); and Terry G. Jordan and Matti Kaups, *The American Backwoods Frontier: An Ethnic and Ecological Interpretation* (Baltimore: Johns Hopkins, 1989).

The business of trans-Atlantic migration is summarized in Kristian Hvidt, *The Westward Journey* (Mankato, Minn.: Creative Education, 1982), and the American promotion of immigration in Lars Ljungmark, *For Sale—Minnesota: Organized Promotion of Scandinavian Immigration 1873–1886* (Chicago: Swedish Pioneer Historical Society, 1973).

Surveys of individual Scandinavian-American national groups include George R. Nielsen, *The Danish Americans* (Boston: Twayne, 1981), and Kristian Hvidt, *Danes Go West: A Book About the Emigration to America* (Copenhagen: Rebild Society, 1976). A. William Hoglund, *Finnish Immigrants in America 1880–1920* (Madison: University of Wisconsin, 1960) surveys the Finnish-American transition from preindustrial to industrial life. Thorstina Jackson Walters, *Modern Sagas: The Story of the Icelanders in North America* (Fargo North Dakota Institute for Regional Studies, 1953) treats Canada as well as the United States. Theodore C. Blegen, *Norwegian Migration to America*, 2 vols. (Northfield, Minn.: Norwegian-American Historical Association, 1931 and 1940), and more recently, Ingrid Semmingsen, *Norway to America: A History of the Migration* (Minneapolis: University of Minnesota, 1978), and Odd S. Lovoll, *The Promise of America: A History of the Norwegian-American People* (Minneapolis: University of Minnesota, 1984), survey Norwegian-American life. Swedish immigration is described concisely by Lars Ljungmark, *Swedish Exodus* (Carbondale: Southern Illinois University and Swedish Pioneer Historical Society, 1979); and in a thick one-volume reference work by Allan Kastrup, *The Swedish Heritage in America* (New York: Swedish Council of America, 1975).

Immigrant letters arranged to survey the history of Scandinavian national groups include H. Arnold Barton, ed., *Letters from its Promised Land: Swedes in America, 1840–1914* (Minneapolis: University of Minnesota, 1975); Theordore C. Blegen, ed., *Land of Their Choice* (Minneapolis: University of Minnesota, 1955); Frederick

Hale, ed., *Danes in North America* (Seattle: University of Washington, 1984); Frederick Hale, ed., *Their Own Saga: Letters from the Norwegian Global Migration* (Minneapolis: Minnesota Press, 1986); and Solveig Zempel, ed., *In Their Own Words: Letters from Norwegian Immigrans* (Minneapolis: University of Minnesota and NAHA, 1991).

There are numerous other collections of primary sources in English translation, including Scandinavian immigrant guidebooks, letters, diaries, ballads, and oral interviews. Many were written by women, such as the letters of an Iowa farm wife in Pauline Farseth and Theodore C. Blegen, eds., *Frontier Mother: The Letters of Gro Svendsen* (Northfield: NAHA, 1950); the diary of a pastor's wife in David T. Nelson, ed., *The Diary of Elisabeth Koren 1853–1855* (Northfield, NAHA, 1955, reprinted 1978 and 1985); the letters of a governess in the antebellum South, Rosalie Roos, *Travels in America 1851–1855*, ed. Carl L. Anderson (Carbondale: Southern Illinois University, 1982); and the writings of a feminist in Texas in Clarence A. Clausen, ed., *The Lady with the Pen: Elise Waerenskjold* (Northfield: NAHA, 1961).

Scandinavian-American settlement is mapped in Carlton C. Qualey, *Norwegian Settlement in the United States* (Northfield: NAHA, 1938), and Helge Nelson, *The Swedes and Swedish Settlements in North America*, 2 vols. (Lund S.: C.W.K. Gleerup, 1943, reprinted 1979).

The classic study of American bilingualism is Einar Haugen, *The Norwegian Language in America*, 2 vols. (Philadelphia: University of Pennsylvania, 1953). Other studies of Scandinavian-American languages include Reino Virtanen, "The Finnish Language in America," *Scandinavian Studies* 51 (1979): 146–61, and Nils Hasselmo, "The Language Question," in *Perspectives on Swedish Immigration*, ed. Nils Hasselmo (Duluth: University of Minnesota, 1978), 225–43.

Community studies of Scandinavian Americans include urban, rural, and utopian communities. Among the best are Ulf Beijbom, *Swedes in Chicago: A Demographic and Social Study of the 1846–1880 Immigration* (Stockholm: Scandinavian University Books, 1971); Odd S. Lovoll, *A Century of Urban Life: The Norwegians in Chicago Before 1830* (Northfield: NAHA, 1988); Jon Gjerde, *From Peasants to Farmers: The Migration from Balestrand, Norway, to the Upper Middle West* (Cambridge, England: Cambridge University, 1985); Robert C. Ostergren, *A Community Transplanted: The Trans-Atlantic Experience of a Swedish Immigrant Settlement in the Upper Middle West, 1835–1915* (Madison: University of Wisconsin, 1988); and Paul Elmen, *Wheat Flour Messiah: Eric Jansson of Bishop Hill* (Carbondale: Southern Illinois University and Swedish Pioneer Historical Society, 1976).

Churches were central institutions in many Scandinavian-American communities. E. Clifford Nelson, ed., *The Lutherans in North America* (Philadelphia: Fortress, 1975), surveys Scandinavian and other Lutheran churches. Karl A. Olsson, *By One Spirit: A History of the Evangelical Convenant Church of America* (Chicago: Convenant Press, 1962), deals with a Swedish-Amerian church with a strong sense of ethnicity. For Methodists, see Arlow W. Andersen, *The Salt of the Earth: A History of Norwegian-Danish Methodism in America* (Nashville: Norwegian-Danish Methodist Historical Society, 1962). Latter-Day Saints are discussed in WIlliam Mulder, *Homeward to Zion: Mormon Migration from Scandinavia* (Minneapolis: University of Minneosta, 1957). Paul Elmen, *Wheat Flour Messiah*, deals with Erik Jansson and his followers. See also Nicholas Tavuchis, *Pastors and Immigrants: The Role of a Religious Elite in the Absorption of Norwegian Immigrants* (The Hague: Martinus Nijhoff, 1963); and Todd W. Nichol, ed., *Vivacious Daughter: Seven Lectures on the Religious Situation Among Norwegians in America by Herman Amberg Preus* (Northfield: NAHA, 1990).

Education among Scandinavian-Americans is the subject of articles by James S. Hamre, including "Norwegian Immigrants Respond to the Common School: A Case Study of American Values and the Lutheran Tradition," *Church History* (September 1981): 302–15. On higher education, see Lloyd Hustvedt, *Rasmus Björn Anderson: Pioneer Scholar* (Northfield: NAHA, 1966); O. Fritiof Ander, *T. N. Hasselquist: The Career and Influence of a Swedish-American Clergyman, Journalist and Educator* (Rock Island, Ill.: Augustana, 1931); and Richard W. Solberg, *Lutheran Higher Education in North America* (Minneapolis: Augsburg, 1985).

The Scandinavian-American press is treated in Marion Tuttle Marzolf, *The Danish-Language Press in America* (New York: Arno, 1979). On editorial policy, see Arlow W. Andersen, *The Immigrant Takes His Stand: The Norwegian-American Press and Public Affairs, 1848–1872* (Northfield: NAHA, 1953), and Finis Herbert Capps, *From Isolationism to Involvement: The Swedish Immigrant Press in America, 1914–1943* (Chicago: Swedish Pioneer Historical Society, 1966). On Scandinavian-American comics, see Peter J. Rosendahl, *Han Ola og han Per: A Norwegian-American Comic Strip*, ed. Joan N. Buckley and Einar Haugen (Northfield: NAHA, 1984). On religious publishing, see Daniel Nystrom, *A Ministry of Printing: A History of the Publication House of the Augustana Lutheran Church* (Rock Island, Ill.: Augustana, 1962).

Novels dealing with Scandinavian-American immigrants include O. E. Rölvaag, *Giants in the Earth* (New York: Harper, 1927); Vilhelm Moberg, *The Emigrants* (New York: Simon & Schuster, 1951); and Sophus Keith Winther, *Take All to Nebraska* (New York: Macmillan, 1936). On Scandinavian-American literature as an historical source, see Dorothy Burton Skårdal, *The Divided Heart: Scandinavian Immigrant Experience Through Literary Sources* (Lincoln: University of Nebraska, 1974).

Music is discussed in Theodore C. Blegen and Martin B. Ruud, *Norwegian Emigrant Songs and Ballads* (Minneapolis: University of Minnesota, 1936); Robert L. Wright, *Swedish Emigrant Ballads* (Lincoln: University of Nebraska, 1965); and Rochelle Wright and Robert L. Wright, *Danish Emigrant Ballads and Songs* (Carbondale: Southern Illinois University, 1983).

Scandinavian-American art is summarized in Mary Towley Swanson, *The Divided Heart: Scandinavian Immigrant Artists, 1850–1950* (Minneapolis: University Gallery, University of Minnesota, 1982); and the whole issue of *Swedish-American Historical Quarterly* 37, no. 2 (April 1986). The impact of Scandinavian design upon America is a theme of Robert Judson Clark et al., *Design in America: The Cranbrook Vision 1925–1950* (New York: Harry N. Abrams, 1983). See also Leonard K. Eaton, *Landscape Artist in America: The Life and Work of Jens Jensen* (Chicago: University of Chicago, 1964).

Scandinavian-American voluntary organizations are described in Erik Friis, ed., *The Scandinavian Presence in North America* (New York: Harper's Magazine Press, 1976); Odd S. Lovoll, *A Folk Epic: The Bygdelag in America* (Boston: Twayne for NAHA, 1975); and many other works on benevolent societies, temperance societies, choral societies, ski clubs, rifle clubs, gymnastic clubs, dramatic societies, literary societies, charitable institutions including hospitals, orphanges and missions, and professional organizations of Scandinavian-American engineers, journalists, and musicians.

Studies of professional groups include Kenneth O. Bjork, *Saga in Steel and Concrete: Norwegian Engineers in America* (Northfield: NAHA, 1947), and Knut Gjerset, *Norwegian Sailors in American Waters* (Northfield: NAHA, 1933). Professional directories include Conrad Bergendoff, *The Augustana Ministerium* (Rock Island, Ill.: Augustana Historical Society, 1980). Many biographies of women, as well as men, are in John Andrew Hofstead, *American Educators of Norwegian Origin: A Biographical Dictionary* (Minneapolis: Augsburg, 1931), and Olaf M. Norlie, *School Calendar, 1824–1924: A Who's Who Among Teachers in the Norwegian Lutheran Synods of America* (Minneapolis: Augsburg, 1924).

The nativist assault on Scandinavian-American "hyphenism" during World War I has been studied by Carl Chrislock, *Ethnicity Challenged: The Upper Midwest Norwegian-American Experience in World War I* (Northfield: NAHA, 1981). See also Peter L. Petersen, "Language and Loyalty: Governor Harding and Iowa's Danish-Americans During World War I," *Annals of Iowa*, 3d series, 42 (1974): 405–17. On the dynamics of ethnic identity, see April Schultz, " 'The Pride of the Race Had Been Touched': The 1925 Norse-American Immigration Centennial and Ethnic Identity," *Journal of American History* 77, no. 4 (March 1991): 1265–95.

Biographical studies of Scandinavian-American political figures range from successful politicians like Hans Mattson, Knut Nelson, John A. Johnson, Charles A. Lindbergh, Sr., and Floyd B. Olson to reformers and social critics like Jacob A. Riis, Thorstein B. Veblen, and the IWW martyr, Joe Hill. On the latter, see Sören Koustrup, *Shattered Dreams: Joe Hill* (Mankato, Minn.: Creative Education, 1982).

Bibliographies on Scandinavians in America are in each issue of *Norwegian-American Studies*, and reviews of books on Scandinavian America appear regularly in the *Swedish-American Historical Quarterly*. Additional serial publications devoted exclusively to Scandinavian-Americans are *Finnish Americana* and *The Bridge: Journal of the Danish American Heritage Society*.

A directory of nearly one hundred North American scholars is H. Arnold Barton, "Scandinavian-Americanists in the United States and Canada: A Preliminary Directory of Academic Scholars," *Scandinavian Studies* 53 (1981): 320–41. See also Robert B. Kvavik, ed., *Directory of Scandinavian Studies in North America* (Madison WI: Society for the Advancement of Scandinavian Study, 1989).

Archival directories include Oivind M. Hovde and Martha E. Henzler, *Norwegian-American Newspapers in Luther College Library* (Decorah, Iowa: Luther College, 1975); Lloyd Hustvedt, *Guide to Manuscript Collections of the Norwegian-American Historical Association* (Northfield: NAHA, 1979); Lilly Setterdahl, *Swedish-American Newspapers: A Guide to the Microfilms held by Swenson Swedish Immigration Research Center* (Rock Island, Ill.: Augustana College Library, 1981); and Wesley M. Westerberg, *Guide to Swedish-American Archival and Manuscript Sources in the United States* (Chicago: Swedish-American Historical Society, 1983).

Archives, museums, and research centers in the field of Scandinavian-American studies include the American-Swedish Historical Museum (1900 Pattison Avenue, Philadelphia, PA 19145), the American-Swedish Institute (2600 Park Avenue, Minneapolis, MN 55407), Archives of Suomi College (Hancock, MI 49930), Dana College Archives (Blair, NE 68008); Augustana Historical Society (Augustana College, Rock Island, IL 61201); Bishop Hill Historical Restoration (Bishop Hill, IL

61419); Danish American Heritage Society (29672 Dane Lane, Junction City, OR 97448); Danish Immigrant Archives (Grand View College, 1200 Grandview Avenue, Des Moines, IA 50316); Danish Immigrant Museum (Elk Horn, IA 51531), Luther College Archives (Decorah, IA 52101); Midwest Institute of Scandinavian Culture (Box 522, Eau Claire, WI 54702); Nordic Heritage Museum (3014 N.W. 67th Street, Seattle, WA 98117); Norwegian-American Historical Association (Northfield, MN 55057); Swedish-American Historical Society (5125 North Spaulding Avenue, Chicago, IL 60625); Swenson Swedish Immigration Research Center (Augustana College, Rock Island, IL 61201); and Vesterheim the Norwegian-American Museum (Decorah, IA 52101).

In addition, there are several research centers in Scandinavia, including the Danes Worldwide Archives (9000 Aalborg, Denmark); House of Emigrants (351 04 Växjö, Sweden); Institute of Migration (Piispankatu 3, 20500 Turku 50, Finland); and the Emigration Museum (Strandveien 100, Hamar, Norway).

6

Polish-Americans

Edward R. Kantowicz

When the Chicago Bears football team defeated the Los Angeles Rams in a playoff game on the way to their Super Bowl victory in 1986, their coach, Mike Ditka, characterized his players as a "Grabowski team" facing a "Smith team." There was no one named Grabowski on the Bears and the team did not have an unusual number of Polish or Slavic players, but Chicagoans recognized what Ditka meant. The Bears played tough, no-nonsense, aggressive, working-class football. Ditka's Grabowski statement symbolized a perfect fit between a sports team, a city, and its people.[1]

Nearly twenty years before, on a less auspicious occasion, a popular television show broadcast a very different view of the Grabowskis. In the spring of 1968, Rowan and Martin's "Laugh In" began airing a series of "Polack" jokes, all based on a simple premise: that Polish-Americans are big, strong, and stupid, with strong backs but weak minds. For example, the classic Polack joke goes like this: "How many Polacks does it take to change a light bulb? Three—one to hold the bulb and two to turn the ladder." Some were more imaginative than that: "Did you hear about the Polish astronauts planning an expedition to the sun? No, they can't do that—the sun is too hot. It's OK, they're planning to go at night." Witty or not, all the jokes made roughly the same point, that Polish-Americans were stupid and vulgar.[2]

Mike Ditka's Grabowski statement expressed admiration for his players and his city. It was intended to be complimentary. Obviously, the Polack jokes appeared more negative and derogatory, and some Polish-Americans took offense. Yet Ditka and "Laugh In" simply presented two sides of the same coin, two attitudes toward the same ethnic stereotype. To call someone big, strong, and stupid is another way of calling him tough, no-nonsense, and aggressive. The connotations are very different but the underlying reality is the same.

Ethnic jokes and stereotypes are controversial subjects, and many people are offended by them. Yet, as a general rule, ethnic jokes only do harm under two circumstances—when they're told with malicious intention (and this is usually quite obvious), or when they're told by politicians (and in this case they're only harmful to the politicians, not to the ethnic group). In most other cases, ethnic jokes are about as harmless as any biting humor can be.

Furthermore, ethnic jokes provide a kind of barometer revealing the degree of acceptance, assimilation, and self-confidence of any ethnic group. Most people feel more comfortable telling a Polish or Italian joke than a Jewish joke. So too with black jokes. Though black comedians freely play upon "nigger" stereotypes, few whites are so bold. In the cases of blacks and Jews, ethnic humor is still a sensitive subject, because the history of prejudice and persecution is still recent and fresh in peoples' minds.

It was no accident that Polish-Americans were singled out for jokes in the late 1960s. Professional comedians, no longer able to rely on traditional racial jokes, due to the Civil Rights Movement, targeted Polish-Americans as perfect replacement candidates, still different enough to be identifiable but secure enough not to be offended. As one historian of folklore has phrased it: "One possible reason for the popularity of the Polack (or Italian) joke cycle is that it takes the heat off the Negro."[3]

Besides providing a barometer of assimilation and acceptance, ethnic jokes also furnish a useful starting point for understanding and analyzing an ethnic group, because ethnic jokes and stereotypes are based on a kernel of truth. Certainly, stereotypes do not portray a complete picture of reality. They are exaggerated and over-simplified, but they are not manufactured out of thin air. They reflect social structures, cultural ideals, and community values shared by members of an ethnic group.[4]

Common Jewish stereotypes, for instance, emphasize money-making, sharp dealing, and professional ambition. These stereotypes reflect, in distorted fashion, the fact that Jewish immigrants clustered disproportionately in occupations dealing with trade and commerce, valued education highly, and often encouraged their sons to pursue medicine, law, or some other profession. Similarly, the stereotype of the strong, no-nonsense, poorly educated Polish-American laborer is based on reality. That is not to say that all Polish-Americans are stupid, as the Polack joke cycle would have it; but there are elements in the background of Polish-Americans that make them seem stupid to certain people in smart social circles (including some academics). In summary form, there are three major elements of Polish-American history: (1) Polish immigrants to America were largely of peasant origin in the old country; (2) once in America, they became overwhelmingly working-class; and (3) they adhered to a militant brand of Roman Catholic religion. Peasant, working-class, and Catholic—these three social realities and the system of values they imply summarize much of Polish-American history. These three elements contain the truth underlying the Polack jokes and the Grabowski stereotype.

PEASANT ORIGINS

The Poland that immigrants left a hundred years ago was a divided country, in several senses. First of all, the country was divided politically; in fact, Poland did not exist as a political entity throughout the nineteenth century. In 1795, Poland's three powerful neighbors, Prussia, Russia, and Austria, had carved up what was left from two earlier partitions and the name of Poland disappeared from the map of Europe for over a century, until after World War I.[5] Perhaps more important, however, than this political partition was the deep social division in Polish society, the great chasm separating the gentry from the peasant classes.

In the days of its independence and in the early years of the partitions, Poland was a nobility nation. The Polish *szlachta*, or gentry, were the most numerous noble class in Europe, forming 8 percent of the country's population. Politically, culturally, and economically, the Polish gentry were the Polish nation—only they held political rights, only they felt deep nationalist longings. In addition, they held a virtual monopoly on Poland's principal economic activity, the grain trade.

Beneath the gentry were the mass of Polish peasants, still serfs bound to the soil they tilled but with no property rights to their land.[6] They owed their gentry landlord burdensome labor services (*panszczyzna*) and were subject to him in matters of civil and criminal justice. Though economically bound together, peasant and gentry could not be more divided socially. Some *szlachta* even believed they were descendants of the ancient Sarmatians, a different race than the peasants, and insisted that their personal servants come from impoverished gentry families, so that their bodies would not be touched by peasants. Poland contained two other social classes, the clergy (often drawn from among peasants but more closely allied with the gentry) and the townsmen and shopkeepers (usually Jews or Germans). Peasants respected the clergy and they patronized the local Jewish innkeeper when necessary, but they kept their distance from both. As a character in Ladislas Reymont's great novel, *The Peasants*, philosophized: "Things have to be so. The husbandman lives on the land he tills, the tradesmen on what he sells, the Squire on his estate, the priest on his parish, and the official, on everybody. It must be so."[7]

Peasants in nineteenth-century Poland were thus not Poles in any meaningful sense. Though they spoke Polish, they had little national feeling. As the leading historian of nineteenth-century Poland has phrased it: "Centuries of feudal oppression had resulted in isolating the peasants from the rest of society. Those who were not peasants were either oppressors (landlords, overseers) or aliens (the government official, the local Jew, the travelling townsman)." Peasants deeply resented the economic advantages of the lords and the aliens ("Plough with a goose-quill, sow paper with sand; ye will get much more pelf [wealth] than by tilling the land"); and most did not support the gentry in their various rebellions against the partitioning powers. Indeed, in 1846 in the Austrian province of Galicia, Polish peasants around the city of Tarnow reacted to a gentry uprising against the partitioning power by attacking the gentry. Rampaging peasants ransacked four hundred manor farms and killed over 1,200 people. They felt their class grievances far more strongly than any national grievances against the Austrians ("The gentry rebel and drive out folk to ruin; but who has to pay, when payday comes? Why, we peasants!") Thus, they confirmed their isolation from the rest of Polish society in "a lake of blood."[8] Occasionally today, well-meaning individuals, affected by the recent "ethnic revival" in America, will flatter a Polish-American by reciting a list of notables from Polish history—Copernicus, who first theorized that the earth revolves around the sun; King John Sobieski, who saved Vienna from the Turks; King Stanislaus Poniatowski, lover of Catherine the Great; Prince Adam Czartoryski, notable European diplomat; Ignace Paderewski, internationally renowned pianist. Such flattery is ahistorical and misses the point. To compliment a Polish-American, who is a descendant of peasants, on his illustrious Polish ancestors is like complimenting an American black man on his illustrious ancestors, George Washington and Thomas Jefferson. Polish peasants were as different from the *szlachta* as American slaves were from plantation owners.

Large social and economic forces eventually transformed the three partitions of Poland and set the peasant masses in motion. In an attempt to modernize their economy, the Polish gentry gradually emancipated the peasantry in the nineteenth century and consolidated their landholdings into more efficient farms. Emancipation followed different timetables in the various sectors of divided Poland. In Prussian Poland and in the large body of central Poland, which Russia administered (the so-called Congress Kingdom of Poland), serfdom was technically abolished in 1807. This theoretical freedom, however, was not followed immediately by a grant of land title to the peasants, so it remained largely symbolic. Indeed, the first effect of the peasant's "freedom" was that the landlord could now evict him from the land he had previously farmed as a serf. Eventually, Prussia granted land title to many of the more ambitious peasants, in a gradual process completed by about 1850; Russia did not confirm peasant title until 1864. In the Austrian province of Galicia, freedom and landowning both came together as a result of the revolution of 1848.

The gradual Prussian emancipation resulted in a highly polarized peasant economy. About 5 percent of the peasants managed to buy enough land to become efficient, productive capitalist farmers, much like the gentry; but over two-thirds of the masses lost their land or else clung to small, inefficient landholdings. In Austria, the process produced a different result. Few became landless, but most peasant landholdings were so small that starvation constantly faced the masses. In Russian Poland, the economic situation fell somewhere between the other two cases. Most peasants became medium-sized landowners; but even here the number of landless swelled by over 600,000 between 1870 and 1891.[9]

Despite these different circumstances in each of the partitions of Poland, we can generalize to some extent about the fate of the emancipated peasants. Some peasants became moderately prosperous farmers as a result of emancipation, but the majority became landless and/or impoverished. The landed peasants stayed where they were, bought more land if possible, acquired some education, and assimilated to the Polish national consciousness preached by the city intelligentsia and some of the more enlightened gentry. The landless, on the other hand, were reduced to marginal subsistence, driven to migratory labor or industrial work in the cities, or else pushed out of Polish territory altogether as immigrants.

The waves of immigration began in the 1870s in the Prussian partition of Poland, where the forces of economic modernization struck earliest. The emigration fever spread to Russian and Austrian Poland after 1890. The process of peasant impoverishment and displacement was greatly accelerated by the general collapse of grain prices in the 1880s, when vast quantities of imported American wheat undercut Poland's traditional markets for grain. By the time of the First World War, 1.2 million Poles had left the Prussian provinces east of the Oder-Neisse line; two-thirds of a million Poles left the Austrian province of Galicia; and 1.3 million abandoned the Russian sector of Poland.[10] Not all of these migrants went to the United States. Some explored other new lands, such as Brazil or Australia, and many settled in industrial cities of western Germany. Yet in the last boom years of unrestricted American immigration, between 1900 and 1914, over 100,000 Poles a year arrived in the United States. According to one recent, careful estimate, between 1,148,649 and 1,780,151 Polish immigrants entered America permanently between 1899 and 1932.[11]

The immigrants from Poland after 1870 came overwhelmingly from the peasant class. A Congressional Immigration Commission reported in 1911 that over 80 percent of the Polish immigrants had been farmers or farm laborers in the old country. There had been politically motivated Polish immigrants before 1870. Each unsuccessful Polish rebellion had sent a small number of gentry patriots into exile in Western Europe or America, but their numbers were small and they had little to do with the peasant masses that came after 1870. The peasant migration was economic in its motivation; in the phrase current at the time, Polish peasants went to *America za chlebem*, after bread. Many emigrating peasants probably intended only a temporary stay in America, long enough to earn money to buy land back in

Poland. More than are generally recognized did return to Poland (perhaps 30 to 40 percent), but through a combination of circumstances the majority stayed in the United States.[12]

The peasant nature of Polish immigration had important consequences. A peasant solidarity, which was neither nationalistic nor socialistic but simply familial and communal, gave the immigrants from Poland a sense of collective fellow-feeling. Their first loyalty was neither to Poland nor to the United States, but simply to themselves and to their families. Peasant origins made them clannish, conservative, fearful of change, intensely land-hungry, and economically acquisitive.

Most of all, however, peasant origins largely determined where the Poles would settle in America and what kind of work they would do here. Polish immigrants came looking for bread, but all they had to offer was their peasant strength. This ensured that most of them would work long and hard as unskilled laborers in America.

WORKING CLASS LIFE AND VALUES

Ironically, the fact that most Polish immigrants were peasants made it nearly inevitable that they would not settle on farms in the United States. As landless peasants in Europe, they had no money to buy land in America; furthermore, they found American farming uncongenial, too individualistic, and too lonely. European peasants lived in villages; and though they owned and worked individual farms, they performed many tasks communally and could always count on a family and village support system in times of need. American prairie farming, with the nearest neighbor miles away, held no allure for them. Besides, many of the Polish peasants wanted to return to Poland and buy land there, so they chose the quickest way to earn money in America, and that was in industrial cities. Most Polish immigrants, there-fore, settled in cities of the Northeast or the Midwest, in the industrial heartland of the nation.

Polish immigrants did not settle in just any city. They gravitated to the newer, fast-growing cities of heavy industry where the demand for unskilled labor was the greatest. As peasants, they had few skills that were useful in an industrial society, but they were strong and they knew how to work hard. Thus, they offered their labor in steel mills, stockyards, mines, tan-neries, or other heavy industries where machine technology had reduced most tasks to a simple routine requiring just brute strength. It is not sur-prising, then, that Chicago—"the city of the broad shoulders; the hog-butcher to the world," as the poet Carl Sandburg phrased it—attracted the largest number of Polish immigrants. By 1930, there were over 400,000 Polish-Americans in Chicago; today there are probably about a million people of Polish ancestry in the Chicago area.[13] Other large industrial cities, such as Detroit, Cleveland, Pittsburgh, and Buffalo, also attracted large numbers of Poles, as did many small mill and mining towns scattered across the landscape of Pennsylvania.

The cities Poles did not settle in are instructive. Like most immigrants, they avoided Southern or semi-Southern cities, such as Richmond, Virginia, Baltimore, or St. Louis, where the black population would have provided stiff competition for the lowest-paying, unskilled jobs. They also avoided cities such as Philadelphia, where industries were old and well-established and put a premium on skilled workers. Though several hundred thousand remained in the New York area after passing through Ellis Island, most settled along the docks of Brooklyn or near the factories of New Jersey, rather than in the commercial heart of Manhattan.[14]

The peasant solidarity of the Poles eased their transition into the working-class and made them good union members. In the early days of trade union-ism, union leaders badly misread the Poles' clannishness and considered them unorganizable. The union's mistake was understandable. Polish peas-ants had come primarily as temporary laborers, intending to stay only long enough to earn a nest-egg and buy land back home. They willingly worked the longest hours, for any wage, and tried to save every penny. Under normal circumstances, then, their limited aspirations in the New World and their peasant submissiveness and dedication to hard work put them at cross-purposes with the militant aims of union organizers. Yet peasants remained submissive only up to a point. If they felt their fundamental rights were being violated, they would resist fiercely; and in such cases, communal solidarity proved a tremendous asset in a strike situation.[15]

This counterpoint between general peasant submissiveness and occasional bursts of fierce communal struggle carried over directly from Europe. After emancipation of the peasants, some vestigial feudal rights and obligations remained as bones of contention. Among the most important were the peasants' forest rights. Though the landlord owned the forests, villages of peasants retained the right to gather firewood in specific sections of the forest and the lord was obliged to consult with them before selling or felling any trees. Reymont's novel, *The Peasants*, climaxes with a tremendous peasant *jaquerie* (revolt) when the local squire secretly fells a portion of his forest to sell it to outsiders. The entire village of Lipka, men, women, and children, marches to the forest to prevent the sale.

There were hand-to-hand fights, there were mass attacks; men were seized by the throat or by the hair of the head, and they tore at each other like wild beasts. The manor servants ... (were led) by the forester, a man of gigantic size, who dearly loved a fight, and had, besides, many a bone to pick with the Lipka folk. He darted onward fighting alone against multitudes, cracking their skulls with the butt of his gun, and making them fly on every side: a scourge to them all, and a terror. ... But he was assailed by a host of women, who flung themselves on him with shrieks, clawed his face, pulled out his hair by handfuls, and piling themselves one upon the other, bore him to the earth along with them: like a lot of curs attacking a shepherd's dog, plunging their fangs in his flesh, and dragging him this way and that way."[16]

Similarly, in America the violent strikes of the Polish workers involved the whole community. In 1921 at the 43rd and Ashland Avenue gate to the Chicago Stockyards, pitched battles broke out between Polish strikers and the packers' strikebreakers. When mounted police charged the strikers, like so many Cossacks in the old country, the Polish women threw red pepper and paprika in the eyes of both police and horses.[17]

In 1915 and 1916, Bayonne, New Jersey, refinery workers mounted two bitter strikes and forced their middle-class community members, mainly local storekeepers, to support them. When violence broke out, the seemingly uncontrolled crowd exercised great selectivity in choosing targets. They sacked three Jewish businesses and an Irish saloon, but did not touch any Polish-owned stores.[18]

The peasant background of immigrant laborers proved to be a two-edged sword. Their initial peasant docility lured employers into hiring them in preference to more skilled American workers, but their fierce communal solidarity made them formidable foes when aroused. Once union organizers broke through the language and cultural barriers, as well as their own craft union limitations, and began to organize the unskilled in industrial unions, they found the Polish immigrant communities fiercely loyal to the workers' cause. Poles and other eastern Europeans with similar peasant backgrounds have formed the backbone of many CIO industrial unions since the 1930s.

As industrial workers, Polish-Americans developed what might be called a working-class mentality. That is, they tended to value good wages and job security more than occupational status or education for their children. In 1890, a young Polish immigrant wrote to his father back in Poland, warning him not to waste any money educating his younger brother: "If he wants to earn a living here with a pen that is not for America. America does not like writers but hard-working people." This attitude persisted in the first two generations of Polish-Americans. In Pittsburgh, two-thirds of the Poles remained in the same low-skill, working-class occupations between 1930 and 1960; in Detroit in 1970, 75 percent of the employed males in a typical Polish neighborhood were blue-collar workers and the average number of years of schooling was 10.1; in Chicago in 1970, census data showed Polish families with a higher than average median income but a low percentage of professionals and managers.[19]

As former peasants, they still had an intense desire to own land, which led them to a high degree of homeownership. In Polish working-class wards of Milwaukee, Wisconsin, around the turn of the century, the immigrant laborers harbored such a strong desire to own their own homes that they bought small frame houses in an undeveloped area. Despite their low wages, they met the payments on these cottages by taking in boarders and by consistently voting down tax assessments for street paving and sewer connections. In other words, these Polish workers made a trade-off: they deferred middle-class amenities in order to own a home.[20]

Success for Polish-Americans with this working-class mentality meant a good-paying, unionized job, without a fancy title but with lots of overtime, and a neat, well-kept house and garden. First-generation Polish-Americans were more likely to send their sons to work in the mills at an early age in order to help pay the mortgage rather than forego home ownership and send them to college. The second generation held more ambiguous attitudes toward work and education. Indeed, many had as their major goal to raise children to have lives that would be significantly different from their own. Yet, as one close student of this phenomenon has described it, "Even though mothers and fathers would like their children to become members of the professional middle-class, or middle-level executives, the prevailing patterns of child-rearing are based on what parents, especially fathers, have learned about the qualities that insure success in the blue collar world: obedience, self-control, respect for authority, and determination." Such traits do not translate into advantages in the professional world.[21]

CATHOLIC SOLIDARITY

The religion of the Polish immigrants reinforced their peasant communalism and their working-class solidarity. Polish peasants were fervent Catholics, though they mixed their religion with numerous vestiges of magic and superstition. Language and religion, far more than any concept of secular nationalism, gave the peasant his identity and distinguished him from foreigners. "Praised be Jesus Christ" was the standard peasant greeting in Poland; "for ever and ever" the ritual reply.

The Roman Catholic Church in the nineteenth century propounded an aggressively defensive brand of dogma—vigorously condemning the modern trends of unbridled individualism and materialism, political and intellectual liberalism. This "circle the wagons" style of religion aptly suited the situation of the Polish peasant. Like the Catholic Church, the Polish peasant felt beleaguered on all sides. In the peasant world of capricious nature, rapacious landlords, and invading armies, the Catholic Church was a rock of solidity and certainty. The Church was eternal and universal, but at the same time it was tangible and concrete, with its rich liturgy, music, and incense. As political partition and agrarian reform slowly crumbled, religion remained to help define who the Polish peasant was. The Catholic priest stood as a pillar in the center of the Polish peasant community.[22]

Upon emigration to America, the Polish peasant needed such a pillar all the more. If it were merely a question of religious services, the Polish immigrant could easily have attended one of the Irish or German Catholic parishes in the United States. Indeed, the Mass was offered in a language equally incomprehensible to all—Latin. But the immigrants' parish church was more than a place for religious services; it was a community center—even an attempt to reestablish the old peasant community itself.

Polish-Americans made the church the central institution of their communities in American cities. These communities formed cities within cities, and the string of Polish churches formed a sort of denomination within a denomination. Fr. Vincent Barzynski, C. R., who served as pastor of the oldest Polish parish in Chicago, St. Stanislaus Kostka from 1872 to 1899, provides a good example. Fr. Barzynski and his flock built a massive cathedral-like church that still stands today; they also built a convent, rectory school, and parish credit union. In the year of Chicago's World's Fair, 1893, St. Stanislaus billed itself as the largest Catholic parish in America, with over 20,000 parishioners organized into seventy-four different parish societies. Nearby, in the same neighborhood, church-related groups also built a Polish Catholic hospital, high school, orphanage, and publishing company.[23]

Polish peasants had been respectful and deferential to the clergy in the old country, often kneeling to hug their legs and kiss their feet; and the clergy held considerable influence over them. On many occasions, when peasant riots threatened, the priest would walk through the village with the Holy Viaticum, the Body of the Lord, and quiet their turbulence. Yet, the priest could not oppose the peasants' most fundamental economic interests. In the *Jaquerie* described above from Reymont's novel, the local priest had tried to stop the peasants but was swept aside.

So too in America. Chicago's Fr. Barzynski, and many other strong-willed pastors, often faced opposition from their parishioners. The Polish laymen had usually taken the initiative in founding a parish in America, forming a confraternity or religious society that bought land and began building a church. These lay trustees of the parish often resisted turning over legal title to the bishop and the pastor. In 1873, for instance, when overcrowding at Chicago's St. Stanislaus Kostka necessitated the building of another church, a lay society founded Holy Trinity church three blocks away and tried to retain title and find a pastor more to their liking than Fr. Barzynski. The bishop and the Resurrectionist religious order (which Fr. Barzynski belonged to) wanted the new church to remain a mission of St. Stanislaus. This dispute dragged on for nearly twenty years, several people were excommunicated, and Holy Trinity was padlocked for long periods of time. Finally, a papal representative had to settle the quarrel personally in 1893. Sometimes, these parish disputes between Polish laity and clergy ended in permanent schism. Fr. Francis Hodur of Scranton, Pennsylvania, eventually gathered together many of these dissident congregations into a new church denomination, the Polish National Church.[24]

Polish-Americans took church politics seriously and played for high stakes. "Salvation was not an individual affair but the consequences of a way of life that could only be lived in a community organizing existence on earth.... Parish organizations could function as artificial families for immigrants separated from the extended family which had offered help and support in the old village."[25]

St. Stanislaus in Chicago, and most large Polish communities in America, attained a high degree of what sociologists call "institutional completeness." This means that the Polish ethnic group built such a wide range of institutions (most of them church-related) that it could perform most of the services its members required—religious, educational, recreational, cultural—without recourse to the host society. Within their ethnic enclaves, Polish-Americans could not only ignore most non-Catholic Americans, they could even remain separate from non-Polish Catholics.[26]

The peasant, working-class, and Catholic background of Polish-Americans, and the resulting separatism of the community, all affected their attitudes toward politics. Poles in America voted overwhelmingly Democratic from the beginning, for they viewed the Democrats as the outsiders's party, more sympathetic to workingmen and more tolerant of the Catholic religion. Republicans, on the other hand, were perceived as puritanical and plutocratic. In Chicago, for example, the identifiably Polish voting precincts gave a majority to the Democratic candidate in all but two of the thirteen presidential elections from 1888 to 1936. The two exceptions reinforce the point. In 1904, Theodore Roosevelt seemed more sympathetic to workers than the conservative Democrat Alton B. Parker, and in 1912 Woodrow Wilson alienated many immigrant voters with an ethnic slur from his published historical writings.

More significant, perhaps, than the voting record is the political strategy pursued by Polish Democratic leaders, a strategy of clannish, solidarity politics. Just as it was initially difficult to unionize the Polish peasant immigrants, it was hard for political leaders to incorporate them into political coalitions. Instead, the Polish politicians organized around in-group concerns, constantly tried to perfect the unity and solidarity of the bloc, and neglected the politics of bridge-building to other groups. Polish leaders were misled by their large numbers in some industrial cities into thinking that political power would fall to them like a ripe fruit if only they would stick together. Sometimes this worked. In the small Polish enclave of Hamtramck, an industrial suburb of Detroit, Poles have dominated politics since the 1930s. So too in the city of Buffalo. But in larger and more diverse cities, such as Chicago, they have enjoyed little success. Since Polish voters never formed a majority in Chicago, their solidarity strategy was doomed to failure. Polish-Americans never elected a mayor of Chicago and they remained weak in the councils of the Democratic central committee until the late 1970s.[27]

Polish immigrants, then, built communities that were worlds unto themselves. But they were never completely successful in transplanting the old-world peasant village. Their new-world communities were neither completely Polish nor completely American, but rather Polish-American. The people inhabiting these Polish-American worlds, collectively called *Polonja Amerykanska*, or simply Polonia, were peasant in origin, unskilled industrial workers by occupation, and fiercely Roman Catholic in their values and loyalties.

IMMIGRANTS AND THE SUCCESS MYTH

A comparative perspective is useful in order to assess whether Polish-Americans have been successful in America, or whether they have proven stupid and unsuccessful, as the Polish jokes imply. First of all, a comparison with one group that most people agree has been successful—the Jews—is instructive.

The experiences of the peasant, working-class Poles contrast strongly with those of Eastern European Jews. Jews had been barred from the land by Tsarist restrictive laws in Russia and thus have lived in towns and cities, working mainly as small merchants and craftsmen. In the two-class Christian social structure of Eastern Europe, divided sharply between gentry and peasant, the Jews performed the despised, but necessary, tasks of financial and commercial middlemen. The Polish gentry, for example, long held a monopoly on the distilling of grain into vodka, but the actual selling of vodka was often contracted to Jewish innkeepers. Thus, the peasants got drunk, the gentry got rich, and the Jews were hated by both. In the process, Jews acquired a background in trade. Furthermore, Eastern European Jews were generally a literate people, who put great value on religious scholarship. It was not uncommon for a Jewish wife to manage the store while her husband sat all day reading the holy Talmud and Torah, for Scriptural learning brought a family high status.

When they came to America, Jews tended to work mainly in semi-skilled trades, particularly the garment industry, which required ability but not much strength; and they often became entrepreneurs and merchants in their own right. Their literate background made them more likely to value education for their children. On the whole, then, the background and values of Jewish immigrants brought them closer to the standard American entrepreneurial tradition and social mobility ideal than the peasant, working-class background of the Poles.[28]

Many Jews have been individualistic risk-takers in business and the professions, whereas Poles have tended to be more security-minded, clinging tightly to labor union, church, family, and community. As Polish-Americans themselves describe their values:

Edward M., when questioned about achieving success, replied, "Yes, I think I did. I never been on welfare, never collected an unemployment check. . . . I never, never collected a dime unemployment or never got a dime from anybody, you know. So I feel good about it. I feel I've progressed." Joseph K., a life-long steel laborer, measured his success another way.... "I was fortunate. I was healthy. I was never sick or anything. I worked steady, that was the main thing, you know."[29]

The point is not that Jews have been more successful in America than Poles, as is often said, but that the two groups have had different definitions of success.

In comparing Poles with Italians, it is the similarities that are immediately striking. Both groups had peasant origins and took up primarily unskilled jobs in America; both groups were largely illiterate in Europe, put a relatively low value on education in America, and showed their peasant land hunger by a high degree of homeownership.

Yet there were important differences as well. The South Italian peasants usually avoided the jobs in heavy industry, such as steel mills and mines, which the Poles took up with such alacrity. Instead, Italians gravitated to seasonal, "outdoor" unskilled labor, to jobs in construction, public works, or on the railroads, which often kept them away from home for weeks or months. This difference is due to the group's social background. In Southern Italy, peasants usually lived in large hillside towns, commuting long distances by the day, the week, or the season, to work in the fields or on construction projects, often in large labor gangs. Many had developed some skills as stone masons or carpenters, and most had become divorced from the land. They were used to outdoor gang labor, therefore, and sought it out in America. Poles, however, with a more communal work tradition, found the hard but steady labor of mills and mines more congenial than migratory work gangs.[30]

These differences in work patterns had both positive and negative effects. The steady factory work of the Poles usually produced more immediate benefits in higher earnings than the unstable work of the Italians. However, the mobile, restless Italian worker might be more likely to take an entrepreneurial gamble and try to leap from construction laborer to construction contractor. In the long run, the Italians tended, therefore, to produce more self-employed, independent businessmen than the Poles, who simply improved their earnings but did not change their status in industry. Again, as in the contrast with Jews, neither group was unsuccessful, but they achieved different kinds of success. Polish-Americans have generally pursued a different dream of success from the standard American ideal of an individualist rise to the top in professions or business. Their success dream values family, religion, and community more highly. If Polish immigrants came to America seeking primarily bread, a home, and a better standard of living for their families and at the same time they tried to preserve their communal lifestyle as much as possible, the conclusion is inescapable that they got what they wanted and have been successful in their own terms.

Yet the Polish-American communities have been changing. Some Polish-Americans, particularly the third and fourth generations, seem to be wondering, in the words of the 1984 Peggy Lee song, "Is that all there is?" Not even a cohesive group like the Poles is immune to the powerful forces of American nationalism and the American success myth. In addition, the working-class communities that Polish peasants found so congenial have been eroding in recent years under the pressure of foreign industrial competition. The industrial heartland of the Northeast and the Midwest, where Polish immigrants settled at the turn of the century, has changed into the "Rust Belt." So partly by choice and partly by necessity, Polish-Americans today are pursuing different career paths from their fathers—attending universities, entering the professions, or driving ahead in business. A 1976 report to the Polish-American Congress, for instance, found an increasing number of Chicago-area Poles attending the three major medical schools in the city.[31] Polish-Americans entered America and lived on their own terms for a long time, but those terms are changing. In the meantime, however, the peasant, working-class, Catholic community mentality still persists in many American cities and even in some suburbs.

John Higham, in one of his many graceful essays on ethnicity in America, has pointed out that both individual assimilation and ethnic cohesion can be recognized as worthy goals in a free and tolerant society. Different individuals will accept one or the other of these goals in different degrees, for the feeling of ethnicity varies enormously in intensity from one person to another. We should stop looking at the melting pot ideal and the ideal of ethnic pluralism as polar opposites, as either/or propositions. The two can and will coexist.[32]

Higham says that on the one hand, many Polish-American communities with the group consciousness I have described in this article will continue to exist for some time in America; and other Americans should be tolerant of them and thankful for the alternate definition of success and the good life that they represent. On the other hand, many individual Polish-Americans will secede from these communities and strike out on their own in a pursuit of individual success; the Polish-American community should be tolerant of them and not look upon them as traitors. A truly pluralist society will have room for both groups and individuals, and for more than one set of values, more than one definition of success.

Above all, I believe we need to keep a sense of humor about all this. One of the most sensitive and perceptive immigrant intellectuals of the twentieth century, Louis Adamic, titled his autobiography *Laughing in the Jungle*.[33] I can't think of any more apt prescription for survival in America. A pluralism of both groups and individuals will only work if we learn how to laugh sympathetically at each others' foibles and failings, and applaud appreciatively at each others' successes, however we define success. If we can't learn to laugh at each other, and at ourselves, America might yet turn out to be not a pluralist utopia, but simply a jungle.

NOTES

1. Paul Galloway, "Grabowski Town," *Chicago Tribune*, January 19, 1986, section 2, pp. 1, 5, is a partly serious, partly humorous discussion of Ditka's statement.

2. William M. Clements, "The Types of the Polack Joke," *Folklore Forum*, 3 (November 1969): 1–45 provides an index of hundreds of Polack jokes found in the University of Indiana folklore collection. The most popular joke book collection was Ed Zewbskewicz, Jerome Kuligowski, Harvey Krulka (probably pseudonymns), *It's Fun to Be a Polack* (Glendale, Calif.: Collectors Publications, 1965). Andrzej Kapiszewski, *Stereotype Amerykanow Polskiego Pochodzenia* (Wroclaw: Biblioteka Polonijna, 1977) is a thorough study of the Polish stereotypes, with a summary in English on pages 188 to 191.

3. Alan Dundes, "A Study of Ethnic Slurs: The Jew and the Polack in the United States," *Journal of American Folklore* 84 (April-June 1971): 202.

4. "Stereotypes," *International Encyclopedia of the Social Sciences* (New York: Macmillan, 1968) 15: 259–269.

5. The best overall history of Poland is a translation of a Polish work, Aleksander Gieysztor et al., *History of Poland* (Warsaw: Polish Scientific Publishers, 1968). The volume on the nineteenth century is written by Stefan Kieniewicz. Some of my remarks about the history of Poland are drawn from two series of lectures Kieniewicz delivered at the University of Chicago from January to June 1968.

6. For the condition of Poland's peasantry at the time of partition, see Stefan Kieniewicz, *The Emancipation of the Polish Peasantry* (Chicago: University of Chicago Press, 1969), 3–43.

7. Ladislas Reymont, *The Peasants*, 4 vols. (New York: Alfred A. Knopf, 1925), 4: 201. Reymont's novel was originally published in Polish as *Chlopi* between 1902 and 1909. It provides a vivid look at all aspects of peasant life in late nineteenth-century Poland. Unless otherwise identified, all peasant sayings or aphorisms in this chapter are quoted from this novel.

8. Kieniewicz, *Emancipation of the Polish Peasantry*, 109, 113–26.

9. The entire discussion is drawn from Kieniewicz, *Emancipation of the Polish Peasantry*.

10. Ibid., 192, 210, 223.

11. Helena Znaniecki Lopata, "Polish Immigration to the United States of America: Problems of Estimation and Parameters," *Polish Review* 21 no. 4 (1976): 105.

12. 61st Congress, 2nd Session, *Reports of the Immigration Commission* (1911), 4: 338–39, 373–75.

13. For background on Poles in Chicago, see Edward R. Kantowicz, *Polish American Politics in Chicago, 1888–1940* (Chicago: University of Chicago Press, 1975), 12–27; and Kantowicz, "Polish Chicago: Survival Through Solidarity," in *The Ethnic Frontier*, ed. Melvin G. Holli and Peter d'A. Jones. (Grand Rapids, Mich.: Wm. Eerdmans Publishers, 1977), 179–209.

14. Caroline Golab, *Immigrant Destinations* (Philadelphia: Temple University Press, 1977), 1–27, ably describes these Polish settlement patterns.

15. Victor Greene, *The Slavic Community on Strike* (Notre Dame, Ind.: University of Notre Dame Press, 1968), was the first to study Polish labor attitudes in detail. John J. Bukowczyk, "Polish Rural Culture and Immigrant Working Class Formation, 1880–1914," *Polish American Studies* 41 (Autumn 1984): 23–44, has described sensitively the complexities of these attitudes.

16. Reymont, *The Peasants* 2 (Winter): 280.

17. Dominic Pacyga, *Polish Chicago: The Making of an Urban Working-Class Community* (forthcoming from University of Illinois Press). Professor Pacyga kindly lent me a copy of his manuscript.

18. John J. Bukowczyk, "The Transformation of Working-Class Ethnicity: Corporate Control, Americanization, and the Polish Immigrant Middle Class in Bayonne, New Jersey 1915–1925," *Labor History* 25 (Winter 1984): 70.

19. Paul Wrobel, *Our Way: Family, Parish, and Neighborhood in a Polish-American Community* (Notre Dame, Ind.: University of Notre Dame Press, 1979) is a sensitive study of a typical Polish working-class neighborhood in Detroit by an anthopologist participant-observer. Dominic Pacyga, *Polish Chicago*, focuses on two premier working-class areas, the Back of the Yards and South Chicago. John Bodnar, Roger Simon, and Michael P. Weber, *Lives of Their Own: Blacks, Italians, and Poles in Pittsburgh, 1900–1960* (Urbana: University of Illinois Press, 1982), studies three working-class groups over time. All figures in this paragraph are from these three works.

20. Roger D. Simon, "Housing and Services in an Immigrant Neighborhood: Milwaukee's Ward 14," *Journal of Urban History* 2 (August 1976): 435–58; and Simon, *The City-Building Process: Housing and Services in New Milwaukee Neighborhoods, 1880–1910* (Philadelphia: American Philosophical Society, 1978).

21. Wrobel, *Our Way*, 77–84.

22. William I. Thomas and Florian Znaniecki, *The Polish Peasant in Europe and America*, 5 vols. (Chicago: University of Chicago Press, 1918), 4: 103–20.

23. Kantowicz, *Polish American Politics*, 30–33; Joseph Parot, *Polish Catholics in Chicago, 1850–1920* (DeKalb: Northern Illinois University Press, 1981), 59–94; Victor Greene, *For God and Country* (Madison: State Historical Society of Wisconsin, 1975).

24. Greene, *For God and Country*, 74–82; Parot, *Polish Catholics in Chicago*, 40–64; Kantowicz, "Polish Chicago," 192–96.

25. Mary Cygan, "Ethnic Parish as Compromise: The Spheres of Clerical and Lay Authority in a Polish American Polish, 1911–1930," Cushwa Center for the Study of American Catholicism, University of Notre Dame, Working Paper Series 13, no. 1 (Spring 1983): 11–12, 23–24.

26. Raymond Breton, "Institutional Completeness of Ethnic Communities and the Personal Relations of Immigrants," *American Journal of Sociology* 70 (1964) 193–205; Kantowicz, "Polish Chicago," 184–92.

27. See Edward R. Kantowicz, *Polish-American Politics in Chicago, 1888–1940* (Chicago: University of Chicago Press, 1975).

28. Moses Rischin, *The Promised City: New York's Jews, 1870–1914* (New York: Harper and Row, 1962); and Irving Howe, *World of Our Fathers* (New York: Simon and Schuster, 1976), have portrayed in vivid detail the background and

lifestyle of East European Jews in Europe and America. Thomas Kessner, *The Golden Door: Italian and Jewish Immigrant Mobility in New York, 1880–1915* (New York: Oxford University Press, 1977), has assessed their mobility in comparative perspective.

29. Bodnar, Simon, and Weber, *Lives of Their Own*, 143.

30. Virginia Yans-McLaughlin, *Family and Community: Italian Immigrants in Buffalo, 1880–1930* (Ithaca, N.Y.: Cornell University Press, 1977), relies mainly on the "outdoor work" explanation of Italian immigrant labor patterns; whereas Bodnar, Simon, and Weber, *Lives of Their Own*, put more emphasis on previous skills acquired in Italy.

31. Dominic Pacyga, "Polish-Americans and Medical Schools," a report to the Polish American Congress, 1976.

32. John Higham, "Another American Dilemma," in *Send These To Me* (New York: Atheneum, 1975), 231–46.

33. Louis Adamic, *Laughing in the Jungle: The Autobiography of an Immigrant* (New York: Harper and Brothers, 1932).

BIBLIOGRAPHICAL ESSAY

For the peasant background in Poland, see Stefan Kieniewicz, *The Emancipation of the Polish Peasantry* (Chicago: University of Chicago Press, 1969); Ladislas Reymond, *The Peasants*, 4 vols., Autumn, Winter, Spring, Summer (New York: Alfred A. Knopf, 1925); and William I. Thomas and Florian Znaniecki, *The Polish Peasant in Europe and America*. Consult the original five-volume edition of *The Polish Peasant* (Chicago: University of Chicago Press, 1918), but also read the lengthy introduction by Eli Zaretsky, in the new, abridged edition (Urbana: University of Illinois Press, 1984).

The best introductions to the Polish-American experience are: Victor Greene, "The Poles," in *Harvard Encyclopedia of American Ethnic Groups*, ed. Stephan Thernstrom (Cambridge, Mass.: Harvard University Press, 1980), 787–803; and Helena Znaniecki Lopata, *Polish Americans: Status Competition in an Ethnic Community* (Englewood Cliffs, N.J.: Prentice-Hall, 1976).

The major monographs in Polish-American history are: Victor Greene, *The Slavic Community on Strike* (Notre Dame, Ind.: University of Notre Dame Press, 1968); Victor Greene, *For God and Country* (Madison: State Historical Society of Wisconsin, 1975); Joseph Parot, *Polish Catholics in Chicago* (DeKalb: Northern Illinois University Press, 1981); Edward R. Kantowicz, *Polish American Politics in Chicago, 1888–1940* (Chicago: University of Chicago Press, 1975); Donald Pienkos, *PNA: A Centennial History of the Polish National Alliance* (Boulder, Colo.: East European Monographs, 1984); Caroline Golab, *Immigrant Destinations* (Philadelphia: Temple University Press, 1977); John Bodnar, Roger Simon, and Michael P. Weber, *Lives of Their Own: Blacks, Italians, and Poles in Pittsburgh, 1900–1960* (Urbana: University of Illinois Press, 1982); Paul Wrobel, *Our Way: Parish and Neighborhood in a Polish-American Community* (Notre Dame, Ind.: University of Notre Dame Press, 1979); John J. Bukowczyk, *And My Children Did Not Know Me: A History of the Polish Americans* (Bloomington, Ind., 1987); and Dominic Pacyga, *Polish Chicago: The Making of an Urban Working Class Community* (Urbana: University of Illinois Press, 1989).

7

Jewish-Americans

Edward Shapiro

Over two hundred years ago in *Letters From An American Farmer,* Hector St. John de Crevecoeur, the French observer of American mores, asked, "What then is the American, this new man?" His answer stressed both the biological and intellectual uniqueness of the transplanted European. The American was an amalgamation of the ethnic strains of Europe, or at least of those of Western Europe. "I could point out to you a family whose grandfather was an Englishman, whose wife was Dutch, whose son married a French woman, and whose present four sons have now four wives of different nations." The true American had also discarded European modes of thought. *He* is an American, who, leaving behind him all the ancient prejudices and manners, "acts upon new principles, entertains new ideas, and forms new opinions."

Crevecoeur waxed poetic as he contemplated the future of this American new man and his land. "Here individuals of all nations are melted into a new race of men, whose labors and posterity will one day cause great changes in the world." American writers of the nineteenth century followed Crevecoeur's cue and stressed the theme of the newness of America and the American. Thus Ralph Waldo Emerson, in his famous 1837 "American Scholar" address delivered before Harvard's Phi Beta Kappa Society, declared that American dependence on the learning of other lands had ended. "The millions that around us are rushing into life cannot always be fed on the sere remains of foreign harvests. Events, actions arise, that must be sung, that will sing themselves." He concluded with a well-known sentence in American literature. "We must have listened too long to the courtly muses of Europe. What is the remedy? . . . We will walk on our own feet; we will work with our own hands; we will speak our own minds."

It is no coincidence that America's Jews, perhaps more than any other group, have followed the advice of Crevecoeur and Emerson to leave behind the prejudices and manners of Europe and to sing of American events. This has been true not only in the defining of American nationality but also in the defining of American Jewish identity. Crevecoeur's "new mode of life" was especially new for the Jew. The definitions of Jewish identity developed elsewhere, "the sere remains of foreign harvests," were hardly relevant for America. In Europe, Africa, and Asia, status and citizenship were based on religion, antisemitism was pervasive, Jews were denied citizenship until the nineteenth century, and the kehillah, the self-contained Jewish community, played a vital role and had an official, or at least semi-official position. In America, there was little public (as distinct from private) antisemitism, citizenship was a matter of right and not sufferance, there were few significant barriers to a Jew's social and economic advance, and the Jewish community had no standing in law, nor did it perform any official tasks. The Jewish attitude toward America was best expressed by Irving Baline (later Americanized as Irving Berlin), a resident of New York City's Lower East Side Jewish ghetto, who wrote "God Bless America."

Pulled in seemingly opposite directions by the force of American hope and the power of Jewish memory, America's Jews were forced to define what it meant to be a Jew in America, to articulate the relationship between American and Jewish identities, and to develop lifestyles both fully American and fully Jewish. No other ethnic group has been as concerned with defining their relationship to America. It is no coincidence that Jews wrote three of the most popular expressions of American identity: Emma Lazarus's poem "The New Colossus," Israel Zangwill's play "The Melting Pot," and Horace Kallen's essay "Democracy Versus the Melting Pot." A disproportionate number of America's most prominent sociologists of ethnicity have been Jews—Arnold Rose, Milton Gordon, and Nathan Glazer, to name just a few. The Harvard historian Oscar Handlin wrote an important monograph on the history of America's Irish, and Jewish historians such as Gilbert Osofsky, Allan Spear, Lawrence Levine, and Herbert Gutman provided much of the intellectual framework for understanding black history and culture. No American novel has probed more perceptively the costs of immigrant acculturation than Abraham Cahan's *The Rise of David Levinsky,* written by the longtime editor of the *Jewish Daily Forward,* the most widely read foreign-language paper in American history.

Jews have had a more difficult problem in defining their status as Americans than any other major ethnic group. Not only did Jews have to adapt to a culture radically different from what they had known in Europe and the Arab lands, but they were also entering a society in which they were both a religious and ethnic minority. Other ethnic groups were at least Christian and thus had a religious bond with native Americans. Furthermore, Jews in Europe, Africa, and Asia were the most isolated, communally organized, and encapsulated of groups, and had to make the radical adaptation to the individualistic and liberal ethos of America.

From the beginning, America's Jews sought to demonstrate that they were at home in America, and that, at least for them, the travail of the wandering, homeless Jew had ended. In 1841, at the dedication of the Beth Elohim synagogue in Charleston, South Carolina, Rabbi Gustav Poznanski rebuked Jews who longed for a return to Zion. "This synagogue is our temple, this city our Jerusalem, this happy land our Palestine." The compatibility of Jewish and American identity was not something that could be taken for granted but had to be asserted and defended. This became the life work of Rabbi Isaac Mayer Wise, the greatest Jewish figure in nineteenth-century America and the founder of Reform Judaism in America.

Wise preferred to use the term "American Judaism" rather than "Reform Judaism" to describe the changes in Jewish theology and ritual he sought in order to reconcile Judaism with the temper of America. His 1857 prayer book was titled *Minhag America (American Custom)*, his organization of synagogues was called the Union of American Hebrew Congregations, and his organization of rabbis was named the Central Conference of American Rabbis. The word "Hebrew" was frequently used by German Jews in describing themselves and in naming their institutions, partially to distinguish themselves from the Eastern European immigrant "Jews" whom they saw as backward and less Americanized. This Americanization of Judaism reached its logical conclusion in a seminal document drawn up by a group of Reform rabbis in Pittsburgh in 1885.

The Pittsburgh Platform not only emphasized the compatibility of Judaism with modern science and biblical criticism, but also stressed the harmony between Judaism and America. It rejected those elements of Judaism that distinguished Jews from other Americans and cast doubt on their Americanness. "We consider ourselves," the rabbis solemnly said, "no longer a nation, but a religious community, and therefore expect neither a return to Palestine, nor a sacrificial worship under the sons of Aaron, nor the restoration of any of the laws concerning the Jewish state." Rabbi Kaufmann Kohler called the Pittsburgh Platform the Reform movement's declaration of independence, because it freed America's Jews from the nationalism and cultural and social separatism of "Mosaico-Talmudical Judaism."

Most Reform spokesmen were intense opponents of Zionism. They strongly opposed Zionism's emphasis on Jewish nationalism, its belief that antisemitism was a permanent aspect of European and American life, and its call for the ingathering of Jews into Palestine. Reform, in contrast, stressed the religious element of Jewish identity, claimed that the dispersion of the Jews was part of God's plan to spread the ethical teachings of Judaism, believed that American antisemitism was insignificant and transitory, and feared that Zionism would result in the raising of legitimate doubts about the patriotism of Jews. "As an American," Jacob Schiff wrote in 1907, "I cannot for a moment concede that one can be at the same time a true American and an honest adherent of the Zionist movement... The Jew should not for a moment feel... that he is in exile and that his abode here is only a temporary or passing one."

For some German Jews, even the tepid Judaism of the Reform movement was too much. Felix Adler, the son of Rabbi Samuel Adler of New York, carried the rationalism and universalism of the left-wing of Reform Judaism to their logical conclusion when he founded the Society for Ethical Culture in 1876. Wishing to free the Jew from any lingering effects of the ghetto and skeptical of traditional religion, Adler favored a humanistic religion that would transcend all racial and religious particularism. To this day, a disproportionate percentage of the members of Ethical Culture and the Unitarian-Universalist Church are Jews seeking to escape from the remnants of an unwanted religious-ethnic heritage.

Despite the ideological challenge of Adler, the vast majority of nineteenth-century German Jews maintained that a denationalized Judaism was perfectly compatible with American identity. Rabbi David Philipson asserted, "From the hills of Palestine the prophet's voice floated down the vestibule of time, enjoining the soulful command, 'Here O Israel, the Eternal is our God.' From the broad plains of the United States the answer is sent back, 'God is one.'" Reformers believed a universalistic Judaism shorn of any distinctive ethnic characteristics could make great strides in the United States, and Wise even rashly predicted that it could eventually become the majority American religion and lead to the salvation of the world.

From the Reform perspective, the mission of the Jew was no longer to preserve a distinctive religious culture and to observe Jewish law. Rather, it was to convert the Gentiles and to usher in the Messianic age. Reformers modified the Jewish liturgy to resemble upper-class Protestantism. Sermons became a central part of the religious service, decorum was stressed, and ethical behavior was emphasized. These services were often conducted in "temples," implying that the Reform temple was here in America now and not in Zion at some future date.

Other Jews besides rabbis were also intent on showing that there was no incompatibility between being an American and being a Jew. In 1892, the American Jewish Historical Society, the nation's oldest ethnic historical society, was established to refute the claims that Jews were not patriotic, were interested solely in making money, could not be integrated into American life, and lacked ties to the colonial period of American history. One of its earliest publications had the revealing title *Christopher Columbus and the Participation of the Jews in the Spanish and Portuguese Discoveries.* The Society's first president was Oscar Straus, who fancied himself an amateur historian. In 1885, Straus had published *The Origins of the Republican Form of Government in the United States,* which argued that the Founding

Fathers had been influenced by the political ideas of the Jewish common-wealth.

Jewish writers during the late nineteenth and early twentieth centuries challenged and supplemented the attempt of the Society to demonstrate that there was no inherent conflict between American and Jewish identity. The sociologist Milton Gordon in his *Assimilation in American Life* (1964) argued that the most important paradigms of American immigrant accul-turation have been Anglo-conformity, the melting pot, and cultural plural-ism. Jews provided the most popular expressions of each model. Anglo-conformity, the belief that America was permanently shaped by the English character of the colonial period and that immigrants should make themselves over into good Yankees, is one of the motifs of Emma Lazarus's 1883 sonnet "The New Colossus." This poem was engraved on a memorial plaque and placed on the pedestal of the Statue of Liberty in 1903.

Lazarus was born in 1849 into an old, respected, and almost completely assimilated Sephardic New York family. One of her earliest references to Jews was in her poem "In the Jewish Synagogue at Newport," appearing in her 1871 collection, *Admetus and Other Poems*. The volume was dedi-cated to "My Friend, Ralph Waldo Emerson." The poem somberly contem-plated the fate of Newport Jewry and, by implication, all of American Jewry.

> No signs of life are here: the very prayers
> Inscribed around are in a language dead.

Lazarus's nearly comatose Jewish identity was revived in the early 1880s when she read George Eliot's novel *Daniel Deronda*, learned of the Russian pogroms of 1881–82, and witnessed the beginning of a massive immigration of Eastern European Jews into New York City. She involved herself in immigrant relief work, and defended the Jewish immigrants against their detractors. To quote the historian John Higham, she became "the first modern American laureate of their history and culture." In 1882, Lazarus wrote a series of essays in *Century Magazine* attacking antisemitism and describing Jews as the agents of progress. In that same year, she published a volume of poems titled *Songs of a Semite*, containing the pro-Zionist "The Banner of the Jew."

> O deem not dead that martial fire,
>   Say not the mystic flame is spent!
> With Moses' law and David's lyre,
>   Your ancient strength remains unbent
> Let but an Ezra rise anew,
>   To life the *Banner of the Jew!*

In *An Epistle to the Hebrews,* which appeared in 1883, Lazarus argued for a Jewish national and cultural revival in Palestine and the United States. She thus undoubtedly had the immigrant Jews primarily in mind in "The New Colossus."

For Lazarus, the Statue of Liberty was a symbol of hope and welcome for Jews and other immigrants.

> Mother of Exiles. From her beacon-hand
> Glows world-wide welcome; her mild eyes command
> The air-bridged harbor that twin cities frame.

And yet the words spoken by the Statue seemingly conflict with the vision of an America whose "golden door" welcomes the immigrants.

> Give me your tired, your poor,
> Your huddled masses yearning to breathe free.
> The wretched refuse of your teeming shore.

Historians have puzzled over Lazarus's seemingly condescending description of the immigrants as "wretched refuse." One interpretation has argued that Lazarus did not use the phrase in a pejorative sense, since in the 1880s "wretched" was often used as a synonym for distressed, and "refuse" often described objects considered to be valueless as well as worthless. There was no doubt, however, as to the attitude of Lazarus's sister toward the immigrant Jews. She forbade the inclusion of "anything Jewish" when Emma's collected works appeared posthumously in 1889. Whatever the original intention of "The New Colossus," the poem was compatible with the ideology of Anglo-conformity that contended that Jews and other immigrants were acceptable only to the extent that they adopted the dominant social and intellectual patterns of American life. Otherwise, they remained "wretched refuse."

Israel Zangwill's 1908 play "The Melting Pot" was the most important literary answer to the doctrine of Anglo-conformity. Zangwill was born in 1864 in the London Jewish ghetto of Whitechapel, the son of poor and Orthodox Russian immigrants. He was the most prominent Jewish writer of his generation in the English-speaking world. In 1856, eight years before his birth, Parliament had granted complete civil rights to Jews. In a series of "ghetto" novels, essays, and plays, Zangwill explored the challenge this presented to Jewish identity.

Zangwill described himself as a man of "violent contraries." Deeply attached to Jewish history and the spiritual values of Judaism, he also believed Judaism was not a viable faith for modern man. The Jew, he wrote, was "like a mother who clasps her dead child to her breast and will not let it go." Although he translated portions of the Jewish liturgy into English, he also published *The Next Religion,* an attack on Judaism. Zangwill wrote nostalgically of the ghetto while proclaiming to be a militant assimilationist. He was one of the founders of British Zionism and was a friend and supporter of Theodor Herzl, yet he advised Western Jews to forego any thought of settling in Palestine and to follow the path of assimilation that he himself had taken.

Zangwill yearned to be accepted as an English writer, not as a Jewish writer. Shortly before his marriage to Edith Ayrton, an English Christian, he defended intermarriage as the solution to antisemitism. "With Israelitish stiffneckedness we have spurned intermarriage, the only natural process by which two alien races can be welded into one. To speak most dispassionately, we have in the long run got only what we deserved." His wife shared his universalism, and the couple rejected all sectarian identification such as Judaism and Christianity, preferring to support such general causes as peace and feminism. Their first son was neither baptized nor circumcised, and belonged, as did his parents, to an abstract humanity. The biological assimilation that Zangwill experienced in his own life was the theme of "The Melting Pot."

Zangwill the Englishmen was entranced by the vision of an American nationality that combined the best that all of the world's ethnic groups had to offer. The purpose of the "The Melting Pot," he said, was to show how "the most violent antitheses of the past may be fused into a higher unity." Contrary to popular belief, Zangwill's melting pot did not refer to a process whereby immigrants were to be transformed into good Anglo-Saxons, but rather to a process whereby native Americans and immigrants alike were to be thrown together into the pot to create something entirely new.

America is God's crucible, the great melting pot where all the races of Europe are melting and reforming.... A fig for your feuds and vendettas, Germans and Frenchmen, Irishmen and Englishmen, Jews and Russians—into the Crucible with you all. God is making the American.

For Zangwill, intermarriage was the fuel that kept the melting pot bubbling. His play recounted the romance between two immigrants—David, a Russian Jew, and Vera, a Russian Christian whose father was responsible for the pogrom that had claimed the lives of David's parents. The play's dramatic focus is whether the love of David and Vera will survive amidst the bitter memories of Europe and the opposition of their relatives. David's last name is Quixano, an unusual name for an eastern European Jew. Some scholars have speculated that Zangwill was alluding to Cervantes' hero's hopeless belief in the power of love to conquer all. At one point David rejects Vera: "Christian love! For this I gave up my people—darkened the home that sheltered me ... Let me go home, let me go home." But, as could be predicted, love triumphs. In its melodramatic finale, David proclaims to

Vera his vision of an American national identity being shaped in the crucible
of New York City.

Yes, East and West, and North and South, and palm and the pine, the pole and the
equator, the crescent and the cross—how the great Alchemist melts and fuses them
with his purging flame! Here shall they all unite to build the Republic of Man and
the Kingdom of God. Ah, Vera, what is the glory of Rome and Jerusalem, where
all nations and races come to worship and look back, compared with the glory of
America, where all races and nations come to labor and look forward!

"The Melting Pot" made a deep impression on American audiences and
was a great commercial success. President Theodore Roosevelt said, "I do
not know when I have seen a play that stirred me as much." Jane Addams
declared that Zangwill's obituaries in 1926 emphasized his authorship of
"The Melting Pot." "Seldom has an author so molded thought by the
instrumentality of a single phrase," declared the New York *Herald Tribune*.
And the magazine *Independent* praised Zangwill for allowing Americans
"to see ourselves as others see us, to learn how the fair Goddess of Liberty
looks to those who have fled to her protection from Russian pogroms."
    Zangwill was not alone in favoring Jewish assimilation through inter-
marriage. Although Hollywood was dominated by Jewish producers, di-
rectors, and owners during the era of the silent screen, that did not prevent
(and perhaps it caused) the production of literally dozens of films endorsing
intermarriage. Most of these featured marriages between Jews and Irish.
Love can conquer all, even religious differences, was the message of *Romance of the Jewess* (1908), *Becky Gets a Husband* (1912), *The Jew's
Christmas* (1913), *For the Love of Mike and Rosie* (1916), *The Cohens and
the Kellys* (1926), *Private Izzy Murphy* (1926), *Kosher Kitty Kelly* (1926),
Clancy's Kosher Wedding (1927), and *Abie's Irish Rose* (1927).
    The most famous treatment of intermarriage was *The Jazz Singer* (1927).
The jazz singer, played by Al Jolson, changes his name from Jackie Rabi-
nowitz to Jack Robin, rejects the religion and culture of his ancestors, sings
in the Winter Garden and not in the synagogue, and marries the Gentile
Mary Dale. "You're of the old world," he tells his father. "Tradition is
alright, but this is another day." In these films, the young Jew symbolizes
Americanization and the melting pot, while their parents personify the ir-
relevant traditions of Europe.
    Not all Americans, however, were so enthusiastic regarding the concept
of the melting pot. Spokesmen for Anglo-Saxon Protestant American had
no objection to immigrants throwing themselves into the melting pot to
purge themselves of their foreign impurities, but they had no intention of
themselves jumping into the pot. Nor did they believe that American identity
was still in the process of being formed. Rather, they maintained, the creation
of American nationality had ended with the close of the eighteenth century.

The *Forum's* review of "The Melting Pot" suggested that its definition of American nationality could only have come from "an author who is himself foreign in nationality and alien in race." And in *The Melting Pot Mistake,* which appeared in the year of Zangwill's death, Henry Pratt Fairchild, a fervent advocate of immigration restriction and a future president of the American Eugenics Society, warned that "a prepondering influence of foreigners . . . take away from a people its most precious possession—its soul."

Zangwill's message of "E Pluribus Unum" was particularly directed at America's Jews. He thought the future held out only two options to them. They could either renationalize themselves and migrate to Palestine, or they could renounce Jewish identity and throw themselves into the American melting pot. Zangwill did not believe that a strong Jewish identity could be reconciled with a strong American identity, and he was convinced that Jewish assimilation was inevitable, although it could be slowed down by continued immigration from Europe and antisemitism. For America's Jews, Zangwill's message was a prescription for cultural and religious extinction. As the *American Hebrew* noted, "Not for this have the million refugees from Russia sought America."

Mary Antin agreed with Zangwill that American and Jewish identities were incompatible. Four years after the appearance of "The Melting Pot," Antin published *The Promised Land,* one of the most famous of American-Jewish autobiographies. Born in Plotzk in White Russia, Antin had immigrated in Boston with her family while a child. Her memoir recounts how the promised land of America replaced the promised land of Zion. The autobiography's chapter recounting her passage across the Atlantic was appropriately titled "The Exodus." For Antin, life in America was a rebirth, and she was entranced by what she learned about America in her American *yeshiva,* the Boston Public Library. Her book ended with a panegyric to her new nation. "America is the youngest of the nations, and inherits all that went before in history. And I am the youngest of all America's children, and into my hands is given all her priceless heritage, to the last white star espied through the telescope, to the last great thought of the philosopher."

For Antin, as well as for David Quixano, the demands of American life required the putting aside of Old World traditions and hatreds. She married Madeus V. Grabau, a Columbia University professor of paleontology and the son of a Lutheran minister. One can only wonder whether she questioned her idealized view of America or her faith in assimilation when her husband left her in 1920 and settled in China.

In contrast to Antin, most American Jews sought to be both American and Jewish. They welcomed Horace Kallen's 1915 essay "Democracy Versus the Melting Pot," which argued that this was not mere wishful thinking. Born in Silesia, Kallen settled in Boston with his family at the age of five. Although his father was an Orthodox rabbi, Kallen gave up any belief in God while a youth. Breaking with Judaism was part of Kallen's repudiation of his Jewish identity, a repudiation that left him permanently estranged from his father. Initially, he believed Jewish identity was an encumbrance to full integration into American life and to becoming a Yankee.

Harvard, and particularly Barrett Wendell, the professor of American literature, showed Kallen the great influence that the Hebraic spirit had had on American literature and culture. While Harvard acquainted him with America's ideals, teaching at the University of Wisconsin prior to World War I acquainted him with America's reality. He was impressed by the extent to which German, Scandinavian, and Irish immigrants had maintained their ethnic identities, and he mistakenly concluded that America was developing as a federation of nationalities similar to Switzerland. Rejecting his earlier efforts at assimilation, Kallen now claimed that being a good American and a good Jew were not antagonistic, as Zangwill had claimed, but complementary.

But how did Kallen define Jewishness? An atheist, his loyalties were not to Judaism but to Hebrew culture, and he referred to himself as a Hebraist rather than a Judaist. Defining Hebraism as "the total biography of the Jewish soul," Kallen became a secular Jewish nationalist, a fervent Zionist, and America's most important advocate of "cultural pluralism." In contrast to Reform Judaism's emphasis on the religion of Judaism, Kallen looked to the ethnic and nationalistic elements of Jewish identity. His was a message of ethnic and not religious survival.

In "Democracy Versus the Melting Pot," which was a direct answer to Zangwill, Kallen replaced the metaphor of a melting pot with that of an orchestra. Just as the beauty of an orchestra stemmed from the different sounds of dozens of instruments harmonizing with one another, so the richness of American culture derived from the contributions of dozens of separate ethnic groups to the American mosaic. The American spirit, he argued, consisted of "this union of the different," and was sustained by the equality among ethnic groups and by "the free trade between these different equals in every good thing the community's life and culture produce."

While comforting to some Jewish spokesmen, it is questionable whether Kallen's belief in a national mosaic of ethnic and religious groups was either accurate or desirable. There is much truth to the complaint of Nicholas Roosevelt that Kallen's scenario would have Balkanized America, and that ethnic identity was an unimportant factor in the lives of many Americans. Kallen argued that ethnic identity was the most intimate, important, and permanent element of a person's life, "the efficacious natural milieu or habitate of his temperament...the center at which he stands, the point of his most intimate social relations, therefore of his intensest emotional life." A person could change many things, he argued, but he could never change the ethnic character of his grandfather. This might be true, but a more important consideration was whether he could predict the ethnic and religious identity of his grandchildren.

As the historian Arthur Mann has noted, Kallen did not anticipate the widespread intermarriage suggested and encouraged by Zangwill. "Democracy Versus the Melting Pot" appeared during the heyday of American immigration from eastern and southern Europe. In 1915, ethnic loyalties remained strong, immigrant groups congregated together in ethnic neighborhoods, and exogamy was relatively rare. Jewish intermarriage in particular was quite low. Zangwill's own life should have altered himself to the malleability of American ethnic patterns.

He had married the daughter of a Methodist minister and hymn writer, his own daughter married a lapsed Quaker, and his grandchild was raised as a Jew. Today Abie's Irish Rose and Bernie's love for Bridget (from "Bridget Loves Bernie," a 1970s TV show about an intermarried couple) are common phenomena. If Irving Berlin could write "White Christmas" and "Easter Parade," if Leonard Bernstein could compose his "Mass," and if Stephen Schwartz could write the popular musical "Godspell" (based on the Gospel according to St. Matthew), then it is possible to forget, if not to change, one's grandparents. And, of course, it is always possible to change one's own name and one's identity. Bernie Schwartz became Tony Curtis, Jules Garfinkel became John Garfield, Theodosia Goodman became Theda Bara (an anagram of "Arab death"), and Max Aronson became Bronco Billy, America's first cowboy movie star.

All definitions of Jewish identity in the twentieth century inevitably have had to confront Zionism and, after 1948, the Jewish state of Israel. Both Zangwill and Kallen were Zionists. For Zangwill, Zionism was the negation of the East European diaspora, a movement with little relevance for Jews living in the West who had no intention of exchanging the good life of America, Canada, and Great Britain for the problems of Palestine. For Kallen, Zionism was an expression of that nationalistic cultural pluralism basic to American identity. American Zionists accepted neither of these formulations, preferring to develop a Zionism that was appropriate both for Americans who had no plan to emigrate to the Holy Land and for a nation in which permanent national divisions were frowned upon.

The major figure in "Americanizing" Zionism was Louis D. Brandeis, the progressive reformer, advisor to Woodrow Wilson, and the first Jew to sit on the United States Supreme Court. The great mystery surrounding Brandeis is why he ever became a Zionist in the first place. There was little in his life prior to 1914 when he became a leader of the American Zionist movement at the age of fifty-eight to suggest such a possibility. A descendant of German Jews who had settled in Louisville, Kentucky, in the mid-nineteenth century, Brandeis had not previously exhibited any particular interest in things Jewish. He was not a member of a synagogue or a Jewish fraternal group, he did not observe Jewish religious rituals, and he opposed the retention of ethnic differences. In 1910, for example, he stated, "Habits of living or of thought which tend to keep alive differences of origin or classify men according to their religious beliefs are inconsistent with the American ideal of brotherhood and are disloyal." And yet two years later, he joined the Federation of American Zionists and became an advocate of cultural pluralism. Various interpretations, ranging from the influence of Kallen to Brandeis's political ambitions, have been offered to explain such seemingly bizarre behavior. There is, however, no confusion as to his impact on American Zionism. He helped transform American Zionism from a plaything of unassimilated Jewish nationalists into a movement that could attract acculturated American Jews.

Under the influence of Brandeis, American Zionism was shorn of both its nationalistic thrust and its underlying assumption that the essence of Zionism was *aliyah,* a Hebrew term signifying immigration to the land of Zion. Brandeisian Zionism resulted in the philanthropy to provide a refuge for persecuted Jews of *other* lands. American Jews had already migrated to the promised land of America, and they had no intention of migrating once more. Brandeisian Zionism, one humorous definition put it, was a movement in which one person gave money to a second person so that a third person could reach Palestine. As a result, American Zionism has been most popular when the needs of non-American Jews have been greatest, such as during World War I and World War II, 1946–48, and the period after 1967 when Israel was directly threatened by her Arab neighbors. For most contemporary American Jews, Zionism rather than Judaism has become the most important manifestation of their Jewishness, the single most important element shaping their identity as Jews. And yet only a tiny number of American Jews have resettled in the Holy Land—the thing which, more than anything else, defined one as a Zionist according to classic European Zionist ideology.

European Zionists lamented this transformation of American Zionism into a charity emphasizing refugee relief, arguing that Brandeisianism had divested the movement of its nationalistic raison d'etre. They were convinced that antisemitism was so strong and economic conditions were so perilous for Jews that *aliyah* was the only realistic Jewish option. For East European Zionists such as Chaim Weizmann and David Ben-Gurion, any movement that rejected Jewish nationalism and the "negation of the diaspora" was hardly Zionistic. Their European Zionist ideology, however, did not resonate in America where there was no "Jewish question" nor any serious attempt to deny American Jews the rights and responsibilities of full citizenship.

For Brandeis, the legitimacy of American Zionism stemmed precisely from what European Zionists objected to—its denial of Jewish nationalism and its definition of Zionism as a political and social movement whose values and goals were similar to those of America. He was careful to describe Jews as a "people" and not a "nation," in part because he did not want Zionists to appear un-American and guilty of "dual loyalty." American Jews who wished to succor Jews in Europe and elsewhere but did not wish to have their Americanism questioned welcomed Brandeis's revision of Zionism.

Brandeis argued that the basic impulses of Zionism resembled those of the American Progressive Movement of the early twentieth century. Just as Zionism sought freedom, social justice, and democracy for the oppressed Jews of Europe, so Progressivism sought freedom, social justice, and democracy for abused Americans. He was particularly impressed by the voluntary kibbutz movement, and helped found a kibbutz that was later named for him, Kibbutz Ein HaShofet—Hebrew for spring of the judge. An American Zionist, Brandeis argued, was not only a better Jew but also a better American, because Zionism exhibited precisely those impulses that Americans characterized as uniquely American. Zionism was thus a fulfillment and not a derogation of Americanism. "To be good Americans," he told a Jewish audience, "we must be better Jews, and to be better Jews, we must become Zionists." An American Zionist was thus by definition an ardent American patriot.

Brandeis's own life demonstrated this symbiosis between Zionism and Americanism. This leader of American Zionism was also the first Jew to give the Fourth of July oration in Boston's Faneuil Hall. Brandeis and his supporters refused to turn their backs on America or Americanization. The relative unimportance of American antisemitism when compared to that of Europe, the improving social and economic status of America's Jews, and American democratic political and social traditions warranted neither a blanket condemnation of the nation nor a wholesale exodus to Palestine.

Supporters of classic Zionism strongly opposed the Brandeisian synthesis of American identity and Zionism. Chaim Weizmann, the future first president of the state of Israel, accused the Brandesians of being ignorant of "all those questions in Zionism which have contributed so much towards the real life of the movement, like the Hebrew revival, like the desire of the Zionists to 'judaize' the Jewish communities of the world... in short, for all those imponderabilia which form a national movement of which Palestine is merely a territorial aspect of a national political upheaval." Louis Lipsky, an American supporter of Weizmann, described Brandeisianism as "a form of opiate for the Jewish masses, which would keep them in the bondage of a culture that could never lead to political rebirth."

From his perspective, Lipsky was correct, but he failed to realize that the political rebirth he sought for American Jews was already taking place in America. The character of Jewish immigration clearly showed the extent to which American Jews identified with their new homeland. Of all the major immigrant groups, Jews had a larger percentage of children and, next to the Irish, a larger percentage of women. When Jews came to the United States, they came with their families, and they came to stay. Their rate of repatriation was far lower than other immigrant groups. With nothing to return to in Europe, Jews had decisively broken their ties with the old country. And once in America, Jews rapidly learned English, flocked to the public schools, and became citizens with alacrity. Only a minuscule minority ever contemplated exchanging the benefits of life in America for a problematic existence in the Middle East. Their support for a Jewish homeland would be restricted to philanthropy, political lobbying, and tourism.

Undoubtedly the most important manifestation of Brandeisian Zionism was Hadassah, the women's auxiliary of the American Zionist Organization. Established by Henrietta Szold of Baltimore in 1912, Hadassah's mission was medical work in Palestine. Hadassah's eschewing of Jewish nationalism and *aliyah,* its ignoring of the political abstractions and ideology so dear to the hearts of European Zionists, and its emphasis on practical and concrete activities to alleviate suffering reflected the fundamental, nonnationalistic, charitable thrust of American Zionism. The Hadassash ideal, Szold correctly stated, "can be embraced by all, no matter what their attitude may be to other Jewish questions." Hadassah would become the largest and arguably the most powerful Jewish organization in the world. By 1980 it had 400,000 members, approximately ten times the membership of the National Organization of Women.

The middle-of-the-road Zionism that identified with Brandeis and Szold was strongly opposed by a variety of ideological purists. Elements within the Reform movement, particularly at the Hebrew Union College in Cincinnati, believed all forms of Zionism were tainted, to a greater or lesser extent, by Jewish tribalism. For them, the Pittsburgh Platform remained the last word regarding Zionism, and they continued to oppose it even when in 1937 in Columbus, Ohio, a new set of principles were adopted by the Central Conference of American Rabbis, the national association of Reform rabbis.

The Columbus Platform sharply revised the traditional American Reform position on Jewish identity and Zionism. No longer was Jewish identity viewed as solely a religious matter, and no longer was Zionism rejected out-of-hand. "We recognize in the group-loyalty of Jews who have become estranged from our religious tradition," the rabbis declared, "a bond that still united them with us." Furthermore, they affirmed, "In the rehabilitation of Palestine, the land hallowed by memories and hopes, we behold the promise of renewed life for many of our brethren. . . . We affirm the obligation of all Jewry to aid in its upbuilding as a Jewish homeland by endeavoring to make it not only a refuge for the oppressed but also a center of Jewish culture and spiritual life."

The Columbus Platform was, of course, a response to the European catastrophe that by 1937 was threatening to engulf European Jewry. The ideological consistency that had marked the Pittsburgh Platform retreated before the tragic reality of the Holocaust. The Reform rabbinate realized that there were more important things than ideological consistency. American Jews had a responsibility for European Jews not because they were members of the same religion but because of "group-loyalty." Some Reform spokesmen, however, remained anti-Zionist platonists.

They refused to allow facts, however disagreeable, to modify that classic Reform ideology that had emptied Jewish identity of any particular ethnic or nationalistic characteristics and had defined Judaism solely as a voluntaristic religion. In 1943, a dissenting group of Reform rabbis organized the American Council for Judaism after the Central Conference of American Rabbis in 1942 had gone on record in support of the formation of a Jewish Army composed of Palestinian Jews. The initial statement of the Council supported the concept of Palestine as a refuge for Jews, but it adamantly opposed the creation of a Jewish state or a Jewish army. Such a state, the Council contended, would detract from the universal teachings of Judaism, would lead to accusations of dual loyalty among Jews, and would confuse "our fellow men about our place and function in society and also divert our own attention from our historical role to live as a religious community wherever we may dwell." As the manichean-like title of Rabbi Elmer Bergner's book *Judaism or Jewish Nationalism* (1957) indicated, the American Council for Judaism believed the alternatives facing America's Jews were unambiguous.

The debate regarding a Jewish state became moot with the creation of Israel in 1948. American Jewry in general, and American Zionism in particular, then faced a vigorous challenge from Israeli officials and intellectuals who partially blamed American Zionism for the failure of American Jewry to migrate en masse to Israel. For them, American Zionism was a mere fund-raising operation and unable to instill into American Jewry either a love of Zion or a commitment to make *aliyah*. Abba Eban expressed the contempt of the Israelis for American Zionism in his quip that American Zionism demonstrated the truth of that fundamental religious belief that there can be life after death.

The confrontation between the Israelis and Americans came to a head in 1950–51 over the Israelis' claim that all Jews were obligated to migrate to Israel. American Jewish leaders promptly demanded that Israel officially acknowledge that American Jews had no political obligations toward Israel. Because of their concern for the future of Israeli-diaspora relationships, David Ben-Gurion, Israel's prime minister, backed down in August 1950. He publicly acknowledged that Jews in America were not living in exile, and that "the state of Israel represents and speaks only on behalf of its own citizens and in no way presumes to represent or speak in the name of Jews who are citizens of any other country. We, the people of Israel, have no desire and no intention to interfere in any way with the internal affairs of Jewish communities abroad." Jacob Blaustein, then president of the American Jewish Committee, welcomed Ben-Gurion's statement, but warned that it was insufficient unless accompanied by unmistakable evidence that Israel's leaders realize relations between Israel and American Jews "must be based on mutual respect for one another's feelings and needs, and on the preservation of the integrity of the two communities and their institutions."

The attempt to define a proper American Jewish stance toward Israel that would allow for a close identification between American Jews and the Jewish state but not derogate from their Americanism masked a growing ideological, psychological, and emotional commitment to Israel. The secularization of American Jewry, the numerical decline in the number of American Jews professing orthodoxy, and the atrophying of Jewish socialism, Yiddish culture, and other forms of Jewish identity prevalent among first-generation Jews left a vacuum in Jewish identity that was filled by Zionism, American-style. That Zionism was the major expression of American Jewish identity became clear only after Israel's incredible victory in the 1967 Six-Day War. It was during the dark days of May and early June, 1967, that American Jews realized the extent of their emotional identification with Israel and the degree to which support for Israel had become the lowest common denominator of American Jewish life.

This identification has been strengthened by another element within recent American Jewish culture—a growing interest in the Holocaust and a passion to learn its lessons. American Jews attend numerous Holocaust remembrance events, write and read a continuing flow of novels and histories of the European catastrophe, avidly view television shows and movies such as "The Holocaust," *The Sorrow and the Pity, The Pawnbroker, Diary of Anne Frank, The Wall*, "Playing for Time," and *Shoah*, endow university chairs and lecture series on the Holocaust, establish Holocaust museums and erect Holocaust statues, pressure state departments of education to establish Holocaust study programs in high schools, and engage in numerable other Holocaust-related activities. The most popular course in many Judaic departments in American universities is the history of the Holocaust. The Hebrew word *zachor* (remember) has become the codeword for this obsession with the Holocaust.

By the 1970s, the American Jewish community was defining its agenda and judging its accomplishments partially by the extent to which these conformed to the Holocaust's teachings. The most important American explicator of the meaning of the Holocaust has been the writer Elie Wiesel, the 1986 winner of the Nobel Peace Prize and himself a survivor of Auschwitz. His book *The Jews of Silence* (1966), which condemned the failure of world Jewry to work for the freedom of Russian Jews, evoked bitter memories of the 1930s and 1940s, when American Jews supposedly stood passively aside and allowed the slaughter of European Jews to occur unimpeded. Wiesel argued that the greatest sin of Jews in the post-Holocaust era was the sin of silence, the failure to hear the cries of help of fellow Jews.

Another eloquent voice in defining the meaning of the Holocaust has been Emil Fackenheim, a refugee from Hitler's Europe and a theologian at the

University of Toronto. Fackenheim proclaimed in his *The Jewish Return Into History: Reflections in the Age of Auschwitz and a New Jerusalem* (1978) the need for a 614th commandment to go with the 613 other commandments that devout Jews observe: "The authentic Jew of today is forbidden to hand Hitler yet another, posthumous victory." The book was dedicated to Yonatan Netanyahu, the hero of the Israeli Entebbe rescue of 1976, and it concluded with a segment from the official Israeli prayer for the state: "Our Father in Heaven, the Rock of Israel and her Redeemer, bless thou the state of Israel, the beginning of the dawn of our redemption. Shield her with the wings of Thy Love, and spread over her the tabernacle of Thy peace." This determination not to allow Adolf Hitler another victory explains the outrage of American Jews in 1985 when President Ronald Reagan visited the Bitburg cemetery.

Some American Jews have suggested that this consuming interest in the Holocaust has been counterproductive. Rabbi Daniel J. Silver of Cleveland, Ohio, for example, complained in 1986 that "the Holocaust cannot, and does not, provide the kind of vitalizing and informing myth around which American Jews could marshall their energies and construct a vital culture." Martyrs command respect, he argued, but the Jewish community's sense of sacred purpose must consist of something "more substantial than tears." Silver especially questioned the decision to build a Holocaust museum in Washington, D.C. "Such a museum," he feared, "will speak of death, not of life, of victimization, not civilization—a less than appropriate statement of the spirit of a people who, throughout their long history, have obeyed God's command: 'Choose life.' " "The fires of Hell are mesmerizing," he concluded, but Jews would be mistaken to organize their future solely by this light.

While there is merit in Silver's concern, it fails to take into consideration the fact that the meaning of the Holocaust for America's Jews is intimately related to the greatest life-giving event in modern Jewish history, the establishment of the state of Israel. For American Jewry, Israel is a contra-Holocaust, rescuing recent Jewish history from its bleakness and providing meaning and purpose to Jewish existence. To emphasize the relationship between the Holocaust and the Jewish state, missions sponsored by the United Jewish Appeal will often first visit Auschwitz before going to Israel. Many of the most popular post–World War II novels by American Jewish writers examined implicitly or explicitly the connection between Israel and the Holocaust. Among the most notable were Herman Wouk's *War and Remembrance* and Leon Uris's *Exodus*. The American-Jewish response to *Exodus* was particularly intense, and one observer dubbed it the Jewish *Uncle Tom's Cabin*.

The relationship between Israel and the Holocaust only became clear for most American Jews in 1967, when Israel and world Jewry were faced with possibility of another holocaust from a united Arab world. For Jews, the

Gentile world in 1967 exhibited the same apathy toward Jewish suffering that had marked its behavior during the 1930s and 1940s when, American Jews were convinced, the destruction of European Jewry could be explained in large part by the indifference of bystanders—officials in the Franklin D. Roosevelt administration fearful of the unfavorable political impact of welcoming a large number of Jewish immigrants to America, American Jewish organizations interested only in their own petty agendas, and British politicians concerned with preserving British interests in the Middle East. A series of historical and quasi-historical books with such titles *While Six Million Died: A Chronical of American Apathy* (Arthur D. Morse, 1967), *The Abandonment of the Jews: America and the Holocaust, 1941–1945* (David Wyman, 1984), and *Were We Our Brothers' Keepers?: The Public Response of Jews to the Holocaust, 1938–1944* (Haskell Lookstein, 1985) catered to this almost morbid obsession with allocating blame for the Holocaust among the Nazis' opponents.

The frantic response of American Jewry to the crisis of 1967—the unprecedented fundraising for Israel, the ears continually glued to radios in search of the latest news, the exultation at the amazing victory of Israeli arms—is understandable only against the backdrop of World War II. It was as if American Jews had spontaneously resolved to prevent another Holocaust, to wash away the strain of guilt carried by American Jewry because of the apathy they and their parents had demonstrated a quarter of a century earlier, and to demonstrate to the non-Jewish world that the period of Jews "going like sheep to the slaughter," as the popular description put it, had ended. Since the 1960s, there has been an upsurge of militancy within American Jewry ranging from acts of violence to a vigorous and blatant political lobbying unknown prior to 1967 on behalf of distinctly Jewish causes. Throughout, the major concern of Jewish spokesmen has been that seemingly ancient and parochial question, "But is it good for the Jews?"

This militancy has encompassed all strains of American Jewish life. Members of the Jewish Defense League and other organizations have bombed pro-Palestinian and Soviet offices in the United States. Other Jews have participated in giant demonstrations on behalf of Soviet Jewry and Israel. Jewish organizations and political action committees have put unprecedented pressure on Congress and the White House to encourage the Soviet Union to allow its Jews to emigrate, to guarantee the military and economic security of Israel, and to speak up for Jewish interests in Ethiopia and elsewhere. This new Jewish militancy has even modified individual behavior.

In the 1930s, the operative principle in Jewish life was *shah* (low profile). Jews were advised to be as inconspicuous as possible for fear of provoking antisemitism. Beginning in the 1960s, however, it became common to see Jewish men wearing skullcaps outside the home, Jewish women wearing stars of David, members of both sexes wearing buttons proclaiming "Kiss me, I'm Jewish," and Jewish comedians such as Lenny Bruce and Woody Allen telling Jewish jokes to largely Gentile audiences.

Jews also came out of the cinematic coast. In the 1960 film *Exodus,* the Israeli Ari Ben Canaan (Paul Newman) tells the Gentile Kitty Fremont (Eva Marie Saint) that she is wrong in believing that people are the same no matter where: "Don't believe it. People have a right to be different." And in the 1979 movie *Norma Rae,* the character Reuben Warshovsky, a northern union organizer, tells Norma Rae that they are different: "History makes us different." Indians speak Yiddish in *Cat Ballou* and *Blazing Saddles,* a black cabbie speaks Yiddish in *Bye Bye Braverman,* and a Japanese career woman speaks Yiddish in *Walk, Don't Run.* Barbara Streisand virtually built her Hollywood career playing Jewish characters. In *Funny Girl, The Way We Were, Yentl,* and other films she refused to dilute the Jewishness of the characters she portrayed, and she refused to get a nose job to modify her less than classic profile. In one song in *Funny Girl* she asks, "Is a nose with a deviation a crime against the nation?"

While these movies were being released, there was a dramatic upsurge of interest in Judaica on the American campus, and no major university was without its Jewish studies program offering courses in Jewish history, theology and philosophy, and Hebrew language. In the fall of 1985, *The New Yorker* magazine even published a lengthy three-part essay titled "Holy Days," which described in favorable terms a Hassidic sect in Brooklyn.

The overriding concern of this new Jewish militancy has been Jewish survival. While the dread of antisemitism has receded, it has been replaced by a fear of cultural assimilation and intermarriage. American Jewish leaders have come to realize that the marriage altar rather than the pogrom is the most immediate threat to American Jewish identity. This fear even affected television programming in the early 1970s with the appearance of the sitcom "Bridget Loves Bernie," featuring the tribulations of an intermarried couple. (Interestingly enough, the show's hero and heroine—the Jewish David Birney and the Gentile Meredith Baxter—were a couple off the tube as well as on it.) Despite their longstanding commitment to freedom of speech, Jewish organizations succeeded in having the program taken off the air.

During the 1970s and 1980s, Jewish task forces examined the condition of the Jewish family and Jewish education, particularly the extent to which they were barriers to intermarriage and transmitters of Jewish identity. The studies of the task forces were generally somber in their conclusions, although Jewish sociologists such as Steven M. Cohen and Calvin Goldscheider claimed that the evidence was more ambiguous than generally assumed and that optimism was as warranted as pessimism regarding the future of the American Jewish community. Pessimism, however, fit the new mood of American Jewry with its overriding concern for demographic and cultural survival. This mood resulted in some startling changes on the American Jewish scene, particularly within the Reform movement, which had always been the segment of American Jewry most willing to make the greatest modifications in Jewish law and practice to conform to the temper of American life.

The Reform movement, which had not welcomed Zionism and had remained unsympathetic to a Jewish state until World War II, now has a branch of its seminary in Jerusalem that all rabbinical students must attend prior to ordination. An even more startling development, because of its tradition of strong support of public schools and distrust of parochial education, has been the establishment under Reform auspices of several Jewish day schools. Reform's most controversial change has been its modification of the very definition of a Jew.

For millennia, to have been considered a Jew required that one either have had a Jewish mother or have been converted according to traditional Jewish law. In 1983, the Reform movement officially stated that it would consider a child of a Jewish father and a non-Jewish mother to be Jewish if the child was being raised Jewishly. The decision on behalf of patrilineal descent was due to a perceived skyrocketing intermarriage rate among American Jews. The Reform movement hoped the revised definition of a Jew and a more open attitude toward religious conversion would provide a sufficiently large enough pool of people to insure a vibrant American Jewish community in general and strong Reform congregations in particular.

For representatives of the Conservative and particularly Orthodox wings of American Jewry, the Reform movement's approval of patrilineal descent was a direct challenge to the integrity of the Jewish legal process and to fundamental Jewish tradition. Traditionalists were adamant that Jewish law could not be made to conform to the Reform movement's latest sociological concerns, particularly when it encouraged a fraudulent Jewish identity. "We can't go half-way," Rabbi Nosson Scherman declared. "I believe Torah is God-given, and I can't compromise on that." Traditionalists pointed out that if the Reform movement did not overturn its decision, no longer could prospective marriage partners assume that their prospective spouses were Jewish. Some marriages between supposed Jews would turn out to be intermarriages, and this would present observant Jews and their children with a whole host of Jewish legal problems, including questions of illegitimacy.

One prospect was that some Jews might not accept others as authentic Jews unless they provided family pedigrees. Orthodox rabbis predicted dire consequences would flow from the patrilineal decision unless the Reform movement recanted. In December 1985, Rabbi Haskell Lookstein claimed the division within the American Jewish community were so deep that it threatened "to isolate Jew from Jew and to rend the fabric of Jewish peoplehood so that we will no longer be one people." Rabbi Irving Greenberg predicted that by 1990 "there will be between three-quarters of a million and a million people whose Jewishness is contested or whose marriageability is denied by a larger group of other Jews." You have, he lamented, "a situation ripe for schism."

This pervasive concern with Jewish survival and Jewish identity arises out of the revolutionary situation in which American Jews found themselves. While America was not the Promised Land, it was the land of promise. America's Jews have been perhaps the major beneficiaries of America's liberal and capitalist social, political, and economic order. America's Jews today comprise the wealthiest and most influential diaspora community in history. Denied none of the benefits America has to offer, the nation's Jews have flocked to the universities, businesses, and professions in search of their share of the American Dream. Overall, they have not been disappointed. But the price Jews have had to pay for their rapid economic and social ascent has been an increasingly attenuated Jewish identity. "The threat of Jewish oblivion in America," Herman Wouk warned in the 1950s, "is the threat of pleasantly vanishing down a broad highway at the wheel of a high-powered station wagon, with the golf clubs piled in the back."

Most American Jews have eliminated those aspects of Jewish existence, such as distinctive dress and diet, that are barriers to economic and social mobility. Attendance at college, and approximately 85 percent of Jewish high school graduates enter college, places Jews at an impressionable age in an intellectual and social environment in which parochial ethnic and religious identities and values are viewed as anachronistic. The secularism of American life and the religious skepticism characteristic of the campus have undermined those Jewish identities largely derived from Judaism. The slogan of the United Jewish Appeal is "We Are One." But the oneness that holds Jews together is no longer Judaism or antisemitism but Israel. "For those without a sense of the Jewish past," the historian Luch Dawidowicz said, "Israel serves as the positively charged nucleus of Jewish identity." Israel provides the link that binds Jews together, no matter how remote they might be from any involvement in Jewish social or religious life. The Jewish thing most Jews have in common is not attendance at the synagogue (even on Yom Kippur) or providing a Jewish education for their children or supporting liberal political causes but contributing at least a nominal sum to United Jewish Appeal. In this respect, the UJA's slogan is apt.

The popularity of the United Jewish Appeal stems from the manner in which it distributes the over half a billion dollars it raises every year from America's six million Jews. While some dollars financed local institutions and other aid impoverished Jews in Europe, Asia, and Africa, over 50 percent of the UJA's allocations support social, welfare, educational, and economic development projects in Israel. And the importance of Israel and the UJA defines status within the Jewish community.

With fundraising the major priority, the emphasis in contemporary Jewish life is on philanthropy rather than Jewish learning or piety. The local Jewish federation, rather than the synagogue or the *yeshiva,* has become the major focal point of Jewish life and the major dispenser of prestige. The fundraising activity of the federation is supplemented by a host of other organizations working independently to raise money for Israeli institutions. Finally, there is the Israel Bond Organization, which every year sells about half a billion dollars in Israeli bonds to American Jews and their friends. Many observers have severely criticized this "check-book" Judaism, but they have been unable to suggest any alternative to even this attenuated Jewish identity that would appeal to acculturated and sophisticated Jews. The sociologist Charles S. Liebman predicted in his *The Ambivalent American Jew: Politics, Religion, and Family in American Jewish Life* (1973) that if Judaism in America was to perpetuate itself, "it must, at least to some extent, reject the value of integration, which I see as sapping its very essence." It is highly unlikely that this will take place.

In 1900, Jacob David Wilowsky, the prominent rabbi of Slutsk, Russia, told a New York audience that Jews who had migrated to America were sinners since they had placed the spiritual welfare of themselves and their children in mortal peril. In coming to America, Jews had left behind "their Torah, their Talmud, their yeshivoth—in a word, their Yiddishkeit, their entire Jewish way of life." Three years later, Wilowsky settled in Chicago and became chief rabbi of a group of orthodox congregations. If Wilowsky, one of the rabbinical giants of his age, could not resist the call of America, it was asking too much of less pious Jews to forego migrating to the "golden land." For every Jew who immigrated to Palestine during the late nineteenth and early twentieth centuries, perhaps fifty risked their souls and came to the United States.

It has been the hospitality of a free and open society to Jewish aspirations that has provided the major challenge to American Jews—to be simultaneously both Jewish and American, to withstand the allure of cultural assimilation while affirming the right to be an integral part of America. Certainly Jews still bear the imprint of the Jewish cultural legacy—in addition to liberal and at time Messianic politics, an educational elitism, and an occupational profile heavily tilted toward business and the professions. What is problematic is the ability of Jews to pass on to future generations a religious and cultural tradition that for many is no longer operative in their daily lives. Although valuable in themselves, cherishing Israel and contributing to Jewish charities are, in the long run, not weighty enough to support a strong Jewish identity. The same problem confronts today's Jews that confronted the first Jewish migrants to America—to establish the delicate balance that can satisfy the demands of both Jewishness and Americanness. Should the center cease to hold, it will not be because Jewishness has assumed a new importance.

BIBLIOGRAPHICAL ESSAY

The history of America's Jews and American Judaism is surveyed in Arthur A. Goren, "Jews," in Stephan Thernstrom, ed., *Harvard Encyclopedia of American Ethnic Groups* (1980), Henry L. Feingold, *Zion in America: The Jewish Experience From Colonial Times to the Present* (1974), Oscar Handlin, *Adventure in Freedom: Three Hundred Years of Jewish Life in America* (1954), and Nathan Glazer, *American Judaism* (1957, rev. 1972). The finest study of America's German Jews is Naomi W. Cohen, *Encounter With Emancipation: The German Jews in the United States, 1830–1914* (1984). The attitude of German Jews in America toward their East European co-religionists is discussed in Edward Shapiro, "German and Russian Jews in America," *Midstream* (April 1979). Goren's *New York Jews and the Quest for Community: The Kehillah Experiment, 1908–1922* (1970) is an important monograph exploring the inability of New York Jewry to establish a communal organization encompassing the city's entire Jewish population. Irving Howe's *World of Our Fathers* (1976) is an eloquent and lengthy elegy on American Jewish socialism, an important element of Jewish identity for a minority within the Yiddish-speaking first generation. A more critical attitude toward the Jewish identity revolving around left-wing politics is found in Shapiro, "Liberalism and Jewish Survival," *Congress Monthly* (June 1978), "Jewish Socialism in America," *Congress Monthly* (May 1980), and "Jews and American Politics," *Midstream* (March 1985).

A perceptive overall view of the status of contemporary American Jewish identity is Stuart E. Rosenberg, *The New Jewish Identity in America* (1985). Marshall Sklare's *America's Jews* (1971) is the best introduction to the economic and sociological status of today's Jews. The phenomena of Jewish involvement in business and American Jewish affluence are examined in Shapiro, "American Jews and the Business Mentality," *Judaism* (Spring 1978) and "Jews With Money," *Judaism* (Winter 1987). Calvin Goldscheider's *Jewish Continuity and Change: Emerging Patterns in America* (1986) comes to some optimistic conclusions regarding the strength of American Jewish identity, at least as far as Boston Jewry is concerned. Charles E. Silberman's *A Certain People: American Jews and Their Lives Today* (1985) is also optimistic, some would say overly so, regarding the contemporary condition of American Jewry. The role of humor in defining American Jewish identity is examined in Shapiro, "Heavy Shtetl," *The World and I* (April 1987). The entire Spring 1987 issue of *Judaism* discusses "Jews and Judaism in the Twenty-First Century Problems and Perils."

Steven M. Cohen and Leonard J. Fein, "From Integration to Survival: American Jewish Anxieties in Transition," *The Annals of the American Academy of Political and Social Sciences* (July 1985) is an excellent, brief discussion of the conflict between integration and ethnic-religious identity. Charles S. Liebman's *The Ambivalent American Jew: Politics, Religion, and Family in American Jewish Life* is an important book by a perceptive observer of American Jewish mores. John Higham, *Send These to Me: Jews and Other Immigrants in America* (1975), Arthur Mann, *The One and the Many: Reflections on the American Identity* (1979), and Milton Gordon, *Assimilation in American Life: The Role and Race, Religion, and National Origins* (1964) place the thinking of Emma Lazarus, Israel Zangwill, and Horace Kallen within their historical context.

The fullest discussion of American Zionism is Melvin I. Urofsky's two-volume study, *American Zionism From Herzl to the Holocaust* (1975) and *We are One! American Jewry and Israel* (1978). Shapiro, "American Jews and the State of Israel," *Journal of Ecumenical Studies* (Winter 1977) examines contemporary attitudes toward Israel. Hillel Halkin's *Letters to an American Jewish Friend: A Zionist's Polemic* (1977) argues that a Jewish life is possible only in Israel. The author settled in Israel in 1970.

Important studies of the various religious expressions of American Judaism are Gilbert Klaperman, *The Story of Yeshiva University: The First Jewish University in America* (1969), Marshall Sklare, *Conservative Judaism: An American Religious Movement* (1955, rev. 1972), Beryl H. Levy, *Reform Judaism in America: A Study in Religious Adaptation* (1937), and Mordecai Kaplan, *The Future of the American Jew* (1948). I have discussed the problems of contemporary Orthodoxy and Conservatism in confronting the challenges of American life in "Does Conservative Judaism Have a Future in America?," *Congress Monthly* (June 1982), "Orthodoxy in Pleasantdale," *Judaism* (Spring, 1985), and "100 Years: Yeshiva University and the Jewish Theological Seminary," *Congress Monthly* (March/April 1987).

American Jewish novelists have perceptively explored the often conflicting demands of being Jewish and American. Among the most important are Abraham Cahan's *The Rise of David Levinsky* (1917) and *Yekl: A Tale of the New York Ghetto* (1896), Anzia Yezierzka's *Hungry Hearts* (1920), and Henry Roth's *Call It Sleep* (1934). The American-Jewish identity of one novelist is explored in Shapiro, "Torah, Torah, Torah: Inside Herman Wouk," *Midstream* (January 1987). Reminiscences that emphasize the attractions of American Life are Yezierzka's *Red Ribbon on a White House* (1950) and Mary Antin's *From Plotzk to Boston* (1899) and *The Promised City* (1912).

Joseph A. D. Sutton's *Magic Carpet: Aleppo-in-Flatbush: The Story of a Unique Ethnic Community* (1979) describes a group that not only has a Jewish and an American identity but a Sephardic one as well. Howard Brotz's *The Black Jews of Harlem: Negro Nationalism and the Dilemma of Negro Leadership* (1970) does the same for another group within the American Jewish mosaic. Egon Mayer's *From Suburb to Shtetl: The Jews of Boro Park* (1979) is a sociological study of the adaptation of right-wing Orthodoxy to American life.

Two analyses of the important role of the Holocaust in defining American Jewish identity are Shapiro, "Historians and the Holocaust," *Congress Monthly* (1986), and Daniel Jeremy Silver, "Choose Life," *Judaism* (Fall 1986).

8

Italian-Americans

Dominic Candeloro

Though sometimes referred to as "The Children of Columbus," Italian-Americans as a people played only a minor role in American history prior to the 1880s.[1] Columbus *did* trigger intellectual, economic, and social revolutions with his discovery of the Western Hemisphere for Europe. Though his heroism endures as a symbol for Italian-Americans, the gap between Columbus's times and the presence of significant numbers of Italians in the United States is almost four hundred years. Nevertheless, we have reports of Venetian glassblowers among the early settlers in Virginia. And certainly, the role of Italian thought in Roman times, the Renaissance, and the Enlightenment had a definite influence on all educated people during the Colonial period. Thomas Jefferson and Benjamin Franklin were both familiar with the Italian language. The embodiment of Italian influence on the American Revolution is Filippo Mazzei, who was brought to Virginia to aid George Washington and Jefferson and their neighbors in scientific agriculture. His effort to bring the grape industry to Virginia failed, but Mazzei became one of the earliest advocates of independence from Britain in his newspaper articles signed "Furioso." Mazzei's close friendship with Jefferson resulted in several governmental appointments, but Mazzei left the country in the 1780s, and the opportunity for the development of an early chain migration of Italians was lost.[2]

The Founding Fathers and educated Americans in the nineteenth century continued to hold Italian art and culture in high esteem. Music teachers, architects, and the artists who embellished the capitol buildings were imported from Italy in that period, and Italian was one of the most frequently studied foreign languages in America. A series of priests, explorers, and opera stars achieved the kinds of things that sometimes merit brief mention in survey textbooks.[3] But there was still no significant Italian colony in the United States until the 1850s.

The 1850 Census reported a total of 5,000 Italians in America, mostly around New York City. The Italian revolutionary, Giuseppe Garibaldi, resided briefly on Staten Island with Antonio Meucci, an inventor of the telephone, during that period. St. Anthony's, the first Italian church in America, was founded in New York in 1866. In the 1880s Italian migration to the United States began in earnest and continued until immigration restriction in the 1920s, reaching reported peaks of 285,000 in 1907, 283,000 in 1914, and 222,000 in 1921.[4] Rough estimates are that five million Italians came to the United States in that forty-year period. With some notable exceptions, they came for economic reasons looking for *pane e lavoro* (bread and work).[5]

As refugees from an overpopulated rural nation, Italian emigrants joined millions in Western Europe and North America in experiencing the rough transition to modernization. Although southern Italy and Sicily sent the most immigrants, all parts of Italy contributed to the migration. The early migrants were mostly unskilled male workers, birds of passage, many of whom returned to Italy several times before they decided to stay in America permanently and to bring their wives and families with them. A good number returned to live in their native villages. The impact of these *rimpatrioti* on Italian social mobility and culture is a fascinating aspect of the unexpected consequences of emigration. These men often served as unofficial agents, expediting the chain migration process and helping to revitalize it in the post–World War II period. Sometimes the *rimpatrioti* successfully advanced their family fortunes by investing savings accumulated in the United States into small businesses or farms. Occasionally aspects of Italian modernization can be traced back to the returnees from industralized America.[6]

Restrictive immigration laws, Benito Mussolini's policies, the Depression of the 1930s, and World War II reduced Italian migration to a trickle from the 1920s to the late 1940s. A second wave of migration from Italy to the United States followed World War II, as residents of war-torn sections of Italy used every connection that they had to find opportunities to migrate to the United States and other countries like Canada, Argentina, and Australia. Waiting lists for migration to the United States were lengthy. Through all the periods of the Italian exodus there developed chains and networks of migration from Italian clans, towns, and regions to specific states, towns, and urban neighborhoods in the United States. For instance, many from the Abruzzi region ended up in the Philadelphia area, and a good percentage of the New Orleans, Louisiana, Italians are of Sicilian origin.[7] There are dozens of U.S. towns and neighborhoods whose population of descendants of an Italian town far exceed the current population of their town of origin. With the exception of New Orleans, Tampa, Florida, and West Virginia, Italian immigrants tended to avoid the South. Because they were capitalless sojourners and because most of the good agricultural land was spoken for, they ended up in the industrialized northeastern and north central cities. A significant segment settled in the West as a result of work on the railroads and in the mines of that region.[8] Perhaps the best established Italian-Americans today are the descendants of the Piedmontese vintners who migrated to California shortly after the Gold Rush. The Italian experience in America was influenced by the mix of ethnic groups, class relationships, and economic structure of the geographic areas where they settled. Thus, Joseph Bernardin (later Cardinal) had a different experience growing up in rural North Carolina with few Italians than did Mario Cuomo in New York City. And Italians in Chicago have played a lesser role in politics than those in New York or Rhode Island, where Italian ethnics make up a larger portion of the population.

Like other immigrant and minority groups, Italians suffered discrimination. They were poor, they were illiterate, they were considered a problem and were stereotyped as criminals, radicals, and buffoons. The largest single lynching in American history that took place in New Orleans in 1891 had as its victims eleven Italians.[9] More subtle discrimination persists into the 1990s in the form of negative stereotypes, and is the only significant "deprivation" of this well-heeled group that has moved from urban slums to middle-class status in barely three generations.[10]

An analysis of the nature and completeness of that transformation of five million immigrants into twelve million ethnics is the subject of this chapter.

Italian immigrants were not helpless entities filtered, Americanized, socialized, and homogenized into squeaky clean middle Americans. Though many of them were illiterate, they brought with them a richly-textured and time-tested folk culture based upon the institution of the family. Even in the migration process, the immigrants only temporarily abandoned their families in order to save them and reconstitute them in America. Italians brought with them a lively rural-paesani culture that, though imbued with class distinctions, lent itself to cooperative survival strategies in their new world. And the failing agricultural economy from which they were fleeing gave them the habit of hard work. The class consciousness of Italians who participated in strikes in Paterson, New Jersey, Lowell, Massachusetts, and Tampa is additional evidence of their inner-directedness. Add to that the religious traditions and folkways of nineteenth-century Italy and you have a substantial cultural base that belies the too-sympathetic notion espoused by Oscar Handlin that the immigrants were hapless victims of the brutal process of migration.[11] And the strength of that Italian cultural base goes far toward explaining ethnic retention.

Like other ethnic groups, Italian immigrants developed a range of self-help organizations. Their mutual benefit societies were based on their towns of origin and provided the early immigrants with minimal sick and death benefits before Medicare and before Social Security. Various national groups such as the Order of Sons of Italy of America (OSIA) tried to combine or federate the thousands of small lodges (average membership 250), but experienced only moderate success. Heavy involvement by the OSIA in Mussolini's Fascist propaganda campaign in the 1920s and 1930s had obvious disastrous consequences for the organization after the outbreak of World War II, and any hope of organizational unity through OSIA was dashed.

We can also consider the Italian-American press as something of a self-help organization. From the time of the founding of the first Italian newspaper in America by Francesco Secchi De Casali in 1849 (*L'Eco d'Italia*), the immigrant press has been there, providing the news of the day in their own language, promoting local political bosses, providing advice for coping in the New World, preaching fascism, preaching socialism, pushing protestantism, and acquiescing in Americanization. Of the dozens of Italian language newspapers once in existence, *Il Progresso Italo-Americano* (New York) remains the only daily. These newspapers depended upon an Italian-speaking public, and the radical newspapers also depended upon a sizeable socialist following. By the 1930s the monocultural Americanization policy had begun to have its effect. The second generation preferred their newspapers in English. This same phenomenon hit radio broadcasting about twenty years later.

Much has been written about Italian radicals.[12] This is both because their story is exciting and because they were by far the most literate element in Italian-American society, and the most literate are always overrepresented in history. Those few Italians who left Italy for reasons other than economic tended to be socialists and "anarchists," (perhaps better described by the term "radical democrat"). Leaders of these movements, like Carlo Tresca and Arturo Giovannitti, had a respectable following in a series of clothing workers strikes in Paterson and Lowell around 1910. The Italian section of the American Socialist party was one of the strongest before the Russian Revolution and the Nicola Sacco and Bartolomeo Vanzetti executions (1927). The 1917 Russian Revolution tainted all socialism with subversiveness, and the Sacco-Vanzetti case proved to Italian-Americans that the system was so prejudiced against Italians that even their most righteous causes could not get a fair hearing in this country. The execution of Sacco and Vanzetti crippled Italian-American radicalism and many of the Italian-language publications that espoused that philosophy.

Though *Il Progresso Italo-Americano* celebrated its 100th anniversary in 1981, its future survival depends upon the existence of a respectable base of Italian-speaking Italian-Americans, which is problematic now that emigration from Italy has ceased. Current Italian-American journalism reflects continued changes in the marketplace. *Fra Noi* (Among Us) is a monthly founded in 1961 by Fr. Armando Pierini to promote his old people's home, Villa Scalabrini in suburban Chicago. In 1983 the paper was taken over by professional journalists who expanded the scope of the paper and developed the Arts and Culture section in an effort to create a national sensitivity to Italian-American culture over and above the organizational life of the community. Slick magazines like *Attenzione, I-AM,* and *Identity* launched in the 1980s could never quite decide whether their constituency consisted of Italophile yuppies or second- and third-generation old-neighborhood types. Though they served a purpose in enhancing the awareness of Italian ethnicity, the slick magazines are gone now, and for the moment Italian-Americans are without an *Ebony*-type mirror.

In addition to mutual benefit societies and newspapers, Italian-American organizations cover a wide range of activities. Italian-American self-help organizations abounded in the post–World War II era to the point of excess. The Center for Migration Studies recently published a National Directory of Italian-American Organizations and a New York City Directory listing almost a thousand organizations of every imaginable size and scope.[13] Each new group presented itself as the one that would bring the elusive unity to the community. One of the roots of Italian-American disunity can be traced to *campanilismo,* an intense loyalty to an Italian town of origin that undermined allegiance on the national level. In addition, the controversy over Fascism, the lack of unifying issues, and the true, but hidden, purpose of all ethnic organizations have worked against organizational unity among Italian-Americans. Italians who were never really unified in Italy should not have expected unity within their immigrant colonies. From a group that had to stretch itself to develop loyalties beyond family to include the village and the region, it would be too much to expect a well-developed sense of national patriotism. Moreover, from 1922–41 the two most articulate elements among Italian-Americans, the Fascists and the anti-Fascists (mostly socialists) were at each others' throats.[14] Flashes of unity appeared after World War II in the relief efforts toward the war-torn old country and in later relief efforts following major Italian earthquakes. Since 1960, however, Italy has been prosperous. There is no need for Italian-American groups to jump to its defense or to lobby the United States on behalf of its survival as do Jewish-Americans for Israel or Polish-Americans for Poland. Thus, the need for unity is not critical.

Unity is also impaired by a natural tendency among social organizations (Italian and non-Italian, ethnic and nonethnic) for proliferation. The basic purpose of ethnic clubs and organizations is not to do good or to support minor charities, though they do that. Their basic purpose is to provide their leaders and their members with a manageable arena in which to achieve social recognition and affirmation. The endless stream of awards dinners, benefit fashion shows, ad books, and other fundraisers do not exist to stamp out disease or to provide scholarships. Their multiplicity serves to pass around the recognition as widely as possible and to affirm the dignity and worth of the leaders and members on a human scale, often creating a sense of community so lacking in mass society.

In the past dozen years, however, the National Italian American Foundation (NIAF) has come onto the scene. Based in Washington, the brain child of Fr. Geno Baroni (former undersecretary of HUD), bankrolled by Jeno Paolucci (of Jeno's Pizza Rolls), and promoted by Italian-American political figures like John Volpe (former governor of Massachusetts), and Congressman Frank Annunzio, the NIAF has established itself as the national spokesman for Italian Americans.[15] As always, Washington politicians are delighted to have only one entity to deal with in satisfying the desires of an ethnic group, especially one that is perceived as an emerging and complex one. By remaining bipartisan, by creating alliances with existing Italian-American organizations, and by developing a broad program of scholarships and cultural endeavors and links to Italy, the NIAF has gone further toward achieving a genuine, unified voice of Italian-Americans than any previous organization. The September 1984 appearance of all four major candidates for president and vice-president of the United States at the NIAF banquet was a high point in the prestige of the organization. Moreover, NIAF's ability to play a role or appear to play a role in the nomination and appointment of high-ranking political figures like Geraldine Ferraro, Supreme Court Justice Antonin Scalia, and Secretary of Defense Frank Carlucci adds to the self-fulfilling process of image building. The success of this national institution will reinforce the retention of ethnic identity among Italian-Americans far into the future and will act to counterbalance such antiretention trends as ethnic intermarriage.

EDUCATION AND SOCIAL MOBILITY

Formal education was not an important part of the experience of the early Italian immigrants. Well over 50 percent of the immigrants from Italy at the turn of the century were illiterate in their own language. And their own language was not likely to be standard Italian, but one of its hundreds of dialects. Illiteracy and the isolation created by Italy's mountainous geography encouraged the development of local dialects significantly different from standard Italian. Even today in Italy with its mass media and effective universal education, differing language patterns are a means of social distinction. The illiteracy of Italian immigrants and their sojourner mentality retarded their mastery of American English and blocked easy access to education as a stepping stone to social mobility. The immigrants valued hard work and family solidarity, and many of them had no intention of remaining long in the United States. They distrusted the conscious and unconscious messages sent back through their children by the middle class, Anglo-oriented school system. The kids got the message, too. Fifty to seventy-five years ago Italian-American kids played the roles of dropouts and cutups and troublemakers in the schools that today are being played by black and Hispanic teens.[16] This lack of opportunity was compounded by conflicts between the immigrant generation and their children. The desire for success without education and the opportunities presented by bootlegging helps to explain why some Italian-American youth turned to gangsterism.[17] Italian-American achievers are divided on the attitudes of their parents toward education.

Leonard Covello (a New York City educator) and Helen Barolini (a New York writer) both report that their parents discouraged them from "wasting time reading books."[18] On the other hand, many successful Italian-Americans report that their parents respected education and scrimped and saved and vowed that their kids would not have to do the heavy manual work that they themselves were condemned to do.

While the attitudes are debatable, the results are not. Italian immigrants were not very successful at passing their language on to their children and grandchildren. Few Italian Americans attended college before the late 1940s when the G.I. Bill began to take effect. College attendance by Italian-American youth was far below average well into the 1970s.[19] And while the ethnic group made inroads into the professions of law, medicine, and dentistry in the post–World War II era, the majority of Italian-Americans who reached middle-class status in the 1960s did so by means other than higher education.

Hard work at steady, unskilled jobs in an America that needed unskilled labor, long hours in small family business, and underconsumption were the elements crucial to Italian-American success in the first two generations. Upwardly mobile Italians turned to small businesses such as groceries, barbershops, shoe repair shops, fruit vending and restaurants because they required little capital and could be staffed by family members near home. Like other immigrant groups, Italians focused early on achieving home-ownership. Paychecks of all family members were turned over to the mother as portrayed in Mario Puzo's *Fortunate Pilgrim,* and the welfare of individual family members was subordinated to that of the family. Gardening skills and construction skills applied to two-flats over time yielded modest accumulations of capital. Mutual assistance within the extended family meant never having to buy in-season produce, to pay for a haircut, hire a plumber, or call a cab. Reciprocity in doing favors and in giving money gifts at birthdays, christenings, weddings, confirmations, and funerals gave extended family members access to spot-cash at critical moments in the life cycle.

The other side of the coin is that family solidarity might be stifling. Young people, especially girls, were subtly and directly discouraged from going away to school. Parents and relatives often pressured the upwardly mobile to refuse promotions that might take them out of town and out of their lives. Perhaps second-generation Italian-Americans, as the children of migrants who had split from their families in order to survive, were especially sensitive to the psychic costs of migration. Many were children of the Depres-

sion who valued security above all else, and a good number were de-ghet-
toized and given technical training by service in World War II. In any case,
until the 1970s Italian-Americans did not use higher education as their major
tool of social mobility into the middle class, and the group was consequently
underrepresented in the ranks of corporate leadership.

Times have changed. The statistics show Italian-Americans attending college at a rate roughly proportional to their presence in the general population.[20] While there might be some quibbling about their majors and the
relative prestige of the schools they are attending, modern Italian-Americans
are worshipping at the shrine of higher education. Upward ripples in the
number of students enrolled in Italian language classes reflect a sensitivity
on the part of Italian-American students and their parents to the importance
of the maintenance of their ethnicity.[21] It also reflects the fact that instruction
in the Italian language is no longer available in the homes and neighborhoods
of Italian-Americans. The language, the culture of Italy, and even the immigrant heritage are available only in the classroom and from cultural
institutions. The migrating generation of the first wave is just about gone.
The semi-ghettoized Italian neighborhoods and their institutions such as
athletic clubs, settlement houses, candy stores and churches, which shaped
the lives of second-generation Italians, have disappeared or worse—been
gentrified. It is ironic that many of the keys to the content of Italian-American ethnicity are no longer in the hands of the ethnics themselves but in
the possession of educational and formal cultural institutions.

Like other ethnic groups, Italians have formed a historical association to
promote the study and dissemination of information about the Italian-American experience. Founded in 1967 by Leonard Covello (the first Italian high
school principal in New York City) and a hardy group of academics, the
American Italian Historical Association (AIHA) adopted its unique name
to emphasize the continuity of Italianita. The group was an American brand
of Italians rather than a hyphenated American group on the verge of melting
into nondescript Americans. The name of the organization does exaggerate
to make its point, but it illustrates the zeal of its founders. AIHA membership
has grown to five hundred college professors, students, and community
amateurs in various fields of the humanities and social sciences. The organization holds annual conferences, publishes its proceedings, and has been
directly or indirectly involved in almost all of the scholarship on the subject
of Italian Americans in the past twenty years. But to say that it is a household
word to the twelve million Italian Americans in the United States would be
a gross exaggeration.

Another indication of a lack of development among Italian Americans of
an intellectual curiosity about themselves is the plight of Italian-American
literature. Aside from Pietro di Donato, Jerre Mangione, and Helen Barolini,
no Italian-American has become self-sufficient by writing on authentic Italian-American themes other than the Mafia. Mario Puzo himself went broke

before *The Godfather,* writing critically acclaimed commercial failures like *Fortunate Pilgrim.* Even the exquisite poet laureate of Italian-Americans, Joseph Tusiani, is almost unknown among his compatriots. Although AIHA and the *Fra Noi* are working to change the situation, Italian-American writers have not found an audience. Especially when compared to Jews and blacks, Italian-Americans, even the college-educated, cannot claim a learned and sophisticated appreciation of their ethnic history or the humanistic heritage of their nation of origin. Whether this will change among the current generation of Italian-American students is yet to be seen.

LABOR UNIONS

Italian-Americans have had considerable success in the labor movement. Though unions no longer represent radical class consciousness as they did seventy years ago, union membership and leadership have added to the welfare and security of a good part of the American population, including Italian-Americans. Italian-Americans have played prominent roles in a number of major unions. The International Laborers' Union has a membership of 500,000 and has been dominated by the Fosco family of Chicago (formerly of Molise) for the past several decades. It appears that ethnic, even regional, Italian considerations were important in the recruitment of membership and the growth of leadership in the union. Italians have shared leadership with the Jews in the Amalgamated Clothing Workers Union and in the Garment Workers Union (ILGWU) and have played important roles in the Teamsters Union. Both New York and Chicago boast Italian-American Labor Councils, composed of the ethnic group's leaders from a wide range of unions. Unions work for social mobility for their leadership at least as hard as they fight for higher wages and better working conditions for their members. This has occurred for Italian-Americans as it has for other ethnic groups.

While they are not always the most prominent as ethnic organizations, unions are among the best financed and organized of the entities that Italian-Americans use. Thus, the support of Italian-Americans union leaders for a fundraiser is often the key to success. Can it be a surprise that so many relatively obscure union leaders end up being "the man of the year" at Italian banquets?

This association has a darker side, because many of the union leaders have image problems that are even more severe for Italian-Americans.

THE NEWEST ORGANIZATION

Complicating the organizational scene among Italian-Americans is the establishment Co. Em. It. (Commitato d'Emigranti Italiana), an elective group to advise the consul general in each of a half dozen major U.S. cities.

Created by a vote of the Italian Parliament, Co. Em. It. is clearly an effort to keep recent Italian immigrants to the United States in the Italian sphere both legally and culturally. Co. Em. It. focuses on those who continue to hold Italian citizenship. Though often ignored by older Italian-American groups, the post–World War II immigrants consider themselves to be the natural leaders of Italian-Americans because of their close ties with contemporary Italian culture. The success or future of this new Co. Em. It. group will shed a good deal of light on the real importance that the Italian government attaches to preserving Italianita in the United States one hundred years after the start of mass migration, and the role of money and power in maintaining ethnicity.

RELIGION

The relationship of Italian-Americans to their religion is a complicated one. Italians are implicitly Roman Catholics. Rome is the seat of the Church. Evidence of the role of Catholicism in Italian culture and Western culture has been pervasive in the architecture, literature, and folkways of the Italian people for almost two thousand years. The Church has also been a political entity, with the popes of Rome scrambling and competing with local strongmen and foreign potentates for political domination of central Italy.

This kind of activity kept Italy from being unified as a modern nation until the latter part of the nineteenth century. The papacy was the last holdout, the final stumbling block to unification. When its temporal power was stripped away in 1870 the Church did not withdraw gracefully, but with a curse of excommunication on all the leaders in the unification movement. Thus, to be an Italian patriot was to be anticlerical. The Church played just the opposite role for Italian nationalism that it has played for Irish and Polish nationalism.

Just as important was the role that the Church played in the social and economic structure of the woebegone towns from which the emigrants fled. The Church was a landlord allied with the establishment with no motivation to encourage reform. Moreover, until the Scalabrini movement, few priests joined the waves of migrants to the new world. When Italians reached American cities in the 1890s and after, they found a Roman Catholic Church dominated by the Irish who sent them to the church basement to pray. This proverbial insult was probably due more to their differences in style of worship than to their language differences. Italians didn't care about Church rules so much; they didn't take to the catechism and puritanical bent of Irish Catholicism; and they were not in the habit of tossing their hardearned cash into the collection basket. Anticlericalism was strong among the socialists and others. Since large numbers were virtually unchurched, a variety of Protestant denominations targeted Italian immigrants for their brand of salvation. With a few notable exceptions, the considerable effort by American Protestants to convert Italians failed.

Probably the most important reason for this failure is that the Italians brought their folk religion with them. The cult of the virgin, devotion to patron saints of each village, and even the superstitious practices associated with the *mal'occhio* (evil eye curses) constituted a virtually indestructible core of culture that immigrants brought with them.

Religious street festivals have been the most outstanding characteristic of old Italian religiosity in America. Italians parading the graven images of saints and madonnas laden with money pinned to their garments was shocking to Protestant Americans and not a little disturbing to the Irish hierarchy and even some Italian priests. The San Rocco feast in the movie *Godfather II* was a masterly portrayal of the tradition. One would have thought that such maudlin folk practices would have been an early casualty to the Americanization process. Twenty years ago the number of such feasts had dwindled to a mere handful, but in recent times there has been a resurgence in the number and intensity of these celebrations. For instance, in Chicago in the 1920s you could attend a different festival each Sunday at the Sicilian St. Philip Benizi Church. In the 1980s in the Chicago area you can still attend a fiesta each Sunday, but you have to travel to different parts of the metropolitan area to do so. Although they are promoted as religious events, these clan-oriented activities have mixed charitable and commercial purposes that keep them alive. In Chicago, Milwaukee, and other cities for the past decade, the commercialized Fiesta Italiana has featured big-name Italian American entertainers, food, art, merchandise, rides and Sunday mass on the lakefront. The organizers (Unico) have attracted hundreds of thousands of people and have used the proceeds to encourage and support Italian-American culture and charitable activities—thus intensifying and perpetrating the identification of all participants and beneficiaries with things Italian. Ethnicity is nothing if not symbolic, and the fests themselves, laden with ancient and modern symbolism, proclaim a convincing challenge to all who would dismiss the importance of Italian ethnicity in the United States.

The anticlerical, superstitious, unchurched aspects of Italian-American religiosity were tempered by the presence in Chicago, New York, and New England of the Scalabrini order. Officially known as the fathers of St. Charles Borromeo, the order was founded in 1887 by Bishop Giovanni Scalabrini of Piacenza, who was moved by the Church's insensitivity to the needs of the immigrant masses. Scalabrini is credited with inspiring Mother Cabrini to shift her attention from Chinese missionary duties to work with Italian immigrants in the Americas. Scalabrini priests led the Italian immigrants in the establishment in the first quarter of the twentieth century of a hundred of schools and churches. The process of organizing to build churches and schools contributed mightily to the development of a sense of community within the Italian sections of larger cities. In Chicago the term "Italian community" would have been inconceivable without the leadership of the Scalabrini fathers, especially Armando Pierini, who established a seminary, an old people's home, and a newspaper (*Fra Noi*), which are today the focal centers for Chicago Italians. Gary Mormino, in *Immigrants on the Hill,* credits St. Ambrose church and its priests with maintaining community identity of St. Louis Italians.[22] In short, the Scalabrini Fathers did for the Italians what other religion orders have done for other ethnic groups: They maintained the combination of religion with national culture and language, preserving and strengthening both. Though the forces of suburbanization have scattered and hibernized Italian Catholics, and though the Scalabrini dedication to the immigrants in America has now extended to Mexican-Americans, the Scalabrini Fathers and their five hundred members around the world continue to play an important role in the maintenance and advancement of Italian ethnicity.

POLITICS

The early immigrants participated in politics as wards of the big-city bosses who got to the immigrants before the social workers. By giving out food baskets to the needy, attending wakes, helping youth out of scrapes with the police, and finding jobs for the immigrants, the bosses won their confidence, helped them apply for citizenship, and saw that they voted the right way. A key Italian-American political hero is Fiorello LaGuardia, who represented Italians and others as a New York City congressman for a decade before becoming mayor of New York in the 1930s. His practice of ethnic coalition politics was a model for all who followed. John Pastore of Rhode Island was elected the first Italian-American U.S. Senator in 1950 based on his popularity in what is now the most Italian state in the Union. Michael Di Salle served as governor of Ohio in the post–World War II period.

Italian-Americans appear to be well-represented in politics today. Mario Cuomo is governor of New York, Richard Celeste was governor of Ohio, some thirty congressmen and senators are Italian-Americans, Judge Scalia recently became the first Italian-American on the U.S. Supreme Court, Geraldine Ferraro was the Democratic nominee for vice-president in 1984 and Frank Carlucci is the current secretary of defense. Italian-American voting strength in New York, New Jersey, Pennsylvania, and some New England states is significant. It is not uncommon in these states to see Italian-Americans running against each other for major office. Politically speaking, it appears that Italian-Americans have arrived. Yet when compared to other ethnic groups, Italian-Americans lack unifying issues. They have not been the victims of racist oppression as have been the blacks; and they lack the forces of unity that motivate Jewish- and Polish-American activism in the political arena. Earlier in the century they had some working-class solidarity, and Italians were part of the Roosevelt Coalition. They voted for fellow

Catholic John F. Kennedy. Increasingly prosperous, middle-class, and small-business-oriented Italian-American voters most recently backed Ronald Reagan in the 1984 presidential election, snubbing their own Geraldine Ferraro, who was on the Democratic ticket as Walter Mondale's vice-presidential running nominee. Catholic leaders balked at supporting Ferraro because of her pro-choice stand on abortion. And, perhaps because she was a woman running in a hopeless race, grassroots and mid-level activity on her behalf by Italian-Americans was surprisingly absent.

Ferraro's experience in dealing with allegations that her husband and long-dead relative has some connection to organized crime demonstrates another unique aspect of Italian-American political participation. Although organized crime is a multi-ethnic industry and only a minuscule percentage of the twelve million Italian-Americans could possibly be part of the organized crime network, the specter of Al Capone and his ilk casts a shadow over the public perception of Italian-Americans, especially politicians. This image is reinforced by the exciting media images of gangsters that ironically, are often created by Italian-American writers, actors, and film makers. And the image is further intensified by the very real need of organized crime to infiltrate the political establishment in order to get protection from strict law enforcement. The result is the popular perception that politicians, especially Italian-American politicians, are "connected." Even a seasoned and well-meaning journalist like Sam Donaldson lent credence to thoughtless Mafia stereotyping when he stated on the Oprah Winfrey TV show that, of course, investigative journalists would look for Mafia connections in the past of any Italian-American candidate for high office. Perhaps the most vicious aspect of this phenomenon is that *Italian-Americans* distrust each other. Politically ambitious Italian-Americans are often satisfied to settle for appointive judgeships rather than subject themselves to the ordeal of Mafia innuendos. The NIAF has been successful in encouraging Italian-Americans to have higher ambitions by promoting Italian-Americans without regard to political philosophy to see "some of our own" in high government positions. Even the NIAF has been frustrated, however, in trying to develop among Italian-Americans a habit of contributing substantial amounts to the political campaigns of their co-ethnics. For the foreseeable future, the group will not come anywhere near the political funding patterns of the Jews and the Greeks.

Aside from power considerations, the chief reason for Italian-Americans to enter the political arena appears to be the desire for respect. Italians are not poor, not unemployed, not grossly discriminated against, or significantly disadvantaged in any other way except for the negative or trivialized image that the larger society has of them and that they sometimes have of themselves. The major task of Italian-American organizations is to get the general society to take an objective look at them, free of the easy stereotypes.

Many inside and outside of the Italian community are convinced that if we only had an Italian-American president like Mario Cuomo or Lee Iaccoca, unfair stereotypes would disappear as they did with the election of our first Catholic president. This is the miraculous solution that makes unnecessary the slow process of building positive self-images based on solid cultural knowledge.

SUBURBANIZATION

Modernization has definitely assaulted Italian-American ethnicity. Suburbanization destroyed the ethnic neighborhoods. They no longer exist as self-perpetrating enclaves but (where they have partially survived) as ethnic theme parks. Ethnic retention can no longer be geographically based. Ethnic newspapers, metropolitan-based ethnic professional organizations, radio and TV broadcasts, and the teaching of the Italian language in the schools and universities are the only basis upon which ethnicity must rely if it is to survive. Though still the best carrier of ethnicity, the Italian-American extended family is not immune from divorce, birth control, and exogamy and fragmentation.

Some aspect of modernization might strengthen Italian-American ethnicity. The growing fascination of yuppie America with food and travel leave them with a positive attitude toward Italian food customs, language and lifestyle. And Italian-Americans stand tall in the reflected light of the Mother Country. Easy international travel and satellite TV will keep post–World War II Italian immigrants bound more closely to Italian culture than were previous generations of immigrants. The spectacular success of the direct broadcast via satellite of Italian soccer matches to Italian-American sports clubs (at 8 A.M. Sunday mornings) is hard evidence of the potential of satellite communication for keeping Italy's immigrants in all parts of the world in touch with their culture. And since it is clearly in the commercial, political, and cultural interest of Italy (population 57 million) to maintain cultural links with its perhaps 50 million immigrants and their descendents in the United States, Canada, Argentina, Australia, and elsewhere, we can expect that modernization will facilitate the maintenance and perhaps growth of Italian culture among Italian-Americans.

What will be lost through modernization are the Italian-American ethnic neighborhood folkways that played such an important role in shaping previous generations of Italian-Americans. In short, modernization can help us conquer the geographic space between America and Italy, but it has the opposite effect on our ability to conquer time and link up with the ethnic neighborhoods of fifty years ago. Popularized ethnic history and the blockbuster authentic Italian-American novel or film are the only ways of recapturing the "old neighborhood" for the modern Italian-American consciousness.

Italian-American ethnicity has come a long way from the time when upwardly mobile immigrants routinely changed their names to avoid identification with the wretched refuse. Third- and fourth-generation Italians seem pretty comfortable with (if not terribly knowledgeable of) their ethnic identity. They are thoroughly American and only part-time consumers of their Italian-American ethnicity. A small minority are Italian-American activitists who can gain entry to the larger social arena through their leadership in ethnic organizations or who have support in their professions from fellow Italian-Americans. The latest emigrants through organizations like Co. Em. It. and through satellite TV links and jet travel back to Italy, may achieve a kind of emigre status.

A tiny fantasy-based minority of second- and third-generation Italian-Americans dream of leaving tawdry America, returning to Italy, and demanding reparations and a homeland for the historical wrong done to them and their families by the forced emigration from Italy.

An idyllic vision of the Italian ethnicity in the United States is projected for a third- or fourth-generation college-educated group. This group will learn the Italian language in high school and college. They will gain an appreciation for their roots in the migration process and the ethnic neighborhoods through Italian-American cultural institutions. This would give them a creative and tolerant understanding of all ethnic groups. Their education would be punctuated by early and frequent trips to Italy. They would approach biculturism and their contacts with Italians all over the world would give them a global perspective. The range of Italian-American modalities is wide, but there are few indeed among them who would deny their identity. American policy on ethnicity seems to have settled into a half-hearted acceptance of the harmless aspects of multiculturalism. For most Italian-Americans, that is all the approval they need. It might not be enough for Co. Em. It. types. Most important, for the maintenance of Italian-American ethnicity, are the socio-psychic needs that individuals and groups have to create a comfortably scaled arena for their lives and the current positive image of Italy in American public opinion.

NOTES

1. Erik Amphiteatrof, *The Children of Columbus: An Informal History of the Italians in the New World* (Boston, 1973).

2. Margherite Marchione, *Selected Writings and Correspondence of Philip Mazzei* (Millwood, N.Y., 1982).

3. Alexander DeConde, *Half Bitter, Half Sweet: An Excursion into Italian American History* (New York, 1971).

4. Luciano Iorizzo and Salvatore Mondello, *The Italian Americans* (Boston, 1980).

5. George Pozzetta, ed., *Pane e Lavoro: The Italian American Working Class* (Toronto, 1980).

6. Betty Boyd Caroli, *Italian Repatriation from the United States* (New York, 1974).

7. Fondazione Giovanni Agnelli, *The Italian Americans: Who They Are, Where They Live, How Many They Are* (Turin, 1980).

8. Andrew Rolle, *The Immigrant Upraised* (Norman, Oklahoma, 1968).

9. Richard Gambino, *Vendetta: A True Story of the Worst Lynching in America,* (Garden City, N.Y., 1977).

10. Stephen Hall, "Italian Americans: Coming Into Their Own," *New York Times Magazine,* May 15, 1983.

11. Oscar Handlin, *The Uprooted* (Boston, 1951).

12. Rudolph Vecoli, "Pane e Giustizia," *La Parola del Popolo* (September-October 1976).

13. Silvano Tomasi, *Italian Culture in the United States: A National Directory of Research Centers, Repositories, and Organizations of Italian Culture in the United States* (New York, 1979), and Andrew Brizzolara, *A Directory of Italian and Italian American Organizations and Community Services in the Metropolitan Area of Greater New York* (New York, 1980).

14. Gaetano Salvemini, *Italian Fascist Activities in the United States* (New York, 1977), and Philip Cannistraro, "Generoso Pope and the Rise of Italian American Politics, 1925–1936," *The Italian Americans: New Perspectives in Italian Immigration and Ethnicity,* ed. Lydio Tomasi (New York, 1985).

15. Frank J. Cavaioli and Salvatore J. LaGumina, *The Ethnic Dimension in American Society* (Boston, 1974).

16. Leonard Covello, *The Social Background of the Italian American School Child* (Leiden, 1967).

17. Humbert Nelli, *The Business of Crime* (New York, 1976).

18. Leonard Covello, *The Heart is the Teacher* (New York, 1958).

19. Richard Gambino, *Blood of My Blood: The Dilemma of Italian Americans* (New York, 1974).

20. Nampeo McKenney, Michael Levin, and Alfred Tella, "A Sociodemographic Profile of Italian Americans," in *Italian Americans: New Perspectives,* ed Tomasi.

21. Edoardo Lebano, "Report to the Conference Linqua e Cultura Italiana negli Stati Uniti," Rome, March 30-April 1, 1987.

22. Gary Mormino, *Immigrants on the Hill: Italian Americans in St. Louis, 1882–1920* (Chicago, 1986).

BIBLIOGRAPHICAL ESSAY

The best brief introduction to Italian-Americans is Humbert S. Nelli, "Italians," in Stephen Thernstrom et al., eds., *Harvard Encyclopedia of American Ethnic Groups,* (Cambridge, Mass. 1980), 545–60. During the past two decades, there has been a significant outpouring of reference works on Italian-Americans, beginning with Wayne Moquin and Charles Van Doren, eds., *A Documentary History of the Italian Americans* (New York, 1974), which includes documents ranging from Columbus to Vince Lombardi, organized around the topics of the age of discovery, the period of mass migration, making a living, organized crime, discrimination, and the emergence of the Italian-American. The record made and the institutional structure developed by generations of Italian-Americans was captured by Silvano Tomasi, *Italian Culture in the United States: A National Directory of Research Centers, Repositories, and Organizations of Italian Culture in the United States* (New York,

1979). The ongoing interest of those remaining in the Old Country in understanding the immigrant experience has led to the publication of Fondazione Giovanni Agnelli, *The Italian-Americans: Who They Are, Where They Live, How Many They Are* (Turin, 1980). Andrew Bruzzoloro, *A Directory of Italian and Italian American Organizations and Community Services in the Metropolitan Area of New York* (New York, 1980) graphically illustrates the significant impact of Italian-American culture on the country's largest city.

The impressive outpouring of literature can best be apprehended in a number of bibliographies. C. M. Diodati et al., *Writings on Italian-American: A Bicentennial Bibliography* (New York, 1975) reflects the ethnic revival of the 1970s. Francesco Cordasco, ed., *Italians in the United States: A Bibliography of Reports, Texts, Critical Studies, and Related Materials* (New York, 1972) is an unannotated compilation designed to present a sufficient representation of Italian-American literature to afford both orientation and resources for further study. His *The Italian-American Experience: An Annotated and Classified Bibliographical Guide, With Selected Publications of the Casa Italiana Educational Bureau* (New York, 1974) contains a list of bibliographies and archives, as well as a bibliography of works dealing with Italian immigration to America, general and regional studies, and analyses of social, political, and economic structure and institutions. His *Italian Mass Immigration: The Exodus of a Latin People: A Bibliographical Guide to "Bolletino dell Emigrazione", 1902–1927* (Towata, N.J., 1980) focuses directly on studies dealing with the peak migration years.

Single-volume overviews of Italian immigration and ethnicity date from the publication, originally in 1919, of Robert F. Foerster, *The Italian Emigration of Our Times* (New York, 1968), which is primarily a detailed examination of the causes of emigration that is highly critical of the Italian government. Michael Musmanno, *The Story of the Italians in America* (New York, 1965), stresses the socioeconomic successes of Italian America in a highly uncritical manner. Two books by Andrew F. Rolle, *The Immigrant Upraised: Italian Adventurers and Colonists in an Expanding America* (Norman, Okla. 1968) and *The American Italians: Their History and Culture* (Belmont, Calif. 1972) both stress immigration, to the western states before the onset of the twentieth century. Silvano Tomasi and Madeline H. Engel, eds., *The Italian Experience in the United States* (Staten Island, N.Y., 1970) is a collection of essays by ten scholars dealing with settlement patterns, institutions, political activity, religion, and return migration. Joseph Lopreato, *Italian Americans* (New York, 1970), investigates settlement patterns, the impact of continuing immigration on social institutions and intergroup relations, the process of adaptation and achievement. Luciano J. Iorizzo and Salvatore Mondello, *The Italian Americans* (New York, 1971), survey the varieties of Italian-American experience on farms, small towns, and large cities, focusing on politics, occupations, crime, religion, and reaction to Mussolini. Alexander De Conde's *Half Bitter, Half Sweet: An Excursion into Italian-American History* (New York, 1971) explores the paradoxical relationship between the Italian and the American peoples, institutions, and cultures, in both the Old World and the New. Erik Amphiteatrof, *The Children of Columbus: An Informal History of the Italians in the New World* (Boston, 1973), stresses the rich diversity of Italian-Americans, as well as their sense of "being looked down upon." In a highly personalized blend of scholarship and experience, Patrick J. Gallo attempts to correct many myths and sterotypes in *Old Bread, New Wine: A Portrait of the Italian-Americans* (New York, 1981). Gallo has also thoughtfully explored the causes of Italian-American discontent in *Ethnic Alienation: The Italian Americans,* (Rutherford, N.J., 1974) and edited the proceedings of the eighth annual conference of the American-Italian Historical Association under the title *The Urban Experience of Italian Americans* (Staten Island, N.Y., 1976).

An appreciation of the importance of locale on the formation of Italian-American identity and culture can be gained from a collateral reading of some of the many works on specific communities. Robert F. Harney and Jean Vincenza Scarpaci, eds., *Little Italies in North America* (Toronto, 1981) includes essays on New York, Toronto, Montreal, Philadelphia, Baltimore, Tampa, St. Louis, and Oswego, New York. The Federal Writers Project of the Works Progress Administration produced a detailed study of the country's largest Little Italy in *The Italians of New York: a Survey* (New York, 1938). Almost a half century later, armed with the insights of the new social history, Donna R. Gabaccia, *From Italy to Elizabeth Street: Housing and Social Change Among Italian Immigrants, 1880–1930* (Albany, N.Y., 1984), explored the changes in family, housing, customs and living conditions of Sicilian immigrants to the same metropolises. Farther north in the Empire State, John W. Briggs, *An Italian Passage: Immigrants to Three American Cities, 1890–1930,* compares and contrasts the communities formed in Utica and Rochester, as well as their counterpart in Kansas City, Missouri. In *Mount Allegro: A Memoir of Italian American Life* (New York, 1981), Jere Mangione describes the phenomenon of growing up Sicilian in Rochester, New York, where the immigrant generation either gradually displaced Italian solutions with American or retained the former while allowing their children to make a free choice. Their counterparts in Buffalo, according to Virginia Yans-McLaughlin, *Family and Community: Italian Americans in Buffalo, 1880–1930* (Ithaca, N.Y.: 1977), resisted outside pressures toward independence and individualism and maintained strict sex role definitions and adult-centered family structures. The Lombards and Sicilians who immigrated to St. Louis built an enduring community by combining extensive ethnic clustering, physical and social isolation, and deep roots with limited geographical and social mobility, according to Gary Mormino, *Immigrants on the Hill: Italian Americans in St. Louis, 1881–1920* (Chicago, 1986). Joseph J. Barton, *Peasants and Strangers: Italians, Rumanians, and Slovaks in an American City* (Cambridge, Mass., 1975), contends that Italians and Slovaks perpetuated particularistic cultural values that kept them in the working class for two generations while the Rumanians experienced much greater upward social mobility. Carlo Bianco, *The Two Rosetos* (Bloomington, Ind., 1975), chronicles the migration of an entire village in southern Italy to southeastern Pennsylvania and analyzes their efforts to keep much of their culture, folklore, and dialect intact. Finally, Humbert S. Nelli, *Italians in Chicago, 1880–1930: A Study in Ethnic Mobility* (New York, 1970), explores settlement patterns, economic and political life, community institutions, crime, and assimilation.

Other scholars have focused their attention primarily on the Italian-American social structure and on the mores that underlie it. Edward C. Banfield, *The Moral Basis of a Backward Society* (New York, 1958), generalizes from his own experiences in a small south Italian village that an "amoral familialism" prevents the development of "public-regarding" civic consciousness among Italian-Americans. That same familial bond, according to Francis A. J. Ianni, *A Family Business: Kinship and Social Control in Organized Crime* (New York, 1972), accounts for the marked similarity in crime families that leads outsiders to see a nationwide network of organized crime. By the same token, Humbert S. Nelli, *The Business of Crime: Italians and Syndicate Crime in the United States* (New York, 1976), insists that the syndicate is really a loose, multiethnic federation. Similarly, according to William F. Whyte, *Street Corner Society: Social Structure of an Italian Slum* (Chicago, 1955), the kinship bonds formed in street gangs in the "Cornerville" section of "Eastern City" carry over into careers in the rackets and in politics. Francesco M. Cordasco and Eugene Bucchioni, *The Italians: Social Backgrounds of an American Group* (Clifton, N.J., 1974), examine chain migration patterns, responses to American life, employment, health, social needs, and the educational experience of Italian children in American schools. Herbert J. Gans, *The Urban Villagers: Group and Class in the Life of Italian Americans* (Glencoe, Ill., 1962), examines Boston's West End, its internal social structure, and its relationship with the larger metropolis. Lawrence Frank Pisani, *The Italians in America: A Social Study and History* (New York, 1957), stresses the role played by Italian-Americans in labor, religion, arts, science, and the urban scene.

The place of community institutions in the adaptive process of Italian-Americans has also received increasing attention. Silvano Tomasi, *Piety and Power: The Role of Italian Parishes in the New York Metropolitan Area, 1880–1930* (Staten Island, N.Y., 1975), contends that the Italian national parish was the primary building block of the ethnic community and the main conservator of culture. He and Edward C. Stibili, *Italian Americans and Religion: An Annotated Bibliography* (New York, 1978), provide an organized guide to numerous parish histories and to over eight hundred books and articles on religion. In two related works, *The Heart Is the Teacher* (New York, 1958) and *The Social Background of the Italo-American School Child* (Towato, N.J., 1972), Leonard Covello provides the historical background and the technical analysis to understand the conflict between Old World culture and public education faced by young Italians. Edwin Fenton, *Immigrants and Unions, a Case Study: Italians and American Labor, 1870–1920* (New York, 1975), argues that while union membership accelerated acculturation and assimilation, Italian workers also forced unions to alter their programs and tactics in significant ways. In *Pane E. Lovoro: The Italian-American Working Class* (Toronto, 1980), George E. Pozzetta, ed., and others explore their role in well-known strikes and nine disasters, the conflict between the padrone system and labor unions, and their reactions to Fascism and to the Vietnam War. Although the title is somewhat restrictive, John H. Mariano, *The Italian Contribution to American Democracy* (Boston, 1924) deals with a range of socioeconomic and demographic issues and draws conclusions regarding acculturation and assimilation, based largely upon responses from questionnaires.

Throughout all the processes of acculturation and community building, Italian-Americans never lost their connections to the homeland. Many Italians continued to function as "birds of passage" as Betty Boyd Caroli, *Italian Repatriation from the United States, 1900–1914* (New York, 1974), clearly demonstrates. Although some of this migration was forced by one government or the other, most of it was voluntary on both sides of the ocean. John P. Diggins, *Mussolini and Fascism: The View from America* (Princeton, N.J., 1972) examines the degree to which the values, symbols, and images of fascism appealed to American Italians of various backgrounds. Gaetano Salvemini, *Italian Fascist Activities in the United States* (New

York, 1977), demonstrates that Mussolini was more attractive to economically successful Italian-Americans than he was to working-class people.

As with every ethnic group, debates still rage over the pace, degree, and contours of the adaptation process. Almost a half century ago, Irvin L. Child, *Italian or American? The Second Generation in Conflict* (New York, 1943), posed the dilemma of acculturation in psychological terms. In *An Ethnic at Large: A Memoir of America in the Thirties and Forties* (New York, 1978), Jere Mangione resolves that dilemma by becoming an "ethnic-at-large," with one foot in his Sicilian heritage, the other in the American mainstream, a "cultural gymnastic stance" that enables him to gain strength from his past and hope from his present. In her biography *Rosa: The Life of an Italian Immigrant* (Minneapolis, 1970), Marie Hall Ets concludes that what Rosa had learned in America was not to be afraid. Confronting the dilemma in 1975, Richard Gambino, *Blood of My Blood: The Dilemma of Italian-Americans* (Garden City, N.Y., 1975), argues that to be Italian in the United States means to develop hyphenated values concerning work, sex, and sex roles, family, religion, education, and politics. Silvano M. Tomasi, ed., *Perspectives in Italian Immigration And Ethnicity* (Staten Island, N.Y., 1977) is a collection of papers by sixteen American and Canadian scholars on new Italian American identity, the state of research on Italian-Americans, and new directions in that research.

9

Chinese-Americans

Bernard Wong

This chapter addresses the problem of assimilation of the Chinese in the United States. Assimilation is defined in this chapter as a process whereby immigrants discard the culture traits of their land of origin and acquire the culture of their host country through marriage, citizenship, participation in the institutions of the host society, internalization of the values of the larger society and adoption of their behavior and attitudes.[1]

Historically, the Chinese have been in the United States longer than many white ethnic groups. The history of the Chinese in America could be traced back to 1781 or even earlier.[2] However, sizable numbers of Chinese immigrants started to arrive only after 1850.[3] The number of immigrants steadily increased and peaked in 1890 with a population of 107,488 (see Table 1). Hereafter, as a result of various discriminatory legislation (to be discussed later), the number of Chinese immigrants dwindled down to 61,639 in 1920. After World War II, there was an increase of Chinese immigration. This influx was hastened further by the passage of the New Immigration Act of 1965. The census of 1980 indicated that there were 806,027 Chinese living in the United States. The 1987 estimate was around one million. Thus, there were several waves of Chinese immigration movements to the United States. One wave occurred before the 1880s, the second after World War II, the third after 1965. The history of the Chinese-Americans can be roughly divided into four periods: 1850–82, 1883–1943, 1943–65, and 1965-present. These periods coincide, more or less, with the immigration waves of the Chinese and demarcated major legislation affecting the Chinese.

Although Chinese-Americans have interacted with U.S. society for more than two hundred years, the rate of assimilation has been relatively slow as compared to European ethnic groups in America. The "melting"

Table 1
Chinese Population in the United States by Sex: 1860–1980

Date	Total	Male	Female
1860	34,933	33,149	1,784
1870	63,199	58,633	4,566
1880	105,465	100,686	4,779
1890	107,488	103,620	3,868
1900	89,863	85,341	4,522
1910	71,531	66,856	4,675
1920	61,639	53,891	7,748
1930	74,954	59,802	15,152
1940	77,504	57,389	20,115
1950	117,629	77,008	40,621
1960	237,292	135,549	101,743
1970	431,583	226,733	204,850
1980	806,040	407,544	398,496

Source: United States Census, 1860–1980

process between the Chinese and the dominant society has been relatively unsuccessful. Thus, the "melting pot" theory, or the "natural history"[4] model have not proven successful in explaining the assimilation of the Chinese.[5] These theories, which asserted the inevitable outcome of assimilation as a result of race contact, could not account for the slow assimilation or nonassimilation of ethnic groups. In the case of Chinese-Americans, assimilation occurred only after World War II. The rate of assimilation quickened after 1965. What accounts for these changes is the subject of this chapter.

The indices used to measure assimilation are varied and debatable, but I consider the following to be significant indicators: interracial marriage, naturalization, participation in the political, social and economic institutions of the host society, internalization of values and adoption of behavioral pattern and attitudes of U.S. society. As measured by these major indices, the process of assimilation was extremely slow in the pre–1945 era but increased speed after 1945 and accelerated further after 1965. The major causes for this pattern of assimilation of the Chinese are macroenvironmental, emanating principally from the encapsulating culture.[6] In this chapter, I will attempt to identify and delineate some of these variables and describe how such exogeneous factors have affected the assimilation of the Chinese in America.

LIMITED PARTICIPATION IN AMERICAN LIFE: 1850–1882

During this period, the participation of the Chinese in the American economy was limited to California and in the construction of the Central Pacific Railroad. The Chinese were recruited to work principally in the exploitation of the mines, the building of the railway and the cultivation of agricultural land. They provided cheap labor for the much needed labor-intensive activities at the frontier and generally worked in jobs disdained by whites. This period is characterized by many historians as a free migration period for the Chinese.[7] Chinese economic activities in this period did not extend to the Midwest or the East Coast.

The need of Chinese laborers in America does not explain the total picture of why the Chinese left China. Considering the hardship involved, there must have been more compelling reasons for departing from China. To leave the Middle Kingdom in order to live among the "savages" was considered to be an apostasy. China was never a migratory nation like some European countries.[8] Chinese were brought up to honor their ancestral land, and to root in their native land to perpetuate their ancestry. The way of life was considered to be superior to any other savage way of life. It was also against the law to leave China. Under the Manchu's law in the 1800s, people caught leaving their country could be decapitated. Furthermore, there were no Chinese embassies or other government organizations that could assist Chinese immigrants.[9] And travel by steamboat crossing the Pacific to a strange new land was hazardous both psychologically and physically. Yet, the Chinese left for America. The reasons for leaving, as it turned out, outweighed the hazards of travel and other considerations.

At the time of the "Gold Rush" in California, the Chinese were encountering insurmountable economic difficulties at home. First, in the southern provinces of Fukien and Kwangtung, the man/land ratio was exceedingly high.[10] The continuing overpopulation did not help in alleviating the economic problem. Second, the Taiping Rebellion (1850–64) and its aftermath laid waste to the livelihood of many. This, coupled with famine, plundering and political corruption, caused many of the people to seek economic opportunities abroad. Many sold themselves as contract coolies to work overseas. Others were recruited by international labor peddlers to work in the "mountain of gold" as miners, farmers, domestics or railroad laborers. Their immediate goal was to work hard and amass some savings and then return home to lead a life of leisure or to become entrepreneurs or landlords in China.[11] They had no intention to stay in America permanently. Some called these early arrivals the "sojourners."[12]

One puzzling question about the Chinese immigrants is: Why did they not think at all of settling down in this new land like some Europeans? Were they antiassimilationists, as purported by some scholars? Granted the early Chinese in America were sojourners, and they looked forward to returning home.[13] Still, it does not explain why so many wanted to stay but so few wanted to assimilate.[14] The reasons for this nonassimilation lie principally in the larger society.

Legally, the Chinese experienced discriminatory legislation against them as soon as they arrived in the United States. As early as 1850, California enacted laws specifically against the Chinese miners. Chinese miners had to pay special head and permit taxes. Chinese miners were subject to abuses. Tax collectors ambushed Chinese miners or ransacked their residences to collect taxes. Tax collectors carried knives and guns, which were used frequently on the Chinese for tax collection purposes.[15]

Economically, there was the fear of competition on the part of white miners.[16] There were mob actions and illegal vigilante groups who attempted to drive the Chinese miners out of the mining business by prohibiting employment of the Chinese in the gold mines or self-employed gold prospecting. In fact, few Chinese miners could operate any gold-prospecting companies due to the lack of capital. Some Chinese miners were able to purchase abandoned mining sites. Using simple tools, they got together to exploit the abandoned mining sites.

Socially, the Chinese were not accepted by the public. Villians and rascals often victimized the miners.[17] These white robbers often made their living from stealing gold nuggets from the Chinese miners. In 1852, the township of Columbia in California had a public meeting encouraging direct action to stop the mining activities of the Chinese. A few weeks later, in Eldorado County, white miners banded together to stop all vehicles carrying Chinese miners from entering the county. In the same year at Weber Creek, white residents set fire on the tents of Chinese miners. In 1856 in Mariposa, California, residents declared that all the Chinese had to leave town in ten days. Any Chinese caught after ten days was to be punished by receiving thirty-nine whips. Often, the wooden huts of the Chinese were set on fire by white vigilante groups. The move to expel Chinese gold miners was also common in other townships and counties of California. In Shasta County, white miners claimed that they had the most effective method to deter the Chinese from mining. In 1859, the so-called "best method" was terrorism. White miners armed themselves with weapons to round up Chinese miners, beat them and throw them out of town. The riot by the white miners alerted the deputies of nearby towns, as well as Governor John B. Weller. He gave order to law enforcement officials to stop the riot and restore order. One hundred seventeen rifles and numerous rounds of bullets were sent to Stockton to supply the local deputies. The riot was later labeled the Shasta Battle.[18]

The Chinese railroad builders did not fare much better than the Chinese miners. Realizing the shortage of manpower, the Central Pacific Railway had decided to hire Chinese laborers. In 1864, the company recruited fifty Chinese laborers on a trial basis.[19] The experiment proved to be a success, and the administration added fifty more laborers. Due to pressure to complete the railroad project on time and the lack of Chinese laborers in the United States, the administration had to send recruiters to Hong Kong to recruit more Chinese laborers. By 1868, there were 5,000 Chinese workers in California, and by 1869, 2,000 more had been recruited. According to an estimate of Y. K. Chu,[20] probably more than 12,000 Chinese were working for the Central Pacific Railroad Company. When the project was completed in 1869, the Chinese had built more than 1,000 miles of railroad tracks. The completion of the railroad not only facilitated the reconstruction of the post–Civil War period, it was also important for the development of the western frontiers.[21]

The employment of the Chinese created conflicts with white laborers. Chinese railroad builders were periodically attacked by white laborers. As soon as the railroad was completed, race conflicts developed. The Chinese laborers had to compete with the white in the labor market. They worked harder for less pay. Competition led to further resentment.[22]

Resentment against the Chinese was so strong that many race riots broke out in California. "The Chinese Must Go!" was echoed throughout the state.[23] Anti-Chinese sentiment in California left a Chinese with three unattractive choices: stay in California; return to China; or leave California to disperse in other states in America. Continuous poverty and instability in nineteenth-century China ruled out the possibility of returning to China. Although some did stay in California, the majority of the Chinese pursued a new adaptive strategy that included lowering their visibility by moving out of the Pacific states, and changing occupations. After 1870, the Chinese started to organize an ethnic niche composed of laundries, restaurants and grocery stores. They also gradually moved out of California, into the metropolitan areas of Portland, Oregon, Tucson, Arizona, Denver, Colorado, Chicago, Detroit, New York, Philadelphia, Boston and other cities to organize their noncompetitive (with the white) Chinese businesses in various parts of the cities.[24] These were the origins of U.S. Chinatowns that, in fact, are testimonies of racial discrimination.

Limited participation in the economic life and discrimination, as mentioned by many writers, were deterrents for assimilation of any ethnic group. The Chinese in this period did not see any advantage in assimilating. Further, legally, socially and economically, the Chinese were not accepted by the larger society. Although periodically there were Chinese who became U.S. citizens, they were often treated as second-class citizens.

EXCLUSION PERIOD: 1882–1943

The infamous "Chinese Exclusion Act" in 1882 was the first such legislation in America. According to this law, no Chinese laborers could be admitted to the United States.[25]

During the exclusion period, the Chinese experienced further discrimination. Socially and legally, they were mistreated. The incident of Rock Springs, Wyoming, is a notorious example. The race riot perpetrated by whites against the Chinese in 1885 caused the death of twenty-eight Chinese miners, the injury of 15 people, and the disappearance of twenty-eight Chinese.[26] Property damage was estimated to be around $150,000. In 1894, a law was enacted to prevent the return of Chinese laborers who had gone abroad.[27] Other discriminatory legislation against the Chinese in 1894, 1900, 1903 prohibited the entry of the Chinese and the naturalization of Chinese residents in the United States. The Act of 1924 specifically prohibited the entry of Chinese wives and thus prevented the union of many Chinese families.[28]

Economically, many occupations were specifically prohibited to the Chinese. In New York State, twenty-seven occupations were legally off-limits to the Chinese. These included lawyer, engineer, doctor, bank director, chauffeur, dentist, pawnbroker, guide, liquor, security guard, embalmer, plumber, horse track employee, veterinarian, architect, CPA, realtor, registered nurse, and teacher. The only areas of employment open to the Chinese were domestic servants or work in the Chinese ethnic niches in the various Chinatowns.

The Chinese were deprived of family life. Due to the lack of Chinese women in the community, the population was highly unbalanced, with males significantly out-numbering females (see Table 1). The community was such that it was often labeled as a "bachelor society."

Social interactions between the Chinese and whites were limited during this period. Many states had also laws against the marriage of Chinese to whites. As a result, intermarriage was infrequent. American-born Chinese were few. Economic activities were confined mainly to Chinatown. During the Exclusion era, the Chinese were denied citizenship. For these reasons, the assimilation rate of the Chinese was exceedingly low. External factors, in particular legal and economic factors, thus played a detrimental role in the assimilation of the Chinese during this period. Some of the barriers did not change until World War II.

IMPACT OF WORLD WAR II ON THE ASSIMILATION OF THE CHINESE: 1943–1965

In this period, the Chinese in the United States experienced a complete change. With the commencement of World War II, many Chinese were drafted to serve in the armed forces. Proportionally, more Chinese served in the armed forces than any other ethnic groups. In a population of 200,000 or so Chinese in America, there were 70,000 Chinese servicemen.[29] Thus, 30 percent of the Chinese in America were in the various branches of the armed forces participating in the war as combat soldiers, staff or support personnel. One reason for so many Chinese being in the armed services was the high number of unmarried single males in the community. Second, even among those who were married, their wives or family were in China since American laws did not permit the migration of wives. Thus, married males were treated the same as single males and were likely to be drafted. Another reason for the participation of the Chinese was that the ancestral land, China, was also at war with Japan. Finally, those who served in the United States armed forces could be naturalized as citizens. Thus, there were incentives as well as political and demographic factors accounting for the relatively large number of Chinese servicemen in the armed forces.

The war definitely had an impact on the assimilation of the Chinese in America. It was, in fact, a turning point in the assimilation process of the Chinese.

New Economic Opportunities

World War II widened the economic opportunities of the Chinese. The war created a manpower shortage in America.[30] Paradoxically, due to the lack of manpower, many Chinese restaurants and laundries had to close their doors. However, employment was not at stake. For those who lost their jobs in the ethnic niche, they could easily find employment in the defense industries. The war had helped the Chinese to move out of their stereotyped businesses. Because the defense industry needed much manpower, many Chinese were recruited to work in the shipyards, for airplane companies, ammunition plants and other defense-related enterprises. According to the research of Y. K. Chu, recruiters were sent by various defense industries to Chinatowns in Chicago, New York, Seattle and San Francisco to attract the Chinese.[31] Many Chinese were trained by their employers first and then offered suitable employment later. For the first time American employers learned that the Chinese could be good workers in the manufacturing sectors. The barrier of employment was thus broken. The tradition of working as engineers and technical personnel among the Chinese today was perhaps set during this period. Many Chinese continue to work in the defense industry today as engineers, scientists and technical personnel, a tradition traceable to the World War II era. The Chinese professionals working in white establishments proved to be more assimilatable than those Chinese working in Chinatown surrounded by their co-ethnics. These professionals had to adapt to the behavioral patterns and attitudes of their white peers.[32] Working with white colleagues also helped break down some of the stereotypes. Some interracial marriages occurred among these professionals. Further, these professionals tended to live in the suburbs and raise their children the American way. They participated in Parent-Teacher Associations (PTA) and church activities and internalized some of the American values. Thus, occupational change among the Chinese had affected their assimilation.

As a result of World War II and subsequent civil wars in China, some Chinese who came to the United States for education or other specific missions got stranded. This group of people was referred to as the "stranded" Chinese by Rose Lee.[33] They were in the professions. After getting their status adjusted, they remained in the country. Most of these people were highly educated and lived outside of Chinatown. Most were more Westernized in their lifestyle and outlook. They, especially their native-born children, tended to be more assimilated than other foreign-born Chinese.

Reorganization of the Ethnic Niche

The large number of young Chinese serving in the armed forces created a ripple effect on the ethnic niche. The lack of manpower led to a pressing need of redevising a strategy to maintain the ethnic niche. First, labor-intensive Chinese laundries could hardly meet the demands of their customers. In order to comply with delivery deadlines and work orders, many Chinese laundries had to resort to technological renovation and specialization. A new division of labor was implemented. The industry was divided into two sections: washing plant and pressing plant. Washing and drying machines had to be deployed. To staff the plants, Chinese and black workers were used. This was the beginning of a semi-automated industry among the Chinese. Few laborers were used, and productivity was increased as a result of modern machinery. Meanwhile, profits grew.

With the influx of women as a result of legal changes after the war and the migration of Chinese war brides, a new industry in various Chinatowns started, that is, the garment factories. New York's and San Francisco's Chinatown were able to tap the new labor resources to organize garment factories. Subsequently, the garment factories became an important lifeline for the Chinese.

In the traditional restaurant sector, the manpower shortage caused many restaurants to install machines for chopping and dishwashing. Meanwhile, many assistant cooks were promoted to principal chefs. As a result of the war, many Chinese sailors also worked in the restaurants. They came with ships that required repair in America. Many left their ships to work in Chinese restaurants as busboys and errand personnel. After the war, they adjusted their immigration status and opened their own restaurants.

Some restaurants made use of the more equitable immigration laws passed in 1943 to sponsor culinary experts in regional cuisines from Hong Kong or China. New specialty restaurants thus got started only after World War II. Before then, the restaurants were almost all Cantonese.

The tourist businesses in Chinatown also got a boost as a result of publicity about the many patriotic Chinese who served in the U.S. armed forces and fought for this country. Because China and the United States were allies, fighting a common enemy, the general public became more friendly toward Chinese-Americans. This changing attitude toward Chinese-Americans became especially evident in San Francisco. The city government provided assistance in helping Chinatown to develop tourism. San Francisco's Chinatown was and still is an important tourist attraction.

Impact on Assimilation

Much of the Chinese assimilation into American life began to take place during this period. On the level of social acceptance, there were gains among the Chinese. First, various restrictive covenants, in San Francisco for instance, were eliminated. Prior to the war, the Chinese could not purchase property outside the Chinatown area. During the war, many of these anti-Chinese regulations were used by Japanese propagandists. Japanese radio broadcasts to American GIs, in particular to Chinese-American GIs, frequently, mentioned that the United States was a racist country and that the Chinese were discriminated against in an attempt to demoralize the Chinese GIs. It appeared also to be incongruent for the United States and China to be allies if the former kept mistreating the Chinese immigrants in the United States. With much persuasion from President Franklin Roosevelt, San Francisco did eliminate many anti-Chinese legislations. This set the stage for assimilation, because the Chinese could then gain entrance to white neighborhoods and various public schools in the white neighborhoods. Previously, many Chinese children in San Francisco had to go to Chinatown's Oriental School.

The movement to the white neighborhoods in San Francisco began after the war when the younger Chinese had obtained a certain degree of economic security. With better jobs, they got better pay. Some of these professionals began to reside in the Richmond and Sunset areas of the city. Previously, no Chinese could rent in these areas. With the improvement of their economic life and the elimination of discriminatory ordinances, many could and indeed did purchase property in these areas as well. Their children went to white schools and interacted with teenagers of the dominant society. Hence, social interaction was facilitated and concomitantly the assimilation rate increased.

The war facilitated the assimilation of the Chinese in other ways too. From interviews I conducted with World War II Chinese-American GIs, it became clear that the war had brought together various segments of American society. For the first time, Chinese-Americans interacted on a face-to-face basis with other Americans. Many of the misunderstandings and racial stereotypes got a chance to be rectified. Through the GI Bill, many Chinese-Americans could go to college to receive a higher education or professional training. After their graduation, they were able to obtain jobs in the larger society.

The VA loan programs also assisted many Chinese-Americans to to purchase houses or to start a business of their own. The G.I. War Bride Act of 1943 helped the development of the second generation. With the influx of war brides, the community for the first time saw the resemblance of Chinese family life. It was also the beginning of the second-generation Chinese-Americans. Second-generation Americans have been important integrators of American life. Chinese-Americans are no exception. They were Americanized like white Americans through the public school system, the media, and various child-rearing complexes of American culture.

During this period, significant gains in the naturalization of the Chinese took place (Table 2). Citizenship was conferred upon many who served in the armed forces. The Act of 1943 no longer debarred the Chinese from becoming U.S. citizens. Chinese who were not in the services could become naturalized U.S. citizens. After the war the Chinese war brides were also eligible for citizenship. Many took the opportunity to become citizens so that they could sponsor their siblings and parents to come to the United States. In 1944, before the end of World War II, only 731 got naturalized. Out of this number, 708 obtained their citizenship through service in the armed forces. After 1945, more and more Chinese were naturalized. During the period between 1944 and 1960, more than 20,000 Chinese became naturalized citizens of the United States (See Table 2).

The war had other impacts on the community. Many Chinese students who became stranded in the United States as a result of the war between China and Japan had their legal status adjusted and gained employment as professionals at the various universities. Similarly, many Chinese sailors who participated in the war effort as workers in Panama-registered vessels, which were used as supply ships for the allies, could also legally get their status adjusted.[34] Later, they became U.S. citizens and sponsored their families to join them as well.[35]

The Chinese war brides also contributed greatly to the economic life of the Chinese-Americans. Finally, savings through frugal living and two wage earners were accumulated. These savings were converted into capital. Some were used for the purchase of stock; others for real estate investment and the establishment of small businesses. It is estimated that the wives' contribution to the economic life of each Chinese family would be at least 50 percent.

Table 2
Chinese Persons Naturalized, 1944–60

Year	Under General Naturalization Provisions	Married to U.S. Citizen	Children of U.S. Citizen Parents	Military	Civilian	Total
1944	0	0	0	708	23	731
1945	0	0	0	459	280	739
1946	0	0	0	334	265	599
1947	0	0	0	352	479	831
1948	0	0	0	56	707	763
1949	340	195	38	257	97	927
1950	375	235	35	86	172	903
1951	327	248	20	23	96	714
1952	386	490	28	23	6	933
1953	560	437	27	16	16	1,056
1954	1,515	158	56	101	50	1,880
1955	3,059	199	133	111	25	3,527
1956	1,951	177	102	82	18	2,330
1957	1,152	178	99	51	11	1,491
1958	1,095	203	102	130	12	1,542
1959	859	277	140	109	10	1,395
1960	1,160	441	186	174	7	1,968
TOTAL	12,779	3,238	966	3,072	2,274	22,329

Source: Annual Report, 1944–60

INCREASED PARTICIPATION: 1965–PRESENT

The Chinese in America have undergone drastic changes since 1965 (Wong 1977, 1987a). At the same time they also have become more open to the larger society. These factors, as well as diminished racial discrimination against the Chinese and elimination of legal and economic barriers, have led to greater assimilation of the Chinese.

The New Immigration Law of 1965 and Assimilation

Two important political changes in the larger society have affected the Chinese in America. One is the enactment of the new immigration law of

1965. The second is the Civil Rights Movement in the United States and the subsequent passage of the Equal Opportunity Act and the Affirmative Action Program. The New Immigration Act of 1965 abolished the inequitable national quota system. Instead, all nations were treated equally. The new law established a preferential system that ranks immediate relatives, family members, specially skilled individuals, refugees and so on in a priority system. Chinese and non-Chinese were to be treated equally under the new law. Chinese immigrants were no longer barred from bringing along their families. These new immigrants are committed to staying in the United States to make America their home to secure a place for themselves and their children. They also welcome the opportunity to become U.S. citizens. Generally, they file their petitions to be naturalized as soon as they are eligible for citizenship.

Before 1945, there were few women and children in Chinatown, and the population consisted mainly of male sojourners. The female population among the Chinese in America has gradually grown since 1945, initially with the influx of Chinese war brides. However, only after 1965 did the sex ratio narrow significantly. In 1960 the male/female ratio was 2:1. In 1980 it was almost equal.[36] The influx of new immigrants thus created an opportunity for a normal family life.

Since the new immigrants came with their spouses, they were also responsible for a new generation of native-born Chinese-Americans. By 1980, there were more native-born Chinese-Americans (297,789) than any time before. These native-born Chinese-Americans will be the facilitators for future assimilation of the Chinese in America. As indicated by many social scientists, the local-born members of an ethnic community have always played an important role in the assimilation of minority populations.[37]

I have found that there is more Chinese willingness to participate in American society than previously.[38] Several reasons explain this kind of willingness to be part of America. First, they come to the United States with the intention of staying here permanently. Second, many of them come from urban backgrounds such as from Taiwan and Hong Kong. They are thus Westernized and more in tune with Western lifestyles. Many, in fact, want to assimilate into American culture and are looking forward to participating in American democracy. Third, many are well-educated and knowledgeable about the American political process. They are eager to use American methods such as voting, petition, and demonstration to pursue the "good life" in America. Thus, there is a predisposition among the new immigrants to participate fully in American society, politically and socially. This kind of attitude will indeed help them assimilate into American life.

Politically, there have been relatively more new immigrants participating in U.S. politics than old immigrants. This is partly because they were better educated and were more familiar with the political process in modern states.[39] The new immigrants came to realize that they were rooted in

Chinese culture but not in Chinese politics.[40] They left Taiwan, Hong Kong and mainland China. Their desire to come to America was to establish themselves in this new soil. Politics is a means to an end, to help establish themselves, to protect their new life in America and to obtain equal treatment in U.S. society. These new immigrants are eager to exercise their political rights. New organizations have been formed to sponsor political rights. New organizations have been formed to sponsor political candidates for elected offices and to lobby for the interests of Chinese-Americans. In San Francisco alone, for instance, there have been efforts to locate a seat on the governing board of supervisors. In 1986, Mayor Dianne Feinstein appointed a Chinese architect, Thomas Hsieh, an immigrant from Shanghai, to sit on the Board. In the election of 1986 the Chinese community campaigned to elect a second supervisor, Julie Tang, a lawyer by training and an immigrant from Hong Kong. A third example is S. B. Wu, an immigrant who won the lieutenant governor race in Delaware. These examples are not merely indications of the interest of the Chinese to establish themselves politically. Their interest to partake in the participatory democracy in America is an important index of assimilation.

The normalization of U.S.-China relations had an impact on the assimilation of the Chinese in the post–1985 era. First, the People's Republic of China advocated explicitly that overseas Chinese should acquire the nationality of the host country. Second, as a result of U.S.-China normalizations, Chinese-Americans became keenly aware of their peculiar situation. They live in America and are committed to the lifestyle here. Culturally, their roots are Chinese. Socially and economically, they embrace the American system. They became convinced that America is their true home when confronted with the question of "belonging." They are members of an ethnic group based on a shared cultural heritage in America. Using their ethnicity, there is the desire to transform the community into an interest group.[41] Thus, contrary to popular perception, Chinese-Americans, especially the new immigrants, have not become more "sinicized" or developed more allegiance to the People's Republic of China as a result of normalization. Instead, as a whole they have become more Americanized, increasing participation in U.S. society and commitment to their life in America. This kind of change has had a great deal to do with the awakening of their ethnic identity in the midst of the triangular relations among the People's Republic of China, Taiwan and the United States.[42]

Economic Opportunity and Assimilation in the Post–1965 Era

The economic aspect of assimilation is an interesting one. Since World War II, and particularly since 1965, economic opportunities have widened for the Chinese. Today, they are no longer limited to the traditional businesses such as restaurants and laundries. Increasingly, Chinese find their employment outside of Chinatown. The Equal Opportunity and Affirmative Action Program play an important role in assisting the Chinese to find jobs with white establishments. Those new immigrants who are professionals tend to work outside of Chinatown. Many second-, third-, or fourth-generation immigrants have attended college or professional schools, and after graduation, they usually prefer to work for white American establishments according to their professional capacity. In fact, the professional Chinese tend not to be related to Chinatown economies and thus not to be Chinatown connected, living instead in middle-class neighborhoods.[43]

Working and living among white Americans allows them to have more contacts with U.S. society through education, institutions, careers, neighborhood connections, professional associations, churches and other secondary institutions. They have the same aspiration as other white Americans: better jobs, better housing, better cars, a better education for their children, better household appliances, better economic mobility. Even the family system resembles that of the majority of white American: a neolocal residence and the nuclear family. Siblings are no longer required to address each other by traditional kinship terminology. Relationships within the nuclear family focus on the husband and wife bond rather than the father and son bond that exists in the traditional Chinese family. The lifestyle of these non-Chinatown-connected professionals is principally a product of their careers, which are intimately connected with the American economy and society. There is also a significant increase of interracial marriages between the Chinese and members of the larger society. D. Y. Yuan noticed that the increase of out-marriages among Chinese males went from 7.4 percent (1940–49) to 13.5 percent (1950–59) to a high of 17.7 percent (1960–69).[44] Correspondingly, the out-marriages among the Chinese female for the same periods rose from 5.6 percent to 10.2 percent and finally to 18 percent for the period of 1960–69. Increased interracial marriage among the Chinese is also an indication of their increased assimilation of the Chinese in recent years. Further, Betty Lee Sung (1987) found that proportionally more Chinese professionals with a higher education married interracially. Here is another example showing that Chinese professionals are more assimilatable than other Chinese in the Chinese ethnic businesses.

The Chinatown residents are connected with the ethnic niche that is composed of Chinese restaurants, grocery stores, garment factories and the various types of Chinese shops interacting in a Chinese environment and reinforcing the Chinese traditional attitudes and behavior. The Chinatown economy does not allow extensive contacts with the larger society. It is true that although they have to deal with white customers, these Chinese residents seldom go beyond minimal business transactions. In fact, many Chinese live in Chinatowns specifically for the convenience of the language and the familiarity with Chinese culture. Some do not speak English and have no English-speaking friends. The social structure established in various American Chinatowns was and still is heavily influenced by traditional Chinese culture with emphasis on kinship, locality of origin and dialect similarities. The traditional pattern of social interaction is fostered. There is also the historical dimension of the nonassimilation of Chinatowns. The formation of Chinatowns in this country since the 1800s has been intimately linked with American racism. Some residents, therefore, do not see any necessity or advantage in assimilating. They prefer not to have anything to do with the larger society. Low visibility and minimal contact are still thought to be useful in avoiding conflicts with the larger society. Although such a mentality is not too common, it does exist among some old Chinese settlers.

Not all Chinatown residents are anti-assimilation. The population in today's Chinatown is not homogeneous. The heterogeneity is due principally to the changes in U.S. immigration law of 1965. In terms of locality of origin, in the post–1965 era there are immigrants from different parts of China. Previously, the community drew its immigrants from the districts close to the city of Canton. They came mostly from rural origins. Old settlers sponsored the new immigrants through kinship, friendship and other social networks. The enactment of the various discriminatory laws against the Chinese in the pre–1965 era, such as the Chinese Exclusion Law of 1882 or the law of 1925 prohibiting the migration of Chinese women, made the community even more homogeneous with adult males outnumbering female. The various Chinatowns in America then had residents principally of rural origin, speaking the Sam Yup and Sze Yup dialects of Kwangtung Province. In the post–1965 era, all this had changed. The new immigration laws permitted the migration of Chinese without kinship connection to any Chinese-American to emigrate to this country, provided that they fall under certain preferences: specially skilled, technical and scientific personnel, refugees and others. The new immigrants could come from different regions of China with diverse social and economic backgrounds. Some came from urban areas; some were from rural districts of China; some were highly educated. Some did come here as dependents or relatives of the old settlers; some were just refugees. Thus, the population in Chinatown became heterogeneous. These are different social and economic groups with different attitudes toward assimilation.

As a group, the old settlers prefer to pursue an isolationist strategy. Many of them are pro-Kuomintang of Taiwan. Having lived in this country and experienced personal discrimination in the United States they see nothing worthwhile in giving up their Chinese identity. In their opinion, the Chinese could never be totally accepted by American society because of prevailing racism. Then, there is the new immigrant group who arrived here after 1965 in a new political climate that stressed the civil rights of a minority and encouraged racial tolerance and cultural pluralism. The new immigrants see something positive in the American system. Values like democracy, equality and dignity of work are of special attraction to the new immigrants. They

aspire to an affluent lifestyle and are impressed by the relatively open educational policy in America. On the other hand, they also see the positive
aspect of Chinese culture, its concerns about people. The new immigrants
as a group prefer to straddle two cultures. They have developed a double
identity that allows them to keep the best of the two cultures: American
affluence and Chinese humanism. A third group of Chinese who live in
Chinatowns are second- and third-generation Chinese-Americans. This
group is dedicated to fight racism and seek unreserved acceptance by the
larger society. They want to do things as other Americans do. They are
Americans and want to be considered as "full-fledged" Americans. They
identify only with America. They speak, behave and think like Americans.
They are totally assimilated.

To complicate the picture, in the post–1965 era, one finds in the various
Chinatowns jump-ship Chinese sailors, over-stayed tourists, boat people
from Vietnam as well as rich entrepreneurs from Hong Kong.[45] For the
above groups, the issue of assimilation is of only superficial interest. They
are here, as they told this author, only to make money." As long as the
influx of immigrants continues to flock to the Chinatowns from overseas,
it will be difficult for the residents of Chinatown to assimilate. However,
it should not be intepreted that Chinatowns are antiassimilation. There are
always groups or individuals in Chinatown that will assimilate, depending
on the acceptance of the larger society. In this regard, the highly successful
example of assimilation is that of the Chinese community of Honolulu. In
the early 1880s, 73 percent of the 5,000 Chinese lived in the Chinatown of
Honolulu. By 1900, only 40 percent of the population lived there; by 1950,
only 10 percent of the 28,000 lived in Chinatown.[46] The majority of the
population had since settled into different neighborhoods outside of Chinatown. The Chinese population there is more assimilated than in any other
Chinatown in the United States, for several reasons. One is the tolerant
attitude of the larger society and the relative lack of legal discrimination
against Chinese in Hawaii. There was no miscegenation law against intermarriage between the Chinese and the natives and there was more respect
for racial equality.[47] A second reason is the relatively large number of local-
born Chinese in Hawaii. Having been born and raised in an American
environment, educated in U.S. schools, the local born have adopted the
speech pattern, behavioral system and attitudes of the larger society.

Barriers to Further Assimilation

Increased assimilation of the Chinese in the past forty years should not
imply that discrimination against the Chinese has ceased in the 1980s. As
compared to the pre–1945 era, there has been great improvement. However,
the Chinese still experience legal, social and economic discrimination. Al-

though citizens of this country, many Chinese find federal employment extremely difficult. The fact that their mother country is a communist country is a barrier for any mid- or top-level employment in the U.S. government. It is still assumed in some quarters that the Chinese are "clannish" and cannot be made good citizens of the United States, although they have fought and died for this country in World War I, World War II, the Korean War and the Vietnam War. Some have been here for five or six generations, yet they are often considered foreigners because of their Chinese ethnicity. Socially, there are educational institutions that still turn away qualified students of Chinese descent.[48] In the job market, Chinese often encounter subtle discrimination. Once employed, Chinese workers often find it difficult to be promoted to higher rank, especially to managerial positions. *Newsweek* called this phenomenon "topping out," meaning that they are already reaching the point beyond further promotion.[49] Although there are new hires at entry levels, they are not promoted to higher levels. This explains why some Chinese leave their jobs after working many years for a company. Realizing that it is a "dead-end" job, they leave and open up their own firms. This strategy of becoming self-employed echoes the old strategy of the Chinese during the exclusion era. In adversary climates, their forebearers withdrew from discrimination and competition with the white labor market by opening their own ethnic restaurants or laundries. Economically, the lifeline for the majority of the Chinese today is still in the ethnic niche composed of restaurants, laundries, grocery stores and other Chinese-type businesses. Although the opportunity structure for the Chinese has widened in the past forty years, it has not been enlarged enough.[50] Most of the Chinese in Chinatown still pursue the traditional business enterprises started by the Chinese in the nineteenth century in order to avoid competition with white business and laborers. The Equal Employment Opportunity Commission reported in 1985 that 4.3 percent of professionals were Asian (mostly Chinese), but only 1.4 percent of managers or officials were Asian. In 1982, a Chinese-American, Vincent Chin, was mistaken as a Japanese and bludgeoned to death by two unemployed autoworkers in Detroit who blamed their unemployment on the importation and sales of Japanese cars in the United States. On October 30, 1985, the *San Francisco Examiner* reporter a series of violent incidents against the Chinese in the United States and, specifically, in California. In the corporate world, the top- and mid-level managerial positions are still difficult to come by. Many are still using old stereotypes such as passivity, lack of verbal skills and so on against the promotion of the Chinese to responsible positions. Poverty still exists in various Chinatowns. The model minority image created by the media often obscures the social reality of the Chinatowns' pressing problems: a decaying housing situation, crowding, aging, juvenile delinquency, deficient health care, underemployment and restrictive economic opportunities.

CONCLUSION

This chapter has demonstrated that during the exclusion era, the Chinese were bitterly discriminated against. As a consequence, there was little progress in assimilation. When the social, political and economic climate improved for the Chinese, assimilation took place. The progress of assimilation over the four historical periods has been reflected in the increase of interracial marriage, naturalization, participation in the American political process and economic life, internalization of values and the absorption of the behavioral patterns and attitudes of the dominant society. These changes have been brought about principally by changes in the larger society. New legislation, new attitudes and new social movements have affected the quality of majority-minority contacts and have produced profound effects on the Chinese by enlarging their economic opportunities, by allowing their movement out of the Chinatowns and by permitting them to be citizens and to bring their families to America. These external factors all act as catalysts and stimulants for the assimilation of the Chinese.

These outside factors affecting the assimilation of the Chinese began to change during World War II. First, the entry of the United States into the war, with China as an ally fighting a common enemy, turned the tide. Many anti-Chinese laws, which were detrimental for the assimilation of the Chinese, were repealed. These laws included the "Chinese Exclusion Law" of 1882, the Scott Act of 1888 prohibiting Chinese re-entry after leaving temporarily, and the Immigration Act of 1924 prohibiting the entry of Chinese women. Second, the enactment of the G.I. War Bride Act of 1945 made possible the development of normal family life and American-born Chinese. The elimination of the miscegenation law made it possible for the Chinese to become integrated through interracial marriage. The passage of the New Immigration Act of 1965 and the political normalizations between the United States and China created a new climate for assimilation. The Civil Rights Act and the Equal Opportunity and Affirmative Action Program created favorable conditions for the assimilation of the Chinese as well. Legislation, with its ripple effects on economic opportunity, the naturalization process and social interaction proved to be an important instrument for the assimilation of the Chinese into American life.

Socially and economically, there is more acceptance of the Chinese than previously, although subtle and blatant racism against the Chinese still exists. If the relative success of assimilation of the Chinese in recent years can serve as any guide, the continued effort of eliminating social, legal and economic injustices against them should be sustained. The elimination of these external barriers will likely entice further assimilation of the Chinese in America.

NOTES

1. The definition is adopted from the work of Milton Gordon, *Assimilation in American Life* (New York: Oxford University Press, 1964).

2. See Jack Chen, *The Chinese of America* (New York: Harper and Row Publishers, 1980), chapter 1, 3–14.

3. See Y. K. Chu, *History of the Chinese People in America* (New York: The China Times, 1975), 9–12.

4. See R. E. Park, "Behind Our Masks," *Survey Graphic* 56 (1926): 135–39.

5. See Bernard Wong, "A Comparative Study of the Assimilation of the Chinese in New York City and Lima, Peru," *Comparative Studies in Society and History* 20, no. 3, (July 1978): 335–58.

6. Ibid.

7. See S. W. Kung, *The Chinese in American Life* (Seattle: University of Washington Press, 1962), 64–80.

8. See Francis L. K. Hsu, *The Challenge of the American Dream* (Belmont: Wadsworth, 1971).

9. See H. F. McNair, *The Chinese Abroad* (Shanghai: Commercial Press, 1925).

10. See Bernard Wong, *A Chinese American Community* (Singapore: Chopmen Enterprises, 1979).

11. See Betty Lee Sung, *Mountain of Gold* (New York: Macmillan, 1967).

12. See Paul Siu, "The Sojourner," *American Journal of Sociology* 8 (July 1952): 32–44.

13. See Bernard Wong, "A Comparative Study of the Assimilation of the Chinese in New York City and Lima, Peru," *Comparative Studies in Society and History,* 20, no. 3 (July 1978): 335–58.

14. See Kung, *The Chinese in American Life.*

15. Y. K. Chu, *History of the Chinese People in America,* 30–35.

16. Elmer Clarence Sandmeyer, *The Anti-Chinese Movement in California* (Urbana: University of Illinois Press, 1939).

17. Chu, *History of the Chinese People in America,* 15–16.

18. Ibid., 17.

19. Ibid., 19.

20. Ibid., 20.

21. Rose H. Lee, *Chinese in the United States of America* (Hong Kong: Hong Kong University Press, 1960), 20–21.

22. Elmer Clarence Sandmeyer, *The Anti-Chinese Movement in California,* 25–40.

23. Ibid.

24. See C. T. Wu, "The Chinese and Chinatown in New York City," Ph.D. Dissertation (Ann Arbor: University Microfilms, 1958).

25. Bernard Wong, *Patronage, Brokerage, Entrepreneurship and the Chinese Community of New York City* (New York: AMS Press, 1984).

26. Y. K. Chu, *History of the Chinese People in America* (New York: The China Times, 1975), 31.

27. Ibid.

28. S. W. Kung, *Chinese in American Life* (Seattle: University of Washington Press, 1962), 64–106.

29. Chu, *History of the Chinese People in America,* 129.

30. Ibid., 128–38. This is augmented by my fieldwork in San Francisco, California, in 1987.

31. Chu, *History of the Chinese People in America,* 128–29.

32. Pei Chi Liu, *A History of the Chinese in the United States of America* (Taipei: Li Min Cultural Enterprises, 1981).

33. Rose H. Lee, *The Chinese in the United States of America,* 231–51.

34. Ibid.

35. Chu, *History of the Chinese in America,* 136.

36. Bernard Wong, "The Role of Ethnicity in Enclave Enterprises: A Study of the Chinese Garment Factories in New York City," *Human Organization* 46, no. 2 (1987): 120–30.

37. Lois Mitchison, *The Overseas Chinese* (London: The Bodley Head, 1961); see also Stanford Lyman, "Contrast in the Community Organization of Chinese and Japanese in North America," *The Canadian Review of Sociology and Anthropology* 5, no. 2 (1968): 1–17.

38. Consult the relevant works of Bernard Wong, published in 1976, 1984, and 1987a. These works are listed in the bibliography at the end of this chapter.

39. Bernard Wong, "The Chinese: New Immigrants in New York's Chinatown" in *New Immigrants in New York,* ed. Nancy Foner (New York: Columbia University Press, 1987), 243–71.

40. Bernard Wong, "The Impact of Changing U.S.-China Policies on Chinese Americans," *Asian Profile* 14, no. 1 (1986): 1–11.

41. Ibid.

42. Ibid.

43. Wong, "The Chinese: New Immigrants in New York's Chinatown," 243–71.

44. D. Y. Yuan "Significant Demographic Change of Chinese Who Intermarried in the U.S.," *California Sociologist* 3, no. 2 (1980): 184–96.

45. Wong, "The Chinese: New Immigrants in New York's Chinatown," 243–71.

46. See S. W. Kung, *The Chinese in American Life* (Seattle: University of Washington Press, 1962), 198.

47. Ibid., 216.

48. See *San Francisco Examiner,* May 15, 1987.

49. See *Newsweek,* May 11, 1987, 48–49.

50. See Pao-Min Chang, *Continuity and Change: A Profile of Chinese Americans* (New York: Vantage Press, 1983).

BIBLIOGRAPHY

Chang, Pao-min

   1983   Continuity and Change: A Profile of Chinese Americans. New York: Vantage Press.

Chen, Jack

1980 The Chinese of America. New York: Harper and Row.

Chu, Y. K.

1975 History of the Chinese People in America. New York: The China Times.

Coolidge, Mary Roberts

1969 Chinese Immigration. New York: Arno Press and the New York Times (originally published in 1909).

Gordon, Milton

1964 Assimilation in American Life. New York: Oxford University Press.

Hsu, Francis, L. K.

1971 The Challenge of the American Dream. Belmont: Wadsworth.

Konvitz, Milton

1946 The Alien and the Asiatic in American Law. Ithaca, New York: Cornell University Press.

Kung, S. W.

1962 Chinese in American Life: Some Aspects of Their History, Status, Problems and Contributions. Seattle: University of Washington Press.

Lee, Rose H.

1960 The Chinese in the United States of America. Hong Kong: Hong Kong University Press.

Liu, Pei Chi

1981 A History of the Chinese in the United States of America. Taipei: Li Min Cultural Enterprises.

Lyman, Stanford

1968 Contrast in the Community Organization of Chinese and Japanese in North America. The Canadian Review of Sociology and Anthropology 5, no. 2: 1–17.

McNair, H. F.

1925 The Chinese Abroad. Shanghai.

Mitchison, Lois

1961 The Overseas Chinese. London: The Bodley Head.

Park, R. E.

1962 Behind Our Masks. Survey Graphic 56: 135–139.

Sandmeyer, Elmer

1939 The Anti-Chinese Movement in California. Urbana: The University of Illinois Press.

Seward, George

1881 Chinese Immigration. New York: Charles Scribner's Sons.

Siu, Paul

1952 The Sojourner. American Journal of Sociology 8 (July): 32–44.

Sung, Betty Lee

    1976   Mountain of Gold. New York: Macmillan.

    1987   Intermarriage Among the Chinese in New York City. Chinese America: History and Perspectives, 1987. San Francisco: Chinese Historical Society of America.

Wong, Bernard

    1958   Chinese People and Chinatown in New York City. Ph.D. Thesis. Ann Arbor: University Microfilms.

    1976   Social Stratification, Adaptive Strategies and the Chinese Community of New York. Urban Life 5, no. 1: 33–52.

    1977   Elites and Ethnic Boundary Maintenance: A Study of the Role of Elites in Chinatown, New York City. Urban Anthropology 6, no. 1: 1–25.

    1978   A Comparative Study of the Assimilation of the Chinese in New York City and Lima, Peru. Comparative Studies in Society and History 20, no. 3: 335–58.

    1979   A Chinese American Community. Singapore: Chopmen Enterprises.

    1982   Chinatown: Economic Adaptation and Ethnic Identity of the Chinese. New York: Holt, Rinehart, and Winston.

    1984   Patronage, Brokerage, Entrepreneurship and the Chinese Community of New York City. New York: AMS Press.

    1985   The Chinese Family of New York with Comparative Remarks on the Chinese Family in Manila and Lima, Peru. Journal of Comparative Family Studies 16, no. 2: 231–54.

    1986   The Impact of Changing U.S.-China Policies on Chinese Americans. Asian Profile 14, no. 1: 1–11.

    1987a   The Role of Ethnicity in Enclave Enterprises: A Study of the Chinese Garment Factories in New York City 46, no. 2: 120–30.

    1987b   The New Immigrants in New York's Chinatown. Manuscript. In press.

Yuan, D. Y.

    1980   Significant Demographic Change of Chinese Who Intermarried in the U.S. California Sociologist 3, no. 2: 184–96.

10

Mexican-Americans

Louise Ano Nuevo Kerr

News magazines ushered in the 1980s with cover stories proclaiming the decade of "the Hispanic." They described and explained demographic trends and projections that pointed not just to the potential political influence of Hispanics, but to their growing importance in the marketplace as consumers and their impact on the culture and social life of the larger community; tacos and burritos were taking their place alongside pizza and hamburgers as favorite American fast foods.

But the economic downturn that shortly followed these same loudly broadcast predictions contributed to a political backlash. Because California was expected to be more than 50 percent Mexican-American by the year 2000 and all Hispanics, including Puerto Ricans, South Americans and Cubans, were predicted to become the United States' largest "minority" in the early twentieth-first century, Hispanics, especially Mexicans, came to be seen as threats rather than as potential contributors.[1] It was in this rather schizophrenic milieu, after many unsuccessful attempts, that Congress was able to pass punitive new immigration legislation intended to alter those prophecies.[2] Most knowledgeable observers were not surprised at the vacillating response of the public and of the Congress, for it was not a new response to Hispanics, especially Mexicans, the most numerous of the Hispanic groups and the one that has had the longest and most complex relationship with the United States.

From their opening encounter with their neighbors to the north, Mexicans repeatedly have been embraced first, later to be rejected or even reviled. The history of Mexicans in the United States is one of ambiguity and duality, a cultural and political, even geographical compound of their mixed Mexican and "American" heritage. The history of Mexicans in the United States is one of survival: endurance of the fearful reactions they have generated; sufferance of the response they receive, particularly when they approach a threatening threshold of achievement; persistence and perseverance in the face of this changeable and unpredictable reaction.

While the history of the Mexicans begins with the Toltecs, the Aztecs and before, and proceeds through the initial encounters between Spaniards and Native Americans to the revolutionary rebellions that gave birth to the Mexican nation in the early nineteenth century, the history of Mexicans and the United States does not begin until the 1820s, immediately after the Mexicans had gained their independence from Spain. The well-known Mexican lamentation decrying the country's remoteness from God and its proximity to the United States no doubt has its origins in these earliest skirmishes.

The almost two centuries of Mexican-American history are divided into five identifiable periods, most of which began with an initial and mutual warm regard soon followed by political and cultural conflict. Each of these eras illustrates the durability, persistence, and inventiveness of Mestizo culture and community under trying and difficult circumstances in the United States.[3]

First, shortly after their initial meetings with Anglos and other Americans in the Mexican territories of Texas and California, it became clear that ownership of the land would come into contention. Fifty years after they first met in the 1820s, the transfer of Mexican-held land titles to Americans in the new American states was virtually completed. Mexicans survived, land poor but dignified.

The first meetings between Mexicans and Americans took place on what were the edges of the frontier for both new nations. While frontier conditions prevailed, pioneer habits and behavior on either side of the "border" differed markedly for historical as well as cultural reasons. Most of those initial nineteenth-century skirmishes took place in the northern Mexican states of Coahuila (Texas) and California, where small groups of people were often supported by retinues of domesticated Indian workers, comforted by parish priests, and sometimes aided and protected by Mexican soldiers. Not numerous, these Mexican settlers had lived in the region for a generation or more with little expectation of change. Distant from the capital of their new nation, they were used to making their own decisions, and to solving their own problems because there was, of necessity, slow response to requests that they made to and that, in turn, were made by the central government.

As a result, Mexicans in these territories remained remote from the protective umbrella of the central authority as well as from its influence. They divided the land among themselves according to Spanish law and achieved a relative harmony with the peaceful if not the more war-like Indian tribes. While they did not expect and apparently were not well-prepared for momentous change, they were not averse to a moderate and manageable increase in the number of settlers in the region who, it was assumed, might participate with them in the gradual transformation of the northern Mexican territory.

The Anglo-Americans, on the other hand, only a generation before, had been settling remote areas east of the Allegheny Mountains that by the 1820s had become virtual metropolises. History had already shown that their habit was to clear the land and alight only for a time before another group moved further west, knowing that their places would be filled shortly.

Almost as soon as the Mexican nation had gained its independence in 1820, Anglo-American settlers began to move into the northern portion of the Mexican state of Coahuila. A vanguard of Anglo pioneers was at about the same time also beginning to find its way to the coastal towns of California, whose settlements and culture were different from that of Texas, but whose political allegiance and relation to the Mexican nation at the time was not in question.

Partly in acknowledgment of the significance of Anglo-American occupation of its northern reaches, but to its later regret, the Mexican government opened its northern reaches to these Americans and welcomed these settlers on the condition that they agree to certain requirements—that they practice the Catholic religion, and that they respect and follow the culture and traditions of their new country, including adoption of Spanish as the primary language of the territory.

Initially, while their numbers remained comparable, relations among the two groups of settlers were warm and friendly. In some respects the frontier squatters had more in common with each other than they did with those who ran their remote governments in Washington and Mexico City. They shared a common desire for greater independence from authority and for self-governance. During these early years the stability of Mexican independence was fragile as a struggle for leadership continued. Mexican and American settlers in Northern Coahuila joined together in rebellion against the Central Mexican authorities and originated a genuinely blended culture in which they all spoke Spanish while moving closer to the establishment and acquisition of Anglo-American political habits and institutions. The famous Battle of the Alamo, celebrated for so many years by Texans as a monument to the bravery of American settlers in the face of Mexican treachery, was in fact fought by a united Mexican and American (Mexican-American) armed force inside the old fort in battle against the Mexican national troops. Many long-time Mexican settlers were killed there along with Jim Bowie. Mexican frontiersmen and their families were prominent in the early government of the quickly-declared Lone Star Republic. Mexico did not recognize the newly self-proclaimed independent nation of Texas, but France, Great Britain, Belgium and several other nations swiftly did.

The Mexican government, inexperienced and insolvent after so many years of bitter armed hostility with Spain, internecine warfare, and inept conflict in Texas, now had neither the ability to reclaim its territory nor the resources to continue to resist further encroachment successfully. The result was a stream of new Anglo-American squatters that became a flood and quickly overwhelmed the demographic equilibrium of the former outpost territory. Outnumbered, Mexicans in the disputed area could claim neither seniority nor the mantle of formerly-agreed upon security. In inverse relation to their declining proportion of the population, Mexican-Americans were increasingly subject to the racial contempt of many of these newest arrivals and, indeed, from the state government itself.

The American government and many of its people, in the throes of their quest for Manifest Destiny, interpreted Mexico's weakness and inefficiency in Texas as a sign from God that the march to the Pacific Ocean had been foreordained. Given the temper of the times, war was expected, even believed inevitable, by Mexicans as well as American, although their reasons and perspectives were quite different. By 1848 the United States and Mexico were at war. In a relatively short encounter, the United States won, and as a result was expanded by more than a third. Mexico, of course, was equally diminished.

In exchange for the new territory, the United States agreed to protect the legal rights of the Mexicans who remained and to allow them to retain their language, religion, and culture. Enforcement of the cultural agreements, however, was ignored by the signers of the Treaty of Guadalupe, was flaunted by the original Anglo-American settlers and was doomed to failure. Despite early Mexican participation in the creation and governance of the now-American territories, conflicting past habits, and new realities led to the eventual disfranchisement of "Mexican Americans." The legally sanctioned removal of their land titles eliminated, in most instances, the basis for their right to vote. Their removal from office took away their political representation and helped set the stage for the next phase.

New Mexico, Nevada, Arizona, parts of Colorado, Utah, and Nebraska, as well as California and Texas were also part of this newly-acquired American territory. Except in New Mexico, which remained remote for most Anglos as well as for new Mexican immigrants for almost half a century, almost none of the southwestern region of the United States that had been acquired after the war by annexation or cession was owned by Mexicans after 1870.

The means by which the transfer of power took place in these states in the next thirty years are not yet completely known; they vary from place to place and time to time. Some United States history books still justify the land transfer in demographic terms. At the time of the Battle of the Alamo, they say, there were only 3,500 Mexicans in Texas as opposed to the estimated 30,000 that had poured across the boundary from the north. Others blame the policies of the dictator Santa Ana for driving Americans and their Mexican allies to rebellion. Still others are fatalistic: "As the experience of Texas showed, the Americans would have moved in anyway. Half of Mexico would have been dominated by Americans."[4]

In the next several decades, especially in New Mexico and Arizona, new

immigrants from Mexico arrived and there followed more conflict, sometimes simply annoying and abrasive, more often brutal and deadly. These
battles lasted for generations. Coinciding with the end of Reconstruction,
the restriction of Chinese immigration, the rise of the nativist movements,
and the elimination of the Native Americans as a threat to westward expansion, this period of Mexican-American history had as its legacy the
creation by borderland Mexicans of barrio sanctuaries that provided protection but at the same time permitted and condoned their isolation from
the mainstream American community.

By mid-century the themes of Mexican-American history had been established: Mexicans adopted or maintained bicultural and binational allegiances out of necessity as well as because of geographic location. Americans
were ambivalent but increasingly hostile as their greed mingled, to some
degree, with guilt. A nascent Mexican-American community and culture
was established and nourished as a means of survival despite attempts to
suppress it. Mexicans born in the former Mexican territories were pro-
gressively and almost completely dispossessed of the land. Most Mexicans
who immigrated to the southwest in the late nineteenth century arrived in
the borderlands frontier as workers on the land, in the mines, or on the
railroads. Although elsewhere in the United States it was the time of the
robber barons and of the new industrial machine, for Mexicans it was a
time of community reconfiguration and consolidation based on the emergence of a very few landed Hispanic and Anglo elites who controlled the
important new railroad and mining industries manned by the now landless
peasants.

Silver and copper mines formed the economic base of Arizona and New
Mexico and "created a greater need for machinery and supplies, which in
turn made freighting one of the largest industries."[5] Heavy equipment previously carted to the remote mining sites by Mexican teamsters and wagons
soon demanded more technologically advanced equipment. As was true
across the United States during the period, routes and rights of way for the
new iron horses also strained social and political relations between Mexicans
and Anglos. The emergence of the railroads insured the inevitable decline
of Mexicans who had little capital and even less political clout than they
had had in an earlier era.

Between 1870 and 1910 Anglos reaped profits from the mines and the
railroads and gradually consolidated their political power, especially in Arizona and New Mexico. Meanwhile, Mexicans provided a large part of the
labor that built, tie by tie, the railroads whose effect would be to destroy
their carting businesses and create a demand for more Mexican manual
labor. On the border, settlements grew gradually, each establishing an individual identity molded by the older Mexican inhabitants, the newest immigrants from Mexico, and those who traveled frequently back and forth
across the invisible boundary that separated the Mexican states from the

United States. Some differences among the settlements reverberated from the blending of people with the place—distance from civilization, and the monetary value that could be extracted. Some differences were extensions of particular historical events. Overall, however, many similarities could also be found among the Mexican-American communities. As was true for blacks during this post-reconstruction period, Mexican-Americans who had previously been active participants in the polity, residentially free to move about in their various communities, increasingly found themselves circumscribed within larger cities and towns. Once residentially segregated, they became more easily excluded from other public facilities such as schools and transportation, and commercial and entertainment facilities. While the intensity of separation varied, the fact of it was undisputed. Ethnic conflict continued to grow and resulted in a larger number of lynchings of Mexicans in the southwest than of blacks in the south.[6]

The transition from landowner to peon between the end of the Mexican War and the end of the century had been undergirded by the imposition of the American legal system on Spanish and Mexican land laws. But it was speeded and made economically feasible by the introduction and rapid spread of the railroad throughout the southwest. "Railroads made possible the full development of California resources, and Mexican labor became essential to this processes."[7] As we have seen, throughout the southwest the building of the railroads had resulted in the disfranchisement of Mexicans, without whose work those railroads might not have been built.

The railroad also played a significant role in the next phase of Mexican-American history that saw settlement expand rapidly and go beyond that historic "Mexican" territory. In 1910, revolutionary conflict in Old Mexico coincided with the opening of opportunities for work in other parts of the United States. The rapidly expanding railroads themselves needed unskilled workers throughout the United States. Automakers, steelworkers, and meatpackers drew hundreds of thousands of new Mexican emigrants to the southwest regions of the United States and beyond.

Many of these newcomers still arrived as farmworkers, as they had for a generation or more, but an increasing proportion headed directly for industrial jobs in already-formed urban barrios in southwestern cities. Mexicans became beet-workers in Nebraska and Wyoming and settled out in Scotts Bluff and Laramie. They became cherry-pickers in Michigan and soon found their way to Saginaw or Bay City. They became pioneer settlers in the ghettos of Chicago and Detroit. The movement was so vast and rapid that between 1920 and 1930 Chicago's population grew from 4,000 to 20,000, making it the largest Spanish-speaking community outside the Southwest and probably the fourth-largest concentration of Mexicans in the country.

Initially having been brought into these northern cities as contract replacement workers for the Europeans who were no longer available during World War I, the first Mexican immigrants in this mass migration were primarily single young men. These workers gradually obtained permanent employment, however. And they began to bring families to their newly-established homes. Soon there were colonies in St. Louis, Kansas City, Omaha, Gary (Indiana), Des Moines (Iowa), Toledo (Ohio), and Altoona (Pennsylvania) as well as Chicago.[8] About one-tenth of the Mexican population could be found outside of the southwest by 1930.

By many measures, Mexicans were doing relatively well during the 1920s, considering the conditions in which they had found themselves at the turn of the century. To be sure, they were still restricted to menial and manual jobs for which they had originally been contracted by American industrialists and the American government: agricultural stoop labor, railroad track labor, steel, auto, and packinghouse unskilled work. But many were making regular wages that, it appeared, would allow them to advance in time.

Times changed, however. The war-time labor shortages were followed in the 1920s by two severe economic recessions that were accompanied by business failure and worker layoffs including many of the Mexicans who had been enticed to come north. Agriculture was also badly affected, along with farm workers. Bad times were blamed on immigrants who seemed to take all the jobs, demand more services, and contribute little but corrupt politics and deteriorating cities.

Sentiment for immigration restriction, which had been growing since before the turn of the century, reached the halls of Congress. While, as we know, nativists wanted to restrict all immigration, the result was to limit the immigration of Europeans and to severely restrict the immigration of Asians. Despite the rapid geographic spread of Mexican settlement, the number of Mexicans in the United States in the early 1920s was still perceived to be quite small and unthreatening in most congressional districts. Rabid anti-Mexican immigration sentiment was geographically isolated and, in the end, neutralized by local agricultural and industrial interests who continued to see docile and cheap Mexican workers as essential to their own continued prosperity.[9] The primary anti-Mexican action to be taken in this legislation provided the embryonic beginnings of the border patrol.

By 1929 the Mexican revolutions and counterrevolutions had ended. Mexico found itself a more stable and tranquil state than it had been for almost a generation. American industry also seemed more stable: a reliable work force, steady growth, unlimited prospects. Fewer Mexicans seemed to be arriving than during the Revolution and World War I. The barrios and colonies that had been established grew with the birth of each new American-born child and bustled with the creation of mutual aid societies, nascent small business communities, and flourishing cultural and social lives.

The Great Depression began in October 1929 and had a profound effect on Mexicans. By 1930 the number of immigrants from Mexico had fallen to less than 20,000 from almost 250,000 per year. By 1939, there were fewer than 10,000 immigrants a year.

Within a year more than a third of all Mexican workers were unemployed, their jobs taken by American workers or cut altogether from company rolls. Mexicans and their families sought help but found themselves, as aliens, ineligible for anything but local, state, and federal assistance in returning to the Mexican border. Between 1900 and 1930, hundreds of thousands had come to work, but one-third to one-half of the immigrants who arrived during the period were eventually returned. Between 1931 and 1934 alone it is estimated that 300,000 to 500,000 Mexicans were "repatriated."[10]

Mexican repatriation marked the end of this phase. Among the deported were many American-born children, some of whom would return to accept another invitation to work and live in the United States during the next important period.

Not long after Pearl Harbor, it was evident that American men were enlisting in the armed services in unprecedented numbers. Defense industries trying to gear up rapidly soon found themselves short of manpower. Potential workers, women as well as men ineligible for the draft, made their way to defense industry sites in Detroit, Chicago, Los Angeles and Seattle. Still there were not enough workers to get the job done and fill the military at the same time.

In 1942, Nelson Rockefeller, who headed the Department of Inter-American Affairs, proposed and began negotiations with the Mexican government for a renewal of Mexican contract labor. Not surprisingly, the industries most in need of workers were those that had brought Mexican workers in during the first World War. It was also not surprising that, remembering the experience of the World War I workers, the Mexican government was more reluctant to enter such an agreement. Citing flagrant violations of the terms of earlier agreements and skepticism about the collective will to abide by the terms of any new agreement, Mexican officials bargained long and hard. The relative tranquility and prosperity of Mexico under the reign of Lazaro Cardenas in the 1930s and the relative amenability of the "good neighbor" government of Franklin Roosevelt gave Mexico a better bargaining position with respect to the United States than it had had previously, or than it would enjoy later.

The resulting *Bracero* Program (from the word *brazo*, meaning arm) began in mid–1942. This agreement guaranteed that for five years there would be a minimum wage of 75 percent of the prevailing rate, government guarantees of humane conditions for the workers, and transportation to and from workers' homes in Mexico at the beginning and ends of the contracts. Reflecting the influence of agribusiness, the agreement also included government subsidies of (and sometimes actual involvement in) the recruitment, maintenance and return of contract workers.

During the war, contract terms were not rigidly fixed. Exigencies of the moment meant that employers were relatively well-monitored, while workers themselves were less closely scrutinized. About 250,000 *braceros* came under contract during the war, most to harvest crops, but some to re-lay track or otherwise work for the railroads. Others came to work in mines steel plants, and packing houses. In addition, just as defense industry work had affected work and settlement patterns in the United States, this government-sponsored and subsidized labor program profoundly affected migration, settlement, and employment patterns inside of Mexico. Recruitment from island cities and the high plateaus drew Mexican migrants from remote villages to those cities and, in ever-increasing numbers, to the Mexico-U.S. border, now not quite as invisible as it once had been, but just as easily permeable. This would affect not just the pattern of Mexico's economy, but the movement of Mexicans to and from the United States. From the beginning of the contract hundreds of thousands of Mexicans arrived at the border and crossed without benefit of papers, knowing that a job would be waiting and that the U.S. government would not object.

Not everyone agreed with the farm owners and the government, however. Provoked by newspaper coverage that characterized Mexican youth as hoodlums and criminals and that apparently manufactured or exaggerated incidents involving youth who wore "pachuco" outfits, American sailors by the hundreds came to East Los Angeles from as far away as San Diego to chastise any "Pachuco" they felt had taken improper advances on American young women. After a series of encounters between the servicemen and Mexican-American youth, it became clear that distinction would be too fine—all Mexican-American young men were vulnerable. The encounters culminated on June 7, 1943, with the gathering of thousands of civilians and servicemen in East Los Angeles to beat Mexicans of all ages. The incidents were called the Pachuco Riots.

These encounters jeopardized the international labor agreements that had just been reached. Redress required the intervention of the federal government to offset the Pachuco Riots, which seemed to belay official efforts to ameliorate the social and political condition of Mexican-Americans.[11]

Local, state, and federal governments made concerted efforts to recognize the enormous contributions being made by Mexican-American servicemen and their families.[12] In Chicago, for example, the school district introduced bilingual education and encouraged its teachers to take advantage of opportunities to travel and study in Mexico to improve their skills. Several Inter-American wartime conferences were held to improve mutual understanding and regard.

But it was the riot sentiment rather than government-sponsored rhetoric that prevailed after the war. Wartime contracts ended but *bracero* labor did not end. A series of *bracero* agreements negotiated between 1947 and 1964 provided less and less protection for Mexican workers and more flexibility for the farm owners. Hundreds of thousands of legally contracted workers arrived and departed throughout this period, some many times. In the meantime, millions of workers and their families arrived without benefit of papers. Authorities, however, now no longer looked the other way. Immigration laws were suddenly and strictly enforced in the early 1950s to prevent the entrance of "subversives." The activity reached a high point in 1954 with "Operation Wetback," which apprehended and deported more than a million Mexicans, many of them American-born.

Despite the importance of Mexican workers to the growth of the agricultural industry, the public recognized and was concerned that contract and undocumented workers who used agricultural labor as a starting point were finding their way to urban industrial centers throughout the southwest and, increasingly, to the urban midwest, where colonies formed earlier now provided shelter.

What the public did not recognize was the role of U.S. policy in precipitating an increased, steady movement from the Mexican hinterlands to cities and the border and beyond. Further effects of these policies would be felt later, but between 1942 and 1964, when *Bracero* legislation finally expired, millions of Mexicans continued to arrive in the United States with their families to join those who had come before, and to form new communities throughout the United States. Between 1940 and 1960, despite the end of contract labor and the lamentable "round-ups," the number of Mexicans grew from 374,433 to 1,735,992.[13] The demise of contract labor marked the end of this period.

Coinciding with the end of the *Bracero* Program was the passage of the 1965 immigration legislation that ended historic national origin quotas. This legislation would have a profound effect upon Mexican immigration, allowing hundreds of thousands of Mexicans and other Latin Americans to enter legally. To be sure, undocumented immigration did not end, nor did American ambivalence toward it. What did change was the impetus for that migration and the mechanisms for imposing control on that historic movement across the border.

Before the Simpson-Mazzoli Act imposed sanctions on employers in 1986, immigration had had ebbs and flows and had not been accurately measurable. Immigration had not abated since World War II. Once begun, immigration grew, with each succeeding immigration generation finding itself in contention with those Mexicans who had come before as well as with the majority population. Barrios in Chicago and Detroit as well as San Antonio and Los Angeles grew steadily well into the 1980s. The 1980 census, in fact, showed that 70 percent of the Mexican-American population could be found in urban centers.

Designed to respond to this apparently unprecedented movement, the sponsors and supporters of the immigration act seemed unaware of the legacy of history or the effects of contemporary U.S. economic policy and practice.

One of the most important developments of this period of which they seemed unaware, affecting both sides of the border, was the rapid growth of "maquiladores"—American-owned factories built along the border on the Mexican side. These factories relocated American teams in cities like El Paso and San Diego to manage a Mexican labor force in Juarez or Tiajuana. The Mexican workers earned one-tenth the wages they would have received had they simply crossed the international bridge or walked across the border. In effect, these business practices, intended once again to take advantage of Mexican labor, contributed in large measure to increased migration across the border. For, once drawn to these cities, Mexican workers increasingly took the opportunity to become guest workers along the border, working on the U.S. side by day and returning to homes on the Mexican side at night. Thus, these factories proved to be magnets to Mexican workers, who quickly learned the advantage they would have if they entered the United States, with or without papers. In addition, of course, as they had for nearly four generations, employers continued to seek Mexican workers in industries ranging from the clothing industry in California to manufacturing in the Midwest and service industries as far away as Florida and Massachusetts.

Since the early 1980s, Mexicans have been hard-pressed to survive the latest and toughest of challenges: the all-American, late-twentieth-century, urban ghetto. They have continued to enter the United States—with or without documents—despite periodic efforts at new immigration restriction. Aimed especially at Mexicans, the most recently passed legislation mandates sanctions against employers who hire newly arrived undocumented Mexican workers. As in days past, exceptions are being sought to allow those same Mexicans to perform unskilled, low-paying jobs. Meanwhile, long-time residents and second- and third-generation Americans of Mexican descent have become targets of reprisal when they enter more technical and more highly-paid occupations.

Between 1965 and 1985 migration from other Latin American countries and Puerto Rico also increased markedly. Often the migration was to the same cities where Mexicans had settled. As the 1980 census had shown, the Hispanic population grew at an even faster rate than the Mexican population alone. And while it was evident that each of the Hispanic groups had a different historical experience and was culturally and ethnically unique, they nevertheless were placed under the same umbrella. Time has shown that Puerto Ricans in the northeast and Cubans in the Southeast have little in common politically or socially. Time has also shown that Mexicans remain the largest of the Hispanic groups, and they will remain so even if immigration diminishes.

As it has from the first encounter between Mexicans and Americans, ambivalence will accompany their relationship, with Americans eager to take advantage of their labor but less enthusiastic about accepting them as permanent residents.

As they have for almost two hundred years, Mexicans have maintained communities established early, communities replenished continuously by newly arrived compatriots. To the consternation of some neighbors, many have remained bilingual, bicultural, and binational, maintaining traditions established at the outset.

Celebration of the Columbian Quincentennial, which opens the decade of the 1990s would seem an appropriate signal for opening yet another decade of the Hispanic.

NOTES

1. John Attinasi et al., *El Filo* (Chicago: Latino Institute of Chicago, 1988).
2. Simpson-Mazzoli bill passed in the fall of 1986.
3. *Mestizo* is a Spanish term that means "mixture," and refers to the people who are a mixture of European and Native American and the culture that has also blended elements of both into something altogether new—in this case the Mexican.
4. G. D. Lillibridge, *Images of American Society: A History of the United States, Vol I* (Boston: Houghton Mifflin Company, 1976), 162.
5. Matt S. Meier and Feliciano Rivera, *The Chicanos: A History of Mexican Americans* (New York: Hill and Wang, 1972), 108.
6. Rodolfo Acuna, *Occupied America* (New York, Harper and Row, 1981), 106–17.
7. Ibid., 115.
8. Meier and Rivera, *The Chicanos*, 131.
9. Until 1924 the international border between the United States and Mexico was virtually unrestricted, allowing free movement. Ibid., 143. "When United States immigration policies were thoroughly revised in 1924, there was another attempt to place Mexican immigration under quota restrictions. Despite a growing exclusionist sentiment, the only restrictive clause pertaining to Mexicans in the 1924 Immigration Act was one that established a $10 visa fee."
10. Meier and Rivera, *The Chicanos*, 161. "There were three types of repatriates: those who were deported by immigration officials, those who returned voluntarily to their home villages in Mexico, and those who were threatened in various ways with deportation and left reluctantly."
11. Carey McWilliams, *North from Mexico: The Spanish Speaking Peoples of the United States* (New York: Greenwood Press, 1968, updated by Matt S. Meier in 1990), 231–37. Carey McWilliams chaired the Sleeply Lagoon Defense Committee, formed to protect the rights of a group of wrongly accused Mexican-American youth in a 1942 incident.
12. Mexican-Americans were over-represented in the military. They earned seventeen Congressional Medals of Honor, including five of the twelve given to Texas servicemen during World War II.
13. U.S. Bureau of the Census, Sixteenth Census of the U.S., vol II, *Population: Characteristics of the Population, 1940* (Washington, D.C., 1943), 42–43; Eight-

eenth Decennial Census of the U.S., vol. I, *Characteristics of the Population, 1960*, 203, 366.

BIBLIOGRAPHICAL ESSAY

The beginning point for an investigation of Mexican-Americans is the essay on "Mexicans" by Carlos E. Cortés in Stephan Thernstrom et al., *The Harvard Encyclopedia of American Ethnic Groups* (Cambridge, Mass., 1980), 697–719. Cortés has also aided significantly the study of Mexican-Americans by editing two major reprint series for Arno Press: *The Chicano Heritage* (New York, 1976), 55 vols., and *The Mexican-American* (New York, 1974), 21 vols. Three other classic works have become somewhat dated by the developments of the past three decades, but still remain valuable for their historical perspective and context: Manuel Gamio, *Mexican Immigration and the United States* (Chicago, 1930) and *The Mexican Immigrant: His Life Story* (Chicago, 1931), and Carey McWilliams, *North from Mexico: The Spanish Speaking Peoples of the United States* (New York, 1968). The last work has been updated by Matt S. Meier and published by Greenwood Press in 1990. Wayne Moquin, ed., with Charles Van Doren, *A Documentary History of the Mexican Americans* (New York, 1971) devotes nearly half of its selections to Mexican immigration from 1911 to 1939 and to the ethnic reawakening of Mexican-Americans from 1940 to 1970. Matt S. Meier and Feliciano Rivera, eds., *Dictionary of Mexican-American History* (Westport, Conn., 1981) is a valuable compendium of the people, events, concepts, and terminology necessary to assess the Mexican-American experience. Arnulfo D. Trejo, Bibliografica Chicano: A Guide to Information Sources (Detroit, 1975) is an annotated bibliography of about five hundred items, including reference works, humanities, social sciences, history, and applied sciences, as well as profiles of Chicano newspapers, periodicals, and publishers. The best detailed scholarship on that phenomenon can be found in such journals as *Aztlan: International Journal of Chicano Studies Research* (Los Angeles), *The Journal of Mexican-American History* (Santa Barbara, Calif.), and *Atisbas: Journal of Chicano Research* (Stanford, Calif.). Renato Rosaldo, Robert A. Calvert, and Gustav L. Seligmann, eds., *Chicano: The Evolution of a People* (Minneapolis, 1973) is a collection of fifty articles from previously published sources that provide a historiography of the subject for use in college courses.

The growing size and importance of the Mexican-American community in the United States in the past two decades is reflected in the significant outpouring of works analyzing their history, culture, and sense of identity. Matt S. Meier and Feliciano Rivera, *The Chicanos: A History of Mexican Americans* (New York, 1972) is a popular overview of the evolution of Mexican-Americans from the conquest of Mexico through the 1960s. John Tebbel and Ramon E. Ruiz, *South by Southwest: The Mexican-American and His Heritage* (Garden City, N.Y., 1969) is a short, readable treatment focusing upon the evolution of ethnic identity and of Mexico from its colonial and revolutionary origins to a modern state interacting with its powerful neighbor to the north. *The Mexican-Americans: An Awakening Minority* (Beverly Hills, Calif. 1970) is a collection of sixteen original and reprinted articles focusing on the twentieth century and edited by Manuel P. Servin. In his *Occupied America: The Chicano's Struggle Toward Liberation* (San Francisco, 1972), Rudolfo Acuna argues that "the experience of Chicanos in the United States parallels that of other Third World peoples who have suffered under the colonialism of technologically superior nations." Stan Steiner's *La Raza: The Mexican Americans* (New York, 1970) is an impressionistic survey of the contemporary Mexican encounter with the dominant culture of the southwestern United States. *Mexican Americans*, written by Joan W. Moore with Harry Pochon (Englewood Cliffs, N.J., 1976), summarizes the findings of the Mexican-American Study Project of the University of California at Los Angeles. David J. Weber, ed., *Foreigners in Their Native Land: Historical Roots of the Mexican-Americans* (Albuquerque, N.M. 1973) is a collection of Spanish, Mexican, and American writings from the sixteenth to the early twentieth centuries demonstrating the continuity and adaptation of Hispanic culture over three centuries.

Several other recent studies have focused on the evolution of Mexican-American communities in particular locales. Leo Grebler, Joan W. Moore, and Ralph C. Guzman, *The Mexican American People: The Nation's Second Largest Minority* (New York, 1970) is a "comprehensive study of the socioeconomic position of Mexican Americans in selected urban areas of the five Southwestern states." Mario T. Garcia, *Desert Immigrants: The Mexicans of El Paso, 1880–1920* (New Haven, Conn., 1981) captures the essence of border town life. Two-way chain migration between El Paso and Mexican villages is the key focus of *Mexican Americans* (New York, 1973) by Ellwyn R. Stoddard. The mythical southwestern small city of "Desconso" is the setting for Ruth D. Tuck's study of the tension between older residents and the more militant veterans who returned there after World War II in *Not With the Fist: Mexican-Americans in a Southwest City* (New York, 1946). The growing militancy of the younger generation of Mexican Americans is detailed in John Staples Schockley, *Chicano Revolt in a Texas Town* (Notre Dame, Ind. 1974). Julian Samora and Richard Lamanno, on the other hand, examine more closely the northern urban experience of Chicanos in *Mexican-Americans in a Mid-West Metropolis: East Chicago*, (Berkeley and Los Angeles, 1967). Taken together, these studies demonstrate the importance of place as a dependent or independent variable in the adaptive process.

The harsh reality that Mexican-Americans have consistently been the victims of economic oppression is brought home by Abraham Hoffman, *Unwanted Mexican Americans in the Great Depression: Repatriation Pressures, 1929–1939*, (Tucson, Ariz. 1974). The ongoing nature of that situation is examined by Mario Berrera, *Race and Class in the Southwest: A Theory of Racial Equality* (Notre Dame, Ind. 1979). The political mobilization of increasingly militant Mexican Americans in response to that situation is the subject of F. Chris Garcia and Rudolph O. de la Garza, *The Chicano Political Experience: Three Perspectives* (North Scituate, Mass. 1977). Carlos Munoz, Jr., *Youth, Identity, Power: The Chicano Movement* (London, 1989), explores the first two decades of the Chicano movement and demonstrates its internal factionalism.

Over the past two decades there has been a significant outpouring of literature on "La Raza" and the Chicano movement. Matt S. Meier and Feliciano Rivera, eds., *Readings on La Raza: The Twentieth Century* (New York, 1974) divides Mexican immigration to and from the United States into six chronological/topical sections. Stanley A. West and June Macklin, eds., *The Chicano Experience* (Boulder, Colo. 1979) contains thirteen essays organized around the topics of immigration and the migrant way of life, boundary maintenance, adaptiveness and change, and voluntary associations and leadership. *The Chicanos: Life and Struggles of the Mexican Minority in the United States* (New York and London, 1973) by Gilberto Lopez y Rivas is a succinct analysis of the origins of the Chicano movement that contains several documents. *The Chicano Struggle: Analyses of Past and Present Efforts* (Binghampton, N.Y., 1984), published by the National Association for Chicano Studies, contains essays by eleven scholars on the community experience, educational policy and programs, and Chicano literature. *Introduction to Chicano Studies: A Reader* (New York, 1973), ed. by Livie Isauro Duran and H. Russell Bernard includes over two dozen essays on Chicano history, their internal and external culture, and perspectives on the future of "la Raza." *Chicano Studies: A Multidisciplinary Approach* (New York and London, 1984), ed. Eugene E. Garcia, Francisco A. Lomeli, and Isidro D. Oritz, examines the development of Chicano studies, its concept of history, social structure, politics, literature, and folklore, its educational perspectives, and suggestions for future research.

Some of the best studies of Mexican-American ethnicity have proceeded from the International Congresses on Mexican Studies, which have been held for nearly two decades. The proceedings of the fourth conference, held in Santa Barbara, California, in 1973, were published under the title *The Chicanos* (Santa Barbara, Calif., 1976), ed. Norris Hundley, Jr., to proclaim the "coming of age" of Mexican-Americans. In *The Chicanos: As We See Ourselves* (Tucson, Ariz. 1980), ed. Arnulfo D. Trejo, twelve Mexican-Americans explicate their views on gender, culture, literature, politics, and bilingualism. Julian Nova's *Viva La Raza! Readings on Mexican Americans* (New York, 1973) deals with the amalgamation of Indian people and Spanish culture, the collision of Anglo and Mexican culture, and with the adaptations made by Mexican-Americans. Luis Valdez and Stan Steiner, *Aztlan: An Anthology of Mexican American Literature* (New York, 1972) contains excerpts from nearly fifty sources dealing with Mexico, Mexican-Americans, and various *causas*—the earth, the woman, the Chicanos, the artist, and the church. Armando B. Rendon, *Chicano Manifesto* (New York, 1971) is an impassioned plea for "a third politics" that bypasses both major U.S. political parties. It should be supplemented with F. Chris Garcia, ed., *La Causa Politica: A Chicano Politics Reader* (Notre Dame, Ind. 1974), which examines the sociohistorical, individual, and organizational foundations of Chicano politics, its relation to conventional and nonconventional U.S. politics, and its prospects for the future.

Less immediate and more dispassionately analytical are four works by social scientists. Ellwyn R. Stoddard, *Mexican Americans* (New York, 1973), examines Chicano origins, identity, values, language, education, income, occupations, and burgeoning organizational structure. Joe L. Martinez, Jr., *Chicano Psychology* (New York, 1977), explores the social psychology, bilingualism, psychological testing, mental health, and psychotherapy of Mexican-Americans in order to establish the "foundations for a Chicano psychology." Nathaniel N. Wagner and Marsha J. Haug, eds., *Chicanos: Social and Psychological Perspectives* contains thirty-two essays on the general topics of interethnic perceptions, sex roles and the family, personality studies, the law, schools, and mental health. Mario T. Garcia, *Mexican Americans: Leadership, Ideology and Identity*, (New Haven, Conn. 1989) attempts to view the Chicano movement from the perspective of political science.

In recent years, scholars have begun to pay increasing attention to Mexican-American women and their peculiar circumstances. Margarita B. Melville, ed., *Twice*

A Minority: Mexican American Women (St. Louis, 1980) contains seventeen essays on "matrescence," gender roles, and cultural conflict. Carmen Tafolle, *To Split A Human* (San Antonio, 1985) argues forcefully for the liberation of Chicanas in popular culture, education, community, career, church, and home. *Chicana Voices: Intersections of Class, Race and Gender* (Austin, Tex. 1990), published by the National Association for Chicano Studies, presents seventeen essays on Mexican American women and education, labor, politics, language, literature, and the theater.

As with all ethnic groups, Mexican-Americans regularly ponder their future as a distinct entity, with conflicting results. *Between Two Cultures: The Life of an American-Mexican as told to John J. Poggie, Jr.* (Tucson, Ariz., 1973) is the life story of Ramon Gonzales, whose ambivalent identity and status is a microcosm of most Chicanos. Rudolph Gomez, ed., *The Changing Mexican American: A Reader* (El Paso, Tex., 1972) speculates on alternative futures in education, work, marriage, politics, and scholarships. Celia S. Heller, *New Converts to the American Dream? Mobility Aspirations of Young Mexican Americans* (New Haven, Conn., 1971) concludes that Chicano young people have the same aspirations and values as do other Americans, but lack only the skills to achieve social mobility. Edward Murguia, *Chicano Intermarriage: A Theoretical and Empirical Study* (San Antonio, 1982) examines the trend toward exogamy and warns that cultural maintenance will become increasingly more problematic as society becomes more open to intermarriage. Especially interesting and enlightening is the growing tendency to compare the Chicano experience to that of other ethnic groups, both within and without the United States. Mario Barrera, *Beyond Aztlan: Ethnic Autonomy in Comparative Perspective* (Notre Dame, Ind., 1988) examines the tension between equality and community among Chicanos as well as in Canada, China, Switzerland, and Nicaragua. Walker Connor, ed., *Mexican Americans In Comparative Perspective* (Washington, D.C., 1985) compares Chicanos to other U.S. ethnic groups with respect to assimilation, economic stratification, political activity, language maintenance, and ethnic revival.

Bibliographical Essay

John D. Buenker and Lorman A. Ratner

Attempting to define the complex process by which myriad ethnic groups have adapted to mainstream American culture over the past two centuries has proven to be a protean task that has resisted the combined efforts of historians, anthropologists, sociologists, linguists, folklorists, geographers, political scientists, psychologists, and scholars of literature, religion, music, art, architecture, and drama. Great has been the temptation to eschew detailed, comparative analysis and to take refuge in a plethora of meta-phorical and rhetorical imagery, such as a melting pot, a salad bowl, a mosaic, or a kaleidoscope. So complex are the variables involved in the adaptive process that they inherently resist reduction to any formula, equa-tion, or definition. Although the approach taken in this book provides an intensive and extensive introduction to the adaptation process as experi-enced by ten of America's myriad ethnic groups in a useful comparative framework, we do not claim to have produced anything more than a stimulus to further study. Even though most of the contributors to this volume are historians by academic training, the complex nature of immigration, eth-nicity, and culture has forced us all to familiarize ourselves with much of the relevant literature from the social sciences and the humanities, as this bibliographical essay clearly demonstrates. Exploring these topics absolutely requires that all of us make a serious effort to break through the disciplinary boundaries that separate us and to develop an appreciation and understand-ing of the perspectives, insights, and contributions that we can make together toward understanding this issue that is so central to the character of the United States and that links Americans to the rest of the world.

Despite the number of sources discussed in the chapter bibliographies and in this bibliographical essay, it is important to remember that they

constitute, in the apt phrase of Rudolph J. Vecoli, "a snapshot of an ava-
lanche." The explosion of ethnic studies in every discipline over the past
quarter century has produced a flood of literature, and the torrent is not
likely to crest in the near future. One of the most difficult tasks faced by
this book's contributors, and by all those who work in this field, is to provide
the reader with reasonably coherent definitions of such slippery terms as
identity, ethnicity, race, acculturation, assimilation, adaptation, integration,
pluralism, diversity, and most vague and controversial of all, Americanization. In the end, each person will formulate his or her own working
definitions and pick and choose among them for the concepts that best
express his or her conceptualization of the adaptive process. In formulating
the essays that comprise this volume, and in constructing the various bibliographical essays, the primary concern has been to provide each reader
with the tools and concepts necessary to undertake this complicated, and
frequently frustrating, task. Although the main focus is on culture and
acculturation, there is no realistic way to avoid focusing on social structure
and assimilation as well. Where that line should be drawn, if it can be drawn
at all, is one of the many topics on which scholars of ethnicity generally
agree to disagree.

Perhaps the most convenient beginning point for a study of ethnicity and
adaptation are the various conceptual essays found in Stephan Thernstrom
et al., *Harvard Encyclopedia of American Ethnic Groups* (Cambridge,
Mass., 1980). The most relevant are: Philip Gleason, "American Identity
and Americanization," 31–58; William Peterson, "Concepts of Ethnicity,"
234–42; Harold J. Abramson, "Assimilation And Pluralism," 150–60; Mi-
chael R. Olneck and Marvin Logenson, "Education," 303–19; Tamara K.
Hareven and John Modell, "Family Patterns," 345–54; Roger D. Abrahams,
"Folklore," 370–79; Richard A. Easterlin, "Immigration: Economic and
Social Characteristics," 476–86; David Ward, "Immigration: Settlement
Patterns," 496–508; David M. Heer, "Intermarriage," 513–21; Joshua A.
Fishman, "Language Maintenance," 629–38; John Higham, "Leadership,"
642–67; Reed Ueda, "Naturalization and Citizenship," 734–48; Edward
R. Kantowicz, "Politics," 803–13; George M. Frederickson and Dale T.
Knobel, "Prejudice and Discrimination, History of," 829–47; and Harold
J. Abramson, "Religion," 869–75. There can be little doubt that the *Harvard
Encyclopedia* itself is the best single reference work on the topic of ethnicity,
both for its conceptual essays and for its articles on virtually every ethnic
group resident in the United States. Much briefer, but still informative, are
the many relevant articles in Francesco Cordasco, ed., *Dictionary of American Immigration History* (Metuchen, N.J., 1990).

Far less comprehensive, but valuable for specific ethnic groups, are several
other reference works. Joan Morrison and Charlotte Fox Zabusky, *American Mosaic: The Immigrant Experience in the Words of Those Who Lived
It* (New York, 1980) is extremely thought-provoking. *By Myself I'm a Book:*

An Oral History of the Immigrant Jewish Women (Waltham, Mass., 1972), published by the National Council of Jewish Women, performs the same function for a more limited category of people. Irving J. Sloan, ed., *The Jews in America, 1621–1977: A Chronology and Fact Book* (Dobbs Ferry, N.Y., 1978) provides a wealth of data. Irving Howe and Kenneth Libo, eds., *How We Lived: A Documentary History of Immigrant Jews in America, 1880–1930* (New York, 1979) contains much valuable information and ambience. Francis Bolek, ed., *Who's Who in Polish America* (New York, 1970), originally published in 1943, is a valuable picture of intergenerational mobility. Hyung-Chan Kim, *Dictionary of Asian American History* (Westport, Conn., 1986) contains many valuable insights into Chinese immigration and ethnicity. W. L. Tung, *The Chinese in America, 1820–1973: A Chronology and Fact Book* (Dobbs Ferry, N.Y., 1974) is a useful map through unfamiliar territory. Frank Chin et al., comps., *AIIIEEE! An Anthropology of Asian American Writers* (Washington, D.C., 1974) presents an inside view, as does Victor G. and Brett de Bary Nee, *Longtime Californian: A Documentary Study of an American Chinatown* (New York, 1973).

The availability of computer-aided search techniques has facilitated the proliferation of bibliographies on immigration and ethnicity during the past two decades. While many of these are extremely useful, all are limited by their dates of publication. John D. Buenker and Nicholas C. Burckel, eds., *Immigration and Ethnicity: A guide to Information Sources* (Detroit, 1977) is the first comprehensive work. A. William Hoglund, *Immigrants and Their Children in the United States: A Bibliography of Doctoral Dissertations, 1885–1982* (New York, 1986) is a treasure trove of largely unpublished works. Paul Wasserman and Jean Morgan, eds., *Ethnic Information Sources of the United States* (Detroit, 1984) is especially helpful in locating nonacademic resources. Richard Kolm, *Bibliography of Ethnicity and Ethnic Groups* (Rockville, Md., 1973) is brief and general. Francesco Cordasco, ed., *A Bibliography of American Immigration History* (Fairfield, N.J., 1978), and Perry L. Weed, *Ethnicity and American Group Life: A Bibliography* (New York, 1972) nicely complement one another. Joseph J. Barton, ed., *An Annotated Guide to the Ethnic Experience in the United States* (Cambridge, Mass., 1976) is especially good on southern and eastern Europeans, while Francesco Cordasco, ed., *The Immigrant Woman in North America: An Annotated Bibliography of Selected References* (Metuchen, N.J., 1985) provides a good introduction to the conjuncture of gender and ethnicity.

Other useful general bibliographies are Judith M. Herman, ed., *White Ethnic America: A Selected Bibliography* (New York, 1969); Wayne C. Miller, ed., *Comprehensive Bibliography for the Study of American Minorities*, 3 vols. (New York, 1976); William Ralph Janeway, ed., *Bibliography of Immigrants in the United States, 1900–1930* (San Francisco, 1972); and Institute for Research in History, *Ethnic and Immigration Groups: The*

United States, Canada, and England (New York, 1983). Two bibliographies that especially focus on creative writing by and about ethnic Americans are Frank Deodene, comp., *The Origins of Ethnicity and Immigrants in America, Including the Immigrant in Fiction* (Chatham, N.J., 1978), and Babette Inglehart and Anthony R. Mangione, comps., *The Image of Pluralism in American Literature: An Annotated Bibliography on the American Experience of European Ethnic Groups* (New York, 1974).

There are also a number of bibliographies that deal with the adaptation process through the prism of a single ethnic group. The University of California at Davis Asian American Studies Program, for example, has issued *Asians in America: A Selected Annotated Bibliography* (Davis, Calif., 1983). Works dealing with Jewish-American ethnicity can be accessed through William W. Brickman, ed., *The Jewish Community in America: An Annotated and Classified Bibliographic Guide* (New York, 1976), and through Jacob R. Marcus, ed., *An Index to Scientific Articles on American Jewish History* (Cincinnati, Ohio, 1971). Entree to Policy-American materials can be gained through Jan Wepsiec, ed., *Policy-American Serial Publications, 1842–1966* (Chicago, 1975); Andrizey Brozek, "Historiography of Polish Immigration to North America," *Immigration History Newsletter* 18 (May, 1986): 1–4; and Joseph W. Zurawski, *Polish-American History and Culture: A Classified Bibliography* (Chicago, 1975). For Norwegian ethnicity, consult John R. Jenswold, "The Missing Dimension: The Historiography of Urban Norwegian Immigration," *Immigration History Newsletter* 18 (May, 1986): 4–7; for Finns, John I. Kolehmanien, ed., *The Finns in America: A Bibliographic Guide to Their History* (Hancock, Mich., 1947; for Danes, Enok Martensen, *Danish-American Life and Letters: A Bibliography* (New York, 1979). The best guides to Swedish-American adaptation are H. Arnold Barton, "Swedish-American Historiography," *Immigration History Newsletter* 15 (May, 1983): 1–5, and Erik Erickson, ed., *Swedish-American Periodicals: A Selective and Description Bibliography* (New York, 1979).

Especially valuable to understanding the adaptation process are a number of interpretive histories of immigration and ethnicity. The pioneer in this field was clearly Marcus Lee Hansen, whose *The Atlantic Migration, 1607–1860: A History of the Continuing Settlement of the United States* (Cambridge, Mass., 1940) and *The Immigrant in American History* (Cambridge, Mass., 1940) not only began the serious study of immigration history, but also turned American historians outward in their search for the meaning of America, away from the frontier thesis of Frederick Jackson Turner and his followers. While Hansen focused his attention on immigration from northern and western Europe and stressed acculturation and assimilation, Oscar Handlin concentrated on immigration from southern and eastern Europe and found alienation in *The Uprooted: The Epic Story of the Great Migrations that Made the American People* (New York, 1951). While the immigrants "made America," Handlin inferred strongly, they were repaid by the destruction of their culture and identities and the alienation of children from parents. Although he modified that pessimistic view somewhat in a revision of *The Uprooted*, Handlin continued to stress the negative impact of immigration on ethnic Americans, a view that largely dominated the field until the late 1960s. Curiously enough, Handlin predicted an optimistic outcome regarding the assimilation of African-Americans and Puerto Ricans as "the last of the immigrants" in *The Newcomers: Negroes and Puerto Ricans in a Changing Metropolis* (Cambridge, Mass., 1959). Over the past quarter century, however, a new generation of immigration historians has departed from the emphasis on alienation and deprivation and built a new consensus around several key points. (1) Immigration was a purposeful and rational choice among viable alternatives, not an involuntary "uprooting"; (2) Most newcomers were part of "migration chains" of families and villages in which the earlier arrivals supplied their successors with information, money, housing, and employment; (3) Immigration was an ongoing process that featured a great deal of repatriation, both temporary and permanent; (4) Every ethnic group was divided internally by class, gender, religion, ideology and pace, and degree of acculturation and assimilation; and (5) Some southern and eastern European immigrant groups shared more in common with earlier northern and western European arrivals than they did with their contemporaries.

This new consensus received a powerful boost from British historian Maldwyn A. Jones, *American Immigration* (New York, 1971), who virtually demolished the invidious distinction between the "old" (northern and western European) and "new" (southern and eastern European) immigration. Leonard Dinnerstern and David M. Reimers, *Ethnic Americans: A History of Immigration and Assimilation* (New York, 1975), stress Handlin's traumatic view of the short-run plight of immigrants and Hansen's notion of long-term success. They and Roy L. Nichols, *Natives And Strangers: Ethnic Groups and the Building of America* (New York, 1979), emphasize the great contributions made by ethnic groups to the growth of the United States despite or because of the hostility of nativists and racists. Maxine Schwartz Seller, *To Seek America: A History of Ethnic Life in the United States* (Englewood Cliffs, N.J., 1977), presents adaptation as an open-ended and ongoing process that is the meaning of America in itself. Alan M. Kraut, *The Huddled Masses: The Immigrant in the United States, 1880–1921* (Arlington Heights, Ill., 1982), concludes that southern and eastern European immigrants "were merely those who looked at what was being done to them, decided to leave their homelands, chose America, and, upon arrival, could not be stopped" (p. 185). John Higham, *Send These to Me: Immigrants in Urban America* (New York, 1984) rejects all existing models of adaptation and substitutes his own concept of "pluralistic integration." And, deliberately choosing a metaphor to offset *The Uprooted*, John E. Bodnar,

The Transplanted: A History of Immigrants in Urban America (Blooming-ton, Ind., 1985), argues that while the lives of immigrants were not entirely of their own making, they made sure that they had something to say about them.

Also of great utility are various collections of eyewitness accounts or series of essays by a variety of scholars of immigration and ethnicity. The classic among the former is Oscar Handlin, ed., *Immigration As a Factor in American History* (New York, 1959), which focuses on the period from 1830 to 1953. Also interesting is Rhoda Hoff, ed., *America's Immigrants: Adventures in Eyewitness History* (New York, 1967), which includes excerpts ranging from Benjamin Franklin (1784) to René Dubos (1966). Joan Morrison and Charlotte Fox Zabusky, *American Mosaic: The Immigrant Experience in the Words of Those Who Lived It* (New York, 1980) includes interviews with nearly a hundred men and women. Thomas Kessner and Betty Boyd Caroli, eds., *Today's Immigrants, Their Stories: A New Look At The Newest Americans* includes stories by an Irish woman, a Russian Jew, an Italian, and a Chinese, and shows the continuity of experiences and issues. Moses Rischin, ed., *Immigration and the American Tradition* (Indianapolis, 1976) contains fifty-five excerpts that demonstrate the persisting ambivalence of America toward immigrants. O. Fritioj Ander, ed., *In the Trek of the Immigrants: Essays Presented to Carl Wittke* (Rock Island, Ill., 1964) includes essays by sixteen scholars on the meaning of immigration for American history. Richard A. Easterlin, David Ward, William S. Bernard, and Reed Ueda, *Immigration* (Cambridge, Mass., 1982), deal with economic and social characteristics, settlement patterns and spatial distribution, and naturalization and citizenship. In *The Immigrant Experience in America* (Boston, 1976), editors Frank J. Coppa and Thomas J. Curran present nine essays on a variety of ethnic groups and the debate over immigration policy in the 1950s. Marjorie P. K. Weiser, ed., *Ethnic America* (New York, 1978) is a collection of two dozen essays that focus on African-Americans, American Indians, and the resurgence of Euro-American ethnicity. Virginia Yans-McLaughlin, ed., *Immigration Reconsidered: History, Sociology, and Politics* (New York, 1990) features eleven essays on migration patterns, ethnicity, and social structure, a new approach to the study of immigration, and the politics of immigration.

Perhaps the most perplexing question of all in trying to understand the nature of the adaptation process in the relationship between ethnicity and identity. Because both are relatively new and abstract concepts, it is difficult to achieve a consensus on much of anything, except to agree that ethnicity, however defined, is a vital component of identity, whatever we believe to be its essence. There can be little doubt that anyone hoping to grasp the meaning of the concept of identity must begin with the works of Erik Erikson. See especially his *Identity, Youth, and Crisis* (New York, 1968); *Identity and the Life Cycle* (New York, 1980); and *Life History and the*

Historical Moment (New York, 1975). The serious psychological damage that can result from a failure to resolve an identity crisis rooted in the disparity between one's ethnic origins and the mainstream society and culture was first explored by Everett V. Stonequist, *The Marginal Man: A Study in Personality and Culture Conflict* (New York, 1937). See also Arnold Dashefsky, ed., *Ethnic Identity in America* (Chicago, 1976) and A. L. Epstein, *Ethos and Identity: Three Studies in Identity* (London, 1978).

Arthur Mann, *The One and the Many: Reflections on the American Identity* (Chicago, 1979), argues that American national identity rests on a persistent faith that the "unum" and the "pluribus" in the national motto are not only mutually compatible, but absolutely essential to the effective exercise of freedom. Perhaps among no ethnic group has this persisting paradox been more perplexing than among Jewish-Americans, who have experienced the greatest sense of alienation because they have enjoyed the greatest degree of upward mobility. Allen Guttmann, *The Jewish Writer In America: Assimilation and the Crisis of Identity* (New York, 1971), analyzes that phenomenon among nearly two dozen Jewish writers, ranging from Emma Lazarus to Saul Bellow. Charles Bezalel Sherman, *The Jew Within American Society: A Study in Ethnic Individuality* (Detroit, 1961), argues that Jews have been virtually unique among American ethnic groups because they have fully integrated into society while retaining their "ethnic individuality." Milton Plesur, *Jewish Life in Twentieth-Century America: Challenge and Accommodation* (Chicago, 1982), finds a complex mixture of anxiety, affluence, and affirmation. David Sidorsky, ed., *The Future of the Jewish Community in America: Essays Prepared for a Task Force on the Future of the Jewish Community in America of the American Jewish Committee* (New York, 1973) features eleven essays on perspectives, profiles, communal institutions, and issues.

Numerous other scholars have focused on establishing a clearer sense of the meaning of ethnicity as it has evolved over generations. William S. Bernard, ed., *Immigrants and Ethnicity: Ten Years of Changing Thought* (New York, 1972) contains excerpts of papers given by seventeen sociologists and historians on the meaning of integration and on the position of ethnic groups within a pluralistic society. William Peterson et al., *Concepts of Ethnicity* (Cambridge, Mass., 1982) consists of essays on the title topic, on pluralism in a humanistic perspective, and on identity and Americanization. Basic to an understanding of the evolution of the concept of ethnicity are three articles by Rudolph J. Vecoli: "Contadini in Chicago: A Critique of *The Uprooted, Journal of American History* 51 (December 1964): 404–17; "Ethnicity: A Neglected Dimension of American History," in *The State of American History*, ed. Herbert Bass (Chicago, 1970); and "European-Americans: From Immigrants to Ethnics," in *The Reinterpretation of American History and Culture*, ed. William H. Cartwright and Richard T. Watson (Washington, D.C., 1973), 87–112. Also instructive are two books by Frank

J. Cavaioli and Salvatore J. La Gumina: *The Ethnic Dimension in American Society* (Boston, 1977), which argues for the centrality of ethnicity to American history over three centuries, and *The Peripheral Americans* (Malabar, Fla., 1984), which focuses on the succession of "ethnic constellations" that have kept group interests, power, and aspirations at the center of American civilization.

Thomas C. Wheeler, ed., *The Immigrant Experience: The Anguish of Becoming American* (New York, 1972), echoes *The Uprooted* in its lament for the destruction of ethnic culture as explicated by writers of Irish, Italian, Norwegian, Puerto Rican, Chinese, African, Jewish, English, and Polish extraction. James S. Olson, *The Ethnic Dimension in American History*, 2 vols. (New York, 1979), insists flatly that "ethnicity is the central theme of American history," that "the most powerful feelings of fidelity and security spring from the values and symbolic associations of the group itself," and that the United States will never become an ethnically homogeneous society, at least for many centuries. Leonard Dinnestein and Frederic Cople Jaher, eds., *Uncertain Americans: Readings in Ethnic History* (New York, 1977), contend that "all groups of non-English origin" are ethnic minorities who have had to undergo a complex and frequently painful process of acculturation. Andrew M. Greeley, *Ethnicity: A Preliminary Reconnaissance* (New York, 1974), argues that the persistence of ethnic attitudes, values, and behaviors are largely subconscious, but can be demonstrated empirically by survey research. See also Richard M. Juliani, *Immigration and Ethnicity* (Philadelphia, 1974).

Central to understanding the concept of ethnicity is the notion of race, a term that has frequently been used interchangeably with ethnicity, especially by nativists. Oscar Handlin, *Race and Nationality in American Life* (Boston, 1957), presents racism as a series of "various divisive doctrines that have attempted to create different categories of men" and as a system of ideas fostered by certain personality types within particular social structures. Mark Haller, *Eugenics: Hereditarian Attitudes in American Thought* (New Brunswick, N.J., 1963), reaches optimistic conclusions by examining a checkered past. The perspective of British anthropologist Ashley Montagu, *Man's Most Dangerous Myth: The Fallacy of Race* (New York, 1964), is apparent from the title. Thomas F. Gossett, *Race: The History of an Idea in America* (New York, 1968), reflects the optimism of the Civil Rights Movement of the 1960s. Peter I. Rose, *The Subject Is Race: Traditional Ideologies and the Teaching of Race Relations* (New York, 1968), calls for a critical, systematic, and objective assessment of this controversial concept. George W. Stocking, Jr., *Race, Culture, and Evolution: Essays in the History of Anthropology* (New York, 1968), features addresses, essays, and lectures on ethnology. Ronald L. Takaki, *Iron Cages: Race and Culture in Nineteenth-Century America* (New York, 1979), contrasts the lot of nonwhite peoples with the American Dream.

Numerous other scholars have written on the interrelationships between race and ethnicity. W. Lloyd Warner and Leo Srole, *Social Systems of American Ethnic Groups* (New Haven, Conn., 1945) is a pioneer work that focuses on the interplay among ethnic and racial groups with respect to residence and occupational patterns, family structure, religion, education, and associational life. Joseph B. Gittler, ed., *Understanding Minority Groups* (New York, 1956) examines a variety of groups, including Indians, Jews, and African-Americans, and discusses the philosophical and ethical dimensions of intergroup relations. James W. Vander Zanden, *American Minority Relations: The Sociology of Race and Ethnic Groups* (New York, 1966) is a theoretical and descriptive analysis of the sociological foundations of race and minority relations, with sections on the sources of prejudice and discrimination, intergroup relations, and reactions to dominance and social change. Vincent M. Parillo, *Strangers to These Shores: Race and Ethnic Relations in the United States* (Boston, 1980), examines majority-minority relations, culture and social structure, and "the American Mosaic." Bernard E. Segal, ed., *Racial and Ethnic Relations* (New York, 1966) contains selections by a wide variety of scholars on such topics as ethic and racial subcultural variation, the scope and quality of social and ethnic attitudes, and prospects for the future in ethnic and racial relations. Norman R. Yetman and C. Hoy Steele, eds., *Majority and Minority: The Dynamics of Racial and Ethnic Relations* (Boston, 1971) is an anthology of nearly forty articles that attempts to analyze the dynamics of racial and ethnic relations within the broader field of majority-minority relations.

Peter I. Rose, ed., *Nation of Nations: The Ethnic Experience and the Racial Crisis* (New York, 1972) contains thirty essays by novelists, journalists, sociologists, and historians on the comparative and competitive experiences of ethnic and racial minorities. Rudolph Gomez, ed., *The Social Reality of Ethnic America* (Lexington, Mass., 1974) concentrates on African-Americans, Mexican-Americans, and American Indians, examining their attitudes, grievances, activities, and leadership. Emerick K. Francis, *Interethnic Relations: An Essay in Sociological Theory* (New York, 1976) presents a worldwide perspective and outlines a theory of interethnic relations. Frank D. Bean and W. Parker Frisbie, *The Demography of Racial and Ethnic Groups* (New York, 1978) compares a variety of groups with respect to residential and school segregation, suburbanization, mental instability, labor force participation, fertility rates, family and household structure, and mortality. Ronald Takaki, ed., *From Different Shores: Perspectives on Race and Ethnicity in America* (New York, 1987) features twenty-seven essays on ethnic patterns, culture, class, gender, and prospects for a more equal society. Lawrence H. Fuchs, *The American Kaleidoscope: Race, Ethnicity and the Civic Culture* (Hanover, N.H., 1991), and Alfred J. Wrobel and Michael J. Eula, eds., *American Ethnics and Minorities: Readings in Ethnic History* (Dubuque, Iowa, 1991), are two important recent additions to the literature.

The debate over the nature, velocity, and eventual outcome, both desired and projected, of the adaptive process has been going on for at least two centuries. Probably the first statement of the "melting pot" concept was J. Hector St. John Crevecour, *Letters From an American Farmer* (London, 1782). Even more well-known is that by Israel Zangwill, *The Melting Pot* (New York, 1909). See also Maurice Wohlgelernter, *Israel Zangwill: A Study* (New York, 1964). The notion that all ethnic groups would and should be eventually amalgamated into the dominant Anglo Protestant society and culture and disappear as identifiable entities, to some extent implied in the melting pot thesis, was made more explicit by the Chicago School of Sociology during the high point of immigration from southern and eastern Europe. See, especially, Robert E. Park and Ernest W. Burgess, *Introduction to the Science of Sociology* (Chicago, 1921) and Fred H. Mathews, *Quest for an American Sociology*, (Montreal, 1977). But the assimilationist theory was quickly challenged by the "cultural pluralism" school led by Julius Draschler, *Democracy and Assimilation: The Blending of Immigrant Heritages in America* (New York, 1920), and Horace M. Kallen, *Culture and Democracy in the United States* (New York, 1924), and *Pluralism and the American Idea: An Essay in Social Philosophy* (Philadelphia, 1956).

All three models are carefully analyzed and compared in Milton M. Gordon, *Assimilation in American Life: The Role of Race, Religion, and National Origins* (New York, 1964), in which he concludes that most ethnic groups eventually embrace "cultural assimilation" (acculturation) but that many are still denied "structural assimilation" (assimilation) years later. In *Human Nature, Class, and Ethnicity* (New York, 1978), Gordon factors in class as an independent variable in the equation. In *Why Can't They Be Like US?" Facts and Fallacies About Ethnic Differences and Group Conflicts in America* (New York, 1969), Andrew M. Greeley posits a six-step process of "ethnogenesis" that runs from "cultural shock" to "emerging adjustment." Higham, as previously noted, discusses a model of "pluralistic integration" in *Send These To Me*. William M. Newman, *American Pluralism: A Study of Minority Groups and Social Theory* (New York, 1973), finds a partial solution to the puzzle in the concept of "multiple realities." Focusing on Detroit, Edward O. Lauman, *Bonds of Pluralism: The Form and Substance of Urban Social Networks* (New York, 1973) argues that religious affiliation and socioeconomic status most affect patterns of social integration. Will Herberg, *Protestant, Catholic, Jew: An Essay In American Religious Sociology* (New York, 1955), concludes that all ethnic groups are being absorbed into a "triple melting pot" organized around three generic "civic religions." Neil C. Sandberg, *Ethnic Identity and Assimilation* (New York, 1974), concludes that the sense of ethnic identity varies with the length of residence, social class, degree of religious identification, and geographical mobility.

One of the most debated issues involving the adaptation process is whether or not it proceeds in a straight line toward some expected outcome or whether it takes a less predictable course. Over half a century ago, Marcus Lee Hansen proposed that "what the son wishes to forget the grandson wishes to remember." Peter Kivisto and Dag Blanck, eds., *American Immigrants and Their Generations: Studies and Commentaries on the Hansen Thesis after Fifty Years* (Urbana and Chicago, 1990) contains essays by ten modern scholars on the implications of Hansen's law of generations and on the switch in perception from process to structure over the past half century. As if to prove Hansen's contention, numerous writers in the 1970s proclaimed the emergence of a "new ethnicity," led by Michael Novak, *The Rise of the Unmeltable Ethnics: Politics and Culture in the Seventies* (New York, 1972). Novak definitely championed the cause of "Poles, Italians, Greeks, and Slavs," proposed their common cause with racial minorities, and chastised liberal intellectuals for their abandonment of the New Deal political alliance. Novak's perspective was reinforced in short order by Michael Werk, Silvano Tomasi, and Gino Baroni, eds., *Pieces Of A Dream: The Ethnic Workers Crisis With America* (New York, 1972), a collection of fifteen essays on the interplay of social class and ethnic pride; by Stanley Feldstein and Lawrence Costello, *The Ordeal of Assimilation: A Documentary History of the White Working Class, 1830s to the 1970s* (Garden City, N.Y., 1974), a compilation of source materials organized around the theme of the ongoing struggling Euro-American laborers for assimilation; by Andrew Levison, *The Working Class Majority* (New York, 1974), which tries to forge a white-black progressive economic and political alliance; by Joseph A. Ryan, ed., *White Ethnics: Life in Working Class America* (Englewood Cliffs, N.J., 1973), which locates the persistence of Euro-American ethnicity in the family, church, and neighborhood and proposes action in the schools, the workplace, and the political arena; and by Richard Krickus, *Pursuing The American Dream: White Ethnics and the New Populism* (Garden City, N.Y., 1976), which urges a new ethnic working-class movement to combat both the "cosmopolitan left" and the ethnic strategy of the (Richard) Nixon Republicans. In *Ethnic Dilemmas, 1964–1982*, Nathan Glazer proposes a plan to deal with bilingualism and affirmative action.

Not surprisingly, the "new ethnicity" quickly gave rise to a critique that regarded its tenets as romantic or reactionary. See, for example, Harold F. Stein and Robert F. Hill, *The Ethnic Imperative: Examining the White Ethnic Movement* (University Park, Penn., 1977); Orlando Patterson, *Ethnic Chauvinism: The Reactionary Impulse* (New York, 1977); Thomas Sowell, *Ethnic America: A History* (New York, 1981); and Stephen Steinberg, *The Ethnic Myth: Race, Ethnicity and Class in America* (New York, 1981). Two works that attempt to present all sides of the controversy over the resurgence of ethnicity in a developmental context are Richard J. Meister, ed., *Race and Ethnicity in Modern America* (Lexington, Mass., 1974), a collection of twenty essays ranging from Crevecour through the 1970s; and David R. Colburn and George E. Pozetta, eds., *America and the New Ethnicity* (Port Washington, N.Y., 1979), an anthology of sixteen essays dealing with the emergence of ethnic awareness, the resurgence of ethnicity, and criticism of the new ethnicity. Robert N. Bellah et al., *Habits of the Heart: Individualism and Commitment in American Life* (Berkeley and Los Angeles, 1985) illustrates that ethnicity still provides many people with a "second language of community solidarity" with which to offset their "first language of the modern individual."

One of the factors that clearly influences the adaptive process is location of settlement. James P. Allen and Eugene J. Turner, eds., *We the People: An Atlas of America's Ethnic Diversity* (New York, 1987) contains a wealth of colored maps by both area and ethnic groups. Wilbur Zelinsky, *The Cultural Geography of the United States* (Englewood Cliffs, N.J., 1973), and Raymond D. Gastil, *Cultural Regions of the United States* (Seattle, 1975) are good introductions to the concept. Donald K. Fellows, in *A Mosaic of Americas' Ethnic Minorities* (New York, 1972), plots the changing distribution of African-, Chinese-, and Mexican-Americans and of American Indians. Caroline Golab, *Immigrant Destinations* (Philadelphia, 1977), specifically interprets "immigrant adaptation as a function of spatial distribution." David Ward, *Cities and Immigrants: A Geography of Change in Nineteenth-Century America* (New York, 1971), concentrates on "the spatial effects of selective urban growth and international differentiation." Dean R. Esslinger, *Immigrants and the City: Ethnicity and Mobility in a Nineteenth-Century Midwestern Community* (Port Washington, N.Y., 1975), compares the geographical mobility of 10,000 immigrants of a variety of ethnic origins in South Bend, Indiana. Odd S. Lovoll, *Scandinavians and Other Immigrants in Urban America* (Northfield, Minn., 1985), demonstrates the significance of the urban environment on the adaptation of different immigrant groups.

The comparative experiences of two or more ethnic groups within a single locale provides a particularly valuable perspective on adaptation, as Esslinger's study of South Bend effectively demonstrates. Robert Ernst, *Immigrant Life in New York City, 1825–1863* (New York, 1965), especially compares Irish and German newcomers, while Nathan Glazer and Daniel Patrick Moynihan, *Beyond the Melting Pot: The Negroes, Puerto Ricans, Jews, Italians, and Irish of New York City* (Cambridge, Mass., 1963), demonstrate the persistence of ethnicity in the country's largest metropolis. John E. Bodnar, ed., *The Ethnic Experience in Pennsylvania* (Lewisburg, Penn., 1973) contains twelve essays, including those on Irish, Poles, Italians, Jews, and African-Americans. In *Lives of Their Own! Blacks, Italians, and Poles in Pittsburgh, 1900–1960* (Urbana, Ill., 1982), Bodnar joins with Roger Simon and Michael P. Weber in a study with both comparative and chronological dimensions. Theodore Hershberg, ed., *Philadelphia: Work, Space,*

Family and Group Experience in the Nineteenth Century (New York, 1981), compares a variety of ethnic groups on those measures over a 120-year period. Donald B. Cole's *Immigrant City: Lawrence, Massachusetts, 1845– 1921* (Chapel Hill, N.C., 1963) traces occupational and residential patterns of two waves of immigrants to a New England mill town. Olivier Zunz, *The Changing Face of Inequality: Urban Industrial Development and Immigrants in Detroit, 1880–1920,* demonstrates that the latest arrivals always inherit the lowest rung of the ladder. In *The Ethnic Frontier: Group Survival in Chicago and the Midwest* (Grand Rapids, Mich., 1977), Melvin G. Holli and Peter d'A. Jones present essays on nine ethnic groups who took their place in "the cauldron of American values." Clyde and Sally Griffin, *Natives and Newcomers: The Structure of Opportunity in Mid-Nineteenth Century Poughkeepsie* (Cambridge, Mass., 1977), and Tamara K. Hareven and Randolph Langenbach, *Amoskeag: Life and Work in an American Factory City* (New York, 1978), demonstrate similar phenomena in smaller locales. And in *The Best Poor Man's County* (Baltimore, 1972), James T. Lemon presents a regional case study of ethnic pluralism in southeastern Pennsylvania.

Another comparative perspective can be gained by matching studies of the same ethnic group in two or more locales. A comparative reading of Stanford M. Lyman, *The Asian in the West* (Reno, Nev., 1970) and James W. Loewen, *The Mississippi Chinese: Between Black and White* (Cambridge, Mass., 1971) graphically illustrates the importance of locale. The bulk of the literature on Jewish-Americans naturally has New York City as its locale. This includes Moses Rischin, *The Promise City: New York's Jews, 1870–1914* (Cambridge, Mass., 1962); Irving Howe, *The World of Our Fathers* (New York, 1976); Stephen Birmingham, *"Our Crowd:" The Great Jewish Families of New York* (New York, 1967); Arthur A. Goren, *New York Jews and the Quest for Community* (New York, 1970); and Ronald Sanders, *The Downtown Jews* (New York, 1969). But these should be compared with a variety of other studies of Jewish-Americans in other locales—Joseph Brandes, *Immigrants to Freedom: Jewish Communities in Rural New Jersey Since 1882* (Philadelphia, 1971); Stuart E. Rosenberg, *The Jewish Community in Rochester, 1843–1925* (New York, 1954); Steven Hertzberg, *Strangers Within the City Gate: The Jews of Atlanta, 1845– 1915* (Philadelphia, 1979); Max Vorspan and Lloyd P. Gartner, *History of the Jews of Los Angeles* (San Marino, Calif., 1970); Marc Lee Raphael, *Jews and Judaism in a Midwestern Community: Columbus, Ohio, 1840– 1875* (Columbus, Ohio, 1979); Louis J. Swichkow and Lloyd P. Gartner, *A History of the Jews of Milwaukee* (Philadelphia, 1963); and Leonard Dinnerstein, *Jews in the South* (Baton Rouge, La., 1970).

Comparative locational influences on Finnish-Americans can be gained from reading Michael J. Karni et al., eds., *The Finnish Experience in the Western Great Lakes Region* (Vammdo, Finland, 1972); John I. Kolehmainen and George W. Hill, *Haven in the Woods: The Story of the Finns in Wisconsin* (Madison, 1965); Hans R. Wasastjerna, ed., *History of the Finns in Minnesota* (Duluth, Minn., 1957); and John I. Kolehmainen, *From Lake Erie's Shores to the Mahoning and Monongahela Valleys: A History of the Finns in Ohio, Western Pennsylvania, and West Virginia* (New York Mills, Minn., 1977). The same perspective on other Scandinavians can be gained from a comparative reading of Harold S. Naess, ed., *The Norwegian Influence in the Upper Midwest* (Duluth, Minn., 1976); Kenneth O. Bjork, *West of the Great Divide: Norwegian Migration to the Pacific Coast, 1847–1893* (Northfield, Minn., 1958); Sture Lindmark, *Swedish-America, 1914–1932: Studies with Emphasis on Illinois and Minnesota* (Uppsala, Sweden, 1971); Byron Nordstrom, ed., *The Swedes in Minnesota* (Minneapolis, 1976); and John L. Davis, *The Danish Texans* (San Antonio, 1979).

Two of the most important concepts developed for comprehending the adaptation process are the realization that every ethnic group is divided internally by social class and a variety of other considerations and that each ethnic community eventually develops a cadre of leaders who serve as conduits or mediators between its members and mainstream society and culture. Gordon, *Human Nature, Class, and Ethnicity*, is an excellent introduction. Donald J. Noel, "A Theory of the Origins of Ethnic Stratification," *Social Problems* 16 (Summer 1968): 157–62, and James A. Henretta, "The Study of Social Mobility: Ideological Assumptions and Conceptual Bias," *Labor History* 18 (Spring 1977): 165–78 provide a good theoretical grounding. Lydio F. Tomasi, *The Ethnic Factor in the Future of Inequality* (Staten Island, N.Y., 1972), explores the tensions generated within individuals and ethnic groups by the interaction of the cultural bond and modernity. Richard Polenberg, *One Nation Divisible: Class, Race, and Ethnicity in the United States Since 1938* (New York, 1980), demonstrates how these three crosscutting realities have restructured society in the past half-century. Michael J. Piore, *Birds of Passage: Migrant Labor and Industrial Societies* (Cambridge, Mass., 1979) examines the lives of a class distinguished by its marginality, both to industrial society and to their own ethnic group. Simon Kuznets and Ernest Rubin, *Immigration and the Foreign Born* (New York, 1954), provide intensive statistical analysis of class differences, both within and among ethnic groups. Robert D. Parmet, *Labor and Immigration in Industrial America* (Boston, 1981), illustrates how ethnicity provides many Americans with a sense of continuity and community denied them in the socioeconomic order. Gerald Rosenblum, *Immigrant Workers: Their Impact on American Labor Radicalism* (New York, 1973) finds that Old World expectations and fears were so powerful that only a small percentage were able to overcome them sufficiently to join unions and become militants. Sally M. Miller, *The Radical Immigrants* (New York, 1974), explores those qualities that separated the relative handful of radicals from their more cautious compatriots. More intensively, Michael J. Karni and Douglas J. Ollila, eds., *For the Common Good: Finnish Immigrants and the Radical*

Response to Industrial America (Superior, Wis., 1977), provide many valuable insights into the qualities and characteristics that caused a relatively small ethnic group to produce a disproportionately large number of radicals.

At the opposite end of the spectrum, at least in some aspects, were the emerging leaders of most ethnic groups. John Higham, ed., *Ethnic Leadership in America* (Baltimore, 1977) contains many indispensible insights into the crucial role played by leaders in the adaptation process. Victor R. Greene, *American Immigrant Leaders, 1800–1910: Marginality and Identity* (Baltimore, 1987), interprets Irish, German, Scandinavian, Jewish, Polish, and Italian community leaders as "traditional progressives" because they urged integration and segregation at the same time. Yonathan Shapiro, *Leadership of the American Zionist Organization, 1897–1930* (Urbana and Chicago, 1971), and Gary Dean Best, *To Free A People: American Jewish Leaders and the Jewish Problem in Eastern Europe, 1890–1914* (Westport, Conn., 1982), both demonstrate the crucial relationship between New York leadership and Old World ties and issues.

Recent scholarship has also begun to focus more attention on the status and function of women in the ethnic experience. Cecyle S. Neidle, *America's Immigrant Women* (Boston, 1975) surveys the broad range of pursuits engaged in by immigrant women from colonial times through the 1960s, ranging from housewives and mothers through clergy, teachers, industrial workers, political radicals, physicians, scientists, musicians, writers, and business leaders. Maxine Schwartz Seller, ed., *Immigrant Women* (Philadelphia, 1981), generates the same impression through the testimony of nearly fifty participants. Joan Younger Dickinson, *The Role of Immigrant Women in the United States Labor Force, 1890–1910* (New York, 1980), and Leslie Woodcock Tentler, *Wage-Earning Women: Industrial Work and Family Life in the United States, 1900–1930* (New York, 1979), both explore the tensions felt and compromises made by millions of ethnic women who worked in one culture and lived in another, neither of which granted them full equality. Charlotte Baum et al., *The Jewish Woman in America* (New York, 1976), and Betty Boyd Caroli et al., eds., *The Italian Immigrant Women in North America* (Toronto, 1978), focus intensively on the impact of American life on two very different cultural perspectives regarding the status and value of women. Jade Snow Wong, *Fifth Chinese Daughter* (New York, 1950), and Maxine Hong Kingston, *The Woman Warrior: Memoirs of a Girlhood Among Ghosts* (New York, 1976), are both sensitive, first-person accounts of the peculiar difficulties faced by Chinese women in adapting to American life.

Changes in family structure and behavior and in marriage patterns have long been recognized as important indices of acculturation and the literature reflects that conviction. Tamara Hareven, *Family Time and Industrial Time: The Relationship Between the Family and Work in a New England Community* (Cambridge, Mass., 1982), explores the creative tension inherent in being caught between two culturally different concepts of the value and meaning of time. Charles H. Mindel and Robert W. Habenstein, eds., *Ethnic Families in America: Patterns and Variations* (New York, 1976), provides a generally excellent synthesis regarding what is known and needs to be known about the varying patterns of ethnic group family life.

Few subjects have stirred up so much controversy in the past two decades as has the African-American family. The conflict dates primarily from the publication of the Moynihan report, "The Negro Family: The Case for National Action" in 1965, which stated flatly that "at the heart of the deterioration of the fabric of Negro society is the deterioration of the Negro family." The reaction led to the publication of Herbert Gutman's *The Black Family in Slavery and Freedom, 1750–1925* (New York, 1976), which specifically contradicted Moynihan and argued that the African-American family had proven to be amazingly resilient, at least until the impact of northern, urban, industrial life. Lee Rainwater and William L. Yancey, eds., *The Moynihan Report and the Politics of Controversy* (Cambridge, Mass., 1967) provides a balanced and enlightening discussion. Charles Vert Willie, *A New Look At Black Families* (Dix Hills, N.Y., 1988) contains eighteen case studies and concludes with a theoretical explanation of family adaptation by race and social class, while his edited work, *The Family Life of Black People* (Columbus, Ohio, 1970), includes essays by two dozen scholars on the general topics of social facts and family life, stability and instability in family life, family structure and interaction among the poor, and family circumstances and social consequences. Willie utilizes case studies of dozens of middle-class, working-class, and poor families, half of them "white" and the other half "black," and concludes that there is an "essential interdependency between all sorts and conditions of families by race and social class."

The general contours and significance of intermarriage as an index of acculturation are sketched briefly in Herr, "Intermarriage," in *Harvard Encyclopedia*, ed. Thernstrom et al., 513–21. Ruth Sharle Cavan's "Annotated Bibliography of Studies on Intermarriage in the United States, 1960–1970 Inclusive," *International Journal of Sociology of the Family* 1 (May, 1971): 157–68 is a helpful guide to the literature. Milton L. Barron, ed., *The Blending American: Patterns of Intermarriage* (Chicago, 1972) contains a wide variety of viewpoints on the attempts of ethnic institutions to regulate intermarriage and on its postmarital consequences. Hugh Carter and Paul C. Glick, *Marriage and Divorce: A Social and Economic Study* (Cambridge, Mass., 1970) contains some interesting data on ethnicity and religion as variables. Richard M. Bernard, *The Melting Pot and The Altar: Marital Assimilation in Early Twentieth Century Wisconsin* (Minneapolis, 1980), finds that exogamy there did produce a veritable melting pot. Harold J. Abramson, *Ethnic Diversity in Catholic America* (New York, 1973), asserts that 55 percent of American Catholics still practiced endogamy in the 1970s.

Richard D. Alba, "Social Assimilation Among American Catholic National-Origin Groups," *American Sociological Review* 41 (December 1976): 1030–48 modifies but does not completely overturn Abramson's findings.

Few conflicts have lent more anxiety to the adaptation process than has the clash between generations. Niles Carpenter, *Immigrants and Their Children, 1920: A Study Based on Census Statistics Relative to the Foreign Born and the Native White of Foreign or Mixed Parentage* (Washington, D.C., 1927), compares the generations with respect to settlement patterns, length of residence, sex ratios, language retention, age, fecundity, vitality, marital status, marriage patterns, illegitimacy, citizenship, and occupation. Edward P. Hutchinson, *Immigrants and Their Children, 1850–1950* (New York, 1956), focuses on the changing composition of immigration, geographical and occupational distribution, contributions to the American economy, and the effects of immigration restriction. Access to much of the best literature can be gained through A. William Hoglund, *Immigrants and Their Children in the United States: A Bibliography of Doctoral Dissertations, 1885–1982* (New York, 1982). June Namias, ed., *First Generation: In the Words of Twentieth-Century America Immigrants* (Boston, 1978) presents the viewpoints of over two dozen newcomers, while Oscar Handlin, ed., *Children of The Uprooted* (New York, 1966) contains nearly three dozen selections dealing with the second generation. Irene D. Jaworski, *Becoming American: The Problem of Immigrants and Their Children* (New York, 1950), compares the nature of the ethnic generation gap in a variety of cultures. Deborah Dash Moore, *At Home in America: Second Generation New York Jews* (New York, 1981), finds a successful model of acculturation, while Judith R. Kramer and Seymour Leventman, *Children Of The Golden Ghetto: Conflict Resolution of Three Generations of American Jews* (New Haven, Conn., 1961), argue that Jewish-Americans in midwestern cities have moved from an ethnic to a status-oriented community due to occupational mobility.

Almost no other single index of acculturation has evoked so much heated controversy as has language retention. Nativists have long regarded the use of English as the ultimate test of loyalty, while traditionalists have insisted with equal fervor on retention as a mark of persisting ethnicity. The leading authority on the topic is certainly Joshua A. Fishman, author of the article "Language Maintenance" in Thernstrom et al., *Harvard Encyclopedia*, 629–38. Fishman's co-edited *Language Loyalty in The United States: The Maintenance and Perpetuation of Non-English Mother Tongues by American Ethnic and Religious Groups* (The Hague, 1966) is the standard work. See also his edited work, *Never Say Die! A Thousand Years of Yiddish in Jewish Life and Letters* (The Hague, Netherlands, 1981). Also insightful into larger issues is Einar Haugen, *Language Conflict and Language Planning: The Case of Modern Norwegian* (Cambridge, Mass., 1966). Francesco Cordasco, ed., "Bilingual Education in American Schools: A Bibliographical Essay," *Immigration History Newsletter* 14 (May, 1982): 1–8, is a useful guide to the literature on that thorny subject. The importance of language in the preservation of ethnic popular culture is evident from a reading of the article on "Folklore," written by Roger D. Abrahams, in Thernstrom et al., eds., *Harvard Encyclopedia*, 370–79. Paradoxically, religion has been an element that has bound some ethnic groups, such as the Irish and the Poles, together, while generating faults lines among others, such as the Germans and American Indians. Edward R. Vollmar, comp., *The Catholic Church in America: An Historical Bibliography* (New York, 1963) and Joseph M. White, "Historiography of Catholic Immigrants and Religion," *Immigration History Newsletter* 14 (November, 1982): 5–11, provide entree to the literature on the most numerically significant religious group. Herberg's *Protestant, Catholic, Jew*, as already noted, sees civic religion as the ultimate melting pot. Gerhard Lenski, *The Religious Factor: A Sociologist's Inquiry* (Garden City, N.Y., 1963), provides a coherent conceptual framework, while John Wilson, *Religion in American Society: The Effective Presence* (Englewood Cliffs, N.J., 1978), makes a strong case for religions importance. John Tracy Ellis, *American Catholicism* (Chicago, 1969); Nathan Glazer, *American Judaism* (Chicago, 1972); and Winthrop S. Hudson, *American Protestantism* (Chicago, 1961), are three cogent overviews. James G. Moseley, *A Cultural History Of Religion in America* (Westport, Conn., 1981), surveys religion as an aspect of national culture. Sydney E. Ahlstrom, *A Religious History of the American People* (New Haven, Conn., 1972), and Winthrop S. Hudson, *Religion in America* (New York, 1965), are comprehensive overviews that focus on the changing character of American religious culture. Martin E. Marty, *Righteous Empire: The Protestant Experience in America* (New York, 1970), illuminates the evolution of the country's core denominations and their response to new religious traditions. Four books authored or co-edited by Robert N. Bellah, *Religions in America* (Boston, 1968); *The New Religious Consciousness* (Berekeley and Los Angeles, 1976); *Varieties of Civil Religion* (San Francisco, 1980); and *The Broken Covenant: American Civil Religion in Time of Trial* (New York, 1975) document the rise of civil religion in the United States.

Randall M. Miller and Thomas D. Marzik, eds., *Immigrants and Religion in Urban America* (Philadelphia, 1977) includes eight essays on various ethnic religious experiences. Besides Abramson, *Ethnic Diversity in Catholic America*, the Catholic experience has been examined thoroughly by Richard M. Linkh, *American Catholicism and European Immigrants, 1900–1924* (Staten Island, N.Y., 1975); Jay P. Dolan, *The Immigrant Church: New York's Irish and German Catholics, 1815–1865* (Baltimore, 1975); and Aaron Abell, *American Catholics and Social Action: A Search for Social Justice, 1865–1900* (Garden City, N.Y., 1960). The Scandinavian experience can be discovered in several works: Paul C. Nyholm, *The Americanization of the Danish Lutheran Church in America* (Copenhagen, 1963); Enok Mortensen, *The Danish Lutheran Church in America* (Philadelphia,

1967); George W. Stephenson, *The Religious Aspects of Swedish Immigration: A Study of the Immigrant Churches* (New York, 1972); Ralph J. Jelkanen, ed., *The Faith of the Finns: Historical Perspectives on the Finnish Lutheran Church in America* (East Lansing, Mich., 1972); and Eugene L. Fevold, *The Lutheran Church among Norwegian-Americans: A History of the Evangelical Lutheran Church*, 2 vols. (Minneapolis, 1960). The Polish religious experience is captured best in Daniel Buczek, *Immigrant Pastor* (Waterbury, Conn. 1974) and Anthony J. Kuzniewski, *Faith and the Fatherhood: The Polish Church Wars in Wisconsin, 1896–1918* (Notre Dame, Ind., 1980). The Jewish experience is also covered well in Marshall Sklare, *Conservative Judaism* (New York, 1972) and Charles S. Liebman, *Aspects of the Religious Behavior of American Jews* (New York, 1974).

For most ethnic groups, the adaptation process has been accomplished largely through the mechanism of a variety of sociocultural institutions that have served as "compression chambers" between the traditional society and culture and that of the mainstream. Although frequently denounced by nativists and assimilationists as "un-American" and separatist, most of these institutions have actually facilitated the transition from immigrant or racial minority to ethnic American by allowing each individual to acculturate and assimilate at the pace and to the degree the person desired, and that mainstream America permitted. Whether these institutions were Old World transplants, copies of those founded by earlier arrivals, or *de novo* creations, they generally passed through a process of evolution from regional through national to hyphenated American orientation. Most weathered crises over such issues as the substitution of English for the mother tongue or the membership status of partners to exogamous marriage, if they endured. Many disappeared with the first generation, while others persisted, in constantly evolving form, through several generations. As late as 1975, Lubomyr R. Wynar et al. eds., *Encyclopedic Directory of Ethnic Organizations in the United States* (Littleton, Colo., 1975) still insisted that there were nearly 1,500 viable ethnic organizations representing over seventy distinct ethnic groups. If anything, the accelerated immigration of the past fifteen years has probably increased their number. Daniel J. Elazar, *Community and Polity: The Organizational Dynamics of American Jewry* (Philadelphia, 1976), analyzes the five spheres of Jewish community activity: religious-congregational, educational-cultural, community relations, communal-welfare, and Zionist, over time. Peter I. Rose, ed., *The Ghetto And Beyond: Essays On Jewish Life In America* (New York, 1969) contains twenty-seven scholarly essays on various institutions that define both the internal life of the American Jewish community and their relationship to other Americans. The significance of one long-standing ethnic organization is related in Naomi W. Cohen, *Not Free To Desist: The American Jewish Committee, 1906–1966* (Philadelphia, 1972). Thomas P. Christensen, *A History of the Danes in Iowa* (Solvang, Calif., 1952); O. Fritiof Ander, *The Cultural Heritage of the Swedish Immigrant: Selected References* (Rock Island, Ill., 1956); and Ralph J. Jalkenen, ed., *The Finns in North America: A Social Symposium* (Hancock, Mich., 1969) provide a sense of the rich diversity of Scandinavian-American institutional life. Ivan H. Light, *Ethnic Enterprise In America: Business and Welfare Among Chinese, Japanese, and Blacks* (Berkeley and Los Angeles, 1972), examines credit associations, business leagues, church societies, and mutual aid and fraternal insurance organizations among those three groups. Maxine Schwartz Seller, ed., *Ethnic Theater in the United States* (Westport, Conn., 1983) includes many selections that document the variety and importance of that particular institution to various cultures. Perry R. Duis, *The Saloon: Public Drinking in Chicago and Boston, 1880–1920* (Urbana, Ill., 1938), amply demonstrates the social and cultural significance of that urban institution to a variety of ethnic groups. Nearly every general history of any ethnic group devotes at least a chapter to its institutions.

Few institutions have been more critical in the adaptation process than has the ethnic press. Frequently challenging the mainstream press for circulation in the heyday of migration, most ethnic newspapers and periodicals eventually fell victim to the loss of the language facility, the passage of generations, and the economics of publishing. However, Lubomyr R. and Anna T. Wynar, eds., *Encyclopedic Directory of Ethnic Newspapers and Periodicals in the United States* (Littleton, Colo., 1975) estimate that there were still nearly 1,500 ethnic newspapers and periodicals in the mid–1970s. Their analysis should be compared to *The Ethnic Press in the United States: Lists of Foreign Language, Nationality and Ethnic Newspapers and Periodicals in the United States* (New York, 1974), published by the American Council for Nationalities Service. Sally M. Miller, ed., *The Ethnic Press in the United States: A Historical Analysis and Handbook* (Westport, Conn., 1987) contains analytical essays on the publications of twenty-seven different ethnic groups. Rita J. Simon, *Public Opinion and the Immigrant: Print Media Coverage, 1880–1980* (Lexington, Mass., 1985), is concerned primarily with how the mainstream press viewed newcomers, while Robert F. Hueston, *The Catholic Press and Nativism, 1840–1860* (New York, 1976), concentrates on how one segment of the ethnic press defended its constituents against prejudice and discrimination. Isaac Metzker, ed., *A Bintel Brief* (New York, 1971) provides translations of scores of letters written by Jewish immigrants to the New York *Daily Forward* that express, eloquently, the myriad problems and frustrations of adaptation.

Equally central to the adaptation process has been the practice of ethnocultural politics. Given the existence of a decentralized political system with myraid loci of power, ethnic groups have been able to capture control of various locales and to utilize that leverage to gain much of what the socioeconomic order might otherwise have denied them. Given the reality of political parties without discipline and without program and of election contests that were largely nonideological struggles for power and office, selecting candidates or affiliating with a party because of its ethnocultural orientation or its positions on issues of ethnocultural salience made as much sense as did any other strategy. Ethnocultural conflict clearly galvanized nineteenth-century voters far more than did any other category of questions, while ethnocultural divisions defined the differences between the major political parties as well or better than any alternative explanation. Not surprisingly, then, the task of defining and evaluating the contours and meaning of American ethnic politics has engaged the talents and concerns of political scientists and historians.

The importance of ethnocultural identification and behavior in American political history was first stated explicitly by Lee Benson, *The Concept of Jacksonian Democracy: New York as a Test Case* (Princeton, N.J., 1970), who challenged the prevailing views of Jacksonian era politics as a conflict among socioeconomic classes. Michael F. Holt, *Forging A Majority: The Formation of the Republican Party in Pittsburgh, 1848–1860* (New York, 1969) and *The Political Crisis of the 1850s* (New York, 1978) emphasizes the interaction between racial and ethnic politics. Ronald P. Formisano, *The Birth of Mass Political Parties, Michigan, 1827–1861* (Princeton, N.J., 1971), makes the same point about a crucial northern state. Richard Jensen, *The Winning of the Midwest: Social and Political Conflict, 1888–1896* (Chicago, 1971), and Paul Kleppner, *The Cross of Culture: A Social Analysis of Midwestern Politics, 1850–1900* (New York, 1970), both stress the importance of religious affiliation to political issues and alignments. Joel H. Silbey and Samuel T. McSeveney, eds., *Voters, Parties and Elections: Quantitative Essays in the History of American Popular Voting Behavior* (Lexington, Mass., 1972) contains twenty-four essays, most of which focus on ethnocultural politics. For a cogent discussion of the strengths and weaknesses of ethnocultural interpretations of American political history, see Richard L. McCormick, *The Party Period And Public Policy: American Politics from the Age of Jackson to the Progressive Era* (New York, 1986).

Much of the theoretical analysis of ethnocultural conflict was provided by political scientists, beginning with the treatment by Robert Dahl, *Pluralist Democracy in the United States: Conflict and Consensus* (Chicago, 1967), who sees ethnicity as one of the key "cross-cutting cleavages" that influence political choice. Edgar Litt, *Beyond Pluralism: Ethnic Politics in America* (Chicago, 1970), discusses the persistent, social, individual, and organizational base of ethnic politics, its patterns and varieties, and focuses on case studies of Irish-, Jewish-, and African-Americans. Thomas J. Pavlak, *Ethnic Identification and Political Behavior* (San Francisco, 1976), and Harold R. Isaacs, *Idols of the Tribe: Group Identity and Political Change* (New York, 1975), both examine the important role played by politics in the formation of individual and group identity. Michael Walzer, Edward R. Kantowicz, John Higham, and Mona Harrington, *The Politics of Ethnicity* (Cambridge,

Mass., 1982), examine pluralism, loyalties, leadership, and voting behavior in the context of ethnic politics. Perry L. Weed, *The White Ethnic Movement and Ethnic Politics* (New York, 1973), examines the role of resurgent ethnic community organizations in the reemergence of ethnic politics and analyzes the latter's impact on the two major political parties.

Numerous anthologies deal with the variety and importance of ethnic politics. Lawrence H. Fuchs, ed., *American Ethnic Politics* (New York, 1968) includes a dozen essays on the operation of ethnocultural politics. Harry A. Bailey, Jr. and Ellis Katz, eds., *Ethnic Group Politics* (Columbus, Ohio, 1969) contains over two dozen treaties on ethnic political behavior, its importance in urban politics, and its persistence. Brett W. Hawkins and Robert A. Lorinskas, eds., *The Ethnic Factor in American Politics*, (Columbus, Ohio, 1970) features ten essays on ethnicity as a durable social and political instrument, ethnic voting and policy attitudes, and ethnicity's impact on political forms and policy outputs. Mark R. Levy and Michael S. Kramer, *The Ethnic Factor: How America's Minorities Decide Elections* (New York, 1972), examine the political behavior of African-, Mexican-, Jewish-, Irish-, Slavic-, and Italian-Americans. S. J. Makielski, Jr., *Beleaguered Minorities: Cultural Politics in America* (San Francisco, 1973), focuses on the political status of African- and Mexican-Americans and American Indians.

Several other works focus on the ethnic politics of a particular locale or a specific group. Roger E. Wyman, *Voting Behavior in the Progressive Era: Wisconsin As A Case Study* (Ann Arbor, Mich., 1975), argues convincingly that ethnocultural politics persisted during the ideological and socioeconomic furor of the reformist era in that critical state. Thomas W. Henderson, *Tammany Hall and the New Immigrants: The Progressive Years* (New York, 1976), gives a mixed review to the efforts of America's most formidable Democratic political machine. John M. Allswang, *A House For All Peoples: Ethnic Politics in Chicago, 1890–1936* (Lexington, Ky., 1971), demonstrates why its midwestern counterpart was eventually much more successful. Angela T. Pienkos, ed., *Ethnic Politics in Urban America: The Polish Experience in Four Cities* (Chicago, 1978), evaluates the performance of Poles in the politics of Buffalo, Detroit, Milwaukee, and Chicago. See also Edward R. Kantowicz, *Polish-Americans Politics in Chicago, 1888–1940* (Chicago, 1975). Jon Wefald, *A Voice of Protest: Norwegians in American Politics* (Northfield, Minn., 1971), argues for the effectiveness and progressivism of that Scandinavian group. Lawrence H. Fuchs, *The Political Behavior of American Jews* (Glencoe, Ill., 1956), and Nathaniel Weyl, *The Jew In American Politics* (New Rochelle, N.Y., 1968), are both chronological surveys of that group's political odyssey. Henry L. Feingold's *The Politics of Rescue: The Roosevelt Administration and the Holocaust, 1938–1945* (New Brunswick, N.J., 1970) is a critical examination of the most important issue in Jewish-American politics. For studies of Irish, German,

African, Mexican and Italian ethnic politics, see the bibliographical essay at the end of each relevant chapter.

Four important books deal with the salience of ethnocultural politics to the resurgence of the Democratic party in the New Deal coalition of the 1930s: Samuel Lubell, *The Future of American Politics* (New York, 1955); J. Joseph Huthmacher, *Massachusetts People and Politics, 1914–1933* (Cambridge, Mass., 1959); David Burner, *The Politics of Provincialism: The Democratic Party in Transition, 1918–1932* (New York, 1968); and Allen J. Lichtman, *Prejudice and the Old Politics: The Presidential Election of 1928* (Chapel Hill, N.C., 1979). Louis Gerson, *The Hyphenate in Recent American Politics and Diplomacy* (New York, 1964), stresses the persisting importance of Old World political issues in American politics. For a discussion of how American immigration policy activates ethnocultural politics, see Robert A. Divine, *American Immigration Policy, 1924–1952* (New York, 1972).

In no other arena has the adaptation process of ethnic minorities generated more bitter and prolonged conflict and produced more ambiguity and soul-searching than in the realm of formal education. "The school," according to two prominent historians of education, "is central to the immigrant epic." Immigrants and other ethnic minorities founded a series of parochial school systems running from kindergarten through graduate and professional school that sometimes educated a fifth to a fourth of the country's school children—a far higher percentage in many locales. While these parochial schools markedly eased the adaptive process for millions of children, they themselves became the objects of great controversy for ethnocultural/religious, political/financial, and ideological reasons. The majority of ethnic children were acculturated in the country's public schools, which were charged with a variety of tasks, from equipping them with the knowledge and skills to become productive and prosperous to inculcating the values of citizenship and social behavior. It was primarily in the public schools that ethnic youngsters daily confronted mainstream language, values, and culture and measured them against those of family, church, and neighborhood.

Prior to the 1960s, there was a prevailing consensus that the public schools had generally adjusted well to meeting the changing needs of a variety of ethnic groups (primarily European immigrants and their descendants) and that these groups, in turn, had utilized public education as a vehicle for significant social mobility. From that it followed, logically and ideologically, that schools would perform the same integrative function for racial minorities and for newer immigrants. The most complete expression of this credo is Ellwood P. Cubberley, *Public Education in the United States* (New York, 1919). This sanguine view was initially challenged by Bernard Bailyn, *Education and the Forming of American Society* (Chapel Hill, N.C., 1960), in which he chastized the Cubberley school for producing "the parasitic literature of a powerful academic ecclesia." It was followed soon by Lawrence Cremin, *The Wonderful World of Ellwood Patterson Cubberley* (New York, 1965), and by his three-volume *American Education* (New York, 1970, 1980, 1988). The relatively moderate revisionism of Bailyn and Cremin quickly gave rise to a thoroughgoing radical critique that viewed public education primarily as the instrument by which an economic, social, and cultural elite established and maintained hegemony over the rest of society, especially the ethnic working class, destroying its members' various cultures and condemning them to a position of virtual indentured servitude. The list of revisionist publications that espoused some variation of the radical revisionist critique is long and impressive: Colin Greer, *The Great School Legend: A Revisionist Interpretation of American Public Education* (New York, 1972); David Nasaw, *Schooled to Order; A Social History of Public Schooling in the United States* (New York, 1979); David B. Tyack, *The One Best System: A History of American Urban Education* (Cambridge, Mass., 1974); Robert Carlson, *The Quest for Conformity: Americanization Through Education* (New York, 1975); Michael Katz, *The Irony of Early School Reform* (Cambridge, Mass., 1962); and Stanley K. Schultz, *The Culture Factory: Boston Public Schools, 1789–1860* (New York, 1973). Although their views have been severely challenged by Diane Ravitch, *The Revisionists Revised: A Critique Of the Radical Attack On The Schools* (New York, 1977), the perception of the public schools as cultural battlegrounds and agents of social conformity remains widely held. Much additional literature may be located in Francesco Cordasco, ed., *Immigrant Children in American Schools: A Classified Annotated Bibliography with Selected Source Documents* (Fairfield, N.J.: 1976).

The persisting nature of cultural and class conflict in the schools is also conveyed in a number of other works. Bernard J. Weiss, ed., *American Education and the European Immigrant, 1840–1940* (Urbana and Chicago, 1982) contains over a dozen essays that deal mostly with the impact of American schooling, at all levels, on various ethnic peoples. Lawrence Cremin, *The Transformation of the School: Progressivism in American Education, 1876–1975* (New York, 1961), elucidates the strong nativist, acculturationist bias in progressive education. Meyer Weinberg, *A Chance To Learn: A History of Race and Education in the United States* (Cambridge, Mass., 1977) makes implicit comparisons among ethnic groups with regard to educational access and payoff. Ronald K. Goodenow and Diane Ravitch, eds., *Schools In Cities: Consensus and Conflict in American Educational History* (New York, 1983) contains eleven essays that explore similar topics in a variety of locales. And Ruth M. Elson, *Guardians of Tradition: American Schoolbooks of the 19th Century* (Lincoln, Neb., 1964), examines one of the issues that generated fierce and protracted ethnocultural conflict in the school system.

Several other works, most of which incorporate many of the tenets of the revisionists, whether liberal or radical, concentrate on the educational experiences of a particular place or a specific ethnic group. Even Diane Ravitch adopts much of that viewpoint and terminology in her *The Great School Wars, New York City, 1805–1973: A History of the Public Schools as Battlefield of Social Change* (New York, 1974). Ronald D. Cohen, *Children of the Mill: School and Society in Gary, Indiana, 1906–1960* (Bloomington, Ind., 1990), examines the long-term effects of the city's "work-study-play" system on various ethnic groups. Cohen and Raymond A. Mohl also collaboratively critique the Gary Plan in *The Paradox of Progressive Education: The Gary Plan of Urban Schooling* (Port Washington, N.Y., 1979). Focusing on another era of educational reform in a different setting is Marvin F. Lazerson, *Origins of the Urban School: Public Education in Massachusetts, 1870–1915* (Cambridge, Mass., 1971). Carl F. Kaestle, *The Evolution of an Urban System: New York City, 1750–1850* (Cambridge, Mass., 1977), covers the fifty years prior to the scope of Ravitch's *Great School Wars*, while Sherry Gorelick, *City College and the Jewish Poor: Education in New York, 1880–1924* (New Brunswick, N.J., 1981), concentrates on that city's most enthusiastic consumers of public education. Alexander M. Dushkin, *Jewish Education in New York City,* (New York, 1918) is a classic eyewitness account.

James W. Sanders, *The Education of an Urban Minority: Catholics in Chicago, 1833–1965* (New York, 1977), finds that the city's parochial schools, ironically enough, were more effective agents of "Americanization" than were its public schools. The passion of Scandinavians for education, especially under their own auspices, is apparent in Enok Mortensen, *Schools for Life: A Danish-American Experiment in Adult Education* (Askov, Denmark, 1977), a history of the Grundtvigian folk schools; William E. Christensen, *Saga of the Tower: A History of Dana College and Trinity Seminary,* (Blair, NE, 1959); Thorvald Hansen, *We Laid Foundations Here: The Early History of Grand View College* (Des Moines, Iowa, 1972); and Leigh D. Jordahl and Harris E. Kaasa, *Stability and Change: Luther College in Its Second Century,* (Decorah, Iowa, 1986). Information regarding the educational experiences of other specific ethnic groups can be gleaned from the sources included in the bibliographical essay at the end of each chapter. For brief general overviews, see Handlin, *The Uprooted,* 244–49; Bodnar, *The Transplanted,* 189–97; and Kraut, *Huddled Masses,* 133–41.

Regardless of origin or time and method of "arrival," every single American ethnic group was, for a time at least, the victim of prejudice and discrimination that frequently culminated in paradoxical campaigns to forcibly acculturate them while seeking to send them "back to where they came from." Contrary to the intent of "Americanizers," forced acculturation drives generally retarded the adaptation process, as ethnic groups determined to resist such campaigns with all their might. And while most Euro-Americans found that partial assimilation, as least, was the reward for acculturation, racial minorities were generally held separate to a great degree, no matter how quickly and completely they attempted to acculturate. Philip Davis and Bertha Schwartz, eds., *Immigration and Americanization* (New York, 1920), is an anthology of works by various scholars and politicians on the effects of immigration of different groups and on the desirability of restriction and Americanization. Kate Holladay Claghorn, *The Immigrant's Day in Court* (New York, 1969), analyzes the difficulties encountered by newcomers in the legal and governmental system as a measurement of acculturation. Edward G. Hartmann's *The Movement to Americanize the Immigrant* (New York, 1967) is a straightforward account of forced acculturation. Paul Boyer, *Urban Masses and Moral Order in America, 1820–1920* (Cambridge, Mass., 1978), contends that much of the urban reform movement of that century was motivated by an attempt to impose upon the unruly and diverse masses of the city the putative moral order of the American village. Barbara M. Solomon, *Ancestors and Immigrants: A Changing New England Tradition* (Cambridge, Mass., 1956), focuses on the efforts of the Immigration Restriction League to stop the influx of "undesirable" immigrants. Ray Allen Billington, *The Protestant Crusade, 1800–1860,* (New York, 1938) is a richly detailed account of the Know-Nothing nativist movement against Catholic immigrants. John Higham, *Strangers in the Land: Patterns of American Nativism, 1860–1925* (New York, 1970), picks up the story where Billington leaves off and carries it through to the passage of the National Origins Quota Act. Gerd Korman, *Industrialization, Immigrants, and Americanizers: The View from Milwaukee* (Madison, Wis., 1967), examines the efforts of zenophobes, uplifters, and industrialists in the Cream City to acculturate their polyglot work force in the name of efficiency and patriotism. Paul McBride, *Culture Clash: Immigrants and Reformers, 1880–1920* (San Francisco, 1975), accuses both the Young Men's Christian Association and the social settlements of promoting forced acculturation. Allen F. Davis, *Spearheads For Reform: The Social Settlements and the Progressive Movement 1890–1914* (New York, 1967), argues strongly that some social settlements genuinely respected the ethnic heritage of their constituents and helped them retain a great deal of it. Stuart C. Miller, *The Unwelcome Immigrant: The American Image of the Chinese* (Berkeley, Calif., 1969), attributes anti-Chinese hostility to a clash of extremely contrasting values and culture. Alexander Saxton, *The Indispensable Enemy: Labor and the Anti-Chinese Movement in California* (Berkeley and Los Angeles, 1971), argues that the experience of Chinese immigrant workers was more similar to that of African-Americans than to that of European immigrants, and that the United States has always had a racial definition of nationality. Robert J. Wechman and David M. Zielonka, *The Eager Immigrants: A Survey of the Life and Americanization of Jewish Immigrants to the United States* (Champaign, Ill., 1972), assert that American Jews have retained their religio-cultural identity while becoming "typically American" in appearance, language, dress, interests, occupations, attitudes, values, and names.

Even while striving to adapt to the pressures for forced acculturation coming from mainstream America, ethnic groups also have contended with one another for recognition, acceptance, and material benefits. Pitted against one another in a critical competition for housing, employment, education, and other necessities of life, ethnic groups have frequently developed strong negative stereotypes about one another. Some ethnic groups have also sought to deflect prejudice directed against them onto other peoples, a strategy that also sometimes curried favor with nativists and racists. Donald E. Gelfand and Russell D. Lee, *Ethnic Conflicts and Power: A Cross National Perspective* (New York, 1973), demonstrate that this phenomenon is not limited to the United States. Arnold and Caroline Rose, *American Divided: Minority Group Relations in the United States* (New York, 1959), examines the legal, economic, and political status of ethnic minorities, their identification, morale, and organization, and the psychology of prejudice. Richard A. Schermerhorn, *Comparative Ethnic Relations: A Framework for Theory and Research* (New York, 1969), attempts to posit a sociology of intergroup relations. Robin M. Williams, *Strangers Next Door: Ethnic Relations in American Communities* (Englewood Cliffs, N.J., 1964), analyzes the psychological and social bases of ethnocentrism, prejudice, and intergroup conflict. Peter I. Rose, *They And We: Racial and Ethnic Relations in the United States* (New York, 1968), discusses race, ethnicity and social status, the nature of prejudice, and varying reactions to discrimination. Milton L. Barron, ed., *Minorities in a Changing World* (New York, 1967), looks at ethnic differentiation and inequality in American society and at various techniques for bettering ethnic relations. In *Ethnic Groups in Conflict*, Donald L. Horowitz (Berkeley and Los Angeles, 1985) posits a theory of ethnic conflict and strategies for reduction of that conflict, while John Slawson and Marc Vosk, *Unequal Americans: Practices and Politics of Intergroup Relations* (Westport, Conn., 1979), examine the principles for treating problems in intergroup relations and analyze the methods used in preventing them.

More concrete and focused are a number of studies that deal directly with the interaction among specific ethnic groups. Charles F. Marden and Gladys Meyer, *Minorities in American Society* (New York, 1968), deal primarily with African-, Mexican-, Chinese-, Jewish-, and Indian-Americans. Charlotte Brooks, ed., *The Outnumbered: Stories, Essays, and Poems about Minority Groups by America's Leading Writers* (New York, 1969) compares Americans of African, Irish, Jewish, and Indian descent. Bruce A. Glasrud and Alan M. Smith, eds., *Promises to Keep: A Portrayal of Non-Whites in the United States* (Chicago, 1972), focus on African-, Mexican-, Chinese-, and Indian-Americans. Stanley Lieberson's *A Piece of the Pie! Blacks and White Immigrants Since 1880* (Berkeley, Calif., 1980) is strong on the similarities and differences between the two. Everett C. and Helen M. Hughes,

Where People Meet: Racial and Ethnic Frontiers (Glencoe, Ill., 1952) de-
lineates the areas where both interaction and conflict frequently occur. Ru-
dolf Glanz, *Jew and Italian: Historical Group Relations and The New
Immigration, 1881–1942* (New York, 1972) concentrates on the interplay
between the two largest segments of the turn-of-the-century immigration.
Thomas Kessner, *The Golden Door: Italian and Jewish Immigrant Mobility
in New York City, 1880–1915* (New York, 1977), explores two different
routes to "the good life." Ronald H. Bayor, *Neighbors in Conflict: The
Irish, Germans, Jews, and Italians of New York City, 1919–1941* (Baltimore, 1978), finds that the key element in initiating interethnic conflict is
a perceived sense of threat. Carlos E. Cortes et al., *Three Perspectives on
Ethnicity: Blacks, Chicanos, and Native Americans* (New York, 1976) compares the adaptive strategies of these three groups. George Eaton Simpson
and Milton J. Yinger, *Racial and Cultural Minorities: An Analysis of Prejudice and Discrimination* (New York, 1965), examine prejudice and discrimination as weapons in group conflict. Edward C. McDonogh and
Eugene S. Richards, *Ethnic Relations in the United States* (New York, 1953),
compare the nature of African-, Jewish-, Mexican-, Chinese-, Indian- and
Euro-Americans with respect to their social, educational, legal, and economic status. Brewton Berry, *Race and Ethnic Relations* (Boston, 1965),
explores what happens when people who differ racially and culturally come
into contact with one another. Ande Manners, *Poor Cousins* (New York,
1972), portrays the initial intragroup conflict and eventual amalgamation
of Germans and Eastern European Jewish-Americans. Finally, J. Anthony
Lukas, *Common Ground: A Turbulent Decade in the Lives of Three American Families* (New York, 1985), sensitively and perceptively portrays the
conflict among Yankees, African-, and Irish-Americans over the issue of
busing for school integration in Boston.

Index

About the Contributors

JAMES M. BERGQUIST is professor of history at Villanova University. He has written extensively on German immigration and his most recent essays have appeared in *Germans in America: Retrospect and Prospect* (1984), *Journal of American Ethnic History* (1984), and *The Ethnic Press in the United States* (1987).

JOHN D. BUENKER is professor of history at the University of Wisconsin, Parkside, and is currently a fellow at the U.W. Institute for Research in the Humanities. He is the author of *Urban Liberalism and Progressive Reform* (1973) and *The Income Tax and the Progressive Era* (1985), co-author of *Progressivism* (1976) and co-editor of five other books, including *Immigration and Ethnicity: A Guide to Information Sources* (1977) and *The Historical Dictionary of the Progressive Era* (1988).

DOMINIC CANDELORO is a professor of social science and director of Workshops and Public Programs at Governors State (Illinois) University. He has written extensively on the Progressive Era and on Italian-Americans in Chicago. He was executive director of the Italians in Chicago Project funded by the National Endowment for the Humanities and is past president of the American Italian Historical Association.

JOHN ROBERT CHRISTIANSON is professor of history at Luther College. He has written extensively on Norwegian immigration to the United States, including an essay "Literary Trends of Norwegian-American Women" in *Makers of an American Immigrant Legacy* (1980).

DENNIS CLARK is a lecturer in history at Temple University and executive director of the Samuel S. Fels Fund of Philadelphia. He is the author of *The*

Irish in Philadelphia: Ten Generations of Urban Experience (1973), *The Irish Relations: Trials of an Immigrant Tradition* (1982), *Hibernia America: The Irish and Regional Cultures* (1986), *The Heart's Own People: A History of the Donegal Association of Philadelphia* (1988), *A History of the Friendly Sons of St. Patrick for the Relief of Emigrants from Ireland in Philadelphia* (1982), and *Irish Blood: Northern Ireland and the American Conscience* (1977).

VINE DELORIA, JR., is professor of American Indian studies at the University of Arizona. He is the author of numerous books on Native Americans, including *Custer Died for Your Sins: An Indian Manifesto* (1969), *We Talk, You Listen: New Tribes, New Turf* (1970), *God Is Red* (1973), co-author of *The Nations Within: The Past and Future of American Indian Sovereignty* (1984), and editor of *American Indian Policy in the Twentieth Century* (1985).

CYNTHIA GREGGS FLEMING is associate professor of history and director of the African and African-American studies program at the University of Tennessee, Knoxville. She has written *The Liberation of Ruby Doris Smith-Robinson: Black Women, Activism, and the Student Nonviolent Coordinating Committee* and has published six articles in journals such as *The Journal of Negro History, Tennessee Historical Quarterly*, and *Phylon*.

EDWARD R. KANTOWICZ is a public historian based in Chicago. He is the author of *Polish-American Politics in Chicago, 1888–1940* (1975), *Corporation Sole: Cardinal Mundelein and Chicago Catholicism* (1983), and *True Value: John Cotter's Seventy Years of Hardware* (1986), and editor of *Modern American Catholicism, 1900–1965: Selected Historical Essays* (1988). He has also written numerous essays on Polish-American ethnicity and on ethnic politics.

LOUISE ANO NUEVO KERR is vice president for instruction and adjunct professor of history at the University of Illinois at Chicago. She is the author of "Mexican Chicago: Chicano Assimilation Aborted, 1939–1954" (*Ethnic Chicago: Revised and Expanded*, 1984) and "The Chicano Experience in Chicago, 1920–1970" (1976). She has written several other articles and papers on Mexican-Americans in the Midwest.

LORMAN A. RATNER is dean of the college of liberal arts and professor of history at the University of Tennessee, Knoxville. He is the author of *Pre-Civil War Reform: The Variety of Principles and Programs* (1967), *Powder Keg: Northern Opposition to the Antislavery Movement, 1831–1840* (1968), and *Antimasonry: The Crusade and the Party* (1969). He co-edited *The Development of an American Culture* with Stanley Cohen.

EDWARD SHAPIRO is professor of history at Seton Hall University. He is the author of numerous essays on Jewish-American religion, culture and politics, on Zionism and on the Holocaust. His writings have appeared in such journals as *Midstream, Congress Monthly, Judaism,* and the *Journal of Ecumenical Studies.*

BERNARD WONG is professor of anthropology at San Francisco State University. He is the author of *Chinatown: Economic Adaptation and Ethnic Identity of the Chinese* (1982), *A Chinese American Community* (1979), and *Patronage, Brokerage, Entrepreneurship and the Chinese Community of New York City* (1984). He has also contributed articles on Chinese Americans to *Urban Life, Urban Anthropology, Comparative Studies in Society and History, Human Organization, Asian Profile* and *New Immigrants in New York.*